THE
PSYCHOLOGY
OF
ADVERSITY

University
of
Massachusetts
Press

Amherst

Edited by Robert S. Feldman

Copyright © 1996 by
The University of Massachusetts Press
All rights reserved
Printed in the United States of America
LC 95-46886
ISBN 1–55849–036–1
Designed by Milenda Nan Ok Lee
Set in Bembo by dix!
Printed and bound by Thomson-Shore, Inc.
Library of Congress Cataloging-in-Publication Data

The psychology of adversity / edited by Robert S. Feldman.
    p.   cm.
  Includes bibliographical references and index.
  ISBN 1-55849-036-1 (cloth : alk. paper)
  1. Social problems—Psychological aspects.   2. Life cycle, Human.
3. Life change events.   I. Feldman, Robert S. (Robert Stephen), 1947–
HN16.P78   1996
361.1—dc20   95-46886
                                          CIP

British Library Cataloguing in Publication data are available.

The Psychology of Adversity

CONTENTS

INTRODUCTION

It is hard to escape from accounts of adversity in today's world. As I write this, the first page of the daily newspaper sitting on the corner of my desk reveals articles about ethnic conflict, fraud, an epidemic, and youth violence. Inside the paper are accounts of other forms of adversity which, although less sensational, still produce unfortunate results to the people involved.

Although identifying various types of adversity is an easy task, finding solutions for them is considerably more difficult. Indeed, the problems of the world defy easy solution, requiring an understanding of how various types of adversity arise and how they are perpetuated.

This volume is designed to highlight the range of approaches to adversity taken by faculty affiliated with the Departments of Psychology at the campuses of the University of Massachusetts. The book, which evolved from a conference in Boston at which the authors discussed theory, research, and applications relating to the topic of psychological adversity, has three specific goals.

First, it is designed to demonstrate how theory and research formulated within the discipline of psychology can help society deal with its major problems. Second, it is meant to illustrate how such psychological theory and research produces practical solutions to difficult problems. The final goal is to illustrate the range of studies being conducted by psychologists who are working in the area of human adversity. Although the chapters are by no means exhaustive in terms of covering the range of human adversity, which could hardly be covered in any single volume, the book does present a sampling of approaches taken by psychologists who are focusing on the types of adversity that afflict the human condition.

To accomplish these goals, this volume is divided into four parts. Part 1 focuses on adversity in infancy and early childhood. In chapter 1, Meyer, Mirochnick, Frank, and Zuckerman seek to separate fact from fiction on the effects of prenatal cocaine exposure on newborn infants—an issue popularized by the media. Based on a review of the literature and their own experimental work, the authors conclude that the widespread presence of "crack babies" who are neurologically impaired due to their mothers' use of cocaine is far from proven. Instead, they suggest that the central problem may lie not in mothers' cocaine use per se but in their lack of general health care during pregnancy and the inadequate care they provide their children after birth.

In chapter 2, Young, Brennan, Baker, and Baker examine a surprisingly common, although often undiscussed, problem of encopresis, inappropriate fecal soiling that occurs past the age of 4. The authors describe an evaluation of a promising program for dealing with encopresis as well as the behavioral and social problems that often accompany the disorder.

Part 2 of the book focuses on adversity in middle childhood and adolescence. Carter, Costa, and Conboy's chapter (chapter 3) addresses the relationship between attention deficit hyperactivity disorder (ADHD) and physical health problems. The discussion of their research shows that children diagnosed with ADHD are at increased risk for a variety of chronic health problems. The authors suggest guidelines for the treatment and prevention of such health difficulties.

In chapter 4, Robbins, Giordano, Hildebrand, and Feldman consider the schooling of children with autism and other developmental disabilities. Describing work conducted in a university preschool, the authors examine techniques for increasing the level of functioning in children with autism as well as in typical children.

Rierdan provides a thorough and comprehensive discussion of adolescent suicide in chapter 5. Her analysis of the underlying causes of suicide begins with an examination of the historical trends that underlie the current increase in adolescent suicide. Rierdan focuses on the adolescent's inability to deal with intolerable psychic pain and the lack of skill in what she calls "self-soothing." The author provides several sets of recommendations for decreasing the current epidemically high incidence of adolescent suicide.

In chapter 6, Staub presents a broad overview of the origins of altruism and aggression in children and youth. Examining the core influences in the family and culture that lead to caring and helping or, alternatively, to hostility and aggression, he suggests several strategies for decreasing aggression and increasing prosocial behavior.

The third part of the book focuses on adversity in adulthood. In chapter

7, Halgin and Vivona present a comprehensive overview of the challenges involved in diagnosing and treating adult survivors of childhood sexual abuse. They describe the challenges faced by therapists who treat adult survivors, including such thorny issues as the validity of survivors' memories and ways of determining the most effective treatment approaches.

Whitbourne, Jacobo, and Muñoz-Ruiz provide an examination of several types of adversity in the elderly, ranging from physical difficulties (such as falls) to psychological adversity (such as depression) in chapter 8. They also address ways in which the elderly can cope with adversity. Ultimately, their message is optimistic, arguing that adversity is neither inevitable nor irreversible.

In chapter 9, Gearan and Rosenbaum examine the question of whether biological factors affect aggression found in relationships. Addressing an issue of significant social importance, the research suggests that physical trauma, such as a head injury, is related to an increase in the incidence of abuse in a relationship. It also raises the possibility that certain classes of drugs may be used to facilitate the acquisition of coping techniques.

Dickman presents a provocative perspective on impulsivity in chapter 10. Although impulsivity has traditionally been viewed as a deficit, he convincingly argues that certain types may actually provide benefits for psychological functioning. However, he emphasizes the importance of differentiating the various sources of impulsivity.

The final part of the book takes a broader perspective on adversity, looking at it in terms of broad societal issues. In chapter 11, Silka considers how geographic considerations color people's responses to the perception of risk. For instance, she raises issues such as "environmental equity," discussing the ways in which poor minority neighborhoods disproportionally become the sites for environmental hazards. She also considers new analytical tools using computer-based geographic information systems that permit a better understanding of the interrelationships among environmental variables. Silka argues that this and similar new approaches will permit a more accurate assessment of environmental risks, by both experts and laypersons.

Ochberg and Chapman address the issue of who chooses to seek higher education in chapter 12. Beginning with the provocative statement that "the habit of higher education appears to be inherited," the authors discuss original research investigating the relationship between social class and the decision to seek a college education and to continue postgraduate studies. The findings suggest ways in which the perceived value of higher education can be increased, especially for those who might not otherwise seek it out.

Finally, in chapter 13, Mandell, Mulvey, and Bond discuss the results of a comprehensive study of sexual harassment on a college campus. The findings show the extent of harassment of women, ranging from seductive behavior to coercive sexual behavior. The authors provide a set of comprehensive suggestions for various solutions and interventions to reduce sexual harassment.

There is great diversity among the chapters in terms of both the level of analysis and analytic approaches employed. However, the authors of all the chapters share a common conviction that adversity is not insurmountable and that problems can be solved. Consequently, each of the chapters concludes with concrete, practical advice based not on abstract, armchair theorizing but on the research and theory discussed within the chapter. The result is a book that offers workable solutions to some of the critical problems that affect people's ability to function successfully.

ACKNOWLEDGMENTS

The President's Office of the University of Massachusetts sponsored the conference on psychological adversity that served as the impetus for this book. Professor James F. Brennan (University of Massachusetts, Boston campus) and Professors Charles Clifton and Susan Fiske (Amherst campus) organized the conference program.

I | ADVERSITY IN INFANCY AND EARLY CHILDHOOD

I ADVERSITY IN THE NEWBORN INFANT

Psychological and Physiological Effects of Prenatal Cocaine Exposure

Jerrold S. Meyer, Mark Mirochnick,
Deborah A. Frank, and Barry S. Zuckerman

Cocaine abuse is currently a serious health problem in the United States. One aspect of this problem that has received considerable media attention is the possible effect of maternal cocaine use on infant development. Over the past few years, researchers at urban public hospitals have reported that at least 10%-15% of newborn infants were exposed to cocaine before birth (Frank et al., 1988; Matera, Warren, Moomjy, Fink, & Fox, 1990; McCalla et al., 1991; Streissguth et al., 1991). Furthermore, as discussed below, these figures may actually represent an underestimate due to the problems associated with obtaining accurate prevalence data for maternal cocaine use.

Human clinical studies as well as research with animal models suggest that *in utero* cocaine exposure may lead to adverse outcomes in the offspring. However, much of this work has been criticized on methodological and other grounds. Is there any way to separate fact from fiction in this debate? To provide the necessary context for understanding the developmental effects of cocaine, we begin this chapter by reviewing some basic features of cocaine pharmacology. The current literature on prenatal cocaine is then summarized and evaluated, followed by a presentation of recent findings from our own research programs. Finally, we close with a brief consideration of some of the social implications of our conclusions.

BASIC PHARMACOLOGY OF COCAINE

Cocaine is extracted from the leaves of the coca shrub, which is grown in the highlands of Peru, Colombia, Bolivia, and Ecuador. On the street, cocaine is available in two different forms: the water-soluble hydrochloride

(HCl) salt and the fat-soluble free base. Cocaine HCl is used for nasal insufflation (snorting) or intravenous (i.v.) injection, but is not normally smoked because it is rapidly degraded at high temperatures. In contrast, cocaine base (crystals of which are called "crack") is suitable for smoking but not for snorting or injection. Smoking leads to a particularly rapid increase in the brain concentration of cocaine, which may account for crack's high addictive potential. It is also important to mention that cocaine is ingested in many different patterns. For example, some individuals take moderate amounts of the drug on a fairly regular basis, whereas others engage in binges in which large amounts of cocaine are taken over a period of hours to days, followed by a "crash" and a variable period of abstinence (Gawin & Kleber, 1986). The relevance of these different patterns for studying the developmental effects of cocaine is discussed below.

Ingestion of cocaine leads to a variety of psychological and physiological effects. The individual experiences a sense of arousal, euphoria, heightened self-confidence, and loss of appetite. Routes of administration that lead to rapid elevations in plasma and brain concentrations (i.e., smoking and i.v. injection) also cause a brief but intense feeling of pleasure called the "rush." Many of the acute physiological effects of cocaine such as increased heart rate, constriction of blood vessels, and elevated blood pressure are mediated by activation of the sympathetic nervous system.

Most of the behavioral effects of cocaine are due to its interaction with neurotransmitters, substances that are responsible for relaying information between nerve cells or from nerve cells to muscles. This process of information transfer is termed *synaptic transmission,* because it occurs at anatomically specialized sites known as synapses. The particular neurotransmitters influenced by cocaine are dopamine (DA), norepinephrine (NE), and serotonin (5-HT). Each is synthesized, stored, and released by specific groups of nerve cells in the brain as well as in other parts of the nervous system. Following release, molecules of the neurotransmitter are taken back up by their cells of origin in order to terminate the chemical signal. For all three neurotransmitters, however, cocaine interferes with this termination process by blocking the reuptake mechanism (Gawin, 1991; Woolverton & Johnson, 1992). Signal transmission is thus enhanced because DA, NE, and 5-HT molecules remain within the synapse for a longer period of time.

Knowledge of cocaine's mechanism of action helps us to understand the psychological and physiological effects of the drug. For example, stimulation of DA transmission in the "reward" pathways of the brain is thought to underlie the reinforcing and perhaps also the euphoric effects of cocaine (Koob, 1992). On the other hand, the nerve cells of the sympathetic system use NE as their transmitter. Hence, the sympathetic activation responsible for the prominent physiological effects of cocaine is mediated partially by a blockade of NE reuptake at various peripheral organs.

REVIEW OF PRENATAL COCAINE EFFECTS

Detection of Prenatal Cocaine Exposure

One of the critical issues in studying cocaine use among pregnant women is correctly identifying users and nonusers. This is important not only for obtaining accurate prevalence data but also for placing offspring into the correct experimental groups. One possibility is to question women directly about their drug use during the course of pregnancy (Day, Wagener, & Taylor, 1985). However, this approach is problematic because of its dependence on the individual's memory of past events as well as her willingness to be honest about an illegal activity. A more widely used method is to screen for the presence of cocaine metabolites (breakdown products) in urine excreted by the mother or the newborn infant (e.g., see Zuckerman et al., 1989). Such metabolites will usually persist for several days after the mother's last usage, thus allowing investigators to verify recent exposure. However, women who used cocaine earlier in pregnancy but not during the last week before giving birth are not identified by this method. Recent studies have shown that cocaine metabolites are also deposited in the hair of the fetus and in a fecal material called meconium that is excreted during the first few days following birth. Thus measurement of cocaine metabolites in the newborn's meconium and/or hair allows investigators to ascertain cocaine exposure during earlier periods of prenatal development (Callahan et al., 1992).

Potential Mechanisms of Prenatal Cocaine Action

Cocaine might influence fetal development by a number of potential mechanisms. For example, the effects of cocaine described earlier on the cardiovascular system occur not only in the mother but also in the fetus due to the transfer of cocaine across the placenta (Schenker et al., 1993). Moreover, cocaine-induced reduction of blood flow to the uterus and placenta leads to a temporary oxygen deprivation by the fetus (Plessinger & Woods, 1991). These effects may be responsible for the intrauterine growth-retarding effects of cocaine as well as for some of the congenital defects observed in a small proportion of cocaine-exposed infants (discussed below).

Another mechanism about which little is known is the direct influence of cocaine on the fetal nervous system. Animal studies discussed below have shown that the neurotransmitter transporters (reuptake sites) influenced by cocaine are present and functional before birth. In humans, these transporters may begin to be expressed as early as 9–10 weeks postconception (discussed below). It is possible, therefore, that inhibition of neurotransmitter reuptake plays a significant role in the effects of prenatal cocaine on central nervous system (CNS) development as well as on postnatal measures of learning and behavior.

Effects of Cocaine on Pregnancy Outcome and Offspring Development

Since the first published reports concerning maternal cocaine use, pregnancy outcome, and infant behavior appeared in the mid-1980s, dozens of studies have been performed by investigators around the country. A number of these studies suggest that pregnant women who use cocaine are more likely to experience placental abruption (detachment of the placenta from the uterine wall) and possibly also spontaneous abortion (see reviews by Kain, Kain, & Scarpelli, 1992; Slutsker, 1992).

As is the case with several other abused substances, cocaine has been reported to exert deleterious effects on fetal growth and development. Consequently, cocaine-exposed neonates (newborn infants) frequently exhibit reductions in birth weight and head circumference (which is an indirect measure of brain size) (Slutsker, 1992). In some cases, this is associated with premature delivery. However, even if the infant is full term, it may be small for its gestational age. Furthermore, prenatal cocaine exposure might increase the risk for certain types of congenital abnormalities, although the data are controversial and more research is needed on this issue.

There is a popular misconception that the offspring of cocaine-using women are born addicted to the drug. In contemporary pharmacological theory, drug-seeking behavior and drug craving are generally considered to be the hallmarks of addiction (Stolerman, 1992). Newborn infants are obviously incapable of exhibiting organized drug-seeking behavior. But we can look for signs of pharmacological dependence (i.e., withdrawal symptoms) that might be construed as including some element of drug craving. Although some cocaine-exposed neonates exhibit behaviors that could be related to drug withdrawal (discussed below), as a group they do not show a consistent withdrawal syndrome such as that observed in the offspring of opiate (i.e., heroin or morphine) users (see Neuspiel & Hamel, 1991). Thus, there is little evidence at this time indicating that prenatal cocaine exposure causes infant addiction to the drug.

Other potential behavioral abnormalities in cocaine-exposed newborns have been investigated using a well-known battery of infant tests called the

Neonatal Behavioral Assessment Scale (NBAS) (Brazelton, 1984). Without going into detail, we can state that cocaine-exposed infants have been reported to show various abnormalities on the NBAS (see reviews by Neuspiel & Hamel, 1991; Singer, Garber, & Kliegman, 1991). One limitation of these findings, however, is that NBAS testing is usually conducted during the first few days of life. Any difference found between cocaine-exposed and unexposed subjects is difficult to interpret because the difference could be due to one or a combination of the following: continued presence of some cocaine in the infant's system; possible withdrawal symptoms from the prior cocaine exposure; cocaine-induced neurological abnormalities that will be repaired or compensated for in time; or neurological abnormalities that are not later repaired. Only in the last case would we expect to find permanent behavioral deficits.

Although prenatal cocaine exposure has been associated with behavioral deficits, there has been little consistency in the *type* of abnormal behavior reported in these offspring. Furthermore, the most recent and well-controlled studies have generally found few or no cocaine-associated deficits on the NBAS (Coles, Platzman, Smith, James, & Falek, 1992; Richardson & Day, 1991; Woods, Eyler, Behnke, & Conlon, 1993), although drug usage may also have been more moderate in these studies than in many of the earlier reports. Finally, cocaine-exposed offspring studied at older ages up to 3 years have, on the average, exhibited cognitive performance similar to that seen in unexposed agemates from similar backgrounds (Azuma & Chasnoff, 1993; Chasnoff, Griffith, Freier, & Murray, 1992; Graham et al., 1992). The meaning of these findings for understanding the prenatal effects of cocaine is considered in the next section.

Evaluation of the Human Prenatal Cocaine Literature

In evaluating this research literature, it should first be noted that except for the frequent presence of intrauterine growth retardation, there is little consensus about what effects are actually associated with cocaine use during pregnancy. Diversity of symptoms in cocaine-exposed offspring could be due partly to the presence of multiple syndromes caused by the cardiovascular versus the direct effects of gestational cocaine exposure on the nervous system (Lester et al., 1991). On the other hand, variability in outcome measures is also attributable to some of the general problems of studying drug use in human populations (Frank, Bresnahan, & Zuckerman, 1993). For example, there is no such thing as a "representative" cocaine user because of the differing routes and patterns of use. Indeed, the effects of maternal cocaine use on the developing fetus depend on the amount consumed at a given time, the frequency and pattern of consumption (e.g., occasional use of moderate amounts versus frequent binging), and when in pregnancy the drug is taken.

Further complicating the interpretation of human prenatal cocaine studies is the problem of obtaining appropriate control groups (Frank et al., 1993). Cocaine-using women often receive little prenatal care, and they almost always take other substances besides cocaine (a practice known as polydrug use). These other substances may be legal, such as tobacco or alcohol, or illegal, such as marijuana or heroin. In any case, few investigators have been able to match their cocaine-exposed and unexposed infants for exposure to other drugs *in utero.* An alternate procedure is to use statistical procedures to remove the effect of confounding factors such as polydrug use, thereby allowing a determination of the influence of cocaine per se. Nevertheless, many studies have not employed this approach, which means that the deleterious effects observed in cocaine-exposed offspring often may have been due to the uncontrolled presence of confounding factors.

Consequently, many researchers now agree that the risks of prenatal cocaine exposure have been seriously overestimated not only by an overzealous, sensationalistic media but even by the scientific community itself (Coles, 1993; Day & Richardson, 1993; Frank & Zuckerman, 1993; Hutchings, 1993; Koren, 1993; Koren, Graham, Shear, & Einarson, 1989). This has led to an unfortunate and unwarranted stigmatization of cocaine or "crack" babies (Mayes, Granger, Bornstein, & Zuckerman, 1992; Zuckerman & Frank, 1992). Nevertheless, the possibility still needs to be tested that infants exposed to particularly high doses of cocaine, possibly in conjunction with other damaging substances such as alcohol or tobacco, do suffer persistent adverse effects. Long-term studies will be particularly important because drug-induced cognitive and/or social deficits may only emerge over time as the nervous system continues to mature (Frank & Zuckerman, 1993).

Effects of Prenatal Cocaine Exposure in Animals

Due to the methodological problems inherent in human cocaine research, even the most sophisticated studies have difficulty in establishing a clear causal connection between gestational cocaine exposure and subsequent behavioral or neurological abnormalities. One way to address this issue is to examine the effects of prenatal cocaine administration in laboratory animals. There are several advantages to using animal models in prenatal drug research. These include control over drug dose, route of administration, and timing of drug exposure; lack of confounding due to group differences in prenatal care or polydrug use (unless drug interactions are specifically being studied); controlling for the effects of drugs on maternal food intake by means of pair-feeding (a procedure in which control animals are given the same amount of food as consumed by the drug-treated subjects); the ability to isolate the effects of prenatal drug treatment from those of the postnatal rearing environment by fostering offspring to normal, untreated surrogate mothers; and the opportunity to examine drug-induced changes in brain structure or functioning. The rapid maturation of species such as rats and mice also facilitates the study of drug-exposed offspring as they develop from infancy to adulthood. On the other hand, there are several disadvantages of using animals (particularly rodents) to investigate the developmental effects of cocaine, including the obvious dissimilarities to humans with respect to behavioral and nervous system complexity, species differences in cocaine metabolism, and the fact that human patterns of cocaine abuse are difficult to mimic in animal models. Despite these limitations, however, animal research can shed much light on whether cocaine has the potential to interfere with normal morphological development, brain anatomy and chemistry, and postnatal behavior, and what mechanisms might underlie such disruptive effects.

Current data are inconsistent as to whether prenatal cocaine induces birth defects in human infants, but recent research using rats and mice has confirmed that cocaine can be teratogenic under certain conditions. In these studies, offspring of cocaine-exposed females displayed congenital malformations of the limbs, the cardiovascular and genitourinary systems, and even the brain (Finnell, Toloyan, van Waes, & Kalivas, 1990; Webster & Brown-Woodman, 1990; Webster, Brown-Woodman, Lipson, & Ritchie, 1991). Such results are intriguing, even though they must be interpreted cautiously because of the high doses of cocaine needed to produce these effects and the general problem of extrapolating teratogenicity from one species to another.

A number of investigators have examined the influence of prenatal cocaine on the development of the DA, NE, and 5-HT neurotransmitter systems. Offspring of mothers given cocaine during pregnancy have been reported to show alterations in DA receptors (Dow-Edwards, Freed, & Fico, 1990; Scalzo, Ali, Frambes, & Spear, 1990), electrical activity of DA nerve cells (Minabe, Ashby Jr., Heyser, Spear, & Wang, 1992), and the density of DA, NE, and 5-HT nerve fibers in several regions of the brain (Akbari & Azmitia, 1992; Akbari, Kramer, Whitaker-Azmitia, Spear, & Azmitia, 1992). Cocaine seems to be capable of interfering with the normal development of all three of these neurotransmitter systems.

A variety of test situations have been used to determine the behavioral effects of prenatal cocaine in animals. For example, subjects that had been exposed to cocaine prenatally showed enhanced reactivity to quinpirole, a drug that stimulates certain receptors for DA (Moody, Frambes, & Spear, 1992). Also of interest are tasks that assess learning ability, because these might predict cognitive deficits in at least some offspring of cocaine-abusing women. Three studies evaluating various types of learning all found deficits associated with gestational cocaine exposure (Heyser, Chen, Miller, Spear, & Spear, 1990; Heyser, Spear, & Spear, 1992; Spear et al., 1989). It is worth noting that the dose of cocaine used in these experiments does not produce intrauterine growth retardation or any other signs of general toxicity in the offspring. Other investigators have reported no cocaine-induced learning deficits (Johns, Means, Anderson, Means, & McMillen, 1992; Smith, Mattran, Kurkjian, & Kurtz, 1989). In general, differences between cocaine-exposed and unexposed offspring are most likely to be observed when the level of task difficulty is high, suggesting that moderate doses of cocaine can lead to cognitive deficits that are revealed only when the subject is appropriately challenged. Human clinical researchers should take these findings into consideration when designing studies to assess possible behavioral impairments associated with prenatal cocaine.

PRENATAL COCAINE RESEARCH AT THE UNIVERSITY OF MASSACHUSETTS AT AMHERST AND BOSTON CITY HOSPITAL

At the University of Massachusetts at Amherst, we have been studying the physiological and behavioral consequences of prenatal cocaine exposure in both human and animal subjects. Following a summary of human infant work carried out in close collaboration with Mark Mirochnick, Deborah Frank, and Barry Zuckerman at the Boston City Hospital, we present a description of our experimental animal research dealing with the possible mechanisms underlying cocaine's effects on brain and behavioral development.

Influence of Prenatal Cocaine on Plasma Catecholamine Concentrations in Human Neonates

Although a number of research groups have examined the behavioral characteristics of newborn infants exposed to cocaine *in utero,* much less is known about the physiological effects of such exposure. Of particular interest in this regard are the substances norepinephrine (NE) and epinephrine (EPI). These substances, which collectively are called catecholamines, are present not only in the brain but also in the bloodstream, where they can readily be measured. NE in the blood comes mainly from the sympathetic nervous system, whereas EPI (also known as adrenaline) is secreted as a hormone by the adrenal gland. The sympathetic nervous system and adrenal gland are major contributors to the classical "fight-or-flight" response elicited by stressful stimuli. Thus cocaine-induced alterations in NE or EPI might reflect disturbances in stress mechanisms, with potentially important consequences for physiological and behavioral adaptability.

We set out to determine whether catecholamine concentrations in blood plasma were affected by prenatal cocaine exposure. The subjects were 24 cocaine-exposed and 22 unexposed infants who were born at the Boston City Hospital between 1992 and 1993 and whose mothers gave informed consent for participation in the study. Maternal cocaine use was documented by either maternal self-report or positive urine and/or meconium assays for the cocaine metabolite benzoylecgonine. Premature infants or those requiring admission to the neonatal intensive care unit were excluded from the study. Birth weight, length, and head circumference were obtained from each infant as indices of intrauterine growth. Between 24 and 72 hours after birth, a blood sample was drawn from each infant for the NE and EPI analyses. Finally, possible behavioral differences between groups were ascertained by means of the NBAS.

The test results revealed no apparent behavioral differences between the infant groups. On the other hand, the cocaine-exposed subjects showed clear signs of intrauterine growth retardation as evidenced by reduced weight and head circumference. Most importantly, these infants also exhibited an elevation in plasma NE, but no change in EPI. An earlier, small study conducted by our research group (Mirochnick, Meyer, Cole, Herren, & Zuckerman, 1991) had found a similar though less-consistent tendency for NE levels to be increased in cocaine-exposed infants. However, Sally Ward and her colleagues (Ward et al., 1989) reported higher plasma NE in 2-month-old offspring exposed to various drugs including cocaine. Taken together, therefore, these studies point to increased NE concentrations as being one possible outcome associated with prenatal cocaine exposure. Because NE in the bloodstream is a marker for sympathetic nervous system activity, we hypothesize that affected infants may be suffering from sympathetic hyperarousal. This conclusion is consistent with the report of Eisen and co-workers that cocaine-exposed neonates showed a higher incidence of stress-related symptoms such as tremors, irritability, high-pitched crying, excessive muscle tone, and gastrointestinal upset than controls showed (Eisen et al., 1991).

The results of this investigation leave many interesting and important questions unanswered. First, we do not know how long the elevation in plasma NE may persist (although the Ward et al. study suggests that the effect is still present at least 2 months after birth). Long-lasting alterations in NE could influence a variety of organ systems that respond to this neurotransmitter. Second, it will be important in future studies to determine whether other measures of sympathetic activity are consistent with our hypothesis of sympathetic hyperarousal. Third, a change in plasma NE raises the issue of whether brain catecholamine systems are also influenced by cocaine. The research group at Boston City Hospital recently examined the concentrations of neurotransmitter metabolites in cerebrospinal fluid (which is the fluid bathing the brain and spinal cord) from cocaine-exposed and unexposed neonates. Although no group difference was found in the NE metabolite 3-methoxy-4-hydroxyphenylglycol, the DA metabolite homovanillic acid was significantly lower in the drug-exposed subjects (Needlman, Zuckerman, Anderson, Mirochnick, and Cohen, 1993). Finally, it is important to note that the cocaine-using mothers in our study differed from the control mothers not only in terms of cocaine but also in their heavier use of other substances such as tobacco, alcohol, and marijuana. There is some reason to believe that these other substances, particularly marijuana, may have contributed to the elevated NE levels seen in the cocaine-exposed offspring.

Neurobehavioral Effects of Cocaine in an Animal Model

Our animal research on the developmental effects of cocaine has two main thrusts: attempting to understand the mechanism of cocaine action during prenatal development by focusing on interactions of the drug with brain neurotransmitter systems; and determining the effects of prenatal cocaine treatment on subsequent brain and behavioral development. Laboratory rats were chosen as subjects for this work because they have a short gestation period (22–23 days), their brain development has already been extensively studied, and their nervous system operates by the same fundamental mechanisms as does that of humans.

Our research has centered around the study of cocaine binding sites because of the importance of such sites for the drug's neural actions. As discussed above, cocaine's effects on adult brain function occur mainly as a result of inhibiting synaptic reuptake of the neurotransmitters DA, NE, and 5-HT. This is accomplished by binding of the drug to the membrane proteins, called transporters, that mediate such reuptake. Consequently, binding experiments using cocaine or related drugs can indicate the presence and characteristics of the cellular components upon which cocaine acts. Other investigators have demonstrated the presence of transporter-related binding sites for radioactively labeled cocaine in brain tissues from adult rats, monkeys, and humans (Calligaro & Eldefrawi, 1988; Madras,

Fahey, Bergman, Canfield, & Spealman, 1989; Reith, Sershen, Allen, & Lajtha, 1983; Schoemaker et al., 1985), but until recently little was known about the possible interaction of cocaine with neurotransmitter transporters in the fetal brain. We set out several years ago to determine whether cocaine binding to these transporters was detectable in the late fetal rat brain, and whether such binding could be related to the above-mentioned reuptake blocking effects of cocaine.

Our initial experiments showed that cocaine binding sites were indeed present in the fetal brain. When studied at day 20 of gestation (GD 20), these sites appeared to represent primarily interaction of cocaine with the transporters for 5-HT and DA (Meyer, Shearman, Collins, & Maguire, 1993). Two other important findings emerged from these studies. First, cocaine was shown to be capable of inhibiting DA uptake into isolated nerve endings obtained from fetal brains. Hence the cocaine binding sites that we had identified could apparently mediate neurotransmitter reuptake, just as in the adult nervous system. Second, cocaine binding sites were first detectable at GD 15 in the rat, after which they showed a steady increase in density up to adulthood (see Figure 1). Human brain development at 15 days gestation obviously is not directly comparable to that of a GD 15 rat fetus. However, we can tentatively extrapolate from rats to humans by adjusting for the stage of development of the neurotransmitter systems that contribute to these binding sites. Based on such an extrapolation, we hypothesize that the human brain probably begins to express cocaine-sensitive neurotransmitter transporters at approximately 9–10 weeks post-conception (Meyer et al., 1993). From this time until birth, the fetus is likely to be vulnerable to the direct reuptake-blocking effects of cocaine.

We have recently begun to use a potent synthetic analog of cocaine known as RTI-55. This compound is valuable for binding studies in part because it binds to the transporters much more tightly than cocaine itself does. Our experiments with RTI-55 have further confirmed the presence of DA and 5-HT transporter-related cocaine binding sites in fetal rat brain (Shearman, Maguire, & Meyer, 1992). We have also found binding sites in rat placenta, which is important because it shows that the placenta as well as the fetus is a target for maternally ingested cocaine (Shearman, Maguire, & Meyer, 1993). Disturbed placental functioning could thus be an alternative mechanism by which prenatal cocaine alters fetal development.

To investigate the influence of prenatal cocaine on later functioning, we have administered various doses of the drug to pregnant females during specific periods of pregnancy and then examined the offspring. For example, Lucille Collins, a graduate student working in the laboratory, was interested in whether cocaine treatment influences later expression of the

ONTOGENY OF WHOLE BRAIN ³H-COCAINE BINDING

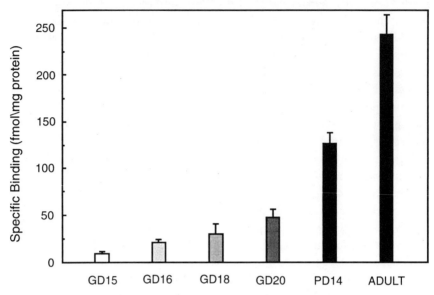

Figure 1. Pre- and postnatal development of cocaine binding sites in the rat brain. GD = gestational day, PD = postnatal day. From "Cocaine binding sites in fetal rat brain: implications for prenatal cocaine action" by J.S. Meyer, L.P. Shearman, L.M. Collins, and R.L. Maguire, 1993, *Psychopharmacology, 112,* p. 447. Reprinted by permission of Springer-Verlag New York, Inc.

DA transporter protein. She injected some pregnant rats once daily with cocaine from GD 8 to GD 21, whereas other animals were given cocaine-containing implants under their skin just from GD 18 to GD 21. The injection procedure is meant to mimic a human user who snorts moderate amounts of cocaine on a daily or near-daily basis, whereas the implants produce persistently elevated levels of cocaine such as might be seen during a cocaine binge. Control rats were treated in similar ways as the other animals, but they received no cocaine. The mothers were allowed to give birth normally, after which the litters were culled to eight and the pups were fostered to untreated lactating dams. As mentioned earlier, fostering the offspring to surrogate mothers ensures that any differences between groups are due to the prenatal treatment rather than to maternal differences in nursing or other behaviors.

At 10, 30, and 60 days of age, offspring from each litter were euthanized and the density of the DA transporter was examined in several brain regions. In this case we used a drug called GBR 12935, which binds more selectively to the DA transporter than either cocaine or RTI-55 does.

Analysis of the results showed that prenatal cocaine treatment by either method caused a decrease in the DA transporter in the dorsolateral region of the corpus striatum, a DA-rich area of the brain. However, the effect was only temporary because it was present at day 10 but not later. The significance of this effect for other aspects of either brain or behavioral development remains to be determined.

In studying the behavioral consequences of prenatal cocaine treatment in rats, we have focused on the use of drug challenges. The rationale for this approach involves the fact that a specific drug may be known to stimulate or antagonize a particular neurotransmitter system. If so, then changes in the behavioral response to the drug following prenatal cocaine exposure are likely to reflect alterations in that neurotransmitter system. In one example of this approach, we investigated the effects of prenatal cocaine on the behavioral reaction of 10-day-old offspring to the drug haloperidol (Meyer, Robinson, & Todtenkopf, 1994). Haloperidol and related drugs are widely used in the treatment of schizophrenia. These antischizophrenic drugs all share the property of blocking a particular type of DA receptor, termed the D2 receptor. The effect of such blockade in rats is to produce a behavioral immobility called catalepsy. Cataleptic animals are not rigid or paralyzed, but they nevertheless show little voluntary movement in the absence of exogenous stimulation. We can quantify the degree of catalepsy in individual subjects by simple methods such as the horizontal bar test. In this procedure, the animal is placed with its forepaws on a horizontally oriented wooden dowel rod elevated above the surface of the apparatus. An experimenter then records the latency (time to respond) for the subject to step off the dowel, up to some maximum time such as 180 sec. Undrugged animals show very short latencies, whereas highly cataleptic subjects may remain on the dowel for the maximum time period. In this particular study, pregnant rats were divided into a cocaine-treated group injected with cocaine daily from GD 8 to GD 20; a control group injected with an inert liquid and pair-fed to the cocaine group (pair-feeding is a procedure that controls for drug-induced changes in the mothers' food intake); and an uninjected, ad lib (unrestricted) fed control group. Litters were culled and the pups were surrogate-fostered as before. When given haloperidol on postnatal day 10, the cocaine-exposed subjects showed less catalepsy than the offspring of the other two groups did (see Figure 2). This behavioral difference may reflect a change in the density or functioning of the D2 receptors, although other explanations are also possible. In future studies, it will be important to determine whether the altered response to haloperidol is long-lasting and whether behaviors related to other types of DA receptors are likewise influenced by prenatal cocaine exposure.

Effect of Maternal Treatment on
Offspring Catalepsy at Postnatal Day 10

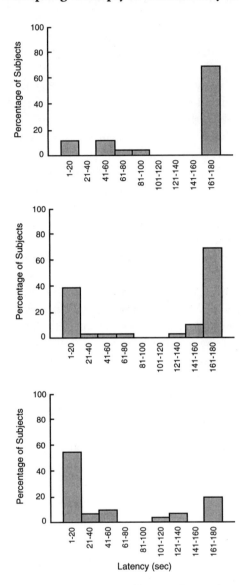

Figure 2. Effect of prenatal treatment on the time (latency) to step off the dowel rod. Pups were given haloperidol on postnatal day 10 and tested 1 h later. The results are expressed as the percentage of subjects in each group that exhibited a latency within the indicated range. From "Prenatal cocaine treatment reduces haloperidol-induced catalepsy on postnatal day 10" by J.S. Meyer, P. Robinson, and M.S. Todtenkopf, 1994, *Neurotoxicology and Teratology, 16,* p. 196. Reprinted by permission of Elsevier Science Ltd., U.K.

CONCLUSIONS AND SOCIAL IMPLICATIONS

The high prevalence of cocaine use, particularly in inner cities, has resulted in the birth of many cocaine-exposed infants. The earliest scientific publications on these infants suggested the presence of significant neurological and behavioral abnormalities. These findings were followed by a barrage of media articles and reports on the new "biological underclass"—a generation of permanently disabled individuals who would soon overwhelm the U.S. system of educational and social services. Research on the psychological and physiological consequences of prenatal cocaine exposure continues, and many important questions remain unanswered. Yet several conclusions can be offered at this time. First, although extrapolation from animal experiments to humans must be done with caution, these studies have shown that cocaine binding sites are present in the fetal brain and that maternal cocaine administration can alter offspring neural and behavioral development. Hence it is premature to conclude that cocaine does not contribute to the abnormalities found in some cocaine-exposed infants. Second, despite such concerns, it is now clear that the majority of these infants show good functioning at birth and probably have the potential for normal cognitive and social development. There is no "biological underclass" threatening to destroy the fabric of American society. Finally, we must come to grips with the central fact that the cocaine epidemic in U.S. inner cities is the manifestation of deep-seated social ills and must be treated as such. Applying this reasoning to the so-called crack baby, we see that cocaine exposure per se is only a small part of the infant's problem. In most cases, greater risk is engendered by the mother's lack of general health concern during pregnancy (e.g., failure to obtain basic prenatal care, cigarette and alcohol use, etc.) and by the adverse postnatal environment in which child may be raised. Therefore, clinicians and social service workers dealing with these women and children should focus on the overall situation, not just on the cocaine use. This change in emphasis should also take place in our governmental policies. To quote Zuckerman and Frank: "We have to provide the basic cost-effective services that support children's health and development and prevent impairment of the child's brain and soul. All children, whether drug-exposed or not, deserve no less" (1992, p. 339).

REFERENCES

Akbari, H. M., & Azmitia, E. C. (1992). Increased tyrosine hydroxylase immuno-reactivity in the rat cortex following prenatal cocaine exposure. *Developmental Brain Research, 66,* 277–281.

Akbari, H. M., Kramer, H. K., Whitaker-Azmitia, P. M., Spear, L. P., & Azmitia, E. C. (1992). Prenatal cocaine exposure disrupts the development of the serotonergic system. *Brain Research, 572,* 57–63.

Azuma, S. D., & Chasnoff, I. J. (1993). Outcome of children prenatally exposed to cocaine or other drugs: a path analysis of three-year data. *Pediatrics, 92,* 396–402.

Brazelton, T. B. (1984). *Neonatal behavioral assessment scale* (2nd ed.). Philadelphia: J. B. Lippincott.

Callahan, C. M., Grant, T. M., Phipps, P., Clark, G., Novack, A. H., Streissguth, A. P., & Raisys, V. A. (1992). Measurement of gestational cocaine exposure: sensitivity of infants' hair, meconium, and urine. *Journal of Pediatrics, 120,* 763–768.

Calligaro, D. O., & Eldefrawi, M. E. (1988). High affinity stereospecific binding of [^{3}H]cocaine in striatum and its relationship to the dopamine transporter. *Membrane Biochemistry, 7,* 87–106.

Chasnoff, I. J., Griffith, D. R., Freier, C., & Murray, J. (1992). Cocaine/polydrug use in pregnancy: Two-year follow-up. *Pediatrics, 89*(2), 284–289.

Coles, C. D. (1993). Saying "goodbye" to the "crack baby." *Neurotoxicology and Teratology, 15,* 290–292.

Coles, C. D., Platzman, K. A., Smith, I., James, M. E., & Falek, A. (1992). Effects of cocaine and alcohol use in pregnancy on neonatal growth and neurobehavioral status. *Neurotoxicology and Teratology, 14,* 23–33.

Day, N. L., & Richardson, G. A. (1993). Cocaine use and crack babies: Science, the media, and miscommunication. *Neurotoxicology and Teratology, 15,* 293–294.

Day, N. L., Wagener, D. K., & Taylor, P. M. (1985). Measurement of substance use during pregnancy: methodologic issues. In T. M. Pinkert (Ed.), *Current Research on the Consequences of Maternal Drug Abuse. NIDA Research Monograph 59* (pp. 36–47). Washington, DC: U.S. Government Printing Office.

Dow-Edwards, D. L., Freed, L. A., & Fico, T. A. (1990). Structural and functional effects of prenatal cocaine exposure in adult rat brain. *Developmental Brain Research, 57,* 263–268.

Eisen, L. N., Field, T. M., Bandstra, E. S., Roberts, J. P., Morrow, C., Larson, S. K., and Steele, B. M. (1991). Perinatal cocaine effects on neonatal stress behavior and performance on the Brazelton scale. *Pediatrics, 88,* 477–480.

Finnell, R. H., Toloyan, S., van Waes, M., & Kalivas, P. W. (1990). Preliminary evidence for a cocaine-induced embryopathy in mice. *Toxicology and Applied Pharmacology, 103,* 228–237.

Frank, D. A., Bresnahan, K., and Zuckerman, B. S. (1993). Maternal cocaine use: Impact on child health and development. In L. A. Barness (Ed.), *Advances in Pediatrics, Vol. 40* (pp. 65–99). Mosby-Year Book.

Frank, D. A., & Zuckerman, B. S. (1993). Children exposed to cocaine prenatally: Pieces of the puzzle. *Neurotoxicology and Teratology, 15,* 298–300.

Frank, D. A., Zuckerman, B. S., Amaro, H., Aboagye, K., Bauchner, H., Cabral, H., Fried, L., Hingson, R., Kayne, H., Levenson, S. M., Parker, S., Reece, H., & Vinci, R. (1988). Cocaine use during pregnancy: Prevalence and correlates. *Pediatrics, 82*(6), 888–895.

Gawin, F. H. (1991). Cocaine addiction: Psychology and neurophysiology. *Science, 251,* 1580–1586.

Gawin, F. H., & Kleber, H. D. (1986). Abstinence symptomatology and psychiatric diagnosis in cocaine abusers. *Archives of General Psychiatry, 43,* 107–113.

Graham, K., Feigenbaum, A., Pastuszak, A., Nulman, I., Weksberg, R., Goldberg, S., Ashby, S., & Koren, G. (1992). Pregnancy outcome and infant development following gestational cocaine use by social cocaine users in Toronto, Canada. *Clinical Investigations in Medicine, 15*(4), 384–394.

Heyser, C. J., Chen, W.-J., Miller, J., Spear, N. E., & Spear, L. P. (1990). Prenatal cocaine exposure induces deficits in Pavlovian conditioning and sensory preconditioning among infant rat pups. *Behavioral Neuroscience, 104*(6), 955–963.

Heyser, C. J., Spear, N. E., & Spear, L. P. (1992). Effects of prenatal exposure to cocaine on conditional discrimination learning in adult rats. *Behavioral Neuroscience, 106*(5), 837–845.

Hutchings, D. E. (1993). The puzzle of cocaine's effects following maternal use during pregnancy: Are there reconcilable differences? *Neurotoxicology and Teratology, 15,* 281–286.

Johns, J. M., Means, M. J., Anderson, D. R., Means, L. W., & McMillen, B. A. (1992). Prenatal exposure to cocaine II: Effects on open-field activity and cognitive behavior in Sprague-Dawley rats. *Neurotoxicology and Teratology, 14,* 343–349.

Kain, Z. N., Kain, T. S., & Scarpelli, E. M. (1992). Cocaine exposure *in utero:* Perinatal development and neonatal manifestations-Review. *Clinical Toxicology, 30*(4), 607–636.

Koob, G. F. (1992). Drugs of abuse: Anatomy, pharmacology and function of reward pathways. *Trends in Pharmacological Sciences, 13,* 177–184.

Koren, G. (1993). Cocaine and the human fetus: The concept of teratophilia. *Neurotoxicology and Teratology, 15,* 301–304.

Koren, G., Graham, K., Shear, H., & Einarson, T. (1989). Bias against the null hypothesis: The reproductive hazards of cocaine. *Lancet, 2,* 1440–1442.

Lester, B. M., Corwin, M. J., Sepkoski, C., Seifer, R., Peucker, M., McLaughlin, S., & Golub, H. L. (1991). Neurobehavioral syndromes in cocaine-exposed newborn infants. *Child Development, 62,* 694–705.

Madras, B. K., Fahey, M. A., Bergman, J., Canfield, D. R., & Spealman, R. D. (1989). Effects of cocaine and related drugs in nonhuman primates. I. [^{3}H]Cocaine binding sites in caudate-putamen. *Journal of Pharmacology and Experimental Therapeutics, 251*(1), 131–141.

Matera, C., Warren, W. B., Moomjy, M., Fink, D. J., & Fox, H. E. (1990). Prevalence of use of cocaine and other substances in an obstetric population. *American Journal of Obstetrics and Gynecology, 163*(3), 797–801.

Mayes, L. C., Granger, R. H., Bornstein, M. H., & Zuckerman, B. (1992). The problem of prenatal cocaine exposure: A rush to judgment. *JAMA, 267*(3), 406–408.

McCalla, S., Minkoff, H. L., Feldman, J., Delke, I., Salwin, M., Valencia, G., & Glass, L. (1991). The biologic and social consequences of perinatal cocaine use in an inner-city population: results of an anonymous cross-sectional study. *American Journal of Obstetrics and Gynecology, 164*(2), 625–630.

Meyer, J. S., Robinson, P., & Todtenkopf, M. S. (1994). Prenatal cocaine treatment reduces haloperidol-induced catalepsy on postnatal day 10. *Neurotoxicology and Teratology, 16,* 193–199.

Meyer, J. S., Shearman, L. P., Collins, L. M., & Maguire, R. L. (1993). Cocaine binding sites in fetal rat brain: Implications for prenatal cocaine action. *Psychopharmacology, 112,* 445–451.

Minabe, Y., Ashby Jr., C. R., Heyser, C., Spear, L. P., & Wang, R. Y. (1992). The effects of prenatal cocaine exposure on spontaneously active midbrain dopamine neurons in adult male offspring: An electrophysiological study. *Brain Research, 586,* 152–156.

Mirochnick, M., Meyer, J., Cole, J., Herren, T., & Zuckerman, B. (1991). Circulating catecholamine concentrations in cocaine-exposed neonates: A pilot study. *Pediatrics, 88*(3), 481–485.

Moody, C. A., Frambes, N. A., & Spear, L. P. (1992). Psychopharmacological responsiveness to the dopamine agonist quinpirole in normal weanlings and in weanling offspring exposed gestationally to cocaine. *Psychopharmacology, 108,* 256–262.

Needlman, R., Zuckerman, B., Anderson, G. M., Mirochnick, M., and Cohen, D. J. (1993). Cerebrospinal fluid monoamine precursors and metabolites in human neonates following in utero cocaine exposure: A preliminary study. *Pediatrics, 92,* 55–60.

Neuspiel, D. R., & Hamel, S. C. (1991). Cocaine and infant behavior. *Developmental and Behavioral Pediatrics, 12*(1), 55–64.

Plessinger, M. A., & Woods, J. R. J. (1991). The cardiovascular effects of cocaine use in pregnancy. *Reproductive Toxicology, 5,* 99–113.

Reith, M. E. A., Sershen, H., Allen, D. L., & Lajtha, A. (1983). A portion of [^{3}H]cocaine binding in brain is associated with serotonergic neurons. *Molecular Pharmacology, 23,* 600–606.

Richardson, G. A., & Day, N. L. (1991). Maternal and neonatal effects of moderate cocaine use during pregnancy. *Neurotoxicology and Teratology, 13,* 455–460.

Scalzo, F. M., Ali, S. F., Frambes, N. A., & Spear, L. P. (1990). Weanling rats exposed prenatally to cocaine exhibit an increase in striatal D2 dopamine binding associated with an increase in ligand affinity. *Pharmacology Biochemistry & Behavior, 37,* 371–373.

Schenker, S., Yang, Y., Johnson, R. F., Downing, J. W., Schenken, R. S., Henderson, G. I., & King, T. S. (1993). The transfer of cocaine and its metabolites across the term human placenta. *Clinical Pharmacology and Therapeutics, 53,* 329–339.

Schoemaker, H., Pimoule, C., Arbilla, S., Scatton, B., Javoy-Agid, F., and Langer, S. Z. (1985). Sodium dependent [³H]cocaine binding associated with dopamine uptake sites in the rat striatum and human putamen decrease after dopaminergic denervation and in Parkinsons disease. *Naunyn-Schmiedeberg's Archives of Pharmacology, 329,* 227–235.

Shearman, L. P., Maguire, R. L., & Meyer, J. S. (1992). Characterization of fetal rat brain cocaine receptors labeled with [³H]cocaine or the potent cocaine analog [¹²⁵I]RTI-55. *Society for Neuroscience Abstracts, 18,* 1434.

Shearman, L. P., Maguire, R. L., & Meyer, J. S. (1993). *Identification of cocaine binding sites in gestational day (GD) 20 rat placenta using the potent phenyltropane analog [¹²⁵I]RTI-55.* Poster presented at the Eleventh International Neurotoxicology Conference: Drugs of Abuse and Developmental Neurotoxicity, Little Rock, AR.

Singer, L. T., Garber, R., & Kliegman, R. (1991). Neurobehavioral sequelae of fetal cocaine exposure. *Journal of Pediatrics, 119*(4), 667–672.

Slutsker, L. (1992). Risks associated with cocaine use during pregnancy. *Obstetrics & Gynecology, 79*(5), 778–789.

Smith, R. F., Mattran, K. M., Kurkjian, M. F., & Kurtz, S. L. (1989). Alterations in offspring behavior induced by chronic prenatal cocaine dosing. *Neurotoxicology and Teratology, 11,* 35–38.

Spear, L. P., Kirstein, C. L., Bell, J., Yoottanasumpun, V., Greenbaum, R., O'Shea, J., Hoffmann, H., & Spear, N. E. (1989). Effects of prenatal cocaine exposure on behavior during the early postnatal period. *Neurotoxicology and Teratology, 11,* 57–63.

Stolerman, I. (1992). Drugs of abuse: behavioural principles, methods and terms. *Trends in Pharmacological Sciences, 13,* 170–176.

Streissguth, A. P., Grant, T. M., Barr, H. M., Brown, Z. A., Martin, J. C., Mayock, D. E., Ramey, S. L., & Moore, L. (1991). Cocaine and the use of alcohol and other drugs during pregnancy. *American Journal of Obstetrics and Gynecology, 164,* 1239–1243.

Ward, S. L. D., Bautista, D. B., Buckley, S., Schuetz, S., Wachsman, L., Bean, Z., & Warburton, D. (1989). Circulating catecholamines and adrenoreceptors in infants of cocaine-abusing mothers. *Annals of the New York Academy of Sciences, 562,* 349–351.

Webster, W. S., & Brown-Woodman, P. D. C. (1990). Cocaine as a cause of congenital malformations of vascular origin: Experimental evidence in the rat. *Teratology, 41,* 689–697.

Webster, W. S., Brown-Woodman, P. D. C., Lipson, A. H., & Ritchie, H. E. (1991). Fetal brain damage in the rat following prenatal exposure to cocaine. *Neurotoxicology and Teratology, 13,* 621–626.

Woods, N. S., Eyler, F. D., Behnke, M., & Conlon, M. (1993). Cocaine use during pregnancy: Maternal depressive symptoms and infant neurobehavior over the first month. *Infant Behavior and Development, 16,* 83–98.

Woolverton, W. L., & Johnson, K. M. (1992). Neurobiology of cocaine abuse. *Trends in Pharmacological Sciences, 13,* 193–200.

Zuckerman, B., & Frank, D. A. (1992). "Crack kids": Not broken. *Pediatrics, 89,* 337–339.

Zuckerman, B., Frank, D. A., Hingson, R., Amaro, H., Levenson, S. M., Kayne, H., Parker, S., Vinci, R., Aboagye, K., Fried, L. E., Cabral, H., Timperi, R., and Bauchner, H. (1989). Effects of maternal marijuana and cocaine use on fetal growth. *New England Journal of Medicine, 320,* 762–768.

AUTHOR'S NOTE

The research reported in this chapter was supported by grants DA06495 (JSM) and DA06532 (DAF, BZ, and MM) from the National Institute on Drug Abuse.

2 FUNCTIONAL ENCOPRESIS

Treatment and Management

Martin H. Young, Lynn C. Brennan, Robert D. Baker and Susan S. Baker

Functional encopresis—inappropriate fecal soiling in children over the age of 4—is a common problem. Use of the terms "functional" and "psychogenic" in conjunction with the term encopresis, are meant to differentiate encopresis from incontinence that is due to a physical disorder such as a spinal cord injury, anal fissure, or Hirschprung's disease (Margolies & Gilstein, 1983). Encopresis appears to be more prevalent in boys than in girls, with some research suggesting that there are as many as six boys for every girl with encopresis (Levine, 1982).

A distinction is often made between primary (or continuous) encopresis and secondary (or discontinuous) encopresis. Children are considered to have primary encopresis when they have never been successfully toilet-trained, whereas with secondary encopresis a child becomes incontinent after having successfully completed bowel training. Previous research has not supported any distinction between these two groups in terms of either etiological or prognostic factors (Bemporad, Kresch, Asnes, & Wilson, 1978; Levine & Bakow, 1976).

Prevalence estimates vary, suggesting that the disorder may affect from 1.5 to 7.5% of all school-aged children (Doleys, Schwartz, & Cineinero, 1981). Further, perhaps due to the embarrassing and unpleasant nature of the problem, underreporting has been consistently noted in the literature. One prominent expert on encopresis has referred to the disorder as "the secret problem" (Rappaport & Levine, 1986). The disorder occurs in every social class and racial group, yet it is little understood and seldom talked about, even among child health clinicians. Given its high incidence in the general population, research on encopresis is relatively scarce. The research that is available presents an inconsistent and confusing picture, with authors differing widely in their views on the nature, etiology, and treatment of the disorder.

Statement of the Problem

The purpose of this study was to examine the relationship between encopresis and the behavioral, emotional, and social problems that often accompany the condition. In addition, treatment effectiveness in terms of both symptom resolution and second-order changes in children with encopresis and their families was studied. An interdisciplinary approach to both the theoretical analysis and treatment was utilized.

Brief Overview of the Literature

Early literature on encopresis, contributed primarily by psychoanalytically oriented authors, is concerned with the role of emotional, behavioral, and family problems in the etiology of the disorder (Bellman, 1966; Bemporad, Pfeifer, Gibbs, Cortner, & Bloom, 1971; Fritz & Armbrust, 1982). This literature suggests that a poor child/mother relationship is frequently the primary etiology for the problem.

Alternatively, the pediatric literature focuses on the physiological aspects of the problem, at times discounting its psychosocial aspects (Stern, Prince, & Stroh, 1988). Perhaps the most glaring shortfall of the available literature on encopresis is the lack of interdisciplinary studies that examine both the physiological and psychosocial factors that contribute to the genesis and maintenance of the problem. The limited research that attempts such an approach tends to utilize small sample case reports and is anecdotal rather than empirical in nature (Landman & Rappaport, 1985; Rydzinski & Kaplan, 1985; Stern et al., 1988). There is also a scarcity of treatment outcome studies.

In one of the very few empirical studies of encopresis treatment outcome, Levine and Bakow (1976) followed a group of 127 children with encopresis treated at Boston Children's Hospital using a behavioral pediatric approach. The findings of this study are especially pertinent to the current study because both Boston Children's Hospital and the University of Massachusetts Medical Center (UMMC) are tertiary-care facilities. Tertiary-care facilities are likely to draw a clientele with greater severity of the disorder than those treated in a primary-care facility.

At one year follow-up, the authors obtained outcome data on 110 of these patients. Four groups were identified; 51% had been soil-free at least six months, 27% showed marked improvement, 14% showed some improvement, and 8% showed no improvement.

Levine and Bakow (1976) compared the four groups with respect to a large number of demographic, developmental, psychosocial, and clinical variables. Findings indicated that 22% of their sample, comprising the latter two groups, had a higher incidence of children with very severe incontinence and constipation at onset, a higher incidence of children who soiled nocturnally and/or while at school, and a higher incidence of behavioral, developmental, and academic problems. It was also noted that lack of compliance with the treatment program was associated with treatment failure.

Only a handful of studies have examined the relationship between encopresis and concomitant behavior problems. Gabel, Hegedus, Wald, Chandra, and Chaponis (1986) used the Child Behavior Checklist (CBCL) to assess the behavioral characteristics of 55 children with encopresis (Achenbach & Edelbrock, 1983). When compared to the normative sample for the CBCL, they found that children with encopresis were rated by their parents as having a high incidence of behavior problems, "but not to the degree usually found in a population of children referred for mental health services" (p. 296).

Using the CBCL, Loening-Baucke, Cruikshank, and Savage (1987) assessed the relationship between behavior problems and defecation dynamics in 38 children with encopresis. Findings indicated a high incidence of poor social competency and behavior problems in the children with encopresis in their sample. While mean T scores were above the mean of the normative standardization sample for the CBCL on all of the behavioral subscales, none were in the abnormal range for the group as a whole, though 21% did obtain scores in the abnormal range. There was no significant relationship between behavior problem scores and recto-anal abnormality, nor was there a significant relationship between behavior problem or social competency scores and treatment outcome. Significant relationships were found, however, between treatment outcome and the ability to defecate rectal balloons (a measure of rectal motility) and the ability to relax the external sphincter.

Two studies (Landman, Rappaport, Fenton, & Levine, 1986; Owens-Stively, 1987) found that children with encopresis demonstrated a diminished sense of self-esteem when compared to control or comparison children with other "low severity high prevalence" disorders such as recurrent abdominal pain, enuresis, and chronic headaches. Landman et al. (1986) found a trend for children with encopresis to make fewer internal attributes when they succeed than children in the comparison group, indicating a diminished sense of efficacy in the encopretic group. It is unclear, however, whether or not the low self-esteem experienced by the children with encopresis is causally related or secondary to the encopretic symptoms.

Several studies (Abrahamian & Lloyd-Still, 1984; Friman, Mathews, Finney, Christophersen, & Leibowitz, 1988; Gabel, Chandra, & Schindledecker, 1988) have found evidence for the existence of a subgroup of children with encopresis with more extreme behavior problems. Between 15% and 20% of the children with encopresis in two studies (Abrahamian & Lloyd-Still, 1984; Friman et al., 1988) were found to have significant psychological problems. Many of these problems were believed to be secondary to the encopresis and did not interfere with treatment outcome.

Friman et al. (1988) posited that successful pediatric management of encopresis may diminish behavioral problems in children who have both, and they suggested this hypothesis as an avenue for future research. According to Owens-Stively (1987), while logistical constraints prevented re-administration of the Piers-Harris (an assessment of self-esteem) in her study, an anecdotal improvement in self-esteem following successful treatment was observed. The author suggested that this second-order change is a topic that warrants further study.

Second-order change has been described in several case studies (Landman & Rappaport, 1985; Stern et al., 1985) that report on focused behavioral treatment to decrease the symptoms of encopresis. Several authors (Margolies & Gilstein, 1983, Rydzinski & Kaplan, 1985) have noted second-order changes following treatment of encopresis with a combination of behavioral techniques within the context of a structural family therapy model.

Hypotheses

1. Children who have encopresis are more likely to demonstrate emotional/behavioral problems than children in a matched nonclinical contrast group.
2. A combined medical and psychotherapeutic intervention is highly successful in the resolution of encopretic symptoms.

WORCESTER ENCOPRESIS STUDY

Study Participants

The total sample in this study was 76 children, ranging in age from 6 years 1 month to 12 years 4 months with a mean of 8.97 years (see Table 1). The group of children with encopresis consisted of 25 boys and 13 girls ($n = 38$), representing close to a 2:1 ratio of boys to girls. This group was drawn from the population of children referred to the Pediatric Gastroenterology (PDGI) Clinic at UMMC, who fit the DSM-III-R criteria for functional encopresis. Nine additional children were excluded from the analysis, one because of physical abnormalities (i.e., Hirschprung's Disease), and eight because they dropped out of treatment prior to 6 months or chose not to participate in behavioral treatment.

Table 1
Sample Characteristics

Characteristics	N	%
Gender		
Male	50	66
Female	26	34
Age		
6	12	16
7	13	17
8	18	24
9	9	12
11	9	12
12	1	1
Race		
White	76	100
SES Group[a]		
1	3	4
2	2	3
3	18	24
4	17	22
5	15	20
6	17	22
7	4	5

[a] In accordance with Hamburger's revision of the Warner, Meeker, Eels Occupational Classification System (Hamburger, 1957).

A nonclinical matched comparison group, the contrast group ($n = 38$), was drawn from the entire population of 6-to 12-year-old children at two local pediatric practices. This group was carefully matched for age, gender, and socioeconomic status (SES) and roughly matched for academic performance. In addition, all children in both groups were Caucasian and all were from the same geographic area. No member of the contrast group was, or had ever been, diagnosed with functional encopresis.

Volunteer subjects in the encopretic group were enrolled in this study following a diagnosis of functional encopresis made by the attending physician in the PDGI Clinic at UMMC. Parents, if interested, met with one of the members of the research team to discuss the research study in detail. Informed consent was obtained for all volunteer subjects in both the encopretic and contrast groups. Twelve-year-old children were asked to sign an informed assent form documenting their willingness to participate in this study. This study was reviewed and approved by the Human Subjects Review Board at UMMC and at Boston University.

Measures

The CBCL was used as a measure of social and behavioral functioning and has a large standardization sample and high reliability and validity (Achenbach & Edelbrock, 1983). Soiling frequency was the measure of the dependent variable.

The CBCL is a checklist consisting of 118 behavior problem items, which takes roughly 20 minutes to complete. Behavior variables are rated by parents using a 3-point response scale. The 20 social competence items record parents reports of the amount and quality of their children's participation in sports, hobbies, games, activities, organizations, jobs, chores, and friendships. The CBCL also records parental responses of how well the child gets along with others, plays and works by himself/herself, and functions in school (Achenbach & Edelbrock, 1983).

Soiling frequency as recorded by mothers and/or fathers was rated on a 6-point scale, 0 indicating no soiling, 1 indicating soiling less than once a week, 2 for soiling once a week, 3 for soiling two or three times per week, 4 for soiling daily, and 5 for soiling more than once a day.

Procedures and Treatment

The CBCL was administered at enrollment and at six months. All children with encopresis received a combined medical and psychotherapeutic treatment. The medical treatment consisted of an initial evacuation procedure (using suppositories, enemas, and/or laxatives, typically performed on an outpatient basis). The typical initial evacuation or "clean-out procedure" consisted of six enemas over a period of three consecutive days. Recommendations for an increase in dietary fiber, the daily use of a stool softener such as mineral oil, and the daily use of a bulking agent such as Unifiber (Dow Hickam, Inc., Texas) were also made.

Patients and their parents were seen by the attending physician for an initial consultation in the PDGI Clinic. Follow-up visits were scheduled for two to four weeks after the initial visit. At the initial visit, consultation with a staff member in Pediatric Psychology was scheduled. During the follow-up medical visit, patients were examined to ascertain whether or not the evacuation procedure was successful. From that point on the patient's treatment was monitored primarily by a pediatric psychologist, with the PDGI Clinic available for consultation. Typically patients were seen by PDGI Clinic staff six months after the completion of the treatment to determine whether any modification of treatment was necessary, such as the gradual phasing out of mineral oil and/or Unifiber.

The psychotherapy treatment component was modified from several published papers and articles, primarily those by Levine (1982), Landman & Rappaport (1985), Walker, Milling & Bonner (1988), White (1984), and Margolies & Gilstein (1983). Treatment consisted of four phases. Phase 1 was the education and demystification process; phase 2 was the behavior modification program within the context of a structural family therapy paradigm; phase 3 was the phasing out of the rewards; and phase 4 was termination.

The goal of the education/demystification procedure was to remove negative attributions for the soiling for either the child or the parent. The importance of a consistent, positive, and supportive parental attitude in all aspects of treatment was stressed. The second component, the behavior modification program, involved scheduled toilet sittings and clean pants checks. As part of this program, children had small rewards for their appropriate toileting behaviors and unsoiled clothing. Although each behavior modification program was tailored to the specific needs of each child and family, the following are some general guidelines.

Children were asked to sit on the toilet and attempt to defecate three times a day, preferably directly following mealtimes to take advantage of the gastro-iliac reflex. If the child produced a bowel movement while on the toilet, he or she earned a previously agreed upon reinforcer. The parent was responsible for checking the toilet and providing the appropriate reward. As the program proceeded, children received different parental rewards depending on the size of the bowel movement.

Rewarding appropriate toileting is very important, especially initially. Many clinicians reward only for clean pants, or the absence of soiling. Since a major part of the child's problem is the withholding of stool, rewarding only for clean pants at the onset of treatment can result in increased withholding rather than appropriate toileting. Typically, there was no punishment for soiling. However, where necessary, an overcorrection procedure was instituted such that children were given responsibility for their own soiled clothing and/or cleaning the entire bathroom if any unnecessary messing was made there. Parents were asked to maintain charts to monitor the child's progress.

The third component of treatment was the phasing-out of rewards. This occurred after children were completely soil-free for eight weeks. Rewards were phased out by making the criteria more stringent. For example, instead of rewarding every large bowel movement, every other large bowel movement would be rewarded. Once children were receiving one reward a week, treatment was terminated.

The termination session was framed for the child and the family as a "graduation" and was celebrated as opposed to merely attended. Relapse prevention was an important aspect at this final session. Families were advised that children occasionally experience recurrence of soiling. They were instructed that in the event of a recurrence they should consider doing a "mini clean-out procedure" on their own (possibly consisting of one to three enemas) and to reinstitute three daily sittings until the child is soil-free for two weeks. Families were invited to contact the clinician for telephone support whenever the need arose.

In treatment-resistant cases a more aggressive treatment can be used. This treatment is outlined in detail by Christophersen and Rainey (1976).

Analyses

Hypothesis 1. *t*-tests for independent means were conducted to measure differences between the two groups' means on the dependent measure of emotional/behavioral problems as measured by the Total Behavior Problems and Total Social Competence pretest scores on the CBCL.

Hypothesis 2. A *t*-test for dependent means was used to compare pre-and posttreatment soiling frequency scores within the encopretic group.

Results

Children with encopresis were found to have significantly more behavioral problems and poorer social skills before treatment than children without toileting problems (Total Behavior Problems [$t(74) = 3.01$, $p<.004$], Total Social Competence [$t(74) = 3.996$, $p<.0001$]). After six months of treatment, children with encopresis were found to have significantly less behavior problems and significantly improved social skills (Total Behavior Problems [$t(37) = 2.70$, $p<.01$], Total Social Competency [$t(37) = 1.989$, $p<.05$]). Boys and girls did not appear to respond differently to treatment [$t(36) = 1.88$, $p< 068$].

Mean soiling frequency before treatment was 3.83, indicating that on average children soiled from two or three times per week to once a day. Six months later, the mean soiling frequency was 1.32, noting that soiling was, on average, eliminated or occurring less than once a week. This change was found to be statistically significant [$t(37) = 11.95$, $p<.0001$].

DISCUSSION

Statistically significant differences were found between pre-and posttest measures of social competence and emotional/behavioral problems for the group of children with encopresis. The observation of second-order symptom resolution has been made anecdotally by a number of authors. However, this is the first study in which this hypothesis has been systematically studied and supported. While all but 3 of the 38 children with encopresis made some improvement in soiling frequency, the amount of improvement varied widely (see Table 2). Nevertheless, the group as a whole made significant improvements on the Total Behavior Problems and Total Social Competence scores. This brings to light the question of whether the change in concomitant social and emotional/behavioral problems is related exclusively to symptom resolution or whether it may be a function of some other effect (or effects) of treatment, such as the manner in which the child experiences the change, improved child-management strategies on the part of parents, or a combination of factors.

Children with encopresis demonstrate significantly more social and emotional/behavioral problems than children who do not have encopresis. However, the problems appear to be secondary to the encopresis rather than causally related to it as has been suggested, especially in the psychodynamic literature (Bellman, 1966; Bemporad et al., 1971; Fritz & Armbrust, 1982).

Of the 38 children in the experimental group, there were 14 children who achieved complete continence within six months of the onset of treatment. An additional 10 children soiled less than once per week. Fourteen children soiled once a week or more six months after the onset of treatment. Children who soiled less than once per week made roughly 69% more improvement in the area of emotional/behavioral problems as measured by the CBCL than those children who continued to soil once per week or more. Children who were soiling less than once per week made roughly 95% more improvement in the area of social competence as measured by the CBCL than those children who were still soiling once per week or more.

While the treatment approach utilized in this study was highly effective, the study is not without its treatment failures. For ease of interpretation and discussion, the 14 children comprising the first outcome group (identified above who experienced a complete alleviation of soiling) are designated as treatment successes (37%) and the 8 children comprising the last two outcome groups (who soiled two to three times per week or more after six months of treatment [21%]) are designated as treatment failures. These children represent the more extreme responders to treatment and, therefore, will make the distinction between the treatment successes and failures more meaningful. Outcome data on the remaining 16 children (42%), comprising the middle two groups, was excluded from only this analysis.

Upon grouping the outcome data in this way, two thematic differences between treatment success and failure groups, which may have been other-

Table 2
Descriptive Statistics for the Soiling Frequency Measure,
Experimental Group Only

Score	Corresponding Frequency	Pre-treatment n	6 Months n
0	None	0	14
1	Less than once a week	1	10
2	Once a week	2	6
3	2–3 times per week	13	4
4	Daily	9	4
5	More than once a day	13	0
	M	3.82	1.32
	SD	1.06	1.36

Note. $n = 38$.

wise obscured, became readily apparent. Only 36% of the treatment success group scored within the abnormal range (above the 90th percentile) on either the Total Social Competence scale or the Total Behavior Problems scale prior to treatment, whereas 75% of the treatment failure group scored within the abnormal range on one or both of these measures prior to treatment.

Furthermore, of the 5 children in the successful treatment group scoring within the abnormal range prior to treatment, only 1 remained within this range after six months of treatment. However, of the 6 children in the treatment failure group that obtained pretreatment scores within the abnormal range, 4 remained within this range on the posttest measure.

Even though these sample sizes are too small to draw inferences to the general population of successfully and nonsuccessfully treated children with encopresis, the trend is in sharp contrast to the findings of the Loening-Baucke et al. (1987) study, in which no relationship between treatment outcome and social competency was found, but it is partially consistent with findings from the Gabel et al. (1988) study, which did find such a relationship. Gabel et al. (1988) posited that parents who perceived their children's behavior as extreme may have demonstrated such a negative view of the child that they were overly punitive and, therefore, not helpful in appropriately motivating the child for treatment.

These data suggest that highly elevated behavior problem scores may be related to poor treatment outcome. Furthermore, the issue of parental negativism ties directly into the second thematic difference between treatment success and treatment failure groups observed in the current study.

Without exception, one or both parents of the 8 children in the treatment failure group were characterized by a negative attitude toward their child, which was most readily apparent in their expressed belief that the child was doing the soiling intentionally. What is noteworthy is that parents of more than half of the children in the treatment success group initially expressed the same belief. However, following the demystification procedure and over the course of treatment, these parents were able to abandon this belief. What was most different between groups regarding the issue of negativism was not whether or not parents began treatment with a negative view of the child but whether or not they were able to change this view.

For virtually all families in the treatment failure group, parents' negative perceptions of their children tended to be fueled or reinforced by oppositional behavior on the part of their children, which was most obvious in terms of noncompliance with the treatment program. This becomes a circular dilemma where the parents' negativism interferes with their ability to give praise and rewards consistently and in a positive way, when such praise and rewards are earned by the child. It is unfortunate that treatment failure can result in strengthening parents' beliefs that their child's soiling is willful, thus perpetuating negativism within the family. The construct of mishandled anger was proposed by Baird (1974) and suggested by Margolies & Gilstein (1983) as a factor that may contribute to the development and, more importantly, to the maintenance of the encopretic symptoms within the family.

As a result of this research, the constructs of family negativism, mishandled anger, family conflict, and low family cohesion, as they relate to treatment outcome, have been suggested as avenues for future study. It may be beneficial to explore these constructs as they relate to both the maintenance and resolution of the encopretic symptoms within the family.

The findings of this research suggest that there may be a small but significant subgroup of children with encopresis for whom concomitant emotional, behavioral, and social problems seem to be more severe and treatment outcome worse. Ultimately, research findings that help to improve upon and refine existing treatment approaches, making them more effective for this subgroup of children with encopresis, are needed.

CASE STUDIES

The following case studies are presented to illustrate the emotional and behavioral impact on the child and the family, the medical and behavioral treatment, and factors that are related to treatment success and failure.

Steven M—A Successful Case

Referral Information. Steven M was diagnosed with Functional Encopresis at UMMC. He was referred to the Pediatric Psychological Clinic for psychological treatment and was seen over a period of 10 months for a total of seven sessions. Steven, a Caucasian male, was 9 years and 9 months of age and lived with his parents and 10-year-old sister at the time of intake.

Pretreatment History. At age 9 Steven had never been toilet-trained, although attempts had been made to do so from the age of 3 1/2. His medical and developmental history was otherwise unremarkable. One previous unsuccessful treatment had been attempted. Upon intake, Steven was soiling daily, often several times a day. He claimed to have little or no awareness of the soiling when it was happening and no bodily sensations that served as cues to the soiling.

Steven's parents attributed his soiling to his willful and defiant behavior and perceived the encopresis as a manifestation of his general noncompliance. This perception led to much family tension. Over the years, Mr. and Mrs. M had attempted to solve the problem using a variety of approaches. They tried punishing him by hitting him with a strap, overcorrection techniques, laxatives, and positive reinforcement, although the latter with questionable consistency. At one point, they promised Steven a ticket to the circus contingent upon his using the toilet. He did use the toilet and earned the ticket. However, the day after the circus he began soiling again. This confirmed his parents' belief that Steven's soiling was willful and defiant.

For the two years preceding treatment, Steven had been made to stay in his soiled clothes all day. As such, he had been in many ways isolated from the rest of the family. He ate dinner alone at the kitchen counter so as not to bother the other members of the family with a noxious odor. For the same reason and so that the living room furniture was not soiled, Steven was not allowed to sit on the couches while watching television and was excluded from almost all family outings in order to avoid a potentially embarrassing situation resulting from the soiling.

Steven demonstrated extremely depressed affect during the intake interview. When asked to rate his desire to work on his problem he responded with a 10 (on a scale from 1 to 10, 10 the highest desire).

Academically, Steven was an average to above-average student. Socially, however, he was identified by his teacher as an isolated, withdrawn, and relatively unresponsive child. Steven's relationships with his parents and sister were negative and conflictual. His mother, who described herself as having never been a "kid person," appeared rigid and overcontrolling as well as emotionally unavailable at times. Mr. M, although not inclined to verbalize his feelings, was clearly angry and highly critical of Steven. He had great difficulty during the first session identifying any of Steven's more positive qualities. Both reported that little of their time was spent with Steven. Mr. and Mrs. M were hard-working individuals and both held full-time jobs. Steven and his sister spent roughly three afternoons a week with their maternal grandmother.

Treatment Summary. During the initial interview, the problem of encopresis was explained in detail to the family in such a way as to reframe all intentionality and to counter previously held beliefs that Steven's encopresis was a willful and defiant maneuver completely under his control. This educational piece needed to be reiterated during the first three treatment sessions. The family was advised to begin Steven on four tablespoons of mineral oil per day.

It was suggested that Steven sit on the toilet three times a day. It was mutually agreed upon that he was to be rewarded five cents for practicing sitting and pushing and 25 cents for defecating any amount in the toilet. The family was asked to keep a log, charting the frequencies of sitting and defecation.

Weekly telephone contact was maintained with the family for ongoing support. Despite the fact that Steven responded immediately to the contingency reinforcement program, his mother did not at first see his progress as encouraging. During the first telephone contact she related her anger with Steven and her ambivalence toward "bribing him" in this way. The reinforcements were reframed as necessary to motivate the "learning."

In the two weeks that elapsed between the first and second session Steven defecated in the toilet seven times. Soiling continued on a daily basis, however. It was hypothesized that Steven had a large amount of soft stool in the colon and a "mini clean-out procedure" was recommended. The mineral oil was also increased by one tablespoon per day.

It was recommended that charting and positive reinforcement continue with the addition of activity rewards, offered intermittently for particularly good days or weeks. This recommendation was made in order to encourage more positive contact between Steven and his parents.

By the third session, one month after the onset of treatment, Steven was consistently sitting and regularly defecating in the toilet. He had defecated in the toilet all but two days of the previous two weeks and had gone for periods of four and five consecutive days without soiling.

A marked change in family interactions was also noted. Both Mr. and

Mrs. M made several positive comments about their son and Steven was visibly more animated. He smiled several times during the session, particularly when his improved toileting behavior was being discussed. The M family reported that Steven had been much more involved in family activities. He earned the privileges of sitting on the living room couch and at the dinner table with the rest of his family during dinner. Steven chose to use the majority of his reinforcement money to buy his lunches at school rather than taking a bag lunch. He did this from the beginning of the reinforcement program.

The phasing out of reinforcement was then recommended. This process began by administering a reinforcement for every other time Steven sat and/or defecated in the toilet. Clean pants checks were also recommended whereby Steven was reinforced three times a day, once at each scheduled toilet sitting, for having clean pants.

Steven and his family continued to make progress for the remaining four treatment sessions. By the fourth session, two months from the onset of treatment, Steven had begun to defecate in the toilet at times other than the scheduled sittings. In addition, his parents frequently noted his improvements in other areas. They reported that Steven had begun to make more friends at school and was getting all As and Bs on his report card. They added that his teacher had noted his becoming less withdrawn; he was participating and smiling more in class. He was demonstrating a more positive attitude toward his chores and seemed generally happier and more independent than prior to treatment.

Treatment recommendations later varied slightly in response to a minor setback, which took place when Mrs. M stopped giving Steven his mineral oil on a regular basis and when the family diet became excessively starchy due to financial problems. Since it was clear that Steven was not yet ready to take complete responsibility for monitoring and charting his own toileting behavior, and since Mrs. M appeared to be tiring of the task, Mr. M was involved more directly in the task. This served the additional purpose of increasing the daily contact between Mr. M and Steven. Steven was also encouraged to take a more active and responsible role. The therapists then instituted a reward called the "daily double," which was a double reward for defecating spontaneously or without being reminded to do so. The same incentive was also offered in a subsequent session to encourage generalization of his toileting behavior to other places, such as at his grandmother's house and at school.

Upon termination, Steven had been soil-free for over five consecutive weeks. The family was advised to continue reinforcement of clean pants on a weekly basis by rewarding Steven with enough money to continue buying his lunches at school.

The family was advised that should the symptoms recur, they should reinstitute the behavioral program as appropriate and they were encouraged to call or to come in for guidance in the form of a booster session if desired. The final session was framed as a graduation of sorts. Steven reported feeling "proud."

A follow-up note from Mrs. M conveyed Steven's continued progress.

> I would like you to know Steven is doing great. He hasn't soiled since the last time we told you back in late June. I still give him oil or I'll have him take his own oil. Most of the time he is using the toilet on his own when he has to go. Steven has also used the toilet at his grandmother's, and since school has started, three times he went at school. He's met a nice friend at school and sees him sometimes on the weekend. He's much happier now. Our family is now relaxed. What a pleasure (a lot less laundry, great). I want to thank you for all your help.

Ann P—An Unsuccessful Case

Referral Information. Ann P was diagnosed with Functional Encopresis at UMMC. She was referred to the Pediatric Psychology Clinic for psychological treatment and was seen over a period of 11 months for a total of 10 sessions. Ann, a Caucasian female, was 8 years and 1 month of age and lived with her mother and 11-year-old sister at the time of intake.

Pretreatment History. Ms. P reports that Ann's biological father had a substance abuse problem and was abusive to her and her two daughters. Their relationship was severed when Ann was 18 months old. Ms. P's present boyfriend, Mr. K, was reported to be an alcoholic, but not physically abusive.

Ann's family was in serious financial distress. While both Ms. P and Mr. K had recently begun working part-time, both had been unemployed for several years prior to this. At the time of intake, the family was living in an insect-and rat-infested tenement building. Their living conditions were a constant source of stress.

According to her mother, Ann had achieved fecal continence at roughly 2 years of age. She remained continent until roughly one year prior to intake. There was no specific stressor coincident with the onset of symptoms. At the time of intake, Ann had infrequent and small bowel movements in the toilet. She soiled many times each day. She claimed to have no awareness of the soiling. A hygiene problem was readily apparent.

According to Ms. P, Ann's behavior was noted to be oppositional both at home and at school. Ann's first grade teacher frequently needed to prod and discipline Ann for her noncompliant and disruptive behavior and excessive daydreaming. Ann had few friends and was reported to have conflictual peer relationships with her classmates. Ann was a B and C student, but Ms. P believed that Ann could have done better if not for her behavioral and attentional problems.

For the six months prior to intake, Ms. P and her two daughters had been attending family therapy sessions at a nearby outpatient mental health clinic to work on the older sister's enuresis and on behavior problems on the part of both children. Ms. P reported that family therapy was not helping and that she had become overwhelmed and discouraged. The family therapist reported that frequently missed appointments, usually without prior cancellation, and general noncompliance with the treatment recommendations were ongoing problems. Ann's mother perceived the soiling as a willful attention-getting maneuver and reported that Mr. K, with whom Ann was particularly oppositional, agreed with her.

Treatment Summary. Treatment began with a thorough education and demystification procedure with a goal of removing any negative attributions for the soiling. The importance of a consistent, positive, and supportive parental attitude in all aspects of the treatment was emphasized. Though Mr. K had been invited to the initial interview, he did not attend. Ms. P and Ann were advised to share this new information with him and it was strongly suggested that he attend the next session.

During the initial interview, Ms. P was also advised to continue giving Ann five tablespoons of mineral oil and one tablespoon of Unifiber as had been prescribed by Dr. Baker. According to Ms. P, Ann had resisted taking the mineral oil from the start, saying she did not like the way it tasted. Several recommendations for preparing the mineral oil in a more palatable form were given.

It was also recommended that Ann sit on the toilet three times per day, for no more than five minutes each sitting. Ann and her mother agreed upon a 20 cent reward for having a bowel movement in the toilet during a scheduled sitting. Due to Ann's history of oppositional behavior and past resistance to taking the mineral oil, an additional 10 cent reward was recommended contingent upon Ann's taking her daily dose of mineral oil and completing her three scheduled sittings. It was also suggested that Ann receive a 20 cent reward for each day that her pants remained clean all day. Ann seemed pleased and enthusiastic at the prospect of earning rewards. Ms. P was asked to keep a log charting the frequencies, consistency, and amounts of defecation and soiling.

Weekly telephone contact was maintained with the family, for ongoing support. During the first phone call Ms. P noted that Ann had continued to refuse the mineral oil. However, the mother admitted to not having prepared the mineral oil as discussed because she had not had time. Ms. P was offered support, and the demanding nature of the regimen was acknowledged. It was suggested that she do her best to help Ann to take the mineral oil by preparing it as previously agreed.

By the second treatment session, Ann had clearly become constipated and was soiling almost continuously throughout the day. A "mini clean-out procedure" was recommended. Mr. K had declined the invitation to attend the session. Ann had continued to refuse taking her mineral oil until a few days before the session.

In addition, Ann reported feeling discouraged by earning almost no rewards. Two separate clean pants checks, once in the morning and once in the evening while under her mother's supervision, were suggested as a means of increasing Ann's opportunities to earn rewards. It was also suggested that on weekends Ann could have three clean pants checks, one at each sitting. Ann was praised for having begun to take her mineral oil.

Despite a brief period of improvement and continued efforts to support and accommodate the family by modifying the program to meet their needs, they remained unable to comply with any of the treatment recommendations and seldom kept either the appointments or the charts. After three months of treatment, Ann was still not doing her three scheduled sittings on a consistent basis.

Ms. P sometimes withheld from Ann the few rewards she had earned, or she failed to follow through with promised rewards, saying that Ann did not deserve them because her behavior had been so bad. She did this repeatedly, even though she had been advised that any rewards Ann earned as a result of her appropriate toileting were not to be withdrawn as punishment for other problem behaviors. She continued to blame Ann's oppositional nature for the family's noncompliance with treatment, and no amount of positive reframing or challenging this belief in any way was helpful in changing her thinking about the willfulness of Ann's soiling.

After the sixth session, four months into treatment, the decision was made in consultation with the PDGI Clinic to move to the more aggressive treatment approach (Christophersen & Rainey, 1976) on a trial basis. This decision was made out of concern that without treatment Ann could develop a serious impaction. Given the frequent displays of hostility between Ann and her mother, this recommendation was made with caution. Ms. P was advised to be firm, consistent, and positive, but not to use physical force in any way for the purpose of giving the enemas, which are sometimes required with this treatment approach. In addition, telephone support was ongoing and Ms. P was urged to contact the therapist with any questions or concerns. Unfortunately, the family was able to comply with the program only partially and only for a part of one week, and it was decided that the family should return to the conservative approach and were again urged to do their best to follow through with the treatment recommendations.

Ten months into treatment Ms. P disclosed that she had beaten both of her daughters with a belt in an effort to gain some control over what she felt was an out-of-control situation. Ultimately, it was decided that more comprehensive and protective services were needed. Although Ms. P had previously elected not to become involved with the Department of Social Services on a voluntary basis, following her disclosure she was advised that social services involvement was essential for the prevention of further abuse.

It was agreed that treatment for the encopresis would not be helpful until such time as organization could be restored within the family. In fact, the treatment may have helped to perpetuate Ann's sense of failure and therefore served only to further undermine her already low self-esteem.

Upon termination of treatment, it was anticipated for Ann that she would likely continue to soil several times daily. Ms. P agreed to purchase a diaper pail and to keep it filled with disinfectant/deodorizing liquid. Ms. P was also advised to instruct Ann on how to rinse out her soiled underpants and leave them in the pail for her to wash. It was suggested that she purchase disposable wipes and teach Ann how to clean her body after an accident, thus reducing the risk of hygiene problems leading to other health and social/peer problems for Ann both at home and at school. The family was encouraged to return to treatment for the encopresis as soon as they felt able and willing as a family to follow through with the treatment recommendations.

A follow-up phone call revealed that immediately following the final treatment session, Ann decided to take her mineral oil each day. After taking the oil and sitting on a somewhat regular basis, Ann had begun having regular bowel movements in the toilet and was soiling only infrequently. According to Ms. P, she and Mr. K were doing their best to praise and reward her good efforts and good progress.

REFERENCES

Abrahamian, F. P., & Lloyd-Still, J. D. (1984). Chronic constipation in children: A longitudinal study of 186 patients. *Journal of Pediatric Gastroenterology and Nutrition, 3*, 460–467.

Achenbach, T. M., & Edelbrock, C. (1983). *Manual for the child behavior checklist and revised child behavior profile*. Burlington, VT: University of Vermont, Department of Psychiatry.

Baird, M. (1974). Characteristic interaction patterns in families of encopretic children. *Menninger Clinic Bulletin, 39,* 144–153.

Bellman, M. (1966). Studies on encopresis. *Acta Pediatrica Scandinavi, 170,*(Sup.), 1–151.

Bemporad, J. R. Pfeifer, C. M., Gibbs, L., Cortner, R. H., & Bloom, W. (1971). Characteristics of encopretic patients and their families. *Journal of the American Academy of Child Psychiatry, 10,* 272–292.

Bemporad, J. R., Kresch, M. D., Asnes, R., & Wilson, A. (1978). Chronic neurotic encopresis as a paradigm of multifactorial psychotic disorder. *Journal of Nervous and Mental Diseases, 166,* 472–479.

Christophersen, E. R., & Rainey, S. K. (1976). Management of encopresis through a pediatric outpatient clinic. *Journal of Pediatric Psychology, 4,* 38–41.

Doleys, D. M., Schwartz, M. S., & Cineinero, A. R. (1981). Elimination problems: Enuresis and encopresis. In E. J. Mash and L. G. Terdal (Eds.), *Behavioral Assessment of Childhood Disorders* (pp. 679–710). New York: Guilford Press.

Friman, P. C. Mathews, J. R., Finney, F. W., Christophersen, E. R., & Leibowitz, J. M. (1988). Do encopretic children have clinically significant behavior problems? *Pediatrics, 82,* 407–409.

Fritz, G. K., & Armbrust, J. (1982). Enuresis and encopresis. *Psychiatric Clinics of North America, 5*(2), 283–296.

Gabel, S., Chandra, R., & Schindledecker, R. (1988). Behavioral ratings and outcome of medical treatment for encopresis. *Developmental and Behavioral Pediatrics, 9*(3), 129–133.

Gabel, S., Hegedus, A. M., Wald, A., Chandra, R., & Chaponis, D. (1986). Prevalence of behavior problems and mental health utilization among encopretic children: Implications for behavioral pediatrics. *Developmental and Behavioral Pediatrics, 7*(5) 293–297.

Hamburger, A. (1957). *A revised occupational scale for rating socioeconomic class.* New York: Columbia University Press.

Landman, G. B., & Rappaport, L. (1985). Pediatric management of severe treatment-resistant encopresis. *Developmental and Behavioral Pediatrics, 6*(6), 349–351.

Landman, G. B., Rappaport, L., Fenton, T., & Levine, M. D. (1986). Locus of control and self-esteem in children with encopresis. *Developmental and Behavioral Pediatrics, 7*(2), 111–113.

Levine, M. D. (1982). Encopresis: Its potentiation, evaluation, and alleviation. *Pediatric Clinics of North America, 29,* 315–330.

Levine, M. D., & Bakow, H. (1976). Children with encopresis: A study of treatment outcome. *Pediatrics, 58,* 845.

Loening-Baucke, V., Cruikshank, B., & Savage, C. (1987). Defecation dynamics and behavior profiles in encopretic children. *Pediatrics, 80*(5), 672–679.

Margolies, R., & Gilstein, K. W. (1983). A systems approach to the treatment of chronic encopresis. *International Journal of Psychology in Medicine, 13*(2), 141–152.

Owens-Stively, J. A. (1987). Self-esteem and compliance in encopretic children. *Child Psychiatry and Human Development, 18*(1), 13–21.

Rappaport, L. A. and Levine, M. D. (1986). The prevention of constipation and encopresis: A developmental model of approach. *Pediatric Clinics of North America, 33*(4), 859–869.

Rydzinski, J. N., & Kaplan, S. L. (1985). A wolf in sheep's clothing? Simultaneous use of structural family therapy and behavior modification in a case of encopresis. *Hillside Journal of Clinical Psychiatry, 7*(1), 71–81.

Stern, H. P., Prince, M. T., & Stroh, S. E. (1988). Encopresis responsive to non-psychiatric interventions with remittance of familial psychopathology. *Clinical Pediatrics, 27*(8), 400–402.

Walker, C. E., Milling, L. S., Bonner, B. L. (1988). Incontinence disorders: Enuresis and encopresis. In D. K., Routh (Ed.); *Handbook of Pediatric Psychology* (pp. 363–397). New York: Guilford Press.

White, M. (1984). Pseudo-encopresis: From avalanche to victory, from vicious to virtuous cycles. *Family Systems Medicine, 2,* 150–160.

2 | ADVERSITY IN MIDDLE CHILDHOOD AND ADOLESCENCE

3 | PHYSICAL HEALTH PROBLEMS IN CHILDREN WITH ATTENTION DEFICIT HYPERACTIVITY DISORDER (ADHD)

Lynn Tondat Carter, Laura Costa, and John K. Conboy

Children with Attention Deficit Hyperactivity Disorder (ADHD) are at increased risk for chronic health problems. These health problems include an increased incidence of infections with a greater use of antibiotics and a higher frequency of physical symptoms associated with allergy. The Children's Symptom/Health Inventory (CSHI; Costa & Carter, 1992) was used to detect these differences. Interestingly, not only did the scores on the health inventory differentiate ADHD from non-ADHD children in frequency of physical health problems, but the scores also predicted both parent and teacher ratings of ADHD and parent ratings of child psychopathology. We conclude that this increase in risk for physical health problems should be considered an important part of the clinical picture for ADHD children, and we offer some specific guidelines for the screening, treatment, and prevention of these physical health problems.

OVERVIEW OF HEALTH AND PSYCHOPATHOLOGY

Some observers stress that specific health and diet problems are central in mental health issues, whereas others are convinced that there is no relationship. The American Psychiatric Association (1994) has included a diagnosis called "Psychological Factors Affecting Physical Illness" (p. 675) in the *Diagnostic and Statistical Manual of Mental Disorders,* 4th edition (DSM-IV). APA suggests that psychological and behavioral factors may affect "every major category of disease, including cardiovascular conditions, dermatological conditions, neurological conditions, pulmonary conditions, renal conditions and rheumatological conditions" (p. 676). This line of research dates back to the early work of Cannon (1929) and Selye (1936, 1976), who provided a foundation for our understanding of the human stress response. More recently, specific links have been established between personality factors and heart disease (Friedman & Rosenman, 1974), life stress events and illness (Holmes & Rahe, 1967), and stress and suppression of the immune system (e.g., Cohen & Williamson, 1991; National Academy of Science, 1984). Among psychologists, the consensus is that psychological factors can influence the development of illness and that the relationship between physical and mental health is very complex.

The connection between health and psychological factors can be examined from a different perspective. If psychological factors influence the development of illness, can the converse idea, that illness leads to specific or even generalized psychopathology, be supported? In the past, the general assumption was that children with poor health are at risk for development of emotional and behavioral problems; specifically, stress associated with illness contributes to childhood psychopathology (Shaw & Lucas, 1970). Other research does not support a clear predictive connection between illness and psychopathology (Garrison & McQuiston, 1989; Roberts, 1986). Examining the literature, Garrison and McQuiston (1989) found that children with chronic illness are not more likely to have specific emotional problems. Furthermore, they conclude that efforts to define personality types associated with specific illness, such as the asthmatic or diabetic or epileptic personality, have failed. Thus an overall consensus of either a predictive or causal relationship between general health problems and psychopathology is lacking. What is clear is that there is a need for more comprehensive research to further an understanding of the relationship between physical health, immune system responses, and mental health.

THE ADHD HEALTH CONNECTION

Our specific area of concern is the study of physical health problems in children with ADHD. Probably the most frequently debated health issue in this area pertains to whether diet and allergy affect ADHD. Reviews of this debate are covered in detail elsewhere (Barkley, 1993; Conners, 1989; Connor, 1991; Egger, 1991; Marshall, 1989; Prinz, 1985; Waksman, 1983; Wender, 1986). The following is a brief summary.

Feingold (1975) began much of the focus on diet and allergy by asserting that toxic reactions to preservatives, dyes, and natural salicylates were at the root of ADHD. His early claims of improvement in 50%-60% of ADHD children, using the Feingold diet, were later questioned. Using double-blind trials, other researchers concluded that Feingold's results were overestimated and applied only to a small sub-group of ADHD children (Conners, Goyette, Southwick, Lees, & Andrulonis, 1976; Consensus Development Conference, 1982; Harley et al., 1978). Despite a general consensus in the medical and psychological communities that food additives have a minimal role in ADHD, researchers such as Egger (1991) have continued to question both this position and the research used to support it. We concur with Egger that serious problems existed in the methodology of the studies that found no behavioral differences between children on diets with additives and those without additives. As an example, both of these diet conditions often contained foods that are now known to cause allergic reactions in some children. Thus, in these early food additive studies, no attempt was made to systematically test or control for children's reactivity to the foods used in the research trials.

Studies reporting a causal or predictive relationship between allergies to foods and hyperactivity include findings by Rapp (1978), O'Shea and Porter (1981), and Tryphonas and Trites (1979). These and other studies were later criticized for various methodological problems, including the lack of a double-blind placebo control group or appropriate comparison group, questionable statistical procedures, and other design issues. Nevertheless, double-blind placebo controlled studies conducted by Egger, Carter, Graham, Gumley, and Soothill (1985) and by Kaplan, McNicol, Conte, and Moghadam (1989) found that ADHD children significantly improved on a nonreactive diet compared to a diet containing reactive foods. Despite this positive evidence, concern for possible allergic reactions to substances in the diet has not been widely accepted as part of the conventional treatment approach for children with ADHD (Barkley, 1993; Goldstein & Ingersoll, 1993). In general, any reactivity to food and/or food additives is believed to be rare or affecting only a small subgroup of ADHD children. Barkley (1993) vigorously attacks diet and allergy treatments as pseudoscience. Yet Conners (1989), a careful researcher and author of several early diet studies, has said, "I have to admit, I have changed my mind about the Feingold idea since the 1970s" (p. 184). Although he recognizes that diet is not a cure, when appropriate Conners recommends very specific and carefully monitored diet changes within a more traditional multifaceted treatment plan. The debate has been heated and as Conners writes, it has contained not just issues of fact, but also "questions of motives and professional bias" (p. 3). These views notwithstanding, a number of persistent questions remain concerning the relationship of specific health issues and ADHD.

One issue facing both ADHD researchers and practitioners is that this area of inquiry is not viewed as "theory driven" or at least not consistent with accepted theory on ADHD, which adheres to use of stimulant medication and behavior management for treatment (Goldstein & Ingersoll, 1993). However, the theoretical approach held within the discipline of clinical ecology offers an explanation (Bell, 1982, 1987). This approach emphasizes the impact of the total stress load of allergens and toxins on the body and brain, implying neural/immune mechanisms that would produce brain and behavioral changes. Recently, researchers in the fields of psychology and neurobiology have proposed specific neurochemical models to explain how allergy might affect both ADHD (Marshall, 1989; Roth, Beyreiss, Schlenzka, & Beyer, 1991) and depression (Marshall, 1993).

In related research, the possibility of immune system differences in ADHD children or in their mothers has been indicated (Beyreiss, et al., 1988; Crawford, Kaplan, & Kinsbourne, 1992). Several studies have examined differences in immediate or atopic allergic reactions between ADHD and non-ADHD children. Since two of these studies found differences (Beyreiss et al., 1988; Roth et al., 1991), and two other studies did not (Crawford et al., 1992; McGee, Stanton & Sears, 1993), the exact nature of immune system involvement requires a closer look. Nonetheless, the hypothesis that some aspects of immune system functioning in ADHD children may be different is interesting in view of past research that has found ADHD children to have increased physical health problems compared to non-ADHD children. These problems include such chronic health problems as asthma, recurring upper respiratory infections (Hartsough & Lambert, 1985), bad breath, skin rash, red cheeks, dry skin, stomach bloat, leg cramps, stuffy-runny nose, headache, sleep problems (Kaplan, McNicol, Conte & Moghadam, 1987a, 1987b), and chronic ear infections (Hagerman & Falkenstein, 1987).

As a continuation of this line of inquiry, we developed an instrument to assess physical health problems in ADHD children thought to be due to allergy. This approach does not assume or imply that allergy and/or health problems are related to ADHD in a causal way. However, if substantiated, this approach does provide clear and practical implications for a more comprehensive treatment plan for ADHD children. This plan would include screening for allergies where allergy-related physical health problems are indicated and providing a treatment plan to reduce these physical health problems.

Although our research does not settle the controversial question of whether diet and allergy affect ADHD, our findings add another voice to the debate and perhaps rekindle interests in specific ADHD/allergy issues.

Our primary goal was to further the understanding of the physical health problems of ADHD children. We also examined the incidence of health problems in children to see if any predictive relationships existed between physical and mental health problems.

STUDY OF A HEALTH INVENTORY FOR CHILDREN

The Children's Symptom/Health Inventory (CSHI) was developed by Costa and Carter (1992) to obtain an index of physical and behavioral symptoms of allergy. The CSHI consists of 111 items that measure various aspects of a child's health, particularly the frequency of physical symptoms that have been associated with food or airborne allergies (Costa & Carter, 1992). The questions were obtained from interviews of parents with children who had confirmed allergies and from research studies/reports on allergy symptoms (e.g., Egger et al., 1985; Egger, Carter, Soothill, & Wilson, 1989; Heiner, 1984; Nsouli, Nsouli, Linde, Scanlon, & Bellanti, 1991; Rapp, 1978, 1991). Questions include specific symptoms in a Prenatal/Infant Section (Items 1–10), a Childhood Section (Items 16–82), and a Behavioral Problem Section (Items 86–97). Other items included questions on infancy and childhood antibiotic use. For each of these sections, a rating scale was used to obtain an index of symptom frequency. We defined high scores as a score of 5 or above on a 7-point scale for the Childhood Section and a 4 or above on a 6-point scale for the Prenatal/Infant Section. The higher the score, the higher the frequency of occurrence for the specific symptom rated. Items from the Childhood Section of the CSHI, with the rating scale, can be found in Figure 1.

In an initial pilot study using the CSHI, Costa and Carter (1992) found significant differences in physical problems between ADHD and non-ADHD children. Carter, Costa, and Conboy (1993) then replicated these findings using a larger sample. Below is a description of this latter study, which focused on the usefulness of several specific CSHI health indices as predictors of behavioral problems and psychopathology in children.

Parents of 42 ADHD and 79 non-ADHD children completed a detailed history (including questions about diagnoses, medication history, and hearing problems), the CSHI, and the following four ADHD scales: Conners Parent Rating Scale (CPRS-48; Conners, 1990), Werry-Weiss-Peters Activity Rating Scale (WWPARS; Routh, Schroeder, & O'Tuama, 1974), Home Situation Questionnaire-Revised (HSQ-R; Barkley, 1990), and the Personality Inventory for Children (PIC; Wirt, Lachar, Klinedinst, & Seat, 1984). Teachers filled out the following ADHD rating scales: Conners Teacher Rating Scale (CTRS-28; Conners, 1990) and School Situation

FIGURE 1 Childhood Section of Children's Symptom/Health Inventory (CSHI)

Using the scale provided, please rate how often your child experiences the following physical symptoms.

7 — CONSTANTLY (every day)
6 — VERY FREQUENTLY (several times per week)
5 — FREQUENTLY (several times per month)
4 — OCCASIONALLY (several times per year)

3 — INFREQUENTLY (once per year)
2 — RARELY (once every 3–5 years)
1 — NEVER (not at all)
0 — NOT SURE or DO NOT REMEMBER

16. _____ ECZEMA
17. _____ ASTHMA
18. _____ NASAL CONGESTION
19. _____ CHEST CONGESTION
20. _____ DIFFICULTY BREATHING
21. _____ MOUTH-BREATHING
22. _____ HEADACHES
23. _____ FATIGUE
24. _____ OVERSENSITIVE TO ODORS
25. _____ OVERSENSITIVE TO LIGHT
26. _____ OVERSENSITIVE TO PAIN
27. _____ OVERSENSITIVE TO COLD
28. _____ RASHES
29. _____ ITCHING
30. _____ HIVES
31. _____ ITCHY THROAT
32. _____ DIZZINESS
33. _____ RINGING IN EARS
34. _____ EAR INFECTIONS
35. _____ SKIN CRACKED
36. _____ DARK EYE CIRCLES
37. _____ PUFFY OR SWOLLEN EYES
38. _____ RED AND/OR ITCHY EYES
39. _____ GLASSY OR GLAZED EYES
40. _____ RUNNY NOSE
41. _____ HIGH BLOOD PRESSURE
42. _____ ULCERS IN MOUTH
43. _____ ITCHY ROOF OF MOUTH
44. _____ ACHES (BACK, MUSCLES, JOINTS)
45. _____ FINGERNAILS/TOENAILS CRACKED
46. _____ STOMACH COMPLAINTS NOT DUE TO APPARENT ILLNESS
47. _____ LEG PAIN NOT DUE TO APPARENT ILLNESS
48. _____ VERY PALE COMPLEXION (LACK OF COLOR)
49. _____ UNUSUAL SENSITIVITY OF SKIN (CLOTHING OR LABELS IRRITATE THE CHILD)
50. _____ NOISY BREATHING THROUGH NOSE
51. _____ CAN'T SLEEP THROUGH NIGHT
52. _____ YEAST OR THRUSH INFECTIONS
53. _____ INFECTIONS (OTHER THAN EAR OR YEAST)
54. _____ OVERSENSITIVE TO THE TOUCH OF OTHERS

55. _____ NIGHTMARES
56. _____ EXCESSIVE PERSPIRATION
57. _____ SNORING
58. _____ BED-WETTING
59. _____ INSOMNIA
60. _____ POOR APPETITE
61. _____ MUSCLE WEAKNESS
62. _____ STOMACH CRAMPS
63. _____ NAUSEA/VOMITING
64. _____ STOMACH BLOATING
65. _____ BAD BREATH
66. _____ DIARRHEA
67. _____ CONSTIPATION
68. _____ LOW-GRADE FEVER
69. _____ TINGLING
70. _____ NUMBNESS
71. _____ SWOLLEN HANDS
72. _____ SORE LIPS
73. _____ THROAT-CLEARING
74. _____ COUGHING
75. _____ WHEEZING
76. _____ FACE FLUSHED
77. _____ RED EARLOBES
78. _____ RED CHEEKS
79. _____ SWOLLEN LYMPH NODES
80. _____ FREQUENT URINATION
81. _____ CONVULSIONS
82. _____ FACIAL TICS

Note: From the Children's Symptom/Health Inventory, copyright 1992 (TXU 516 091) by Costa and Carter. Reprinted by permission.

FIGURE 1. Childhood Section of the Children's Symptom/Health Inventory (CSHI). From "Differences in allergy symptoms between ADHD and normal children" by L. Costa and L.T. Carter, 1992. Poster presented at the Eastern Psychological Association Annual Conference, Boston, MA. Reprinted by permission.

Questionnaire-Revised (SSQ-R; Barkley, 1990). The CPRS-48, CTRS-28, WWPARS, HSQ-R, and SSQ-R are commonly used to aid in the diagnosis of ADHD (Barkley, 1990). The PIC is a multidimensional test for a variety of child psychopathology issues and contains a scale useful in the diagnosis of ADHD (Wirt et al., 1984). All children were administered the Carter-Conboy Auditory Vigilance Task (AVT; Conboy et al., 1993), which is a continuous performance test of auditory attention.

The 79 non-ADHD children were from local schools. The 42 ADHD children were from local schools and a local ADHD clinic or were recruited when their parents volunteered to participate after attending regional ADHD workshops given by J. K. Conboy. The non-ADHD children had no more than one indicator of ADHD on the four parent and two teacher scales of ADHD, while the ADHD children had independent diagnoses and at least four of the six indicators of ADHD (Conboy et al., 1993).[1] Children whose PIC Lie Scale scores exceeded the criterion ($T > 59$) and three others who had outlier scores on the CSHI were not included in the study.

HEALTH DIFFERENCES BETWEEN ADHD AND NON-ADHD CHILDREN

Compared to the non-ADHD children, ADHD children had significantly more frequent prenatal/infant and childhood physical symptoms. ADHD children were also found to have a significantly higher use of antibiotics during both infancy and childhood (see Table 1). These differences existed regardless of use of stimulant medication for ADHD children. As expected from our previous research (Costa & Carter, 1992), the number of physical symptoms was not significantly different between ADHD and non-ADHD children for either the Childhood or Prenatal/Infant sections. The reader should note that the term *frequency* of a rated symptom refers to how frequent the parent felt the child experienced the symptom (e.g., 7 = constantly, 6 = very frequently, etc.; see rating scale in Figure 1). The term *number* of symptoms refers to the total number of symptoms rated by parents to have some frequency rating (a rating other than 1 = "never" or 0 = "not sure").

As predicted a priori, several physical symptoms (inability to sleep, rashes, infections, and skin sensitivity) were found to be significantly more frequent in ADHD compared to non-ADHD children. In addition, poor appetite and excessive mucous in infancy were found to be more frequent in ADHD children (see Table 2). We also found that significantly more ADHD children were reported to complain about being overheated (said they were hot when others were comfortable or cold) than non-ADHD

Table 1

Significant Group Differences on the Children's Symptom/Health Inventory

Variable	ADHD group		non-ADHD group		
	M	(n)	M	(n)	p
Frequency of prenatal/infant physical symptoms	20.5	(40)	16.1	(74)	< .05[a]
Frequency of childhood physical symptoms	107.7	(42)	76.4	(79)	<.005[a]
Antibiotics during infancy	2.7	(34)	1.7	(63)	<.001
Antibiotics during childhood	3.0	(37)	1.9	(71)	< .01[a]

Note: The ADHD group consisted of children with Attention Deficit Hyperactivity Disorder. The non-ADHD group consisted of children not diagnosed with ADHD.

[a] Corrected for unequal variances

Table 2

Group Differences for Frequency Ratings on the Children's Symptom/Health Inventory

Variable	ADHD group		non-ADHD group		
	M	(n)	M	(n)	p
Inability to sleep through night	3.1	(39)	2.0	(79)	< .005[a]
Poor appetite	3.2	(42)	2.1	(79)	< .001[a]
Unusual sensitivity of skin	3.0	(41)	1.8	(79)	<.0005[a]
Excess mucous in infancy	2.4	(31)	1.5	(64)	< .005[a]
Rashes	2.5	(42)	1.9	(76)	< .05[a]
Infections (other than ear)	2.4	(41)	1.5	(79)	< .001[a]

Note: The ADHD group consisted of children with Attention Deficit Hyperactivity Disorder. The non-ADHD group consisted of children not diagnosed with ADHD.

[a] Corrected for unequal variances

children. Mothers of ADHD children reported themselves as having significantly more physical symptoms such as nose and throat problems (CSHI Items 102–105) compared to mothers of non-ADHD children. Although these CSHI items are associated with allergy symptoms, none of the mothers of ADHD children answered that they themselves had allergies.

As expected, ADHD children were reported by parents to have significantly more frequent behavioral problems on the CSHI Behavioral Section compared to non-ADHD children.

HIGH SCORE INDICATORS

As noted earlier, we found that the number of physical symptoms rated by parents was not significantly higher in ADHD children than in non-ADHD children. However, when we analyzed just the high scores on these sections, there were significantly more high scores for the ADHD group. As indicated above, a high score was defined as a score of 5 or above for the Childhood Section, and as a score of 4 or above for the Prenatal/Infant Section. On the Childhood Section, 88% of the ADHD children compared to 44% of non-ADHD children had two or more high scores and the average number of high scores was seven for ADHD children compared to only two for non-ADHD children. Statistically, there is less than a one in 10,000 chance that this difference could occur by chance ($p < .0001$). On the Prenatal/Infant Section, 31% of ADHD children had high scores on at least five of the symptoms compared to only 5% of the non-ADHD children; the average was three high scores for ADHD children and two for non-ADHD children ($p < .01$).

TEST-RETEST RELIABILITY

For an additional sample of ADHD children ($n = 18$) from a local ADHD clinic, parents completed the CSHI ratings twice (with two to four weeks between tests) in order to obtain test-retest reliability for the CSHI. Reliability coefficients were calculated for the following CSHI measures: childhood and prenatal/infant high scores, child and infant antibiotic use, and behavioral problems; these were all found to be $+ .90$ or above.

CORRELATIONS OF HEALTH SYMPTOMS WITH BEHAVIORAL MEASURES

There were significant positive correlations for all children ($N = 121$) between the frequency of physical symptoms and behavioral problems as measured by the CSHI. Children with a high frequency of physical symptoms were more likely to have behavioral problems. Infant and childhood use of antibiotics also correlated positively with behavioral problems as rated by the CSHI. Furthermore, as can be seen in Table 3, there were significant positive correlations between the high scores on the Childhood Section of the CSHI and each of the parent and teacher measures of ADHD. This demonstrates that a higher frequency of physical health problems was associated with a higher incidence of behavioral problems as rated by both parents and teachers.

Table 3

Correlations of High Scores on Childhood Section of the CSHI
with ADHD Rating Scales

Conners Parent Rating Scale ($\underline{n}$ = 121)	r
Conduct Problems	+ .50[a]
Learning Problems	+ .55[a]
Psychosomatic	+ .59[a]
Impulsivity-Hyperactivity	+ .43[a]
Anxiety	+ .44[a]
Hyperactivity Index	+ .55[a]
Conners Teacher Rating Scales ($\underline{n}$ = 105)	r
Conduct Problems	+ .38[a]
Hyperactivity	+ .45[a]
Inattention-Passivity	+ .29[b]
Hyperactivity Index	+ .45[a]
Werry-Weiss-Peters Activity Rating Scale ($\underline{n}$ = 94)	+ .49[a]
Home Situation Questionnaire-Revised ($\underline{n}$ = 120)	+ .42[a]
School Situation Questionnaire-Revised ($\underline{n}$ = 96)	+ .33[b]

[a] p <.0001
[b] p <.005

Childhood high scores also correlated significantly with the number of errors on an auditory attention task (the Carter-Conboy AVT); this analysis did not include medicated children or children with reported hearing problems. Thus, we found that children with frequent physical health problems were more likely to have poor auditory attention.

CORRELATIONS OF HEALTH SYMPTOMS WITH PSYCHOPATHOLOGY MEASURES

The CSHI Childhood high scores also correlated significantly with each of the clinical subscales of the PIC, except intellectual screening. Examples of these correlations include depression (r= + .56), delinquency (r= + .48), psychosis (r= + .51), and anxiety (r= + .51; p < .0001). Therefore, a greater number of high scores predicted a rating of greater severity of child psychopathology.

SUMMARY OF PHYSICAL HEALTH PROBLEMS IN ADHD CHILDREN

Children with ADHD were found to have significantly more frequent physical health symptoms as rated on the CSHI compared to non-ADHD children. Prenatal and infant physical symptoms of allergy and use of infant antibiotics were significantly related to later behavioral symptoms as measured by both the CSHI and by ADHD indicators.

Perhaps the most important finding of the current study pertains to the potential usefulness of high scores in screening children for allergies. A high score indicates a high frequency of occurrence for a specific physical problem. Based on the extensive literature on physical symptoms and allergy (e.g., Egger et al., 1985, 1989, 1992; Heiner, 1984; Nsouli et al., 1991; Pelikan, 1987), we strongly suggest that the incidence of high scores may indicate allergy-related problems. Significantly more high scores were found for ADHD children compared to non-ADHD children for both the Childhood and Prenatal/Infant Sections.

Another important finding of the current study pertains to the possibility that high scores may signal an increased likelihood of ADHD or other types of psychopathology. We report here that high scores for the Childhood Section resulted in significant positive correlations with each of the parent and teacher measures of ADHD, as well as a measure of auditory attention (AVT). In addition, these high scores also correlated significantly with 12 of the 13 clinical subscales of the PIC, including ratings of depression, anxiety, and delinquency. Whereas other researchers and clinicians have reported significantly more physical health problems in ADHD children compared to non-ADHD children (e.g., Barkley, 1990; Kaplan et al., 1987b), to our knowledge this is the first study that identifies a single indicator of childhood physical health (the number of high scores) as a correlate of ADHD, child psychopathology, and a measure of auditory attention.

Regarding the group differences, it is possible that a bias by ADHD parents could have made them more aware or sensitive to their child's health problems. Thus they could have overrated their child's complaints or symptoms compared to the parents of non-ADHD children. We note, however, that parents of ADHD children did not report a higher number of physical symptoms than parents of non-ADHD children. If rater bias were an issue, it is likely that parents of ADHD children would have consistently overrated their children on the number of symptoms, as well as the frequency. However, this did not occur. Furthermore, as mentioned earlier, all parents whose Lie scale on the PIC exceeded t-score 59 were excluded from the study. Thus those included in the study were less likely to have an unusual response bias. This procedure is not a guarantee that response bias was eliminated, but it increased the likelihood of including valid responders. Finally, in other research an extensive investigation on health ratings by parents of ADHD children did not reveal a rater bias

(Kaplan et al., 1987b). In view of the past research on the topic (e.g., Egger et al., 1985, 1992; Kaplan et al., 1987a, 1987b; Tryphonas & Trites, 1979), it would be more parsimonious to attribute the differences in physical symptoms to real differences between ADHD children and non-ADHD children and not to parental bias.

The benefit of using a screening tool such as the CSHI is to determine early risk of allergy so that appropriate allergy testing and treatment can be sought. This can be very important, since our observations suggest that few of the parents who completed the CSHI realized that the chronic physical symptoms measured could be associated with allergy. Although ADHD children had a mean of 7 high scores that may be indicative of allergy, and 88% of them had two or more high scores on the Childhood Section, less than 1% of these children had been tested for allergy (e.g., blood testing and elimination diet with challenge). We note that the majority of the symptoms listed on the CSHI are considered delayed allergy reactions, which are typically not associated with positive scratch tests or RAST IgE blood test results. This might help to explain the negative findings of a recent study on allergy and ADHD by McGee et al. (1993), which looked at ADHD and allergy symptoms in children with immediate allergy responses (atopic responsiveness). These investigators measured allergy using scratch and IgE blood tests, which are both considered measures of immediate allergy reaction and not the delayed reactions.

SUGGESTIONS FOR FUTURE RESEARCH

Further study is necessary to confirm these findings. Research concerning the validity of the CSHI to accurately predict those who have allergies is needed. Our initial feedback from parents who pursued allergy testing of their children indicates that a greater incidence of high scores is indeed associated with high positive RAST IgG tests and positive ELISA/ACT tests (e.g., positive allergy blood tests). Informal feedback from these parents, who then used elimination diets for the treatment of the physical symptoms, has been very encouraging.

Future research might also examine the nature of the relationship between antibiotic use and later behavioral problems. Significant correlations were found between both infancy and childhood antibiotic use and ADHD indicators. It may be worthwhile to investigate this further. The benefits of antibiotics are obvious, but overuse of antibiotics may play a role in decreasing immune system functioning and in increasing the risk of chronic illness for children (Schmidt, Smith, & Sehnert, 1993).

TYPICAL PROFILE

ADHD children are heterogeneous for many measures and the CSHI is no exception. Although we are suggesting that the physical symptoms of allergies are problematic for many ADHD children, we note that this is not the case for all ADHD children. Nonetheless, when the CSHI files were reviewed, a general picture emerged which seemed to describe the majority of these children. They were typically very active *in utero*. Colic was often a problem along with frequent changes in infant formula and treatment with antibiotics. Infections, including recurrent ear infections, were also common. High scores on other symptoms were also typical, particularly those found in Table 2.

SPECIFIC GUIDELINES

In addition to standard treatments for ADHD, we suggest that children who resemble the profile given above be seen by a medical doctor who will first rule out other medical causes and then help parents identify food or airborne substances that could be causing the chronic physical problems. It would be preferable to find a doctor who will provide blood testing for allergies that includes RAST IgE and RAST IgG antibody screening[2] or Elisa/Act testing[3] and who will assist the family with an elimination diet and/or procedures to reduce exposure to airborne allergens (J. Hubbuch, M. D., personal communication, February 1994). It is recommended that the following foods be tested: milk, wheat, eggs, corn, soy, chocolate, oranges, and peanuts, as well as other foods common in the child's diet. Some airborne allergens to consider are dust mites, mold, pollen (especially with seasonal problems), animal dander, and natural gas. Allergy testing is not yet an exact procedure, and negative test results can be misleading. Therefore, placing the child on an elimination diet with the supervision of a doctor may provide clues not revealed by allergy testing (Rapp, 1991; Schmidt et al., 1993).

Finally, we recommend the following preventative measures that are aimed at increasing immune system functioning: with the aid of a nutritionist, try a rotation diet, increase green vegetables and fruits, decrease refined foods, sugar, animal protein, food dyes, and additives, use vitamins including Vitamin C, E, and beta carotene and mineral supplements (particularly calcium if milk products are a problem); with the aid of an environmentally aware health care professional, reduce exposure to hidden toxins in water, air, and food that can seriously impair immune system functioning (Warren, 1991); and with the aid of a psychologist, reduce sources of stress and learn adaptive coping mechanisms (Morter, 1992; Schmidt et al., 1993).

In conclusion, while there may be ample reason to question the role of diet and allergy in the etiology and treatment of ADHD, there is evidence that ADHD children have more physical health problems than other children and that the frequency of these physical problems are related in a predictive way to parent and teacher ratings of child psychopathology. Furthermore, there is evidence that diet and allergy do affect physical health. It would not be prudent to ignore the effect diet and allergy might have on physical health simply because diet and allergy have not been proven to be causally related to ADHD or to child psychopathology in general. Therefore, we contend that the treatment approach for an ADHD child should address not only the usual issues of poor attention, impulsivity, hyperactivity, behavioral problems, and academic difficulties, but also the prevention and treatment of any chronic physical health problems.

REFERENCES

American Psychiatric Association (1994). *Diagnostic and Statistical Manual of Mental Disorders* (4th ed.). Washington, DC: American Psychiatric Association.

Barkley, R. A. (1990). *Attention Deficit Hyperactivity Disorder: A Handbook for diagnosis and treatment.* New York: Guilford Press.

Barkley, R. A. (1993). Pseudoscience in treatments for ADHD. *The ADHD Report,* 1(6), 1–3.

Bell, I. (1982). *Clinical Ecology.* Bolina, CA: Common Knowledge Press.

Bell, I. (1987). Effects of food allergy on the central nervous system. In J. Brostoff & S. Challacombe (Eds.), *Food allergy and intolerance* (pp. 709–722). Philadelphia: Baillier Tindall.

Beyreiss, J., Roth, N., Beyer, H., Kropf, S., Shlenzka, K., Schmidt, A., & Roscher, G. (1988). Coincidence of immune (atopic dermatitis) and behavioral (attention deficit) disorders in children: Empirical data. *Activita Nervosa Superior,* 30(2), 127–128.

Cannon, W. B. (1929). *Bodily changes in pain, hunger, fear, and rage.* New York: Branford.

Carter, L. T., Costa, L., & Conboy, J. K. (1993). Differences in allergy symptoms between ADHD and normal children: Study of a screening inventory for professionals. Poster presented at the American Association of Applied and Preventive Psychology Conference, Chicago, IL.

Cohen, S., & Williamson, G. M. (1991). Stress and infectious disease in humans. *Psychological Bulletin, 109,* 5–24.

Conboy, J. K., Carter, L. T., Burns, K. A., Souza, K. A., Faria, K. L., Brunner, J. K., Cordeiro, C. M., & Holland, M. (1993). Development of an auditory vigilance task to diagnose attention deficit hyperactivity disorder in children. Poster presented at the American Psychological Society Conference, Chicago, IL.

Conners, C. K. (1989). *Feeding the brain: How foods affect children.* New York: Plenum Press.

Conners, C. K. (1990). *Manual for Conners' rating scales: Conners' Teacher Rating Scales, Conners' Parent Rating Scales.* Toronto: Multi Health Systems.

Conners, C. K., Goyette, C. H., Southwick, D. A., Lees, J. M., & Andrulonis, P. A. (1976). Food additives and hyperkinesis: A controlled double-blind experiment. *Pediatrics, 58,* 154–166.

Connor, M. J. (1991). Diet and performance in children. *Educational Psychology in Practice, 7*(3) 131–139.

Consensus Development Conference (1982). Defined diets and childhood hyperactivity. *Clinical Pediatrics, 21*(10), 627–630.

Costa, L., & Carter, L. T. (1992). Differences in allergy symptoms between ADHD and normal children: Preliminary study of a screening inventory for professionals. Poster presented at the Eastern Psychological Association Annual Conference, Boston, MA.

Crawford, S. G., Kaplan, B. J., & Kinsbourne, M. (1992). The effects of parental immunoreactivity on pregnancy, birth, and cognitive development: Maternal immune attack on the fetus? *Cortex, 28,* 483–491.

Egger, J. (1991). Psychoneurological aspects of food allergy. *European Journal of Clinical Nutrition, 45*(1), 35–45.

Egger, J., Carter, C. M., Graham, P. J., Gumley, D., & Soothill, J. F. (1985). Controlled trial of oligoantigenic treatment in the hyperkinetic syndrome. *The Lancet, 14,* 540–545.

Egger, J., Carter, C. M., Soothill, J. F., & Wilson, J. (1989). Oligoantigenic diet treatment of children with epilepsy and migraine. *The Journal of Pediatrics, 114*(1), 51–58.

Egger, J., Carter, C. H., Soothill, J. F., & Wilson, J. (1992). Effect of diet treatment on enuresis in children with migraine or hyperkinetic behavior. *Clinical Pediatrics, 31,* 302–307.

Feingold, B. F. (1975). *Why your child is hyperactive.* New York: Random House.

Friedman, M., & Rosenman, R. H. (1974). *Type A behavior and your heart.* New York: Knopf.

Garrison, W. T., & McQuiston, S. (1989). *Chronic illness during childhood and adolescence: Psychological aspect.* Newbury Park, CA: Sage.

Goldstein, S., & Ingersoll, B. (1993). Controversial treatments for ADHD: Essential information for clinicians. *The ADHD Report, 1*(4) 4–5.

Hagerman, R., & Falkenstein, A. (1987). An association between recurrent otitis media in infancy and later hyperactivity. *Clinical Pediatrics, 26*(5), 253–257.

Harley, J. O., Ray, R. D., Tomasi, L., Eichman, P. L., Matthews, C. G., Chun, R., Cleeland, C. S., & Traisman, E. (1978). Hyperkinesis and food additives: Testing the Feingold hypothesis. *Pediatrics, 61,* 818–828.

Hartsough C. S., & Lambert, N. M. (1985). Medical factors in hyperactive and normal children: Prenatal, developmental, and health history findings. *American Journal of Orthopsychiatry, 55*(2), 190–201.

Heiner, D. C. (1984). Respiratory diseases and food allergy. *Annals of Allergy, 53,* 657–664.

Holmes, T. H., & Rahe, R. H. (1967). The social readjustment rating scale. *Journal of Psychosomatic Research, 11,* 213–218.

Kaplan, B. J., McNicol, J., Conte, R. A., & Moghadam, H. K. (1987a). Sleep disturbance in preschool-aged hyperactive and nonhyperactive children. *Pediatrics, 80*(6), 839–844.

Kaplan, B. J., McNicol, J., Conte, R. A., & Moghadam, H. K. (1987b). Physical signs and symptoms in preschool-age hyperactive and normal children. *Developmental and Behavioral Pediatrics, 8*(6), 305–310.

Kaplan, B. J., McNicol, J., Conte, R. A., & Moghadam, H. K. (1989). Dietary replacement in preschool-aged hyperactive boys. *Pediatrics, 83*(1), 7–17.

Marshall, P. S. (1989). Attention deficit disorder and allergy: A neurochemical model of the relation between the illnesses. *Psychological Bulletin, 106*(3), 434–446.

Marshall, P. S. (1993). Allergy and depression: A neurochemical threshold model of the relation between the illnesses. *Psychological Bulletin, 113*(1), 23–43.

McGee, R., Stanton, W. R., & Sears, M. R. (1993) Allergic disorders and attention deficit disorder in children. *Journal of Abnormal Child Psychology, 21*(1), 79–88.

Morter, M. T. (1992). *Your health, your choice: Your complete personal guide to wellness, nutrition and disease prevention.* Hollywood, FL: Fell Publishers.

National Academy of Science (1984). *Bereavement: Reactions, consequences and cure.* Washington, DC: National Academy Press.

Nsouli, T. M., Nsouli, S. M., Linde, R. E., Scanlon, T. M., & Bellanti, J. A. (1991). The role of food allergy in serous otitis media. *Immunology and Allergy Practice, 8*(8), 37–41.

O'Shea, J. A., & Porter, S. F. (1981). Double-blind study of children with hyperkinetic syndrome treated with multi-allergen extract sublingually. *Journal of Learning Disabilities, 14*(4), 189–192.

Pelikan, Z. (1987). Rhinitis and secretory otitis media: A possible role of food allergy. In J. Brostoff & S. J. Challacombe (Eds.), *Food allergy and intolerance* (pp. 467–485). Philadelphia, PA: Bailliere Tindall.

Prinz, R. J. (1985). Diet-behavior research with children: Methodological and substantive issues. *Advances in Learning and Behavioral Disabilities, 4,* 181–199.

Rapp, D. J. (1978). Does diet affect hypersensitivity? *Journal of Learning Disabilities, 11*(6), 56–62.

Rapp, D. J. (1991). *Is this your child?: Discovering and treating unrecognized allergies.* New York: W. Morrow & Co.

Roberts, M. C. (1986). *Pediatric psychology: Psychological intervention and strategies for pediatric problems.* New York: Pergamon.

Roth, N., Beyreiss, J., Schlenzka, K., & Beyer, H. (1991). Coincidence of attention deficit disorder and atopic disorders in children: Empirical findings and hypothetical background. *Journal of Abnormal Child Psychology, 19*(1), 1–13.

Routh, D. K., Schroeder, C. S., & O'Tuama, L. A. (1974). Development of activity level in children. *Developmental Psychology, 10*(2), 163–168.

Selye, H. (1936). A syndrome produced by diverse nocuous agents. *Nature, 138,* 32.

Selye, H. (1976). *The stress of life* (2nd ed.). New York: McGraw-Hill.

Schmidt, M. A., Smith, L. H., & Sehnert, K. W. (1993). *Beyond antibiotics: Healthier options for families.* Berkeley, CA: North Atlantic Books.

Shaw, C. R., & Lucas, A. R. (1970). *The psychiatric disorders of childhood* (2nd ed.). New York: Appleton-Century-Croft.

Tryphonas, H., & Trites, R. (1979). Food allergy in children with hyperactivity, learning disabilities, and/or minimal brain dysfunction. *Annals of Allergy, 42,* 22–27.

Waksman, S. A. (1983). Diet and children's behavior disorders: A review of the research. *Clinical Psychology Review, 3,* 201–213.

Warren, T. (1991). *Beating Alzheimer's: A step toward unlocking the mysteries of brain diseases.* Garden City Park, New York: Avery Publishing Group.

Wender, E. H. (1986). The food additive free diet in treatment of behavior disorders: A review. *Development and Behavioral Pediatrics, 7,* 35–42.

Wirt, R. D., Lachar, D., Klinedinst, J. K., & Seat, P. D. (1984). *Multidimensional description of child personality: A manual for the Personality Inventory for Children* (2nd ed.). Los Angeles: Western Psychological Services.

AUTHOR'S NOTE

This research was funded in part by the University of Massachusetts at Dartmouth University Research Committee and Psychology Department. Different portions of this research were presented at the annual meetings of the American Association of Applied and Preventive Psychology in Chicago, 1993, and the Eastern Psychological Association in Boston, MA, 1992, and in Providence, RI, 1994. We wish to thank Jeanne Hubbuch, M. D. for her advice, as well as the following psychology student research assistants: Jennifer Brunner, Kim Burns, Vivian Bussiere, Kevin Cook, Christine Cordeiro, Anne Marie Dialessi, Susan Esteves, Kristen Faria, Tim Gallagher, Mia Holland, Ann Lynch, Stacey Marcosa, Kris Mason, Wendy Montembault, Karen Souza, and Jayda Woodman.

NOTES

[1] ADHD indicators used were as follows: $T > 64$ for Hyperactivity Index CPRS-48 and CTRS-28; $T > 69$ for WWPARS (if age >9, then WWPARS raw

score >14); greater than 3 "yes" responses on SSQ-R; greater than 6 "yes" responses on HSQ-R; $T > 64$ for the hyperactivity scale of the PIC.

[2] Combined RAST IgE and RAST IgG food antibody panels test for up to 30 foods for immediate reactions (IgE) and 90 foods for delayed reactions (IgG) and are available through MetaMetrix Medical Laboratory of Norcross, Georgia.

[3] The ELISA/ACT tests for delayed immune reactions for up to 235 foods, preservatives, yeast, and pesticides, and is available through Serammune Physicians Lab of Reston, Virginia.

4 | PRESCHOOL CHILDREN WITH AUTISM

Current Conceptualizations and Best Practices

Frank R. Robbins, Susan Giordano, Susan Rhoads, and Robert Feldman

CRAIG'S STORY

Craig was a full-term baby who appeared normal and healthy at birth. According to his mother, his only notable features were that he was remarkably attractive and in her view, an excessively "good" baby who demanded little attention. In his parents eyes, aside from a little colic, his first year of life was quite uneventful. Although his motor development was slightly advanced, his family became concerned over his growing lack of social responsiveness, poor eye contact, and failure to acquire any speech by age 18 months. By age 2, Craig's family was quite concerned about his frequent tantrums, long periods of screaming, odd stereotypic behaviors (staring at lights and waving his fingers in front of his eyes), and lack of play skills. Family life was further disrupted by his sleeping problems and refusal to eat most foods. At their wits' end, Craig's parents brought him for a full evaluation at a nearby children's hospital, fearing that their son might be deaf. After several days of tests, the team of professionals reached a conclusion; Craig was a child with autism. In one sense, his parents were relieved that they had a label for their son's puzzling constellation of behaviors. Along with this small sense of relief, they experienced conflicting emotions of depression, anger, guilt, and frustration. What was autism and what did it mean for their son and their family?

WHAT IS AUTISM?

The question on "What is autism?" is far easier to ask than it is to answer. In fact, for many aspects of this puzzling disability the most accurate answer is simply, "We don't know." Since its discovery in 1943, autism has attracted a variety of conceptualizations and an even broader array of therapeutic approaches. Early in its history, autism was marked by professional disagreement and lack of consensus. Fortunately, through research and clinical practice over the last 50 years autism has become less of an enigma. Although there are still numerous theoretical and therapeutic debates, there has emerged an increased consistency in describing the etiological, diagnostic, therapeutic, and prognostic aspects of this disorder. In this chapter, a framework is provided for understanding autism through information that has been amassed over the syndrome's half century of existence as well as through case examples that help to illustrate many of the features of autism.

Autism is a developmental disability that is evident during a child's development, usually at quite an early age, and continues to some degree throughout the child's life. It is a disability that affects many areas of functioning. Like mental retardation and other developmental disabilities, autism presents many challenges. Unlike mental retardation, the child with autism presents inconsistencies and an array of difficulties that magnify the challenges for the child's family and those involved in habilitative efforts.

Currently, autism is categorized as a "pervasive developmental disorder" (PDD) in the *Diagnostic and Statistical Manual,* 4th edition (DSM-IV) (APA, 1994). This label describes a core clinical picture in which many areas of development are affected simultaneously and severely. In the DSM-IV, five types of PDD are described: autism (or "Autistic Disorder"), Rett's Disorder, Asperger's Disorder, Childhood Disintegrative Disorder, and Pervasive Developmental Disorder Not Otherwise Specified (PDDNOS). A diagnosis of PDDNOS is made when the child does not exhibit enough behaviors to receive a diagnosis of autism or another pervasive developmental disorder but has qualitative impairments in social and communication skills (APA, 1994). Although DSM-IV contains additional subgroups of PDD as compared to DSM III-R (APA, 1987), little evidence exists that these diagnostic categories carry specific prescriptions for intervention.

Autism is a behavioral syndrome. A diagnosis of autism can only be made based on the presence or absence of certain behaviors. There are no medical tests that can be used to make this judgment because autism is not an infection, virus, or chromosomal abnormality that can be detected through blood tests, EEG recordings, or CAT scans. At one very basic level, autism is simply a term that is used to describe children and adults who share a set of similar behaviors.

The keystone features in the syndrome of autism are disabilities in social relatedness and communication skills. People with autism exhibit great difficulties, and often little interest, in the social contexts and relationships that most of us take for granted. Although this feature is always present with people who are described as having autism, there exists a great deal of variation in the expression of this trait. Some people with autism show almost no interest in other people and seem to have little ability or motivation to communicate. Other people with the same diagnosis are described as having almost "excessive speech" and may have at least an interest in social exchanges with others. Although in many ways this group may appear on the surface to be less disabled, the fact remains that these people still experience significant difficulties in some dimensions of socialization and communication. For example, a child we worked with had a narrow and excessive interest in the esoteric topic of weather records at the local airport. Although in one sense this child's ability to communicate was not problematic, social relationships were drastically affected since this was the only topic this child had interest in talking about. None of his peers had any interest in this child's long diatribes about relative humidity, wind speed, and daily high and low temperatures.

Another defining aspect of autism is the fact that these children have a restricted or limited repertoire of activities and interests. People with autism also have a variety of repetitive and stereotypic behaviors and other unusual traits. These behaviors, often referred to as "self-stimulation" vary in form (e.g., Craig would spend extended periods of time waving his fingers in front of his eyes) and intensity. Other forms include body rocking, finger or arm flapping, noise making, and head weaving. Some other behaviors that fit this general category include attachment to certain objects (e.g., one child we worked with insisted on wearing two combination locks on the belt loops of his pants), ritualistic and perseverative response patterns, poor play skills, following routines in precise detail, and distress over even trivial changes in the environment (e.g., a child may become upset when a picture is moved from one wall to another). In addition, this characteristic may be manifested in restricted, narrow, idiosyncratic, or bizarre topics of conversation.

Autism is also associated with other characteristics which are not defining aspects of the disorder. For example, although 75%-80% of people with autism have accompanying cognitive impairments, some individuals may possess unusual abilities in certain areas (e.g., in art, music, or mathematical areas) that are at least inconsistent with their overall level of functioning. In some cases, à la Hollywood's "Rain Man" character, these skills may be truly exceptional for any person (e.g., the ability to do rapid mental calculations with large numbers), whereas in other cases these skills may represent relative strengths (e.g., the ability to do complex puzzles in the context of severely impaired communication skills). In some cases, autism is also accompanied by disruptive and violent behaviors, such as tantrums, aggression, and self-injury. Current conceptualizations of these behaviors indicate that they are reflective of the person's limitations in other areas, particularly communication skills (e.g., Donnellan, Mirenda, Mesaros, & Fassbender, 1984; Durand, 1990). A label of autism may also be accompanied by odd responses to sensory input (overresponsive to some sensations and underresponsive to others), difficulties with eating and sleeping, and abnormalities of mood (APA, 1994).

Several comments regarding etiology are pertinent, although it must be stated that at this time more remains unknown than known about the cause(s) of autism. One conclusion that has been reached involves the causative role of parents in their children's disability. Early conceptualizations (e.g., Bettelheim, 1967) scapegoated the mothers of children with autism, indicating that they were cold, aloof, and disinterested, which caused their children to "retreat" into an autistic shell. The therapeutic implications were to separate these "refrigerator mothers" from their children, providing play therapy for the child and individual psychotherapy for the mother. Put most simply, it is now known that autism is not caused by poor parenting with study after study failing to uncover the traits that Bettelheim posited (e.g., Koegel, Schreibman, O'Neill, & Burke, 1983). Although broadly speaking there is agreement that autism is a physiologically based disorder, no precise, consistent cause has been discovered (e.g., Simpson & Zionts, 1992). In fact, a large number of research investigations have examined various structural, electrical, and biochemical aspects of the brains of people with autism, with few consistencies emerging (Rutter & Schopler, 1988).

One final note. People with autism are a heterogeneous group, in many ways more different than alike. Across all developmental and behavioral dimensions, a great diversity exists. Some people remain nonverbal and relatively uncommunicative, whereas others develop impressive speech. Some individuals are active and difficult to manage behaviorally, but others are lethargic, passive, and unresponsive. Later in life, some people with autism are able to live independently, even though others require lifelong, 24-hour supervision and support. Overall, individuals may be distinguished along a continuum that ranges from mild to severe autism, with the severe end referring to the more extreme profiles of social and emotional aloneness. A parallel and independent dimension concerns a person's cognitive functioning. People with autism span the gamut of intellectual functioning from genius level to severe and profound mental retardation. Thus, an infinite number of combinations of autism severity and intellectual abilities are possible. With this in mind, the extraordinary diversity in this population should not be surprising.

EARLY INTERVENTION

A consensus has emerged that if children with autism are identified and treated at an early age, then outcomes will be improved compared to children who do not receive such early services (e.g., Fenske, Zalenski, Krantz, & McClannahan, 1985). These authors reported significantly greater improvements when children with autism entered treatment before the age of 5 in comparison with children who began the same intervention program after age 5. To date, the most compelling data on the effectiveness of early intervention for children with autism comes from the work of Ivar Lovaas and his colleagues (Lovaas, 1980, 1987; McEachin, Smith, & Lovaas, 1993). Lovaas (1987) provided 40 hours per week of intensive behavioral intervention over a two-year period for a group of 19 preschool children (under age 4) diagnosed with autism. Follow-up data indicated that of these 19 participants, 9 successfully completed first grade in regular education classrooms. In contrast to these positive outcomes, only 1 of the children in the control group achieved similar levels of success. Longer term follow-up by McEachin et al. (1993) indicated that the children in the treatment group had maintained their successes and that 8 of the 9 were "indistinguishable from average children on tests of intelligence and adaptive behavior" (p. 359). Although the work of the Lovaas group has encountered methodological criticisms and debate (e.g., Schopler, Short, & Mesibov, 1989), the essential message is that if children with autism receive early and intensive intervention then impressive outcomes can be realized.

Although Lovaas is considered one of the pioneers of early intervention for young children with autism, he is not the only one who has developed, evaluated, and disseminated quality programs. Across the country, a number of high-quality, successful early intervention programs have been developed which have resulted in impressive gains for the young children they have served (e.g., Anderson, Campbell, & Cannon, 1994; Strain & Cordisco, 1994). Space limitations here prohibit descriptions of these programs, but the interested reader is referred to an excellent book that provides detailed information on 10 preschool education programs for children with autism (Harris & Handleman, 1994).

Over the years many diverse programs and service delivery models have been developed for young children with autism. Despite this diversity, a consensus on what constitutes "best practice" for this population is emerging. In the next section, we discuss five aspects of best practice in programs for preschoolers with autism based on both clinical experience and the available research literature.

BEST PRACTICES IN EARLY INTERVENTION FOR CHILDREN WITH AUTISM

Inclusion as a Reference Point

Consistent with the national movements toward mainstreaming, least restrictive environments, and full inclusion is the growing consensus that preschoolers with autism are best educated alongside typically developing peers. As has been described elsewhere (e.g., Dunlap & Robbins, 1991), young children with autism need to take part in the same kinds of educational and community activities that children without disabilities experience. This includes attending preschool or daycare programs with typically developing children as well as participating in afterschool activities with peers and visiting community settings such as the mall and supermarket. Clinical practice and research suggest that peers are invaluable assets that can be utilized in teaching young children with autism key social and communicative skills (e.g., Strain, 1981). Although empirical evidence for the benefits of inclusive education is growing (Odom & McEvoy, 1988; Strain, 1983; Strain & Cordisco, 1994), the fact remains that unequivocal data in favor of this approach do not exist. However, inclusion is not only an increasing phenomenon, but one of the standards by which quality programs are judged (Dunlap & Robbins, 1991). Of the 10 programs described in Harris and Handleman's (1994) book, every one indicates that, at a minimum, opportunities for integration exist as part of its program.

Individualizing Programs

As has been already discussed, a tremendous diversity exists within the diagnostic category of autism across a number of behavioral dimensions. One obvious implication is that all aspects of programming must be specifically tailored to address individual differences and meet the needs of each child. Simply knowing that a child has a label of autism does little as far as providing relevant information that will be helpful in educational planning and behavioral programming. Even children with autism who appear similar often need vastly different approaches to intervention. This is particularly the case when dealing with challenging behaviors such as tantrums or aggression. Imagine two children, Jonny and Michael. Both are 3-year-olds with autism who engage in aggressive behavior. Jonny exhibits aggression and other disruptive behaviors when he is asked to make transitions from more preferred to less preferred activities (e.g., from free play to the bathroom), while Michael exhibits behaviors that are similar in topography when his teacher is unable to sit and read story books to him. These behaviors are emitted because both children lack more appropriate ways to communicate (Durand, 1990). Through a process of functional assessment (Lennox & Miltenberger, 1989), it can be demonstrated that these behaviors serve vastly different functions for the two boys (an escape function for Jonny and an attention-seeking purpose for Michael). With this knowledge, it should be clear that the same approach to treatment cannot possibly be effective for both children (e.g., Carr & Durand, 1985; Repp, Felce, & Barton, 1988). In fact, if a brief time-out were applied to both children, Michael's behavior would likely improve, while Jonny's behavior would likely get worse.

Other aspects of individualizing programs involves curriculum planning, teaching techniques, and motivational strategies. A whole series of questions pertinent to these areas must be answered for each child. What are the child's strengths? Weaknesses? Priorities for intervention? What is the best communication system for the child? How best to teach the child to independently use the bathroom? What does the child like? Dislike? Which things can function as reinforcers for teaching the child new skills? These are just a few of the myriad of questions that must be asked if quality educational services are to be delivered. Again, simply knowing the child's diagnosis offers little information as a parent, teacher, or other professional attempts to address these questions.

Family Support and Collaboration

The role of parents in the etiology and the treatment of their children with autism has evolved substantially over the years. The days when parents were viewed as the causative agents of autism have ended, largely replaced with the orientation that parents need to be actively involved at several levels for the overall benefit of their children. Current thinking views parents as collaborators in the process of intervention with the recognition that not all families may want (or need) the same kind of support services (e.g., Turnbull & Turnbull, 1990).

The evolution of the field's views on parents has several phases. First, when psychodynamic theories were popular, parents (particularly mothers) were viewed as the cause of their child's autism (e.g., Bettelheim, 1967). Specifically, the disastrous parenting these children received led to their withdrawal and profound inabilities to socialize, play, and communicate. The logical extension of this orientation was to separate the child and parent, providing supportive play therapy for the "damaged" child and intensive, individual psychotherapy for the mother. Not only did this approach fail miserably, but it destroyed families, casting blame when support, training, and education should have been provided.

The next phase characterized parents as "teachers" who could provide important learning opportunities for their children. During this time an emphasis was placed on "parent training," which was designed to help parents teach their children new skills while reducing problematic behaviors (e.g., Koegel, Glahn, & Nieminen, 1978; Schopler & Reichler, 1971). A plethora of manuals were published designed to help parents learn how to deliver good instructions, utilize effective prompting strategies, and provide reinforcement (e.g., Baker & Heifetz, 1976; Koegel & Schreibman, 1982; Kozloff, 1973; Schopler, Reichler, & Lansing, 1980). This approach has been successfully extended to teaching young children with autism, most notably through the work of Lovaas (1987) and Anderson, Avery, DiRietro, Edwards, & Christian (1987).

Although the "parents as teachers" approach continues to be the foundation of many quality programs, it has undergone some alteration and broadening over the last 10 years. This evolution has been stimulated by clinical practice, research, and the input of families themselves. Clinically, it was commonplace to see some families and their children make impressive gains in acquiring new skills while others made little to no progress. Research (both within and outside the disability of autism) has begun to identify some of the child and family variables that may affect the progress of families and their children (e.g., Clark & Baker, 1983; Griest & Forehand, 1982; Robbins, Dunlap, & Plienis, 1991). Some of the factors identified have included socioeconomic status and parenting stress in addition to child factors including cognitive and language abilities. Finally, families themselves have called for a more collaborative approach characterized by mutual respect and understanding (e.g., Turnbull & Turnbull, 1990). Taken together, these convergent data suggest that families must be recognized as individual systems with individual needs. Therefore, intervention programs increasingly include multiple components, including "traditional" parent training, respite care, in-home supports (e.g., a home health aide), referrals to other service agencies, and groups that help "connect" parents to other parents with children with autism. In addition, families must be seen as essential and enduring resources on behalf of their children with unique expertise regarding their child. If all these premises are accepted, then viewing families as collaborators represents the only logical conclusion.

Behavioral/Educational Approach

Consistent with the shifting perspectives on etiology has been a growing consensus that children with autism are best served through what can be termed a behavioral/educational approach. This orientation replaces one that could primarily be conceptualized as symptom-oriented in that individual behaviors or "symptoms" were targeted for reduction. "Bizarre" or stigmatizing behaviors such as echolalia, stereotypies, self-injury, and other idiosyncrasies were conceptualized as behavioral excesses that should be the targets of elimination (e.g., Lovaas, 1977; Lovaas & Simmons, 1969). Work in the areas of functional analysis (e.g., Carr & Durand, 1985; Iwata, Dorsey, Slifer, Bauman, & Richman, 1982) and communication (e.g., Prizant, 1987; Wetherby, 1986) have helped shift the perspectives on these problematic behaviors. What has emerged is the understanding that these behaviors are representative of the skill deficits that children with autism display, particularly in the area of communication (e.g., Durand, 1990; Evans & Meyer, 1985; Van Bourgondien, 1993).

The trend toward a behavioral/educational approach is particularly evident in early intervention, though this approach has drawn criticism (e.g., Berkeley & Ludlow, 1989) from proponents of "developmentally appropriate practice" (Bredekamp, 1987). Developmentally appropriate practice (DAP) has been advocated by a number of organizations, most notably the National Association for the Education of Young Children (NAEYC). Key aspects of this approach involve an emphasis on child-directed exploratory play activities, as well as on age appropriateness and individual appropriateness, which highlights the uniqueness of each child (Bredekamp, 1987). Formal academic instruction is eschewed with the position that tightly structured, adult-directed activities are counterproductive for young children. While DAP has enjoyed widespread support, a number of authors have cogently and persuasively argued for the blending of developmentally appropriate practice and more structured behavioral approaches for children with autism and other disabilities (e.g., Carta, Schwartz, Atwater, & McConnell, 1991; Wolery, Strain, & Bailey, 1994).

Taken together, available research and clinical experience suggest that young children with autism are best served through interventions that are designed to develop new skills and competencies (Dunlap, Johnson, & Robbins, 1990). Optimally, these skills are taught in the most natural, normalized, and least restrictive contexts possible, capitalizing on children's initiations, preferences, and interests. However, it must be emphasized that in order for some children to learn, instruction must be more adult-directed, planned, and structured (Wolery & Fleming, 1993). For some children with autism, a more structured approach may be necessary at first, followed by a more natural, less intrusive approach after children have acquired some basic skills (Anderson et al., 1994). In any case, the ultimate criterion involves the simple question, "Is *this* child learning under a given set of conditions?"

Effective, Data-Based Procedures

Along with the fantastic variety of conceptualizations that autism has attracted over the years, an equally large number of interventions have been proposed, advocated, and to a lesser extent, evaluated. A variety of psychodynamically oriented approaches (e.g., Bettelheim, 1967; DesLauriers, 1978), pharmacological interventions (e.g., Campbell et al., 1978; Ritvo, Freeman, Geller, & Yuwiler, 1983), megavitamin regimens (Rimland, 1973), and behavioral techniques (Lovaas, 1977) have been prescribed for children with autism over the years. Other "therapies"—including sensory integration, holding, auditory training, facilitated communication, and even swimming with dolphins—have been implemented for children with autism. Although such treatments have been highly touted, systematic study has typically failed to demonstrate effectiveness empirically. For example, a number of investigators have recently reported data that call into great question the validity of facilitated communication with people with autism (e.g., Wheeler, Jacobson, Paglieri, & Schwartz, 1993). Broadly speaking, the literature concludes that effective interventions for people with autism fall into the behavioral, educational, and to a lesser extent, pharmacological approaches. With this in mind, the essential message is that therapeutic approaches need to be systematically evaluated to assess their effectiveness for individual children. Adhering to this guideline will help insure that "treatment fads" are not put into practice without adequate evaluation (Schopler, 1987).

Although thus far the discussion has centered on the overall effectiveness of various therapeutic approaches, the focus on the individual child remains important. As described earlier, the diversity of children with autism is tremendous and the working with each child as a unique individual is paramount. At this level it is important to consistently and objectively monitor progress such that decisions can be made based on both quantitative and qualitative data. This is deemed vital, as ongoing monitoring is necessary to ensure that children move on to more advanced competencies as they acquire simpler skills. In addition, it is not uncommon for a given intervention to fail to produce the desired outcomes. Under these circumstances, programs must be continually modified and adjusted if children are to make meaningful progress. To make these alterations without objective data is tantamount to reading a roadmap in the dark.

In the next section, we describe our work with a program designed to provide services for preschool-aged children with autism and related disorders of learning and behavior. This description illustrates programmatic features that are seen as important for young children with autism, their families, and those community-based professionals involved in habilitative efforts on behalf of these children.

A PROGRAM EXAMPLE:
THE EARLY CHILDHOOD LEARNING CENTER

The Early Childhood Learning Center (ECLC) began providing services to young children with special needs in 1991. Through a unique arrangement, this program is a collaborative endeavor between the University of Massachusetts at Amherst's Department of Psychology and the May Institute, a private, nonprofit organization involved with education, training, and research for people with autism and other developmental disabilities.

General Program Structure

The Early Childhood Learning Center is a center-based preschool program that serves children with autism and related developmental disorders alongside typically developing children. This full-day (6-hour), 12-month program typically serves seven children with autism and eight typically developing children in its one preschool classroom. This program is staffed by a full-time lead teacher/educational coordinator, three full-time teachers/case managers, and one part-time teacher. A ratio of four adults to 15 children is maintained at all times. This highly trained staff is knowledgeable about best practices in the areas of early childhood education and behavioral approaches to working with children with autism. It is our belief that the program combines the best aspects of developmentally appropriate practice (Bredekamp, 1987) and a more structured behavioral approach and places a high emphasis on the individual nature of all participating children. Only well-documented educational practices are utilized and instruction is conducted in the most natural contexts possible. The program also provides home-based parent training and family support services, with each child's case manager making weekly phone calls and monthly home visits. These visits are designed to address concerns unique to the home environment or to assist with the follow-through of school programs (e.g., a communication system) to the home setting. Finally, the program provides consultation and support to help ensure a successful transition back to public school settings. The program is funded by tuition paid by sending school districts (about $26,000 per year for the 1994 school year) and nominal fees paid by parents of typically developing children.

Population Served

An average of seven children with disabilities a year have participated in this preschool program meeting the following criteria: they were 5 years old or younger at the time of admission, and they carried a variety of diagnostic labels including autism, pervasive developmental disorder, and severe language disorder. The majority of these children were referred by their parents, although some were referred by their local school districts, pediatricians, and early intervention programs. The mean age of these children at admission was 3 years 11 months (range 2 years 9 months to 5 years 4 months).

Screening and Assessment Procedures

An initial screening is conducted to determine the ability of the program to meet the child's needs. The screening is not a formal assessment of the child's abilities. This process involves a comprehensive review of the child's records and previous evaluations; a visit to the program by the child's parents so that they may gather information about ECLC's services, ask questions of program staff, and observe interactions within the classroom; a formal screening where one staff member spends about 45 minutes with the child loosely following the Developmental Play Assessment Instrument developed by Lifter, Edwards, Avery, Anderson, and Sulzer-Azaroff (1988); and an in-depth parent interview to collect information about the child's skills and behaviors at home and to get parental input on educational priorities. Based on this information, staff meet and determine whether the program can adequately meet the needs of the child and his or her family. Once a child is accepted for admission into the program, final placement is made contingent upon space in the classroom and the willingness of the child's school district to fund program tuition.

Once the child is enrolled in the program, a variety of information is gathered so that the most appropriate Individualized Education Plan (IEP) can be developed. The development of the IEP is always a team process involving the child's family, school district, and program staff. For the most part, assessment data are collected in the context of the child's involvement in classroom activities. During the first 4–6 weeks of the child's enrollment, baseline data are collected in the classroom on problem behaviors, language and communication skills, social interactions with adults and peers, self-care skills, and school readiness skills. When needed, these in-classroom data may be supplemented by standardized tests (e.g., Early Learning Accomplishment Profile, Learning Accomplishment Profile, Vineland Adaptive Behavior Scales) to further assess the child's skills at program entry.

Teaching and Administrative Staff

A full-time, master's-level lead teacher/educational coordinator has the responsibility for the day-to-day operation of the classroom. The preschool classroom is also staffed by one part-time and three full-time teachers, all of whom are at least bachelor's-level individuals with educational backgrounds in psychology, special education, early childhood education, speech/language pathology, or a related human services field. The program also employs a part-time (half a day a week) speech/language therapist who functions as a consultant within the classroom program. The program contracts with other specialists (i.e., physical and occupational therapists) on an as-needed basis. For the most part, these ancillary services are integrated into the classroom curriculum, with specialists serving as consultants rather than delivering individual "pull-out" services for children.

Both the training and supervision of staff are approached in a systematic manner. Although some initial training could be described as didactic, virtually all of the training is conducted in vivo. That is, each individual receives in-classroom monitoring by the lead teacher, who is responsible for providing supervision, training, and regular feedback. In addition, each staff member receives a clear set of job performance standards prior to employment that delineates and operationalizes specific job responsibilities. All staff evaluations occur within the context of these job performance standards.

In addition to in-classroom responsibilities, each full-time member of the classroom staff serves as case manager for two children. With the close supervision of the lead teacher/educational coordinator, case managers are required to develop educational and behavioral objectives, write detailed programs, monitor individual student progress, and serve as the primary liaison with the child's family (i.e., make weekly phone contact with the family and conduct monthly home visits).

In addition to full-time professional staff, by virtue of the relationship between the Early Childhood Learning Center and the University of Massachusetts, both undergraduate and graduate students have opportunities to complete clinical or research practica or internships within the context of the program. In addition, students from other area colleges and universities have taken advantage of the training experiences offered within the program. Students from various university departments (e.g., psychology, special education, communication disorders) participate in these training experiences, which may last one semester or involve several semesters of increasing responsibility. The primary purpose of this aspect of the program is to train students, and not for students to provide service (i.e., replace full-time staff or reduce ratios).

Curriculum

One of the primary programmatic goals is to teach children the necessary skills that will allow for successful functioning at home, in the community, and public school classrooms. In this context, the classroom curriculum addresses a child's needs in areas of communication, socialization, play, self-care, self-management/behavioral, and school readiness skills. Although a broad range of materials are utilized, no single curriculum is followed. Each child's program is developed individually based on extensive in-classroom observations, input from parents and school personnel, and the administration of standardized instruments (when necessary). Based on all available information, the child's case manager identifies 15–20 objectives to be targeted in the classroom for a given school year.

Classroom instruction on individual children's objectives occurs in a variety of contexts. As a general rule, instruction is provided to maximize skill acquisition, generalization, and maintenance. The secondary criteria involves conducting instruction in the most natural context possible. For most children, the majority of the objectives on their IEPs are addressed throughout the day in natural settings. For example, much of the work on communication skills takes place during snack or lunch, times when situations are ripe for children to practice requesting, protesting, and other communicative functions. Work on socialization may take place at the beginning of the day in the context of children greeting staff, or in one of the free play centers interacting with peers. At other times of the day, children receive instruction in both small and large group activities. For example, additional work on social interaction occurs during "social games" where children work in integrated groups of 3–5 children on sharing and turn-taking activities. Large group instruction occurs during "morning meeting" when children work on following group directions, group responding, and attentional skills in a large group format. Finally, for educational objectives that are less easily embedded into play and other natural contexts, children are removed from "free play" and receive brief periods (5–15 minutes) of one-to-one instruction.

When examining the daily schedule (see Table 1) the variety of activities and contexts should be immediately apparent. The day begins with a period of child-directed discovery referred to as "free play." To an outside observer this may appear to be a free period without goals, but in reality these periods are thoroughly planned and carefully arranged by teachers. Six "centers" comprise the free play area; puzzles, books, table top toys, art, dramatic play, and blocks. Materials are frequently rotated to keep children interested. With some exceptions, children are free to choose the areas and

Table 1
Daily Schedule

Time	Activity
9:00– 9:45 am	Free play
9:45–10:05	Morning meeting
10:05–10:20	Snack
10:20–10:50	Art/social games
10:50–11:20	Free play
11:20–11:50	Outside
11:50–12:00	Story/wash hands
12:00–12:30 pm	Lunch
12:30– 1:15	Rest period
1:15– 1:45	Outside
1:45– 2:00	Story/wash hands
2:00– 2:20	Snack
2:20– 2:50	Free play
2:50– 3:00	Afternoon meeting

other children with whom they play and may move from center to center as space permits (given the size of the centers, there is a limit on the number of children in a given center at one time). These periods provide perfect opportunities for incidental instruction on communication, play, and social skills. Also during this time children are taken to the bathroom (many of the participating children are not yet toilet-trained) and others are pulled out for short periods of one-to-one instruction.

Free play is followed by "morning meeting" (often referred to as "circle time"), which is a large group activity led by one of the teachers on a rotating basis. A variety of activities centered around the theme and color of the month are incorporated into this time period with individual IEP objectives addressed for each child (e.g., motor imitation, group responding). This activity often requires some modification for children who lack the attentional and self-management skills to successfully participate in a 20-minute group activity. Therefore, for some children, this activity is shortened or additional incentives are incorporated to encourage at least sitting with the group.

Following morning meeting is a snack period, where many social, self-help, and communication objectives are incorporated. Such objectives range from requesting more of a particular snack using a communication board to asking a peer to pass more food. Snack is followed by a 30-minute block that incorporates an art activity and a time for social games. The class is divided in two, with half the children starting in art and half starting in social games. These smaller group activities allow for the incorporation of social, communication, self-care, and fine motor goals. The morning is filled out by a second free play period, time outside (an inside gross motor period on days where weather is a problem), story time, and lunch.

Given the age of the participating children, the afternoon contains less intensive kinds of activities. After lunch, a 45-minute rest period is scheduled, during which children are allowed small quiet toys and the opportunity to watch children's videotapes. During this time, some children sleep, whereas others quietly engage themselves with toys. This is followed by an outside time, story, afternoon snack, a final free play period, and an afternoon meeting (which has some of the same goals as morning circle but lasts only about 10 minutes). This group activity helps provide children with a clear "end of the day" cue.

Overall, the approach to instruction can best be described as behaviorally based and involves detailed lesson plans ("short-term objectives" or STOs), which provide behaviorally stated objectives, acquisition criteria, teaching procedures, methods of evaluation, reinforcers, and a task analysis, and address generalization and maintenance issues. The STOs serve as the framework for collecting data on child progress and allow for data-based decisions to be made about when to move children up a step, or when to modify objectives or teaching procedures based on lack of progress.

Integration

Integrating children with special needs with typically developing children is a concept that is not new, but nonetheless it is one that still encounters debate. There are those who advocate full inclusion of all children with disabilities at all ages with their agemates in neighborhood schools (e.g., Stainback & Stainback, 1984), but others advocate a less fully inclusive approach. For example, Lovaas (1987) describes an intensive, systematic, and one-to-one approach to instruction that needs to precede students' placement in typical preschool settings. That is, children must exhibit certain "readiness" skills in order to benefit from socially integrated experiences.

At the Early Childhood Learning Center, all children who are accepted into our program begin in our integrated classroom from their first day in the program (a few children have not been considered for admission due to their size and/or severity of behavior problems). Although all children begin in our integrated classroom, children require different levels of support to be successful in the program. Many children have entered the program and have been quite successful with our structured approach to teaching along with teacher-student ratios that are much lower than in most public school or private preschool settings. Other children have needed additional (often temporary) program modifications to be successful (e.g., participating in morning meeting for only 10 minutes), and still others have needed more extensive one-to-one support to help integrate them into the classroom routine. In all cases we have been able to reduce the need for extensive adult assistance, although it is expected that some children may require full-time individual assistance in order to be maximally successful.

Of course, the main goal of the program is to provide children with the skills to be able to benefit from integrated experiences in their community public schools. We believe that because children are educated (with the necessary supports) alongside typically developing peers from the outset that inclusion (again, with the right supports) in typical kindergarten programs in the public schools can often be a successful experience.

Behavior Management

As has been well-documented in the clinical and research literature, children with autism often display challenging behaviors that interfere with learning. Many of the preschool-aged children who enter the program engage in problematic behaviors including tantrums, aggression, noncompliance, other disruptive and destructive behaviors, and stereotypic behaviors. These behaviors not only interfere with learning but can be quite disruptive to other students in the classroom.

A comprehensive and systematic approach to addressing problem behaviors is fully incorporated into the program. Generally, the approach can best be characterized as one that utilizes both formal and informal functional assessment data paired with positive strategies for managing behavior problems (e.g., Dunlap, Robbins, & Kern, 1994). As has been described in many other contexts, most of the program's "behavior management" occurs when behavior problems are *not* being exhibited. That is, a number of programmatic and curricular components are in place whose purpose is largely to *prevent* problematic behaviors from occurring. Some of the proactive aspects of the program include: (1) staff members who are directed to keep children engaged in appropriate activities as much as possible; (2) a consistent and predictable classroom schedule; (3) a mixture of activities that allow children to make choices and those that are more adult-directed; (4) clear instructions and classroom rules; (5) high density of behavior-specific social/physical reinforcement for appropriate behavior; (6) an emphasis on teaching children appropriate, alternative skills (e.g., communication, play, social) that can replace problematic behavior (Carr, 1988); and (7) varying materials and activities to keep children's interest.

Although these general components are in place, program modifications are typically made in a child-specific fashion. For example, one child had extreme difficulty transitioning from free play to the bathroom. After a preferred toy was introduced to signal the transition, the tantrums were greatly reduced.

Although the preventative aspects of the program go a long way in solving many of the children's behavior problems, given the nature of the population, it should not be surprising that behavior problems still occur with regularity. Again, given that this is a community-based, integrated program, positive, community-referenced approaches to handle misbehavior are the rule (e.g., Horner et al., 1990). First and foremost, behaviors are responded to (or not responded to) based on their presumed function. For example, if a child is hitting the teacher to escape a work session, the teacher may redirect/ignore the behavior while continuing to present instruction. Alternately, if the child is crying to gain access to a toy that has been removed, the behavior will be ignored. Most behavior problems are successfully managed through a combination of reinforcement of appropriate behavior, redirection, ignoring, and differential attention. The only exception to this rule is a classroom-wide consequence for *peer* aggression. All typical and special needs children (except for those whose individual programs dictate otherwise) receive a brief, one-minute period of contingent observation (i.e., they are removed from the activity and must "sit and watch" for one minute) if they are aggressive toward a peer.

Taken together, the proactive and reactive strategies employed at the Early Childhood Learning Center are sufficient to address most, if not all, behavior problems that children have exhibited. In particular, we feel strongly that the "teaching alternative skills" component is critical as the behavior problems manifested by children with autism are best conceptualized as behavioral deficits. These deficits, particularly in the areas of communication, play, and social skills are the typical driving factors behind the behavior problems of young children. Thus an "educative approach" (Meyer & Evans, 1989) is one that is likely to be most successful with this group.

Family Training and Support

A central part of any program that provides services for young children with autism should involve family training and support (Dunlap & Robbins, 1991). Families must be viewed as their child's most enduring resource as well as their lifelong advocate. If families are to be successful in the latter of these two roles, they need information, training, and support that can be offered by professionals. In much the same way that services are tailored to meet the unique needs of the children that are served, so too are the services to participating families. Thus, in one sense, families have their own IEPs.

Family involvement at the Early Childhood Learning Center consists of several interrelated services that are offered to family members. First, families are involved from the very start in the development of their child's IEP. Parental input on this document is viewed as an essential part of the process. Second, each family has an identified case manager who serves as primary liaison between the program and the family. In this capacity, daily notes and weekly phones calls are made to describe the child's progress and to allow the family an opportunity to ask questions about their child's day-to-day activities. With this regular contact, it is easy to keep parents abreast of program changes, seek their input on which reinforcer may be most effective, or to ask them to follow through with changes in the home (e.g., keeping a child in underwear rather than a diaper to facilitate toilet training). Third, parents are invited to their child's clinical case review meetings, which occur approximately every six weeks. At this meeting, all staff members meet to review each of the child's objectives, discuss progress, and troubleshoot problems. Families are encouraged to attend these meetings to get a clear and comprehensive picture of their child's progress (for families unable to attend, written summaries are sent to them for review).

Fourth, on approximately a monthly basis, case managers (sometimes accompanied by the lead teacher/educational coordinator) make visits to the child in his or her home setting. The purpose of these visits is threefold. Case managers use these visits to provide family members with programmatic updates on all the child's IEP objectives. These visits are also used to provide parents with basic training on how to deal with problems that may be unique to the home setting (e.g., bedtime problems). Finally, parents also receive training in following through on certain programs that are being conducted in the classroom (e.g., use of a communication board, toilet training, etc.). Fifth, on a monthly basis, group parent training and informational meetings are held. These meetings center around specific topics (e.g., behavior management in community settings, teaching play skills, advocating for your child) and allow for the provision of information as well as the opportunity for parents to interact with one another sharing both their successes and failures. This parent-to-parent support is seen as vital and often extends to settings outside these meetings, when individual small groups of parents may gather on a regular basis to talk about their children.

Finally, parents are encouraged to visit the classroom as frequently as they wish. For some parents this is virtually a daily occurrence (for parents that drive their children to and from school), whereas others visit less frequently. This "open door" policy extends to parents calling their child's case manager or any member of the program staff to discuss virtually any issue. For example, a parent may call with questions on how to approach their child's school district on some issue, or need a referral to a dentist. The overriding goal of all these service components is to provide parents with the training, information, and support they need. Some families avail themselves of all these services, but others are much more selective.

Transition

The transition from preschool to public school can be a time of significant stress for both child and family (e.g., Fowler, Schwartz, & Atwater, 1991). In the case of our program, some of these stressors are intensified due to the small, intimate, and supportive nature of the program and its staff. It has been our experience that parents do not always have these same positive experiences when interacting with individuals from large, public school districts charged with serving hundreds, or even thousands of children. Due to these circumstances, the transition of children to public school classrooms is addressed in a careful, systematic, and proactive manner.

Most children begin their enrollment in the ECLC when they are 3 or 4 years of age. Thus, most children are enrolled in our classroom program for two (and sometimes three) school years. Although there could be exceptions, children have not been transitioned from the ECLC into preschool classrooms in their public schools. Children are typically transitioned into kindergarten (or in some cases first grade) classrooms in their home communities. Thus, when it is known that a child will be in the public school in September (whether it has been decided that the child is ready or the child ages out of the ECLC), the team begins having transition meetings in December or January (8–9 months prior to the actual transition). These meetings are attended by the child's parents, school district personnel, and program staff members. The first meeting is spent discussing the child's progress, current levels of performance, and needs in the context of future placements. During this meeting the child's family articulates the kind of setting they would most like to see their child in and a representative from the school district describes current placement options within the system (with the understanding that an appropriate setting may not currently exist).

As the transition process continues, representatives from the district may come to the classroom to observe the child to help in generating placement options. At the same time, an ECLC representative arranges with the parents and the school district to visit potential school and classroom settings for the child. During these visits, special attention is paid to the classroom structure, the willingness of general educators to take children with special needs into their programs, and other programmatic variables that are relevant to the child's needs. Additional meetings are held to discuss placement options as well as the necessary ingredients of support that the child needs in order to increase the likelihood of success in the new setting. These aspects of support may include an individually assigned aide, the provision of a certain number of hours of speech, physical, or occupational therapy, contractually arranging follow-up consultation services with the ECLC, and regular team meetings in the new setting.

Once a setting and additional supports are determined, every effort is made to identify the specific staff members who will be working with the child. Unfortunately, given the realities of teacher contracts, unions, and the like, this is not always possible. For the most part, we have been successful at getting future teachers and classroom assistants to visit the classroom and observe how the child functions under current conditions. Sometimes, districts are able to send future staff for extended periods (several days to a week) to receive child-specific training. These program visits are supplemented by detailed "exit summaries" that are written on each transitioning child, which contain very specific information about communication skills, behavior problems, self-care skills, and so forth.

Although there are never guarantees, we have found that the time invested in transition planning has been well spent. It can be time consuming and difficulties still arise, but children are at least positioned for the best transition possible, capitalizing on the substantial (often years' worth) information that has been accrued on each child. Potential problems can be averted through proactive strategies, and ineffective strategies are delineated such that staff in the new setting do not waste time in their implementation.

Outcomes and Program Evaluation

One trend in the field of developmental disabilities concerns the consideration of a broader range of outcomes than have been typically articulated (e.g., Meyer & Evans, 1989). Thus, in the context of the ECLC, the description of child and programmatic outcomes can be described at a variety of levels.

At the broadest level, we can report that over the last two school years that 12 children with autism have "graduated" from the ECLC program. Of these children, 11 (92%) are currently enrolled in mainstreamed public school classrooms. Of course, many of these children require additional supports to be successful, including individual aides, curricular adaptations, specialized consultation, and child-specific behavior programs. One child (8%) is enrolled in a private, segregated special education setting. It is important to note while these data may appear impressive, the high percentage of children in mainstreamed settings is a combination of "local philosophy" (many districts are highly inclusive at young ages), parent advocacy, and child skills.

Another outcome that can be reported involves children's progress on Individualized Education Plan objectives. Although IEPs are an imprecise instrument, we can report that, over the last 18 months, children have either achieved or are progressing on 89% of the objectives targeted. This is an indication that objectives appropriate to the child's level are being addressed and that children are making steady gains in language, socialization, self-care, and preacademic skills.

Another dimension of program effectiveness involves how engaged children are in appropriate, preschool activities. Regular planned activities checks ("PLA-CHECKS") have been conducted to determine the percentage of children actively engaged in appropriate activities. On average, over the last 18 months, 90% or more of the special needs and typically developing children have been appropriately engaged when random probes were conducted by the educational coordinator.

A final measure of program effectiveness concerns program satisfaction data, which are gathered at six month intervals. Questionnaires are sent out to parents and individual school districts by May Institute staff not directly affiliated with the ECLC (i.e., corporate-level staff based on Cape Cod). The parent questionnaires tap a wide variety of programmatic variables, including satisfaction with their child's progress, cooperativeness of staff, and the quality of home consultation. Information gathered from school districts includes overall satisfaction with services, cost-effectiveness of services, quality of reports, and cooperativeness of staff. Over the last 18 months, the reports we have received from parents and school districts have been overwhelmingly positive, with virtually all respondents reporting either satisfaction or complete satisfaction on every program dimension.

One final point. Many parents have asked about the effects of our program on their typically developing children. While we cannot report systematic data, we have not observed any negative effects on peers and in most cases believe that the typical children derive great behavioral, developmental, and social benefits from placement in our socially integrated program. This is consistent with reviews of the literature (e.g., Esposito, 1987)

FUTURE DIRECTIONS

An empirically based technology for educating children with autism in integrated settings continues to evolve with new developments reported in the research and clinical literature each year. Despite the increased attention to early intervention for children with autism and related disabilities, much work remains if the goal is for all children and their families to receive maximal benefit from these early services.

The first priority must be to identify and serve all children at the earliest possible time. The three main impediments to meeting this objective involve difficulties with getting accurate diagnoses at very young ages, ensuring equal access to programs for underserved (often minority or low-income) children, and the availability of quality educational programs. In this vein, the early identification of children may help prevent the development of more serious problems (i.e., severe behavior problems) at a later point (Dunlap et al., 1990).

For those children already receiving services, a goal of highest importance concerns the identification of the child, family, community, and programmatic variables that influence positive outcomes for young children. A better understanding of these factors will help professionals better tailor programs and provide more individualized supports to maximize child progress. In addition, it is important to follow and document the development of these children over time, carefully articulating the kinds of services they receive each year so that long-term prognosis can be better studied.

Another important area for investigation concerns some of the programmatic variations in currently operating "state of the art" preschool programs (see Harris & Handleman, 1994). For example, do children need certain prerequisite skills to benefit from being educated in integrated settings? Or can all children be educated in socially integrated classrooms with the necessary individualized supports? What are the best ways to increase generalized social and communicative interactions between children with autism and typically developing children? What curricular approach is best? Perhaps some of these questions cannot be directly answered, but research is necessary to begin to understand which variations are important for which children.

Finally, the field must find better ways of disseminating an already impressive technology to parents and professionals in the community. So much of what is routinely applied in programs such as the ECLC may be foreign to parents, preschool teachers, and school administrators who are responsible for educating young children with disabilities in their respective communities.

In sum, it should be clear that although much has been accomplished, much work remains if we are to realize our goal of improving the lives of all children with autism and of their families.

REFERENCES

American Psychiatric Association (1987). *Diagnostic and Statistical Manual of Mental Disorders* (3rd ed., rev.). Washington, DC: American Psychiatric Association.

American Psychiatric Association (1994). *Diagnostic and Statistical Manual of Mental Disorders* (4th ed.). Washington, DC: American Psychiatric Association.

Anderson, S. R., Avery, D. L., DiPietro, E. K., Edwards, G. L., & Christian, W. P. (1987). Intensive home-based early intervention with autistic children. *Education and Treatment of Children, 10,* 352–366.

Anderson, S. R., Campbell, S, & Cannon, B. O. (1994). The May Center for Early Childhood Education. In S. L. Harris & J. S. Handleman (Eds.), *Preschool education programs for children with autism* (pp. 15–36). Austin, TX: Pro-Ed.

Baker, B. L., & Heifetz, L. J. (1976). The READ Project: Teaching manuals for parents of retarded children. In T. D. Tjossem (Ed.), *Intervention strategies for high risk infants and young children* (pp. 351–369). Baltimore: University Park Press.

Berkeley, T. R., & Ludlow, B. L. (1989). Toward a reconceptualization of the developmental model. *Topics in Early Childhood Special Education, 9,* 51–66.

Bettelheim, B. (1967). *The empty fortress.* New York: The Free Press.

Bredekamp, S. (Ed.). (1987). *Developmentally appropriate practice in early childhood programs serving children birth through age 8.* Washington, DC: National Association for the Education of Young Children.

Campbell, M., Anderson, L. T., Meier, M., Cohen, I. L., Small, A. M., Samit, C., & Sachar, E. J. (1978). A comparison of haloperidol and behavior therapy and their interaction in autistic children. *Journal of the American Academy of Child Psychiatry, 17,* 640–655.

Carr, E. G. (1988). Functional equivalence as a mechanism for response maintenance. In R. H. Horner, G. Dunlap, & R. L. Koegel (Eds.), *Generalization and maintenance: Lifestyle changes in applied settings* (pp. 221–241). Baltimore, MD: Paul H. Brookes.

Carr, E. G., & Durand, V. M. (1985). Reducing behavioral problems through functional communication training. *Journal of Applied Behavior Analysis, 18,* 111–126.

Carta, J. J., Schwartz, I. S., Atwater, J. B., & McConnell, S. R. (1991). Developmentally appropriate practice: Appraising its usefulness for young children with disabilities. *Topics in Early Childhood Special Education, 11,* 1–20.

Clark, D. B., & Baker, B. L. (1983). Predicting outcome in parent training. *Journal of Consulting and Clinical Psychology, 51,* 309–311.

DesLauriers, A. M. (1978). Play, symbols, and the development of language. In

M. Rutter & E. Schopler (Eds.), *Autism: A reappraisal of concepts and treatment* (pp. 313–326). New York: Plenum Press.

Donnellan, A. M., Mirenda, P. L., Mesaros, R. A., & Fassbender, L. L. (1984). Analyzing the communicative functions of aberrant behavior. *Journal of the Association for Persons with Severe Handicaps, 2,* 201–212.

Dunlap, G., Johnson, L. F., & Robbins, F. R. (1990). Preventing serious behavior problems through skill development and early intervention. In A. C. Repp & N. N. Singh (Eds.), *Perspectives on the use of nonaversive and aversive interventions for persons with developmental disabilities* (pp. 273–286). Sycamore, IL: Sycamore Press.

Dunlap, G., & Robbins, F. R. (1991). Current perspectives in service delivery for young children with autism. *Comprehensive Mental Health Care, 1,* 177–194.

Dunlap, G., Robbins, F. R., & Kern, L. (1994). Some characteristics of nonaversive intervention for severe behavior problems. In E. Schopler & G. Mesibov (Eds.), *Behavioral issues in autism* (pp. 227–245). New York: Plenum Press.

Durand, V. M. (1990). *Functional communication training: An intervention program for severe behavior problems.* New York: Guilford Press.

Esposito, B. G. (1987). The effects of preschool integration on the development of nonhandicapped children. *Journal of the Division for Early Childhood, 12,* 31–46.

Evans, I. M., & Meyer, L. H. (1985). *An educative approach to behavior problems: A practical decision model for interventions with severely handicapped learners.* Baltimore: Paul H. Brookes.

Fenske, E. C., Zalenski, S., Krantz, P. J., & McClannahan, L. E. (1985). Age at intervention and treatment outcome for autistic children in a comprehensive intervention program. *Analysis and Intervention in Developmental Disabilities, 5,* 49–58.

Fowler, S. A., Schwartz, I., & Atwater, J. (1991). Perspectives on the transition from preschool to kindergarten for children with disabilities and their families. *Exceptional Children, 58,* 136–145.

Griest, D. L., & Forehand, R. (1982). How can I get any parent training done with all these other problems going on? The role of family variables in child behavior therapy. *Child and Family Behavior Therapy, 4,* 73–80.

Harris, S. L., & Handleman, J. S. (Eds.). (1994). *Preschool education programs for children with autism.* Austin, TX: Pro-Ed.

Horner, R. H., Dunlap, G., Koegel, R. L., Carr, E. G., Sailor, W., Anderson, J., Albin, R. W., & O'Neill, R. E. (1990). Toward a technology of "nonaversive" behavioral support. *Journal of the Association for Persons with Severe Handicaps, 15,* 91–97.

Iwata, B. A., Dorsey, M. F., Slifer, K. J., Bauman, K. E., & Richman, G. S. (1982). Toward a functional analysis of self-injury. *Analysis and Intervention in Developmental Disabilities, 2,* 3–20.

Koegel, R. L., Glahn, T. J., & Nieminen, G. S. (1978). Generalization of parent training results. *Journal of Applied Behavior Analysis, 11,* 95–109.

Koegel, R. L., Schreibman, L. (1982). *How to teach autistic and other severely handicapped children.* Lawrence, KS: H & H Enterprises.

Koegel, R. L., Schreibman, L., O'Neill, R. E., & Burke, J. C. (1983). The personality and family-interaction characteristics of parents of autistic children. *Journal of Consulting and Clinical Psychology, 51,* 683–692.

Kozloff, M. A. (1973). *Reaching the autistic child: A parent training program.* Champaign, IL: Research Press.

Lennox, D. B., & Miltenberger, R. G. (1989). Conducting a functional assessment of problem behavior in applied settings. *Journal of the Association for Persons with Severe Handicaps, 14,* 304–311.

Lifter, K., Edwards, G., Avery, D., Anderson, S. R., & Sulzer-Azaroff, B. (1988). *Developmental assessment of children's play: Implications for intervention.* Miniseminar presented at the Annual Convention of the American Speech-Language-Hearing Association, Boston, MA.

Lovaas, O. I. (1977). *The autistic child.* New York: Irvington Publishers

Lovaas, O. I. (1980). Behavioral teaching with young autistic children. In B. Wilcox & A. Thompson (Eds.), *Critical issues in educating autistic children and youth* (pp. 220–233). U.S. Department of Special Education, Office of Special Education.

Lovaas, O. I. (1987). Behavioral treatment and normal educational and intellectual functioning in young autistic children. *Journal of Consulting and Clinical Psychology, 55,* 3–9.

Lovaas, O. I., & Simmons, J. Q. (1969). Manipulation of self-destruction in three retarded children. *Journal of Applied Behavior Analysis, 2,* 143–157.

McEachin, J. J., Smith, T., & Lovaas, O. I. (1993). Long-term outcome for children with autism who received early intensive behavioral treatment. *American Journal on Mental Retardation, 97,* 359–372.

Meyer, L. H., & Evans, I. M. (1989). *Nonaversive intervention for behavior problems: A manual for home and community.* Baltimore, MD: Paul Brookes.

Odom, S. L., & McEvoy, M. A. (1988). Integration of young children with handicaps and normally developing children. In S. L. Odom & M. B. Karnes (Eds.), *Early intervention for infants and children with handicaps: An empirical base* (pp. 241–268). Baltimore: Paul H. Brookes.

Prizant, B. M. (1987). Theoretical and clinical implications of echolalic behaviors in autism. In T. Layton (Ed.), *Language and the treatment of autistic and developmentally disordered children* (pp. 65–88). Springfield, IL: Charles Thomas.

Repp, A. C., Felce, D., & Barton, L. E. (1988). Basing the treatment of stereotypic and self-injurious behaviors on hypotheses of their causes. *Journal of Applied Behavior Analysis, 21,* 281–289.

Rimland, B. (1973). High dosage levels of certain vitamins in the treatment of children with severe mental disorders. In D. R. Hawkins and L. Pauling (Eds.), *Orthomolecular psychiatry* (pp. 513–539). New York: W. H. Freeman.

Ritvo, E. R., Freeman, B. J., Geller, E., & Yuwiler, A. (1983). Effects of fenfluramine on 14 outpatients with the syndrome of autism. *Journal of the American Academy of Child Psychiatry, 22,* 549–558.

Robbins, F. R., Dunlap, G., & Plienis, A. J. (1991). Family characteristics, family training, and the progress of young children with autism. *Journal of Early Intervention, 15,* 173–184.

Rutter, M., & Schopler, E. (1988). Autism and pervasive developmental disorders: Concepts and diagnostic issues. In E. Schopler & G. Mesibov (Eds.), *Diagnosis and assessment in autism* (pp. 15–36). New York: Plenum Press.

Schopler, E. (1987). Specific and nonspecific factors in the effectiveness of a treatment system. *American Psychologist, 42,* 376–383.

Schopler, E., & Reichler, R. J. (1971). Parents as cotherapists in the treatment of psychotic children. *Journal of Autism and Childhood Schizophrenia, 1,* 87–102.

Schopler, E., Reichler, R. J., & Lansing, M. (1980). *Individualized assessment and treatment for autistic and developmentally disabled children: Volume II, Teaching strategies for parents and professionals.* Baltimore, MD: University Park Press.

Schopler, E., Short, A., & Mesibov, G. (1989). Relation of behavioral treatment to "normal functioning": Comment on Lovaas. *Journal of Consulting and Clinical Psychology, 57,* 162–164.

Simpson, R. L., & Zionts, P. (1992). *Autism: Information and resources for parents, families, and professionals.* Austin, TX: Pro-Ed.

Stainback, W., & Stainback, S. (1984). A rationale for the merger of regular and special education. *Exceptional Children, 51,* 102–111.

Strain, P. S. (1981). Modification of sociometric status and social interactions with mainstreamed developmentally disabled children. *Analysis and Intervention in Developmental Disabilities, 1,* 157–169.

Strain, P. S. (1983). Generalization of autistic children's social behavior change: Effects of developmentally integrated and segregated settings. *Analysis and Intervention in Developmental Disabilities, 3.* 23–34.

Strain, P. S., & Cordisco, L. K. (1994). LEAP Preschool. In S. L. Harris & J. S. Handleman (Eds.), *Preschool education programs for children with autism* (pp. 225–244). Austin, TX: Pro-Ed.

Turnbull, A. P., & Turnbull, H. R. (1990). *Families, professionals, and exceptionality: A special partnership* (2nd ed.). Columbus, OH: Merrill Publishing Co.

Van Bourgondien, M. E. (1993). Behavior management in the preschool years. In E. Schopler, M. E. Van Bourgondien, & M. Bristol (Eds.), *Preschool issues in autism* (pp. 129–145). New York: Plenum.

Wetherby, A. M. (1986). Ontogeny of communicative functions in autism. *Journal of Autism and Developmental Disorders, 16,* 295–316.

Wheeler, D. L., Jacobson, J. W., Paglieri, R. A., & Schwartz, A. A. (1993). An experimental assessment of facilitated communication. *Mental Retardation, 31,* 49–60.

Wolery, M., & Fleming, L. A. (1993). Implementing individualized curricula in integrated settings. In C. A. Peck, S. L. Odom, & D. D. Bricker (Eds.),

Integrating young children with disabilities into community programs (pp. 109–132). Baltimore, MD: Paul H. Brookes.

Wolery, M, Strain, P. S., & Bailey, D. B. (1994). Reaching potentials of children with special needs. In S. Bredekamp & T. Rosegrant (Eds.), *Reaching potentials: Appropriate curriculum and assessment for young children* (pp. 92–111). Washington, DC: National Association for the Education of Young Children.

5 ADOLESCENT SUICIDE

One Response to Adversity

Jill Rierdan

On April 18, 1994, the headline on the cover of *Newsweek* magazine was "Suicide: Why Do People Kill Themselves?" The shotgun-suicide of Kurt Cobain, "the authentic voice of the 20-plus generation" (Gelman, 1994, p. 46), prompted this query. Prominent in the mass media—at least for a week —variants of this question have been the focus of hundreds, even thousands, of less conspicuously displayed and less widely circulated publications. These are the empirical and theoretical considerations of suicide published in the last several decades in the journals and texts of psychology, psychiatry, sociology, and philosophy.

The question Why do people kill themselves? has received increasingly extensive and urgent attention in recent years, especially with respect to adolescents and young adults. There are three major reasons for this increased focus. First, there is a dramatic increase in rates of suicide from childhood to adolescence. In 1988, 243 children younger than age 15 were identified as committing suicide, while 2,059 adolescents aged 15–19 were confirmed as suicides, a 700% increase in absolute terms (National Center for Health Statistics, 1991). Second, the rate of adolescent suicide has increased in recent decades. Whereas the suicide rate in the general population of the United States rose by 17% from 1960 to 1988, the rate for adolescents aged 15–19 rose by 200% (Garland & Zigler, 1993). Third, suicide today is recognized as the second leading cause of death for 15–19 year olds (National Center for Health Statistics, 1991). These statistics, all the more alarming because they probably underestimate the prevalence of adolescent suicide (Berman & Jobes, 1991), prompt the two major questions of this chapter: Why do adolescents kill themselves? Why are they killing themselves in increasing numbers?

In posing these two questions, I am taking the position that adolescent suicide is a serious problem in contemporary society. This view is not shared by all. Offer and Schonert-Reichl (1992) consider as essentially mythical the view that adolescence is a time of increased risk for suicide.

They point out that the adolescent suicide rate is still the lowest in the life cycle, save that for younger children. While this is quite accurate, as is the fact that the absolute risk of suicide is still very low in adolescence (Gans, 1990), it is still the case that rates of completed suicide increase from childhood to adolescence and that rates of suicidal ideation and attempted suicide increase even more dramatically (e.g., Carlson & Cantwell, 1982; Garrison, Addy, Jackson, McKeown, & Waller, 1991; Kovacs, Coldston, & Gatsonis, 1993).

Mack (1986) has suggested that suicide has become "an option" for current adolescents, to a degree that far exceeds the level of acceptance by previous cohorts. Sixty percent of adolescents in a 1990 Gallop poll (cited by Ackerman, 1993) said they personally knew someone who had attempted suicide. Even assuming this figure is inflated, it nevertheless means that many of today's adolescents have been introduced to suicidal behavior as an "option" for dealing with adversity. How are we to understand, and thus have a basis for altering, this alarming presence of suicide in adolescent lives?

ADOLESCENT SUICIDE: HISTORICAL TRENDS

As noted above, the incidence of adolescent suicide in the United States has increased dramatically over the last three decades, far exceeding the increase for the population as a whole. Possible explanations for this historical trend might provide some directions for understanding suicide in the lives of adolescents today.

Some have suggested that the increase in the adolescent suicide rate is epiphenomenal, attributable to the greater proportion of adolescents in the population as a whole, as the "baby boomers" reached adolescence in the 1960s and 1970s. Sociological studies confirm that rates of suicide increase in adolescence as the proportion of adolescents in the total population increases (Holinger, Offer, & Zola, 1988). Possible explanations are as follows. With greater numbers of adolescents, competition for stable or even shrinking resources (jobs, college acceptance, places on sports teams) is greater, resulting in more frequent experiences of failure (Holinger et al., 1988). In this context, social comparison processes—with larger referent groups—may become even more intense than is typically the case in adolescence, leading more adolescents to feel they fall short of acceptable standards (Holinger & Offer, 1982). Finally, with more adolescents feeling marginalized, a deviant peer group culture may arise as a basis for belonging and identity. By its very size, such an adolescent culture may become increasingly deviant and also more influential in the lives of distressed teenagers (Holinger et al., 1988). Whether as a basis for identity in a deviant peer culture or as an expression of isolated marginality and low self-worth, maladaptive behaviors such as suicide may then become more prevalent. This may be associated with increasing social contagion effects, where adolescents exposed to peer suicide or suicide attempts are more likely to engage in such behavior (Harkavy-Friedman, Asnis, Boeck, & DiFiore, 1987; Shafii, Carrigan, Whittinghill, & Derrick, 1985). Since social imitation of suicide seems stronger in adolescence than in childhood or adulthood (Stack, 1991), most likely because of the greater need for conformity, the effects of peer suicide are likely to have an especially large ripple effect for adolescents.

These sociological explanations might lead one to anticipate a decrease in adolescent suicide simply by waiting a few years, as suggested by Offer and Schonert-Reichl (1992). This comforting prediction seems unlikely to be valid. Today's adolescents may be launched on a suicidal "career" (Maris, 1991), currently engaging in the kind of self-destructive thoughts and behaviors that may eventuate in suicide when they are older adults, with a resultant exaggeration of the usual increase in suicide rates in middle age (Berman & Jobes, 1991). Alternatively, the large majority of today's adolescents, who will not commit suicide, will have children, resulting in another adolescent population bulge in future decades (Holinger et al., 1988), when adolescents again will comprise an unusually large proportion of the population. We can not wait to understand and intervene in prevention of adolescent suicide.

Five other social trends are noteworthy correlates of the increasing prevalence of adolescent suicide. First, parallel to increasing suicide rates has been an increasing rate of homicide (Gans, 1990). Violence overall has increased dramatically among adolescents in the United States in the last three decades. Second, and related, accessibility of guns has increased since 1950 (Garland & Zigler, 1993). Studies have suggested that increasing rates of adolescent suicide in some countries can be fully explained by the increasing availability of firearms (Berman, 1986), the means of attempting suicide that is most likely to be fatal (Berman & Jobes, 1991). Explanation of adolescent suicide thus needs to be placed in the context of increasing violence, overall.

The third and fourth social trends correlated with increasing adolescent suicide relate to dimensions of social integration and support. A factor apparently not considered in relation to adolescent suicide is that of residential mobility. Families move much more frequently than they did a generation ago, with the result that social support, from community, school, and stable peer relations, is likely to be less available. Furthermore, the rate of divorce and single parenthood has increased dramatically over the last several decades. The result of this is not only that the likelihood of two available parents is lower, but that the custodial parent—usually the mother —is necessarily less available to her adolescents, as she is often employed out of the home, as well as perhaps suffering her own personal distress over the end of a marriage and an uncertain financial future supporting herself and her children (Hawton, 1986). Since social support from family and community has been reliably associated with depression and suicide risk, as we shall see below, the psychological significance of this social-historical trend cannot be minimized.

A fifth social trend, related both to the categories of violence and social support/integration, is the rising rate of child maltreatment. Numerous reports (Gans, 1990) have confirmed that increasing reports of child sexual and physical abuse are not simply artifacts of greater public awareness and reporting, however much these have contributed to identifying the magnitude of this problem. Since early experience of maltreatment has been related to suicide, suicide attempts, and nonsuicidal self-injurious behavior (e.g., DeWilde, Kienhorst, Diekstra, & Wolters; 1992; Smith & Crawford, 1986; Walsh & Rosen, 1988), the contribution of this social trend should not be ignored.

These five correlates of increasing suicide rates involve broad social trends. There are three additional trends, paralleling the increasing rate of adolescent suicide, that can be related even more immediately to suicide. These pertain to historical changes in aspects of adolescent development, on the one hand, and adolescent psychopathology, on the other.

The first of these relates to the secular trend (Tanner, 1990) toward earlier onset of puberty. For example, in the last century, the average age at menarche, the onset of menstruation for girls, has decreased approximately three months per decade. While this historical decrease in age of pubertal development has not been directly related to increasing suicidality, there may yet be an important relationship. Rates of depression increase with puberty, especially for girls (Angold & Rutter, 1992), and most especially for early maturing girls (Rierdan & Koff, 1993), who may lack the psychological maturity and social support to deal with this developmental challenge. If decreasing age at menarche, especially in the context of decreasing social support, were paralleled by increasing levels of depression, rates of suicide would also be expected to rise.

There is some evidence to support this speculation. A number of studies (e.g., Klerman & Weissman, 1989) have reported a secular trend toward earlier onset of depression in recent generations, paralleling that of earlier puberty. Since the relation between depression and suicide has been well-established—people who commit suicide have higher rates of depression, and people who are depressed have higher rates of suicide (e.g., Brent, Perper, Allman et al., 1993; Klerman, 1987)—the historical changes in normal development, on the one hand, and psychopathology, on the other, may be significantly related to the trend toward increasing prevalence of adolescent suicides.

A final secular trend related to psychopathology is the increased use of drugs, most especially alcohol, by today's adolescents (Garland & Zigler, 1993). For adolescents in particular, suicide and suicide attempts frequently occur in the context of intoxication or alcohol ingestion (Brent, Perper, Allman et al. 1993; King, Hill, Naylor, Evans, & Shain, 1993). Increasing use of alcohol sets the stage for a greater likelihood of self-destructive behavior, in part because its disinhibiting effect may impair judgment and increase potentially lethal risk-taking behavior. Moreover, substance abuse represents an attempt at coping through alteration of consciousness, which may be a forerunner to the use of suicide to *end* consciousness.

Summary and Implications for Intervention

Explanations for the increasing rate of adolescent suicide have been couched in terms of changes over the decades in biology (earlier puberty), family experience (maltreatment, family disintegration), sociocultural experience (decreased social support, increased socialization for deviance, increased violence), and psychopathology (increased and earlier onset of depression and substance abuse). The most immediate implication for intervention, and the most concrete, is to make guns less accessible to adolescents. It has been estimated that the rate of adolescent suicide would decrease dramatically if guns were not available as a means for killing oneself (Garland & Zigler, 1993). Other suggestions—reducing child maltreatment, decreasing drug use, preventing depression, restructuring schools and community groups to provide more social support—while highly desirable, are extremely broad. To generate more specific targets for intervention, we need to know more specifically who the adolescents are today who are attempting or succeeding in killing themselves.

ADOLESCENT SUICIDE: THE VULNERABLE ADOLESCENT

There is an enormous literature on adolescent suicide, but a poverty of approaches to investigation. The same sets of variables have been studied again and again as risk factors for suicidal behavior. The assumption has been that identification of risk factors will permit identification of particular groups of adolescents vulnerable to suicide. The reader is pointed to the excellent monograph by Berman and Jobes (1991) for a comprehensive and current review of this literature.

In terms of demographic (categorical) variables, gender, race, sexual orientation, and socioeconomic status have been investigated. Gender effects are striking, and more extreme than found in adulthood. In the United State, adolescent boys are five times more likely than adolescent girls to commit suicide (Berman & Jobes, 1991). In contrast, girls are three times more likely to report thinking about or attempting suicide. These findings prompt two related questions: Why do adolescent boys commit suicide more than girls? Why do adolescent girls contemplate and attempt suicide more frequently than boys? There are a number of possible explanations.

Most writers have focused on gender differences in the method of attempting suicide; boys use more lethal means—guns and hanging—than girls, and so are more likely to consummate the act (e.g., Marttunen, Aro, & Lonnqvist, 1992). While some have inferred, therefore, greater intentionality on the part of boys, this need not be the case. As Spirito, Brown, Overholser, and Fritz (1989) have pointed out, boys engage in all varieties of risk-taking behavior more than girls; the greater lethality of boys to girls is not unique to the suicidal act and may represent a more general gender difference in all classes of risk-taking behavior, especially those which involve more violence. An alternative explanation involves accessibility of information about, and treatment for, medication overdoses. Adolescents are often quite misinformed about the potential lethality of drug overdoses (Myers, Otto, Harris, Diaco, & Moreno, 1992); girls may overdose believing they are taking an amount sufficient for death, but they can be treated successfully through prompt medical intervention, resulting in their being classified as attempting, but not completing, suicide. Interestingly, Spirito et al. (1989) point out that in India, where medical care is less accessible, the gender difference in suicide completions and attempts does not exist. Girls may be classified as making more "attempts" and fewer "suicides" in the United States because their method of self-harm is one that permits intervention by available medical personnel.

Other explanations have been offered for the finding that girls are more likely to engage in suicidal ideation and suicide attempts than boys. Some of these have been faintly pejorative, as girls are described as manipulative and melodramatic. Such descriptions miss a crucial point, as Leenaars and Wenckstern (1991) point out: One must be desperate and impaired to choose self-injury as the means to get attention. At the same time that girls who attempt suicide must be desperate, it may also be that they, to a greater degree than boys, have some hope of a helpful response from others, leading them to communicate about or engage in suicide acts where others can intervene.

A final consideration regarding the higher levels of suicide attempts by girls than boys is the possibility that their self-destructive behavior is mislabeled. Clinicians make the distinction between suicide attempts (i.e., self-destructive behavior intended, however transiently, to be life-threatening) and nonsuicidal, self-injurious behavior (Walsh & Rosen, 1988). The latter behavior, including inflicting cuts and cigarettes burns, is characteristic of girls who have special difficulty in their own sense of identity, in their respect for their own body integrity, and in their interpersonal relatedness. Their intent is to focus and reduce a diffuse and overwhelming anxiety, and their self-injurious behavior is often experienced by the girl as a way of avoiding suicide—as a way of feeling alive instead of dissociated. One former adolescent patient of mine carved the greeting "HI!" on her forearm, so that when she looked at it she would feel less lonely. On most surveys of suicidal behavior, this would be regarded as a suicide attempt. It most definitely was not, but rather was a poignant, if equivocal, affirmation of a life that was extremely bleak. To understand gender differences in suicide and suicide attempts, we need to start by defining what we mean by each (Meehan, Lamb, Saltzman, & O'Carroll, 1992; Pfeffer, 1989). Only then can we consider the range of plausible explanations.

Along with clear gender differences in the United States, there are also racial differences in rates of completed suicides (GAP, 1989), which are most striking among males. Among 15–24 year olds, native Americans have the highest rates, followed by whites, Hispanics, blacks and Asians. Explanations of race differences have related to religion, social isolation, acculturation stress, alcohol use, alternative forms of risk taking and violence, and degree of oppression (Earls & Jemison, 1986). As well, there are significant differences in suicide rates between heterosexual and homosexual youth (Hammelman, 1993; Harry, 1989), a finding that may be related to a plethora of psychosocial factors, including issues of identity, loss of family support, social isolation and oppression, and health concerns.

Repeatedly, social class has not been found to be a significant risk factor. Thus the adversity of poverty is not as significant as biopsychosocial factors involved in gender and race.

Knowledge of demographic risk factors does not help much in terms of preventing adolescent suicides. Since suicide is still a rare response, it seems unlikely that broad gender or racial differences in normally distributed characteristics—e.g., self-esteem, sex roles, aggression—would explain this highly atypical act. Instead, it seems more likely that important determinants would be related to extremes of normally distributed traits and dimensions of psychopathology. Knowledge of demographic risk factors needs to be complemented by identification of other risk factors that would delimit the number of adolescents who are validly identified as vulnerable to suicide (Berman, 1991).

One such risk factor pertains to social support. Perhaps because of the seminal writings of Durkheim (1897/1951), who placed suicide in the context of the individual's relationship with society, many studies have examined the relationship between social support and suicide. The oft-replicated findings are that adolescents who lack social support have higher rates of suicidal ideation, attempts, and completions (e.g., Dubow, Kausch, Blum, Reed, & Bush, 1989; Harter, Marold, & Whitesell, 1992; Joffe, Offord, & Boyle, 1988). One dimension of social support relates to family functioning, which has been found to be significant as a predictor of suicidality, in terms not only of support but also in terms of the presence of violence in intimate relationships (Spirito et al., 1989).

Social support seems to function as a moderator of life stress—people with higher levels of social support are able to avoid pathology or, if distressed, to bear it better than people with fewer social supports. Furthermore, it is the actual or anticipated loss of social support—in the form of a breakup of an intimate relationship, fights with parents, or anticipation of parental disapproval—that has been reported to precipitate suicidal acts in vulnerable adolescents (Shaffer, Garland, Gould, Fisher, & Trautman, 1988). The fact that diminishing social support has been suggested as a partial explanation of the historical increase in suicide makes it attractive as an explanation of current adolescent suicides. At the same time, such limitations of social support have been related to many other aspects of pathology—in particular, depression—and are quite common during the adolescent years, so social support in itself is not sufficient for identifying the subset of adolescents most vulnerable to suicide.

Social support does deserve our particular attention, though, in a way that has received scant consideration. This concerns the social response of family and peers when adolescents reveal that they are thinking about suicide or have engaged in self-destructive behaviors. For those adolescents who do disclose suicidal thoughts and actions, the response is often minimal and ineffective. This is especially true for peers, who are most often the confidants of suicidal adolescents (Overholser, Hemstreet, Spirito, & Vyse, 1989). It has been reported (Mishara, 1982) that peers laugh off or minimize the seriousness of a peer's suicidal statements, a response particularly characteristic of adolescent boys (Norton, Durlak, & Richards, 1989), or simply don't know what to do (Lawrence & Ureda, 1990). This finding may help to explain adolescent boys' higher rate of suicide, if the availability of social support in the form of constructive caring response to statements of suicide is less available than for girls.

A second large category of factors putting adolescents at risk for suicide pertains to cognitive and personality dimensions. It has been suggested that difficulty generating coping strategies enhances the likelihood of suicide (e.g., Prezant & Neimeyer, 1988), as does hopelessness as a general cognitive stance (Brent, Kalas, Edelbrock, Costello, Dulcan, & Conover, 1986), although the latter cognitive variable seems less characteristic of adolescent than adult suicides (Carlson & Cantwell, 1982). It would be interesting to consider whether adolescents today are less cognitively flexible, or more hopeless, than were adolescents 50 years ago. If so, this variable would relate both to the historical trend regarding adolescent suicide and also to current predictions of suicidality.

Curiously, very little work has been done looking at specific dimensions of emotions as predictors of suicide (Spirito et al, 1989), despite Shneidman's (1987) view that one of the three determinants of suicide is unbearable psychic pain. Furthermore, very little work has been done looking at personality traits as vulnerabilities to suicide.

The strongest predictors of adolescent suicide are two aspects of psychopathology: depression and substance abuse. Depression and alcohol abuse frequently co-occur, and each independently has been associated with contemplating, attempting, and committing suicide (Klerman, 1987). Of course, not all adolescents who are clinically depressed do attempt or commit suicide (DeWilde et al., 1992), but certainly the pessimism, self-hatred, sadness, and guilt associated with depression conduce to thoughts of suicide (Klerman, 1987). The use of alcohol, which may begin as a way of relieving depression, may then augment it and increase the likelihood of suicidal behavior as thought disorganizes and action becomes more impulsive. Linking this finding with historical trends, it should be noted that depression in adolescence is by definition early onset depression, which has increased in prevalence during this century (Klerman & Weissman, 1987), as has alcohol abuse among adolescents.

It is important to note that the best established fact about adolescent suicides is their history of psychological disorders (Brent, Perper, Allman et al., 1993). It is the rare adolescent who commits suicide in the absence of a diagnosable psychological disorder (Brent, Perper, Maritz, Baugher, & Allman, 1993). This single fact greatly reduces the pool of potential suicides.

Summary and Implications for Intervention

Berman and Jobes (1991) suggest that for variables to constitute risk factors for adolescent suicide, they must have two qualities. First, they must frequently be present in adolescents who commit suicide. Second, they must be largely absent in adolescents who don't. Of the variables considered above, the ones that best meet these criteria are depression and alcoholism. Other dimensions, such as diminished social support, cognitive inflexibility, family dysfunction—while present to a greater degree among suicidal adolescents than their peers—are nevertheless so often present among nonsuicidal adolescents as to constitute nonspecific stressors rather than specific vulnerabilities for suicide. This conclusion is in keeping with those of Garland and Zigler (1993), who reject the view that suicide is a stress-induced phenomenon and argue that it must be viewed as an expression of psychopathology. While it is the case that stressors seem to precipitate suicidal behavior, they can not explain it; these stressful events—usually interpersonal rejection and family crises—are exceedingly common among adolescents (Shaffer et al. 1988) and therefore cannot explain an event as rare as suicide.

The implications for intervention that do ensue from the literature just reviewed are twofold. First, we might screen in school and health care settings for relevant dimensions of psychopathology among adolescents, to identify higher risk individuals who might warrant assessment and intervention. Second, we might educate adolescents about the pathological significance of suicide threats and attempts and teach them appropriate responses when peers reveal such suicidal preoccupations to them. In that way, such "cries for help" might indeed lead to helpful intervention instead of anxious laughs and disparagement.

Such interventions will still be of limited usefulness since they require the expression of considerable dysfunction by the adolescent before targeted intervention can begin. Further, research on risk factors still do not answer the two questions of this chapter: Why do adolescents commit suicide, and why are they doing so in increasing numbers?

To address these questions, we need to assume a developmental perspective. We need to understand why some individuals, by the time they reach adolescence, come to view their lives as so intolerable that they choose to end them prematurely. At the same time, we need to remember that adolescent suicide is still very rare, even if it is more prevalent than it was four decades ago. And we need to consider more fully the nature of the suicidal act. Adolescents who commit suicide kill themselves. This is the most stunningly dramatic and important decision a person can make regarding his or her life, and the most fundamental rejection of life itself. Surely, the explanation of adolescent suicide must involve some variables that are themselves atypical and dramatic, if not singly then in their confluence.

ADOLESCENT SUICIDE: CONTINUITY/DISCONTINUITY

When confronting the issue of adolescent suicide, one is immediately confronted with two sides of the developmental coin: continuity and change. Many developmental theorists and suicidologists emphasize the basic continuity in the life of the suicide (e.g., Maris, 1991; Shneidman, 1987). It is argued that people do not suddenly become suicidal; the onset of suicidal thinking and engagement in suicidal behavior is meaningfully related to the individual's history. At the same time, the act of suicide is the act of profound discontinuity. By definition, one has never done it before. Since this act increasingly emerges in adolescence, we need to ask: What are the early life experiences and childhood biopsychosocial characteristics that render some individuals vulnerable to suicide by adolescence? What are the demands of adolescence that so stress the vulnerable individual that suicide is contemplated or committed? First, though, we should consider more fully the issue of continuity and change as it relates to adolescent suicide. There are three aspects to this issue.

Continuum of Suicidal Behavior

What are the relationships among suicidal ideation, suicide attempts, and completed suicides? Szasz (1980), for one, contends that people who commit suicide want to die, while people who threaten or attempt suicide want to improve their lives (i.e., he sees the motivation behind suicide and attempted suicide as entirely different and therefore as likely to be engaged in by very different people). Others have argued that since these dimensions of suicidality are differentially associated with demographically defined groups (e.g., adolescent girls more likely attempt, and adolescent boys are more likely commit suicide), there must be little overlap in the population of individuals who contemplate, attempt, and commit suicide and, accordingly, little continuity in the lifetime of any particular individual. This ignores the fact that boys who complete suicide are frequently reported to have previously attempted and girls who attempt may subsequently succeed.

What seems more viable as a perspective is the idea of a continuum from ephemeral thoughts of suicide, to persistent suicidal thinking and planning, to action, and then to completion (cf. Meehan, Lamb, Saltzman, & O'Carroll, 1992). The largest subset of adolescents would not be in this continuum at all (e.g., Dubow et al., 1989; Garrison, Addy, Jackson, McKeown &

Waller, 1991; Garrison, Jackson, Addy, McKeown, & Waller, 1991), a substantial minority of adolescents would think of suicide (Harkavy-Freidman et al., 1987), a smaller number of these would generate plans (Harkavy-Friedman et al., 1987) and an even smaller subset of these ideators would go on to attempt (e.g., Dubow et al., 1989) or commit suicide (e.g., Brent, Perper, Allman et al., 1993). It has been demonstrated again and again that previous suicidal thoughts and attempts are the best predictors of subsequent suicide completions (Farberow, 1989); while far from inevitable (there is change as well as continuity in development), continuity in levels of suicidality should not be overlooked.

Continuity over Development

The idea of continuity in suicidality also applies when considering the emergence of suicidal actions and the completion of suicide in the lives of individual adolescents; this view stands in contrast to some empirical reports which have suggested that adolescent suicide is largely impulsive and unplanned. Hawton, Cole, O'Grady, and Osborn (1982), in their study of adolescents who overdosed and were treated in hospital emergency rooms, reported that only 20% had planned their suicide attempt. These data suggest a profound discontinuity and utter unpredictability in accounting for adolescent suicide. It should be noted, though, that these conclusions are based largely on cross-sectional data, i.e., data collected at one point in time, and often are in reference to minimally lethal self-destructive behaviors. Myers et al. (1992) note that there is a significant relationship between premeditation and lethality, with fatal attempts more likely to be well-planned.

The few available longitudinal studies suggest considerable continuity. Marttunen et al. (1992), in a study of Finnish adolescent suicides, conducted psychological autopsies, including interviews with family members, and reported that 33% of suicides have made previous attempts and approximately 60% had expressed suicidal ideas, suggesting significant continuity. At the same time, the precipitating event had occurred within 24 hours for most adolescents (Marttunen, Aro, & Lonnqvist, 1993), and all but three of the parents of the 57 suicides found the suicide unexpected. The sense of unexpectedness may come from parents' inability to conceive of their children actually killing themselves and not from the absence of suicidal indicators in the past.

Consistent with the idea of continuity in suicidality over the course of development are the findings of Kovacs et al. (1993), who found significant continuity in the suicidal ideation and behavior of children and adolescent outpatients followed over time, and Brent, Perper, Allman et al. (1993) and DeWilde et al. (1992). Brent's group reported that about 75% of adolescents who had committed suicide had formulated plans during the week before their deaths and had warranted diagnoses of major depression and substance abuse disorders; DeWilde and colleagues found that suicide attemptors had longstanding histories of problems which had escalated with puberty. There is some evidence, then, from longitudinal and/or retrospective studies that the life history of adolescent suicides reveals significant psychological stability over time.

Suicidal Careers

Evidence of a continuum of suicidal behaviors, with such behavior escalating in lethality for some individuals from childhood to adolescence, constitutes the basis for a theoretical model of continuity in the life of the suicide. Shneidman (1991), one of the premier suicidologists in our time, asserted that suicide was consistent with lifelong patterns of living, however much its act—by definition something the individual has never done before—has no precedent. Similarly, Maris (1981/1991) argued that "the suicide's biography or 'career' is always relevant to his or her self-destructive reaction to crises and . . . it is precisely this history . . . which tends to be neglected" (p. 25). To begin to understand the relevant aspects of history and the developmental crises that lead an adolescent to begin or complete a suicidal career, we need to consider the essence of suicide.

It is surprising and disconcerting that in the vast majority of empirical reports of adolescent suicide, the act of suicide is treated no differently than any other behavioral act. One gets no sense that we are trying to explain why 15-year-olds are killing themselves in increasing numbers. And yet surely our theory and research and interventions will be inadequate if we don't consider what this act entails.

In a provocative volume, *Suicide: The Philosophical Issue,* Clements (1980) writes that suicide implies a fundamental attitude concerning the universe and oneself—a nay-saying attitude, a fundamental orientation away from life and toward death. How could one come to adopt such an attitude? There is a fundamental negation of the value of one's own life (Windt, 1980), an inability to conceive of a reason and means for living a personally acceptable life. How could one become so desperate?

The model I suggest to address these questions is based on the empirical literature on adolescent suicide, general understandings about adolescent development, and understandings of normal and maladaptive personality development.

ADOLESCENT SUICIDE: LAUNCHING A SUICIDAL CAREER

The following comments on suicide were written by a young woman, some 20 years after her hospitalization as an adolescent, at which time she was regarded as dangerously suicidal.

> Suicide is a form of murder—premeditated murder. It isn't something you do the first time you think of doing it. It takes getting used to. And you need the means, the opportunity, the motive. . . .
>
> It's important to cultivate detachment. One way to do this is to practice imagining yourself dead, or in the process of dying. If there's a window, you must imagine your body falling out the window. If there's a knife, you must imagine the knife piercing your skin. If there's a train coming, you must imagine your torso flattened under its wheels. These exercises are necessary to achieving the proper distance.
>
> The motive is paramount. (Kaysen, 1993, p. 36)

Kaysen makes several important points that are consistent with research reported in this chapter. She points out that the decision to suicide is not a sudden decision; it has a history in the psychic life of the individual. She emphasizes that one must have a compelling reason, one that somehow is related to the motivation for murder. She points out, as few do, that a kind of attitude of detachment or estrangement must be acquired, one that allows for imagining the mutilation of one's body, as well as the severing of all interpersonal connections.

My own belief is that the core motivation for suicide is the relief of intolerable psychic pain—whether it be grief, guilt, emptiness, or rage. This very general assumption subsumes the three motivations enumerated by Menninger (1938) as causes of suicide—the wish to kill (rage), the wish to be killed (guilt), and the wish to die (emptiness, grief)—and assumes that all are present to some degree and that some are present to an intolerable degree. It is consistent also with the view of Shneidman (1991), who thought the primary motivation for suicide was the urge to end psychic pain. One difference between Shneidman's formulation and my own is my elaboration of the early developmental characteristics of suicide-engendering psychic pain.

To explain how an adolescent would come to have such an unbearable degree and quality of psychic pain, it is important to consider, first, what childhood experiences would likely create a vulnerability to suicide and, second, what adolescent experiences would so exceed an individual's capacities for bearing psychic pain that suicide would be precipitated.

As reviewed above, recent empirical research suggests that individuals who are launched on a suicidal career have experienced, to an unusual degree, disruptive and inconsistent parenting and/or outright abuse and neglect. It is assumed that this kind of early experience has a twofold significance. First, there are the direct effects of assault on a developing child's sense of self: internalization of a sense of inner badness, distrust of interpersonal relationships, learning of self-directed assault as a way of responding to one's self-perceived limitations. Second, there is the failure to acquire a fundamental adaptive human capacity. This is the capacity to soothe oneself—the capacity, when feeling the pain of loneliness, loss, abandonment, rage, panic, guilt, or depression, to know how to feel compassionate and caring toward oneself in a way that makes such feelings bearable.

Numerous psychodynamic writers have written variously of the capacity to soothe oneself (Adler, 1985), to be alone (Winnicott, 1958), or to bear depression (Zetzel, 1965/1970). The basic idea is that part of normal development is the internalization of good-enough parenting from relatively secure parents, whereby the experience of soothing and care from parents or caretakers provides the basis for coming gradually to be able to soothe oneself in their absence, both in childhood and adulthood. The assumption is that ordinary life may entail considerable pain, and that one must develop the capacity to bear such pain. Self-soothing is part of the basis for such a capacity.

It seems inevitable that children abused and neglected by parents have great difficulty acquiring this capacity, both because of their exceptional pain and also because of the absence of a model of caring to be internalized. It also seems likely that quite well-intentioned parents, with unusual demands and anxieties, may also inadvertently undermine a child's capacity for self-soothing if, as they strive to be attentive and caring in the time they have available for child care, they convey a sense that only they can soothe and/or that the world is full of unbearable disappointments and dangers. Whatever the etiology in terms of particular early experiences, I assume that the essential vulnerability underlying suicidality is the incapacity to self-soothe.

This model is consistent with the early life experiences reported in the history of adolescent suicides. What other research findings support this model? If a deficiency in the capacity to self-soothe is the vulnerability underlying suicidality, it seems likely that a child who is relatively lacking in the capacity and who is therefore likely to begin a suicidal career would show difficulty moderating his or her emotions, and tend toward extremes of depression and/or rage. As noted above, depression and anger is reported in the history of adolescents who attempt and commit suicide. Furthermore, since emotional regulation is thought to be one domain of ego functioning (Loevinger, 1976), it seems likely that suicidal adolescents have lower levels of ego development than their peers do. There is limited evidence, some of which is consistent (Borst & Noam, 1993). Difficulty with self-soothing also likely leads to a generalized paucity of coping techniques—not much would be experienced as "working," since feelings would remain painful. This is a characteristic description of suicidal youth, who have been described by Rich and Bonner (1987) as having "coping vulnerability." Furthermore, such difficulty with self-soothing is likely to lead to thoughts and feelings of hopelessness. Again, this quality has been characteristic of those who suicide (Brent et al., 1986). It also seems that individuals unable to soothe themselves would be unusually dependent on others for assuming responsibility for the relief of their pain, leading them to be unusually pained by ruptures in relationships. Findings reviewed above support this hypothesis, as disrupted relationships are a prime precipitant of adolescent suicide attempts. In summary, it is suggested that the child vulnerable to suicide as an adolescent is likely to have a core deficiency in self-soothing, related intrapsychically to lower levels of ego development, interpersonally to dependency, affectively to depression and anger, behaviorally to a paucity of coping skills, and cognitively to a sense of hopelessness. While the capacity to self-soothe has not been investigated directly, the other qualities that are thought to proceed from this deficiency have been found to characterize suicidal youth.

If a deficiency in self-soothing is the vulnerability that puts some children at risk for subsequent suicide, what is it about adolescence that so escalates the sense of unbearable pain that suicide begins to be considered? Adolescence is the most profound period of change in the life span, save that of prenatal development. In the decade between ages 10 and 20, the individual must develop a mature and positively valued body image, a sense of sexual orientation, the beginning of significant attachments and intimacy outside the family, a greater separation from and renegotiated integration in the family of origin, a vocational direction, and—through all of this change— a continuing sense of the sameness of self. The adolescent transition is a challenge for all, and a crisis for some. It has been recognized by developmental theorists that off-time development, particularly early puberty for girls and late puberty for boys (e.g., Brooks-Gunn, Petersen, & Eichorn, 1985), and the simultaneous occurrence of multiple difficult life events (Coleman, 1978), are especially stressful, whereas the sequential unfolding of biological, psychological, and social changes are more easily assimilated.

For the vulnerable child, the challenges of adolescence are likely to be crises. Intrapsychically, the increased self-consciousness (Cheek, Carpentieri, Smith, Rierdan, & Koff, 1986) associated with adolescence should be difficult to bear, given a limited capacity to self-soothe. Limitations in ego development are likely to make it difficult to maintain a sense of continuity over time and to project oneself into a positive future. Dependency on others should make it difficult to separate from parents and make the adolescent exquisitely vulnerable to disruption of interpersonal relationships and loss of social support in peer relations, increasing the risk of depression and anger. Depression and anger, in turn, would likely make the adolescent less accepting and valuing of the limited coping strategies he or she has, and exacerbate negative cognitions about the possibility of a satisfactory life. It would not be surprising, subsequently, for such adolescents to turn to alcohol to blunt awareness of increasingly less bearable pain.

It seems likely that the child deficient in self-soothing, who has the misfortune to experience exceptional stress or an unusual confluence of otherwise normative stresses, comes to experience intolerable psychic pain and eventually adopts a nay-saying attitude and belief that there is no possibility of leading a personally satisfying life. The thought of suicide may be particularly congenial to such adolescents who, immature in ego development, may have a misconception of the finality of death, and instead see it as a temporary coping means that blocks out, in lieu of soothing, a sense of intolerable pain.

The proposed model is consistent with both well-established and recently articulated explanations of suicide across the life span. It is easily integrated into Shneidman's (1987) trifold explanation of suicide. Shneidman suggested that individuals commit suicide when there is a concurrence of extreme pain (i.e., psychological suffering), extreme press (e.g., co-occurring, stressful life events), and perturbation (i.e., the inclination to action). The proposed model places the Shneidman model in a developmental context, suggesting that psychic pain becomes intolerable for adolescents who have not acquired the capacity to self-soothe, press increases in adolescence with the demands to integrate biological, social, and psychological change, and perturbation increases in adolescence with the increase in risk-taking behavior. This model is also complementary to the elegant formulation of Baumeister (1990) who argues that people attempt suicide when, by virtue of their psychological pain, they can no longer tolerate self-consciousness or self-awareness. Such a wish to avoid self-consciousness may be akin to the detachment that Kaysen (1993) suggests is essential if one is to suicide.

As well, the proposed model is consistent with the limited number of empirical efforts placing the issue of adolescent suicide in developmental context. Predictions from the model are consistent with the work of Harter et al. (1992), who clarify how the stresses of adolescence increase vulnerability for suicidal ideation, and with the findings of DeWilde et al. (1992), who found that adolescents who made suicide attempts had experienced a greater number of difficult life events than normal adolescents or adolescents who were depressed without being suicidal. The model is consistent also with the work of Ball and Chandler (1989), who found that suicidal adolescents were less able to maintain an integrated sense of identity which they could project into the future. Clearly, suicide is a way to avoid having a future. Similarly, this model is complementary to the thinking of Wade (1987), who suggested that suicide was a way of ending, given pessimism about resolving, the adolescent crisis of separating from the family of origin psychically and interpersonally. Further, the model places in a somewhat broader context the view of Kovacs et al. (1993). They argue that intolerance of depression leads to suicide attempts. The proposed model suggests a vulnerability antedating the onset of depression—the intolerance of painful affect, given a deficiency in self-soothing—which both creates a predisposition for depression and then an intolerance of it.

This developmental model of adolescent suicide clearly needs elaboration, testing against the available empirical literature, and assessment in future research. Its advantage, at a conceptual level, is that it provides an explanation of developmental trends—ontogenetic and historical—in suicide by reference to the well-established literature of normal and maladaptive personality development. In the last century, there has been an increase in the kind of early life experiences thought to interfere with the development of self-soothing capacity, and an increase in the challenges of adolescence. As well, there is a more ready access to alcohol for use as a maladaptive coping strategy, and prescription drugs, which are often used by girls in suicide attempts. Finally, there has been a greater acceptability of suicide as an "option" for dealing with life.

At the same time that I have sought to explain increases in the rate of adolescent suicide—relative to childhood and relative to cohorts 40 years ago—the goal has been to generate a model that is consistent with the reality that adolescent suicide is still (thankfully) a rarity. It is the unusual adolescent who has the misfortune to have early experiences destructive enough to interfere with the development of a self-soothing capacity, who then experiences an unusual confluence of normative and nonnormative life stresses during adolescence, and who also has available a ready means for suicide.

Further, the model makes sense of the phenomenology of suicide, which has more frequently been considered by suicidologists and philosophers than by empirical researchers. The pain prompting thoughts of suicide must be extreme, indeed, to lead to cultivation of the kind of detachment that Kaysen (1993) describes, which permits imaging oneself mangled and maimed.

Summary and Implications for Intervention

The view that adolescents have "suicidal careers" that develop over time suggests that there may be many points of intervention and prevention. First, if it is true that a relative incapacity for self-soothing is a fundamental vulnerability to suicide, and that this is related to early childhood experiences, the most fundamental line of intervention is on parent and early childhood education. Second, if it is the case that diminished ability to soothe oneself leads to depression and alcohol use (two risk factors reliably associated with adolescent suicide), monitoring of these behavior problems in the preteen and early adolescent years is indicated. Third, if there is a continuum from suicidal thoughts, to actions, and to completions, careful assessment of suicidal ideation may identify vulnerable youngsters before they engage in self-destructive acts. Fourth, school-and clinic-based support systems for vulnerable youngsters may help those who do not have or are not able to employ ordinarily available supports.

A view of adolescent suicide as an impulsive, stress-related response offers little direction for intervention—most of the precipitating events associated with adolescent suicide are widely experienced challenges of adolescent life (Shaffer et al., 1988). We need to turn our attention to the years preceding an individual's beginning a "suicidal career" and think about what changes need to be made in our approach to child rearing and education, at home and in the myriad of small and large institutions in which children spend their lives, so that we can reduce the likelihood of vulnerable adolescents believing that suicide is their only possible way of coping with adversity.

REFERENCES

Ackerman, G. L. (1993). A congressional view of youth suicide. *American Psychologist, 48,* 183–184

Adler, G. (1985). *Borderline psychopathology and its treatment.* New York: Jason Aronson.

Angold, A., & Rutter, M. (1992). Effects of age and pubertal status on depression in a large clinical sample. *Development and Psychopathology, 4,* 5–28.

Ball, L., & Chandler, M. (1989). Identity formation in suicidal youth: The role of self-continuity. *Development and Psychopathology, 1,* 257–275.

Baumeister, R. F. (1990). Suicide as escape from self. *Psychological Review, 97,* 90–113.

Berman, A. L. (1986). Helping suicidal adolescents: Needs and responses. In C. C. Corr & J. N. McNeil (Eds.), *Adolescence and death* (pp. 151–166). New York: Springer.

Berman, A. L. (1991). Child and adolescent suicide: From the nomothetic to the idiographic. In A. A. Leenars (Ed.), *Life span perspectives of suicide* (pp. 109–120). New York: Plenum.

Berman, A. L., & Jobes, D. A. (1991). *Adolescent suicide: Assessment and intervention.* Washington, DC: American Psychological Association.

Bonner, R. L., & Rich, A. R. (1987). Toward a predictive model of suicidal ideation and behavior: Some preliminary data in college students. *Suicide and Life-Threatening Behavior, 17,* 50–63.

Borst, S. R., & Noam, G. G. (1993). Developmental psychopathology in suicidal and nonsuicidal adolescent girls. *Journal of the American Academy of Child and Adolescent Psychology, 32,* 501–508.

Brent, D. A., Kalas, R., Edelbrock, C., Costello, A. J., Dulcan, M. L., & Conover, N. (1986). Psychopathology and its relationship to suicidal ideation in childhood and adolescence. *Journal of the American Academy of Child Psychiatry, 25,* 666–673.

Brent, D. A., Perper, J. A., Allman, C., Friend, A., Roth, C., Schweers, J., Balach, L., & Baugher, M. (1993). Psychiatric risk factors for adolescent suicide: A case-control study. *Journal of the American Academy of Child and Adolescent Psychiatry, 32,* 521–529.

Brent, D. A., Perper, J., Mortiz, C. Baugher, M., & Allman, C. (1993). Suicide in adolescents with no apparent psychopathology. *Journal of the American Academy of Child and Adolescent Psychiatry, 32,* 494–500.

Brooks-Gunn, J., Petersen, A. C., & Eichorn, D. (1985). The study of maturational timing effects in adolescence. *Journal of Youth and Adolescence, 14,* 149–161.

Carlson, G. A., & Cantwell, D. P. (1982). Suicidal behavior and depression in children and adolescents. *Journal of the American Academy of Child Psychiatry, 21,* 361–368.

Cheek, J. M., Carpentieri, A. M., Smith, T., Rierdan, J., & Koff, E. (1986). Adolescent shyness. In W. H. Jones, J. M. Cheek, & S. R. Briggs (Eds.), *Shyness: Perspectives on research and treatment* (pp. 105–115). New York: Plenum.

Clements, C. D. (1980). The ethics of not-being: Individual options for suicide. In M. P. Battin & D. J. Mayo (Eds.), *Suicide: The philosophical issues* (pp. 104–114). New York: St. Martin's Press.

Coleman, J. C. (1978). Current contradictions in adolescent theory. *Journal of Youth and Adolescence, 7,* 1–11.

DeWilde, E. J., Kienhorst, I. C. W. M., Diekstra, R. F. W., & Wolters, W. H. G. (1992). The relationship between adolescent suicidal behavior and life events in childhood and adolescence. *American Journal of Psychiatry, 149,* 45–51.

Dubow, E. F., Kausch, D. F., Blum, M. C., Reed, J., & Bush, E. (1989). Correlates of suicidal ideation and attempts in a community sample of Junior High and High School students. *Journal of Clinical Child Psychology, 18,* 158–166.

Durkheim, E. (1897/1951). *Suicide.* New York: Free Press.

Earls, F., & Jemison, A. (1986). Suicidal behavior in American Blacks. In G. L. Klerman (Ed.), *Suicide and depression among adolescents and young adults* (pp. 131–146). Washington, DC: American Psychiatric Press.

Farberow, N. L. (1989). Preparatory and prior suicidal behavior factors. In Alcohol, Drug Abuse, and Mental Health Administration, *Report of the secretary's task force on youth suicide: Vol. 2. Risk factors for youth suicide* (pp. 34–55). (DHHS Publication No. ADM 89–1622). Washington, DC: U.S. Government Printing Office.

Gans, J. E. (1990). *American's adolescents: How healthy are they?,* Vol 1. Chicago, IL: American Medical Association.

Garland, A. F., & Zigler, E. (1993). Adolescent suicide prevention: Current research and social policy implications. *American Psychologist, 48,* 169–182.

Garrison, C. Z., Addy, C., Jackson, K. L., McKeown, R. E., & Waller, J. L. (1991). A longitudinal study of suicidal ideation in young adolescents. *Journal of the American Academy of Child and Adolescent Psychiatry, 30,* 597–603.

Garrison, C. Z., Jackson, K. L., Addy, C. L., McKeown, R. E., & Waller, J. L. (1991). Suicidal behavior in young adolescents. *American Journal of Epidemiology, 133,* 1005–1014.

Gelman, D. (1994, April 18). Lifestyle. *Newsweek,* pp. 45–49.

Group for the Advancement of Psychiatry (GAP). (1989). *Suicide and ethnicity in the United States.* New York: Brunner/Mazel.

Hammelman, T. L. (1993). Gay and lesbian youth: Contributing factors to serious attempts or considerations of suicide. *Journal of Gay and Lesbian Psychotherapy, 2,* 77–89.

Harry, J. (1989). Sexual identity issues. In Alcohol, Drug Abuse, and Mental Health Administration, *Report of the secretary's task force on youth suicide: Vol. 2. Risk factors for youth suicide* (pp. 131–142). (DHHS Publication No. ADM 89–1622). Washington, DC: U.S. Government Printing Office.

Harkavy-Friedman, J. M., Asnis, G. M., Boeck, M., & DiFiore, J. (1987). Prevalence of specific suicidal behaviors in a high school sample. *American Journal of Psychiatry, 144,* 1203–1206.

Harter, S., Marold, D. B., & Whitesell, N. R. (1992). Model of psychosocial risk factors leading to suicidal ideation in young adolescents. *Developmental Psychopathology, 4,* 167–188.

Hawton, K. (1986). *Suicide and attempted suicide among children and adolescents.* Beverly Hills, CA: Sage Publications.

Hawton, K., Cole, D., O'Grady, J., & Osborn, M. (1982). Motivational aspects of deliberate self-poisoning in adolescents. *British Journal of Psychiatry, 14,* 286–291.

Holinger, P. C., & Offer, D. (1982). Prediction of adolescent suicide: A population model. *American Journal of Psychiatry, 139,* 302–307.

Holinger, P. C., Offer, D., & Zola, M. A. (1988). A prediction model of suicide among youth. *Journal of Nervous and Mental Disease, 176,* 275–279.

Joffe, R. T., Offord, D. R., & Boyle, M. H. (1988). Ontario Child Health Study: Suicidal behavior in youth age 12–16 years. *American Journal of Psychiatry, 145,* 1420–1423.

Kaysen, S. (1993). *Girl, interrupted.* New York: Random House.

King, C. A., Hill, E. M., Naylor, M., Evans, T., & Shain, B. (1993). Alcohol consumption in relation to other predictors of suicidality among adolescent inpatient girls. *Journal of the American Academy of Child and Adolescent Psychiatry, 32,* 82–88.

Klerman, G. (1987). Clinical epidemiology of suicide. *Journal of Clinical Psychiatry, 48,* 33–53.

Klerman, G. L., & Weissman, M. M. (1989). Increasing rates of depression. *Journal of the American Medication Association, 261,* 2229–2235.

Kovacs, M., Goldston, D., & Gatsonis, C. (1993). Suicidal behaviors and childhood onset depressive disorders: A longitudinal investigation. *Journal of the American Academy of Child and Adolescent Psychiatry, 32,* 8–20.

Lawrence, M. T., & Ureda, J. R. (1990). Student recognition of and response to suicidal peers. *Suicide and Life-Threatening Behavior, 20,* 164–176.

Leenaars, A. A., & Wenckstern, S. (1991). Suicide in the school-age child and adolescent. In A. A. Leenaars (Ed.), *Life span perspectives of suicide* (pp. 95–107). New York: Plenum.

Loevinger, J. (1976). *Ego development.* San Francisco: Jossey-Bass.

Mack, J. E. (1986). Adolescent suicide: An architectural model. In G. L. Klerman (Ed.), *Suicide and depression among adolescents and young adults* (pp. 53–76). Washington, DC: American Psychiatric Press.

Maris, R. W. (1981/1991). The developmental perspective of suicide. In A. A. Leenaars (Ed.), *Life span perspective of suicide* (pp. 25–38). New York: Plenum.

Marttunen, M. J., Aro, H. M., & Lonnqvist, J. K. (1992). Adolescent suicide: Endpoint of long-term difficulties. *Journal of the American Academy of Child and Adolescent Psychiatry, 31,* 649–654.

Marttunen, M. J., Aro, H. M., & Lonnqvist, J. K. (1993). Precipitant stressors in adolescent suicide. *Journal of the American Academy of Child and Adolescent Psychiatry, 32,* 1178–1183.

Meehan, P. J., Lamb, J. A., Saltzman, L. E., & O'Carroll, P. W. (1992). Attempted suicide among young adults: Progress toward a meaningful estimate of prevalence. *American Journal of Psychiatry, 149,* 41–44.

Menninger, K. (1938). *Man against himself.* New York: Harcourt Brace.

Mishara, B. L. (1982). College students' experiences with suicide and reactions to suicidal verbalizations: A model for prevention. *Journal of Community Psychology, 10,* 142–150.

Myers, W. C., Otto, T. A., Harris, E., Diaco, D., & Moreno, A. (1992). Acetaminophen overdose as a suicide gesture: A survey of adolescents' knowledge of its potential for toxicity. *Journal of the American Academy of Child and Adolescent Psychiatry, 31,* 686–690.

National Center for Health Statistics. (1968–1991). *Vital statistics of the United States; Vol. 2, Mortality—Part A.* Washington, DC: U.S. Government Printing Office.

Norton, E. M., Durlak, J. A., & Richards, M. H. (1989). Peer knowledge of and reactions to adolescent suicide. *Journal of Youth and Adolescence,* 427–437.

Offer, D., & Schonert-Reichl, K. A. (1992). Debunking the myths of adolescence: Findings from recent research. *Journal of the American Academy of Child and Adolescent Psychiatry, 31,* 1003–1014.

Overholser, J. C., Hemstreet, A. H., Spirito, A., & Vyse, S. (1989). Suicide awareness programs in the schools: Effects of gender and personal experience. *Journal of the American Academy of Child and Adolescent Psychiatry, 28,* 925–930.

Pfeffer, C. R. (1989). Studies of suicidal preadolescent and adolescent inpatients: A critique of research methods. *Suicide and Life-Threatening Behavior, 19,* 58–77.

Prezant, D. W., & Neimeyer, R. A. (1988). Cognitive predictors of depression and suicide ideation. *Suicide and Life-Threatening Behavior, 18,* 259–264.

Rich, A. R., & Bonner, R. L. (1987). Concurrent validity of a stress-vulnerability model of suicidal ideation and behavior: A fellow-up study. *Suicide and Life-Threatening Behavior, 17,* 265–270.

Rierdan, J., & Koff, E. (1993). Developmental variables in relation to depressive symptoms in adolescent girls. *Development and Psychopathology, 5,* 485–496.

Shaffer, D., Garland, A., Gould, M., Fisher, P., & Trautman, P. (1988). Preventing teenage suicide: A critical review. *Journal of the American Academy of Child and Adolescent Psychiatry, 27,* 675–687.

Shafii, M., Carrigan, S., Whittinghill, J. R., & Derrick, A. (1985) Psychological autopsy of completed suicide in children and adolescents. *American Journal of Psychiatry, 142,* 1061–1062.

Shneidman, E. S. (1987). A psychological approach to suicide. In. G. R. VandenBos & B. K. Bryant (Eds.), *Cataclysms, crises, and catastrophes: Psychology in action.* Washington, DC: American Psychological Press.

Shneidman, E. S. (1991). The commonalities of suicide across the life span. In A. A. Leenaars (Ed.), *Life span perspectives of suicide* (pp. 39–52). New York: Plenum.

Smith, K., & Crawford, S. (1986). Suicidal behavior among "normal" high school students. *Suicide and Life-Threatening Behavior, 16,* 313–325.

Spirito, A., Brown, L., Overholser, J., & Fritz, G. (1989). Attempted suicide in adolescence: A review and critique of the literature. *Clinical Psychology Review, 9,* 335–363.

Stack, S. (1991). Social correlates of suicide by age: Media impacts. In A. A. Leenaars (Ed). *Life span perspective of suicide* (pp. 187–213). New York: Plenum.

Szasz, T. S. (1980). The ethics of suicide. In M. P. Battin & D. J. Mayo (Eds.), *Suicide: The philosophical issues* (pp. 185–195). New York: St. Martin's Press.

Tanner, J. M. (1990). *Foetus into man: Physical growth from conception to maturity, Revised*. Cambridge, MA: Harvard University Press.

Wade, N. L. (1987). Suicide as a resolution of separation-individuation among adolescent girls. *Adolescence, 22,* 169–177.

Walsh, B. W., & Rosen, P. M. (1988). *Self-mutilation: Theory, research, and treatment*. New York: Guilford.

Windt, P. Y. (1980). The concept of suicide. In M. P. Battin & D. J. Mayo (Eds.), *Suicide: The philosophical issues* (pp. 39–47). New York: St. Martin's Press.

Winnicott, D. W. (1958). The capacity to be alone. *International Journal of Psychoanalysis, 39,* 416–420.

Zetzel, E. R. (1965/1970). On the incapacity to bear depression. In E. R. Zetzel (Ed.), *The capacity for emotional growth* (pp. 82–114). London: Hogarth Press.

6 ALTRUISM AND AGGRESSION IN CHILDREN AND YOUTH

Origins and Cures

Ervin Staub

Caring about others' welfare, helping others, and altruism bind individuals together and create the experience of connection and community. Hostility and aggression in everyday life create the experience of separateness and division. Aggression tends to evolve into greater aggression, without social forces that inhibit this evolution (Staub, 1989).

The United States is a violent country, in terms of criminal violence and murder substantially more violent than any Western democracy (Prothrow-Stith, 1991). Since the mid-1980s, there has been a dramatic increase in violence by and against adolescents. Homicide was the leading cause of death for African-American youth, both male and female, between 1978 and 1988 (Hammond and Yung, 1991; National Center for Health Statistics, 1992; Prothrow-Stith, 1991, Rodriguez, 1990; Summary Report of the APA's Commission on Violence and Youth, 1993). The understanding of the origins of violence and reasons for its increase among youth in contemporary America is important as a scientific enterprise. It is essential to help us take steps to reduce youth violence.

In this chapter I discuss the core experiences in the family that develop caring about other people's welfare, helping others, and altruism in children and youth and the core experiences that develop lack of caring, hostility, and aggression. A primary thesis is that just as helping and harming are opposites in that they respectively enhance and diminish others' welfare, so the psychological processes, socialization, and experience that contribute to one or the other are opposites of each other. The emphasis is on the origins and "cures" (prevention) of aggression. Examining the origins of caring and helping provides a comparison or baseline for understanding the origins of aggression.

A primary focus is the impact on children of love and nurturant caretaking versus neglect, rejection, hostility, and aggression. Positive connection leads to connection and turning toward others, negative connection leads to disconnection and turning against others. Structure and guidance are also required for the development of caring and altruism, whereas their absence contributes to disorganization in personality, hostility, and aggression. Another focus of the chapter is on reasons for lack of care, neglect, mistreatment, and violence by parents against children and adolescents, especially their sources in cultural characteristics and societal conditions. Finally, I consider what can be done to create positive socialization and to help children and adolescents overcome the effects of neglect and harsh treatment. My concerns include the impact of the family and to a lesser extent of the school on the child and adolescent, as well as that of the overall culture in which the youth, family, and school are located.

A variety of conditions and influences that contribute to violence in the United States and elsewhere are not discussed. One of these is the easy access to guns in the United States (Prothrow-Stith, 1991), which makes violence lethal. Another is drug use and drug trade. Another is the long-term impact of the experience of war, especially on children. Political terrorism used to accidentally involve youth; increasingly, it is directed at them as a means of intimidating communities (Garbarino, Dubrow, Kostelny, & Pardo, 1992). Adolescents are frequently inducted into revolutionary movements and armies such as the Khmer Rouge, as well as into regular armies (Etcheson, 1984; Staub, 1989). Killing others, the danger of being killed, and the loss of comrades have profound impact, like posttraumatic stress disorder. Being victimized, as in ethnic conflicts, appears to increase the likelihood of victimizing others (Staub, 1989; 1993a). Violent neighborhoods and violence among teenagers (Garbarino et al., 1992) greatly affect the lives of children and adolescents, their security, perception of the world as dangerous, experience of stress, capacity for organized thought and action, and aggressiveness. Violence against children in families and violence in neighborhoods are likely to increase each other's impact.

THE ORIGINS OF CARING AND HELPING

"Positive socialization" (Staub, 1992) in the family provides the basis not only for caring about others' welfare, but also for the development of a positive identity, interest in socially valued activities, and the capacity for sustained engagement in goal directed action (Eisenberg, 1992; Radke-Yarrow, Zahn-Waxler, & Chapman, 1984; Staub, 1979, 1986, 1992; Zahn-Waxler et al., 1986). What is its nature?

The Experience of Love and Affection

The core element is love, affection, and nurturance. Starting at birth, responsiveness to the child's needs and affectionate social stimulation (touching, gazing, etc.) contribute to secure attachment to caretakers (Shaffer, 1988). Secure attachment is in turn associated with positive peer relationships in the early school years (Sroufe, 1979; Troy and Sroufe, 1987; Waters, Wippman, & Sroufe, 1979).

Bowlby (1980) suggested that infants develop a mental model of relationships that guides their later interactions with people. Early experiences of love also create emotional orientations, both towards others and the self. Early and ongoing affection and nurturance create the experience of people and the world as benevolent, a positive view of and orientation to people, and a positive view of the self (Staub, 1979, 1986).

The research findings indicate that parental affection and nurturance contribute to caring about people and helpful and/or altruistic behavior in children (Eisenberg, 1992; Hoffman, 1970a, 1975b; Radke-Yarrow et al., 1984; Staub, 1979). Benevolence by parents and the children's perception that the parents care about their welfare are central to the development of positive self-esteem in boys (Coopersmith, 1967). In simple societies that are peaceful and cooperative children receive warm, affectionate caretaking, whereas in aggressive, selfish ones they receive harsh, punitive child rearing (Eisenberg, 1992), practices that presumably perpetuate the characteristics of these societies. Children's experience also affects what they perceive and remember. Children supervised in a group on several occasions by warm, affectionate versus distant, indifferent caretakers remember the same amount from diorama scenes enacted for them, but the former children remember more of the helpful, positive behaviors of the diorama characters (Yarrow & Scott, 1972).

The experience of love, affection, and nurturance are core requirements for the development of both caring about other people and a positive identity, but not sufficient by themselves. A pattern of parent-child relations and child-rearing practices is required.

Positive Guidance, Discipline, and Learning by Participation

Positive guidance is another component of this pattern. One form of it is reasoning, instead of authoritarian rule setting. Effective guidance has to be appropriate to the child's age and developmental level, but reasoning can be established at an early age, at the very least as a mode of interaction. Children to whom the reasons for rules are explained can internalize the values that underlie rules. They can later engage in flexible self-guidance.

An important form of reasoning for the development of caring and helping is "induction" (Hoffman, 1970b, 1975a; Radke-Yarrow et. al., 1984; Staub, 1971, 1979), the pointing out to children the consequences of their behavior for other people, both the hurt, distress, or pain created by selfish, inconsiderate, or aggressive behavior and good feelings and enhanced well-being that result from sensitive, helpful behavior. This leads children to consider others' internal states and promotes role-taking and empathy. It also develops awareness of one's capacity to influence others' welfare and a feeling of responsibility for others. Another form of positive guidance is inherent in setting standards for children that are challenging but reasonable, appropriate for the child's level of development (Coopersmith, 1967).

Discipline or effective control by parents (Baumrind, 1971, 1975) is a component of guidance. While it is important to allow children autonomy, and to an increasing degree as they get older, it is essential for them to learn that adults consider certain values and the rules and behaviors that express them of great importance (Staub, 1979, 1981). By placing standards and rules in the context of essential values, parents can help children develop a view of the world as meaningful (Janoff-Bulman, 1992). This should contribute to internalization and self-guidance. Parents who use effective but flexible control have children who are more prosocial in their interactions with peers and more effective in pursuing varied activities (Baumrind, 1967, 1975). In contrast, nurturance is not associated with prosocial behavior when it is combined with parental permissiveness (Eisenberg, 1992). And the benevolent parents of high self-esteem boys are firm in their expectations that their children adhere to and strive to fulfill certain standards (Coopersmith, 1967).

It is essential, however, that parents use discipline techniques that do not undo the child's experience of love and nurturance. Reasoning is a form of guidance and also a nonforceful method of control, but at times more is required. However, the extensive use by parents of their power to punish or deprive, and especially of physical punishment, creates hostility rather than caring and positive identity (see further discussion below).

"Natural socialization" (Staub, 1979)—parents guiding their children to engage in various activities—is another important part of the pattern. The experience of engagement produces learning, given supporting external conditions. Children (and adults) learn by doing, or participation, in many realms. It is an important avenue for the development of caring and helping (Whiting and Whiting, 1975). Children who make toys for poor, hospitalized children or teach younger children are subsequently more helpful than children in control groups (Staub, 1975, 1979). They probably come to both value the welfare of people and perceive themselves (Grusec, 1982; Grusec, Kuczynski, Rushton, & Simutis, 1978) as helpful. Adults who are provided an opportunity to help are subsequently also more helpful (Harris, 1972).

Rescuers of Jews in Nazi Germany who endangered their lives to save others' lives frequently started out with a limited commitment, such as hiding a person or family for a short time in a cellar. As they helped, many of them became intensely committed to further helping (Oliner and Oliner, 1988; Staub, 1989, 1993a; Tec, 1986). People who engage in aggressive acts also change and become more aggressive. "Teachers" who administer shocks to "learners," when they have control over shock intensity, raise the shock level over time (Buss, 1966; Goldstein, Davis, and Herman, 1975). Whole groups of people change, and the possibilities of violence evolve, as they begin to discriminate against and harm victim groups (Staub, 1989).

Natural socialization and learning by doing seem of central significance for developing skills and interests in many realms. Children have to engage in reading, work on math problems, or play baseball to develop relevant skills and the interest to engage in these activities. Guidance that leads to engagement is essential for growth.

Modeling, the Role of Examples

Exposure to the example of other people who are caring or helpful is an important avenue for learning that helping is expected, valued, or satisfying (Eisenberg, 1992). The example of significant people in the child's life is especially important. Many committed civil rights activists had parents who worked for and made sacrifices for justice or social change (Rosenhan, 1970).

Personal Characteristics that Promote Helping

Affectionate, loving relationships, reasoning, discipline, guidance to act or participate, and others' example represent structures and order in the external environment which contribute to the growth of internal structures. These include self-esteem and components of a positive identity such as a feeling of efficacy and the capacity for sustained engagement and effective self-guidance. The perception of self-efficacy (Bandura, 1986; Bandura and Cervone, 1983) and internal locus of control (Lefcourt, 1976) are associated with people actively pursuing their goals. The belief in one's capacity to improve others' welfare is strongly associated with self-reports of varied kinds of helping (Staub, 1991b). However, the motivation to benefit others also has to be present.

What are the motives that children acquire that lead to helpful or altruistic actions? What are the personal characteristics out of which these motives arise? Hoffman (1975b) stressed the expanding capacity with age and corresponding experience of taking others' role and understanding others' condition, and the concomitant enlargement of the capacity for empathy. Personal distress evoked by another's condition is only associated with helping when escape from the situation is difficult (Batson, 1990). But empathy that is based on concern for anothers' distress (sympathy) is associated with helping under varied conditions (Eisenberg, 1992; Staub and Feinberg, 1980).

In many situations a feeling of responsibility for others' welfare also has to be present to move a person from empathy to helping. Research has shown that beyond witnessing another's need, conditions that focus responsibility on a person for helping, such as being the only witness (Latane and Darley, 1970), occupying a leadership role (Baumeister, Chesner, Senders, & Tice, 1988), or other people assigning responsibility to the person (Staub, 1970), increase helping.

A personal disposition that I have called *prosocial value orientation,* which combines a positive evaluation of human beings, concern about others' welfare, and feelings of personal responsibility for their welfare, is substantially associated with varied forms of helping (Feinberg, 1978; Grodman, 1979; Oliner & Oliner, 1988; Staub, 1974, 1978, 1991b). A feeling of responsibility has also been found to inhibit people from harming others (Kohlberg and Candee, 1984). The properties of the childrearing practices I emphasized—affection, inductive reasoning, setting standards, and guiding children to help (and to not harm) others—are likely to contribute to the development of both empathy and a prosocial value orientation.

The characteristics children acquire through positive socialization enable them to function effectively with peers and in school. Delinquent and antisocial children lack positive connection to school or other prosocial institutions. When such connections are present, they can ameliorate the impact of difficult conditions in a child's life (Ziegler, Taussig, & Block, 1992).

THE ORIGINS OF HOSTILITY AND AGGRESSION

When affection and nurturance are absent and especially when there is hostility and violence against the child, the likelihood of aggression increases and the child's capacity to function effectively in the world—in terms of interpersonal relations, school performance, and adjustment to school—decreases. The research literature has begun to delineate the influences, and at times their combinations, that lead to aggressiveness, to its frequent correlate ineffectiveness in socially (conventionally) valued realms, and to the psychological processes, the feelings and modes of thinking, that mediate these outcomes.

The Origins of Aggression in Neglect, Harsh Treatment, Violence, and Lack of Guidance

Parental negativity, hostility, and punitiveness stand out as core elements in the pattern of childrearing that creates aggression and ineffectiveness in socially valued realms. The degree of punitiveness and whether punishment expresses hostility or occurs in an otherwise affectionate or caring context appear to determine their impact.

What is the meaning of the terms *child neglect, maltreatment,* and *abuse* (Kinard, 1979; Youngblade and Belsky, 1990)? Parental neglect and punitiveness are often treated as a single dimension. At one endpoint is lack of care so that the child's physical needs are not satisfied, progressing to lack of nurturance, affirmation, and support so that the child's emotional and identity needs remain unfulfilled. This side of the dimension points to omissions and corresponds to what is usually identified as neglect. It moves on to increasing degrees of commission or harmful behavior: punitive discipline or the use of parental power to withhold privileges and restrict the child's freedom and rights, rejection of the child in the form of criticism and negative evaluation, verbal abuse, the use of physical punishment of varying intensity and frequency, and finally physical abuse (violence that leads to physical injury) and sexual abuse. In reality, there may be two separate dimensions, one involving neglect, the other punitiveness. A child can receive good physical caretaking and affection from parents who regularly use physical punishment (see below).

Harsh discipline consisting of physical punishment or abuse is associated with aggression in children, youth, and adults (Dodge, Bates, & Pettit, 1990; Gelles & Conte, 1990; Weiss, Dodge, Bates, & Pettit, 1992; Widom, 1989b; Youngblade & Belsky, 1990). Weiss et al. (1992) found that harsh (severe, strict, often physical) discipline early in life was associated with aggression by children. In most research, however, physical punishment and abuse on the one hand and neglect on the other hand are not treated independently. Moreover, different points on the neglect-abuse dimension are often not identified. The influence of the context is usually not separated, for example, whether physical punishment is used in a generally hostile or affectionate context, or in an orderly functioning or disorganized family.

Maltreated (both neglected and abused) toddlers are more aggressive, less prosocial, and respond to others' distress with aggression rather than empathy. Maltreated children exhibit more anger, have more conflict in their families, and are more aggressive with peers (see Youngblade & Belsky, 1990). Vissing, Straus, Gelles, and Harrop (1991) found that the physical punishment of young children was associated with aggression, delinquency, and interpersonal problems at age 18; the more intense the physical aggression against the child, the stronger the relationship. The frequency of verbal aggression by parents, such as swearing at and insulting the child, was independently related to aggression, delinquency, and interpersonal problems (Vissing et al., 1991).

Researchers who study aggressive boys find that they have experienced more rejection, hostility, physical punishment or abuse by parents (Bandura & Walters, 1959; Huesmann, Eron, Lefkowitz, & Walder, 1984; Olweus, 1979). Moreover, a high percentage of violent adult criminals have been abused as children (Lewis, Mallouh, & Webb, 1989). Widom (1989b) found, comparing validated cases of abuse and neglect 20 years earlier with a control group of nonabused cases, that children who were abused and neglected were later more frequently arrested for delinquency, adult criminality, and violent criminal behavior.

Aggressive behavior shows at least moderate stability with age, with greater stability in males than females (Huesmann et al., 1984; Olweus, 1980). Peer-rated aggression when a child is 8 years old is related to later aggression against spouse, physical punishment of one's children, and criminality at age 30. There is, moreover, intergenerational stability of aggression in families. First, parents' aggression (physical punitiveness) when their children are 8 years old relates to the children's aggression at age 8 and to these children's use of aggression when they are 30 against their own children, whose modal age is 8. Second, the strongest relationship has been found between a person's aggression at age 8 and the aggressive fantasy of this person's child when the child is about age 8 (Huessmann et al., 1984).

A variety of studies have shown that people who were abused as children tend to abuse their own children (Kaufman & Zigler, 1987), and young unmarried adults who were abused show a heightened potential to abuse (Milner, Robertson, & Rogers, 1990). The majority of physically abused children do not become abusive parents, however (Widom, 1989a). According to one estimate, the rate of intergenerational transmission is 30% (Kaufman & Zigler, 1987), in comparison to the 2%-4% percent abuse rate found in the general population (Gelles & Conte, 1990). This should not be surprising, for several reasons. Aggression can have varied objects. Some abused children maybe partly or wholly healed through contact with caring adults (Garmezy & Rutter, 1983), peers, or later in life. Others may become fearful and avoidant rather than aggressive; this would also affect their parenting.

Punitiveness is not the only source of the development of aggression. Permissiveness, a lack of standards, or lax discipline was associated with high aggressiveness as measured by the recorded offenses of a group of delinquent youths (DiLalla, Mitchell, Arthur, & Pagliococca, 1988). In a permissive setting, aggression may be reinforced by its consequences (Patterson, 1986; Patterson, Littman, & Bricker, 1967), teaching children that aggression pays (Buss, 1971). This may occur especially in environments that instigate but do not control aggression. Permissiveness also means a lack of guidance, contributing to ineffectiveness and poor self-control. However, the motivations for aggression would differ as a function of its origins in permissiveness or punitiveness, and of the reasons for permissiveness.

Permissiveness can be a form of neglect associated with lack of love or disinterest in the child. However, it can also have other origins: an at least theoretically benevolent desire not to stifle the child, based on an ideology of children's inherent potential for growth; family disorganization and chaos; or parents' incapacity to exercise control.

Sexual abuse is a significant form of aggression against children and adolescents. So far primarily female victims have received attention, but boys are also abused sexually, with the extent, nature, and consequences less well known. When the abuser is an older male with power who is part of the family, that is, the father or stepfather, the traumatic impact is especially great (Finkelhor, 1979; Herman and Hirschman, 1981). The use of force adds to the traumatic impact (Browne and Finkelhor, 1986). Females have historically been less likely to respond to abuse and trauma by becoming aggressive, but with an increase in the United States in antisocial aggression by females (Summary Report of the APA's Commission on Violence and Youth, 1993), this may be changing. One reason that sexual abuse by fathers or stepfathers is especially traumatic may be that the child has no "safe haven" to escape to and therefore lives in constant insecurity and danger. The same is true of children in physically abusive families.

Aggression against the child not only impacts the child, but also teaches by modeling. So does violence by one parent against the other. In abusive couples, frequently males and females are both violent (Morgan, 1993), but male violence against females has more destructive effects. The many forms of modeling of aggression—others' aggression toward oneself, toward others, on TV and in films, in neighborhoods—lead to a strongly established view in which aggression is normal, acceptable, even the right form of behavior, at least in dealing with conflict (Huessmann & Eron, 1984).

In some families a coercive pattern of interaction leads to the use of aggression both to defend oneself and to get what one wants (Patterson, 1982, 1986). Both the reinforcement of aggression (Buss, 1971) and principles of reciprocity (Rausch, 1965; Staub and Feinberg, 1980) create and maintain aggressive behavior in the children.

Parents abusing each other, or spouse battering, contributes to aggressive behavior by children. In some studies its influence is even greater than that of physical punishment of children (Widom, 1989a). In one study, parental conflict and general aggressiveness (yelling, throwing things, attempting to injure someone when frustrated) was associated with a greater degree of criminality in children than parental punitiveness (McCord, 1988).

External influences, like TV watching, interact with parental negativity toward the child and negativity in the family. The amount of violent television 8-year-old boys watch is associated with more fantasy aggression at a later age and with aggressively delinquent behavior at age 19 (Eron, Walder, & Lefkowitz, 1971). However, rather than TV watching itself, the interaction of large amount of TV viewing and the experience of abuse by either mother or father has been found related to violent crime (Health, Krutt Schitt, & Ward, 1986). As the findings of Yarrow and Scott (1972) reported earlier suggest, whether an environment is affectionate or indifferent (or hostile) is likely to affect what children remember of their experience. It is also likely to effect how they process the television aggression they are exposed to.

How does heredity affect the development of individual aggressiveness? To the extent it does, it is likely to be through temperamental characteristics, as they evoke or simply interact with certain parental behaviors or environmental influence. For example, temperamentally difficult children raised in unsupportive environments by disorganized, distressed caretakers are more likely to develop delinquency than those with nurturant caretakers in a supportive environment (Werner, 1987). Both premature and temperamentally difficult children are more likely to be abused (Widom, 1989a), presumably because the attachment ties that parents develop to them are weaker and the parents' frustration in their caretaking efforts are greater.

Physical Punishment in an Affectionate Context

Like caring and altruism, aggression is a function of a pattern of child-rearing and environmental influences. While frequent and severe physical punishment often occurs in the context of neglect and lack of love, physical punishment can also occur in the context of affection, care, and guidance, which moderate its effects. A limited amount of physical punishment, in the context of love and responsiveness, was associated with "humanistic" values in children (Hoffman, 1970b). The combination of an affectionate, loving relationship with mother, consistent standards, physical punishment for violating standards, and church attendance by mother and child (which suggests the presence of guiding values) characterized nonaggressive African-American boys, in contrast to institutionalized aggressive and noninstitutionalized aggressive boys (Boone, 1991). The physical punishment of the nonaggressive boys may have also been of lesser magnitude, since parents were likely to be less provoked. The investigator suggests that in the context of caring and guidance, adolescents seem to experience the physical punishment as an indication of parental love (Boone, 1991).

In the first phase of their longitudinal study, Eron and his associates (1971) found that the less nurturant and accepting parents were and the more they punished the child for aggression at home, the more aggressive were the children in school. But boys who were punished for aggression and strongly identified with their fathers tended not to be aggressive either at home or in school. The presumably more benevolent pattern of child-rearing that led to boys' identification with their fathers also influenced the meaning and effect of punishment. However, when punitiveness is intense and chronic, it is likely to be the primary determining influence of the child's experience in the family, and to shape his or her relationship to the adults.

THE EFFECTS OF PARENTAL NEGATIVITY AND PERMISSIVENESS: MEDIATORS OF AGGRESSION IN CHILDREN AND YOUTH

Beliefs, Norms, and Cognitive Structures

Current views of the acquisition of aggression stress the reinforcement of aggression (Patterson, 1982, 1986), the imitation of aggressive models (learning aggressive behavior and the expectation that it leads to rewards) (Bandura, 1986), learning norms and developing cognitive structures that make aggressive behavior acceptable and appropriate (or even right)(Huesmann & Eron, 1984), and the acquisition of sociocognitive processes such as schemas, scripts, perceptions, and attributions of hostility to people (Dodge, 1993). Neglect, hostility, or physical aggression by parents, or psychological, physical, or sexual abuse can define for the child the nature of the world and the way life is lived. Aggressive children and adolescents (Dodge, 1993, Dodge et al., 1990), as well as adults (Toch, 1969), see people as hostile. Aggressive children see hostility especially toward themselves, but also see and describe others' behavior not directed toward them in terms of aggression (Steinberg and Dodge, 1987; Stromguist & Strauman, 1992). The child develops "memory structures of the world as a hostile place that requires coercive behavior to achieve desired outcomes" (Dodge,

1993, p. 579). These theoretical views, while extremely useful and supported by research findings, place insufficient emphasis on the emotional consequences of the child's experiences and on the resulting emotional orientations and motives as the sources of aggression.

Motives for Aggression

Persistent motives may result from parental negativity. Cognitive schemas and attributional styles, which guide the perception and interpretation of current events and of one's relationship to them, are both rooted in and activate feelings and motives. A view of other people or of the world as hostile toward the self (Dodge, 1993), or as malevolent in general, and low self-esteem and an insecure self (Staub, 1993b) can jointly activate strong needs to protect and elevate the self. Aggression can provide feelings of strength, power, and control.

Intense parental negativity, especially abuse, is likely to lead to hostility toward people. An antisocial value orientation may develop, the opposite of a prosocial value orientation, a personal disposition embodying a negative evaluation of people and a desire and intention to harm them. That childhood victimization leads to hostility is suggested by a strong association between physical abuse in childhood and expressive but not instrumental crimes of violence in adulthood (Widom, 1989a), or angry reactive violence but not proactive aggression or nonviolent criminal behavior (Dodge, 1993).

For young children, parental negativity intensifies the need for security, which they can only gain through connection to the hostile or abusive parent(s). An early psychological strategy to increase a feeling of security may be to see oneself as bad and deserving of punishment. This offers the hope of avoiding punishment by learning how to be good. While this places the focus of responsibility within the self and creates a negative self-concept, it does not stop children from also learning that the world is a hostile place, at least for them. In adolescence, perhaps because parental punitiveness paradoxically intensifies the need for connection to the abusive parents, the normal process of separation from parents and developing psychological independence becomes more difficult.

Types of Attachment

Parental negativity is related to insecure infant attachment to caretakers. Neglect is associated with resistant attachment, abuse with avoidant attachment, and their combination with a composite of resistant and avoidant attachments (Youngblade & Belsky, 1990). After World War II there were reports of the absence of attachment in children reared in extremely neglectful institutions (Thompson and Grusec, 1970). Some writers now again mention "unattached" children (Keogh, 1993), whose affective connections to caretakers and by generalization to other people have not developed or have been disrupted. They are usually children who have been passed around in child care agencies and foster homes and may well have been abused.

Resistant and avoidant attachment in infants is associated in the preschool years with aggressive behavior (Youngsblade & Belsky, 1990). Boys who had been classified as avoidant, when paired with another insecurely attached child, are either aggressors or victims in the interaction or alternate between the two. This is not the case when they are paired with securely attached children, who manage to create friendly interactions regardless of the other child's attachment classification (Troy and Sroufe, 1987). Avoidant attachment creates a disconnection from people in general, perhaps of a lesser degree and without the disorganized emotionality that is found in unattached children.

As noted above, recent research and theory has focused on schemas, scripts, or the social-cognitive consequences of child maltreatment as moderators of aggressive behavior in children (Dodge, 1993; Huesmann & Eron, 1984). However, attachment is primarily an affective relationship. Different types of attachments, as they generalize to other people (possibly cognitively encoded in mental models or assumptions about and evaluations of people), represent a continuum of emotional connection to, ambivalence toward, disconnection from, or hostile turning against people.

The Self-Concept

Experiences of hostility and abuse are likely to lead to problems with self-esteem. In a recent study, aggressive boys did not differ from others in their perceived self-competence (see Dodge, 1993). However, incarcerated violent criminals (Newman, 1974; Toch, 1969), first-time violent offenders (Gillooly & Bond, 1976), and violent gang members (Copeland, 1974) all had lower self-esteem than either control groups or nonviolent delinquents who themselves differed from control subjects (Offer, Marohn, & Ostrov, 1975). Moreover, college students who had low self-esteem found aggressive reactions more acceptable in their responses to vignettes that described frustrating, threatening, or aggressive behavior directed at them than students with high self-esteem did (Theiss, 1985).

Subcultural beliefs and norms may teach strength and power as the ideal male characteristic and strong response to provocation as the required behavior (Nisbett, 1993). A need to look strong in one's own and others' eyes can lead to the tendency to perceive and react aggressively to slight or even imagined provocation (Staub, 1971; Toch, 1969). The combination of personal experience, subcultural norms, cultural influence through TV and film, and violent neighborhoods with rules of reciprocity explain why retaliation-revenge for past insult or harm is the most frequent reason adolescents give for their violent acts (Agnew, 1990).

Socialization Void and Self-socialization

Some hostile and abusive parents set firm rules in an authoritarian fashion, but others are permissive or neglectful, so that guidance and structure are lacking. This makes it unlikely that children learn impulse control and effective self-guidance. The combination of abuse with neglect and lack of guidance combine the child's victimization with the absence of socialization. One conceptualization of this is as a "socialization void" (Friedrich & Stein, 1973). The environment does not provide learning opportunities for prosocial behavior and skills in effective interaction. Children do not learn how to satisfy their goals by prosocial means. They are not guided to participation in activities that develop socially and academically useful skills and interests. They lack, as a result, the cognitive capacities, motivation, and self-regulatory skills required for effective participation in school. Young children who experience physically punitive discipline are less likely to attend to relevant social cues and to use competent responses (Dodge, 1993; Dodge et al., 1990).

Aggressive behavior toward peers leads to unpopularity in school (Hartup, 1970). Unpopularity and poor school performance both express and perpetuate lack of stable connections to people and social institutions. Engagement in school makes delinquency less likely (Ziegler et al., 1992).

Aggressive boys' perception of hostility toward themselves is correct; in a new group more aggression is directed toward them (Dodge and Frame, 1982). This is a form of self-socialization. Aggressive boys' behaviors create reactions toward them that presumably further develop their already existing perceptions, feelings, and behavioral tendencies. Given strong reciprocity in aggressive behavior (Rausch, 1965; Staub & Feinberg, 1980), children's own aggression may elicit reciprocal aggression, or their poor social skills and inappropriateness in joining with others (Dodge, 1993) may lead to aggression against them. In contrast, securely attached children create peaceful interactions with normally aggressive, avoidantly attached children (Troy and Sroufe, 1987). Empathic children (especially girls) are the recipients of more positive behavior from their classmates (Staub & Feinberg, 1980).

One form of self-socialization occurs when already existing characteristics lead to behavior that elicits reactions that strengthen and further evolve these characteristics. Another form is the selection of associates, contexts, or environments that further develop these existing characteristics. Delinquent, antisocial friends or gangs may serve important and developmentally appropriate needs for belonging, identity, and security. Aggressive adolescents may select antisocial friends or antisocial groups partly because of a match in inclinations, partly because they are the only ones available to them.

A new form of grouping that has received attention, as a result of "wildings" (Gibbs, 1989), has been named a pack (Scheidlinger, 1992; Staub & Rosenthal, 1995). The pack is a relatively temporary joining together by a group of teenagers in antisocial acts, without the rules and stability of traditional gangs. As yet we know little about packs' frequency and nature. It might be that a reason for their appearance is that adolescents are not developing the capacities required for sustained friendship or social organization.

Bystander Behavior and Perceptions of Abandonment or Benevolence

The impact of bad treatment by parents may be modified if the child or adolescent realizes that his or her experience is not universal. The child may come to feel betrayed at home and abandoned by "bystanders," other family members, or people outside the family who are in a position to know but do nothing. In families with father-daughter incest, mothers who know frequently remain passive (Scott and Flowers, 1988). Their reactions to daughters who approach them for help is often punitive, which intensifies the trauma (Browne & Finkelhor, 1986; Herman & Hirschman 1981). Similar abandonment by the other parent or other bystanders may be experienced by sons and daughters who are neglected, badly treated, or physically abused. While an awareness of one's own bad fate relative to others can intensify hostility, realizing the existence of benevolence and especially experiencing benevolence can build connections and create hope for the future. The experience of benevolence, or of an affectionate connection with people outside the immediate family, has been identified as an important source of resilience in children who grow up in difficult home environments (Garmezy & Rutter, 1983). We know little as yet about the consequences for children of different roles that nonabusive parents and relatives assume: supporter of the perpetrator (as sometimes happens in father/daughter incest, see Staub 1991a), passive bystander, silent ally, active defender, or source of love and affection.

Spouse abuse not only provides aggressive models, but also interferes with the child's relationship to both parents. Depending on the child's experience with each parent, it may create hostility to, identification with, or ambivalence toward the perpetrator. Empathy with the victim gives rise to empathic distress. Given the child's incapacity to help, as in the case of other passive observers of victimization (Staub, 1989), over time the child is likely to distance himself or herself by devaluing the abused parent.

THE ORIGINS OF NEGLECT AND MISTREATMENT OF CHILDREN

Why do parents treat children badly? The sources of child maltreatment include (see Belsky & Vondra, 1992) parental characteristics, including the parents' own experience of abuse, child characteristics like difficult temperament and prematurity, and sources of stress in parental life like marital difficulties, economic problems (especially as they combine with certain parental characteristics)(Elder & Caspi, 1985), and lack of a social support network and the frustrations such conditions create, which parents direct at the child (Staub, 1995). Here I will focus on cultural characteristics and societal conditions that affect many parents and may account for the recent increase in youth violence in the United States.

Negative Assumptions about Children

There has been a long Western tradition to see children as willful and inclined to disobedience, with forceful means considered necessary to ensure that they are obedient and manageable. This tradition has a partly religious basis and has been strongly present in Germany (Miller, 1983), England, and other European countries (Stone, 1977), as well as in the United States (Greven, 1991). It is still with us today in the widely held view that physical punishment is required for raising children (Strauss and Gelles, 1986; Strauss, Gelles, & Steinmetz 1980). In actuality, affectionate caretaking is associated in young children with the development of secure attachment, greater cooperation, and better self-regulation (Scarr & Eisenberg, 1993; Shaffer, 1988).

Difficult Life Conditions, Societal Changes, and Their Impact on Individuals and Family Life

There have been many difficult, socially disorganizing events and changes in the United States in the last 25 years, giving rise to intense needs in people (Staub, 1989). These conditions included the assassination of leaders; social movements such as civil rights, opposition to the Vietnam war and feminism—which, even as they brought about positive societal changes by creating political conflict and changes in roles, lifestyles, and relationships, have placed great demands on people; tremendous changes in sexual and social mores, family structure, family life, and drug use; and a less central role of the United States in the world, reduced economic power, and reduced expectations by citizens for better economic conditions for themselves. Some of these events and changes led to some of the others, but they all join in their impact on people as they create new social realities, which require adjustment.

Substantial, rapid social changes have called into question traditional values and made it difficult to identify new values to live by. Many parents lack the conviction to offer the guidance required for transmitting values and a sense of purpose to their children. With a cultural emphasis on the development of the self and on one's own needs and rights, the feeling of obligation by parents to children has also declined (Baumeister, 1992; Bellah, Madsen, Sullivan, Swindler, & Lipton, 1985).

The great changes in family life, and especially the growth of single-parent families, have affected parenting. Single parents, especially when poor and/or young, use substantially more violence against their children than parents in dual-parent households (Gelles, 1981). Increase in divorce, which impoverishes people, especially women, and single teenage parenting have both contributed to violence against children. While most single parents are women, the findings hold to an even greater degree for single fathers (Gelles, 1981).

Basic human needs are activated by difficult life conditions, like economic problems or rapid, substantial social change. Needs for security, for a positive identity, for a world view in changing times that helps to comprehend new realities, and for connection to other people are often frustrated when social conditions are difficult (Staub, 1989; 1975). Stress, threats, and frustrated basic needs in turn affect family relations and parenting.

Prejudice, Discrimination, Poverty, and Violence (Hate Crimes) against Certain Groups and their Psychological Consequences

They create frustration, anger and aggression, self-devaluation (Tajfel, 1982), and compensatory processes such as a culture of toughness in which honor becomes highly valued and an image of strength is essential to maintain (Hammond & Yung, 1991). Bad economic conditions, bad housing, and especially the unresponsiveness of societal institutions to grievances contribute to riots (Staub & Rosenthal, 1995). Poverty alone, and even poverty combined with discrimination, does not inevitably lead to violence in families, or communities. Strong guiding values and community and family cohesion can counteract their effects. For example, Chinatown in San Francisco at one time was one of the poorest areas of the city, yet the murder rate was extremely low (Wilson & Herrnstein, 1985). A cohesive, supportive internal community makes it less likely that devaluation by outside groups becomes ingroup devaluation (Tajfel, 1982). This, however, is a best-case scenario, and frequently poverty, disadvantage, discrimination, and their disorganizing impact do give rise to violence within homes and whole communities (Belsky & Vondra, 1992; Garbarino et al., 1992).

A conception of the world or an ideology that provides hope can lead to constructive efforts by members of a group to improve their lives. Garbarino and his associates (1992) described how a belief that living well is the best revenge has energized efforts by Cambodians in their own behalf, following the Khmer Rouge "autogenocide" (see Staub, 1989). Lack of hope makes it unlikely that people engage in constructive efforts and create a supportive community. A strong sense of relative deprivation and injustice, combined with lack of hope, make poverty and discrimination less tolerable, and violence as a means of expressing frustration and affirming the self probable.

Wilson (1987) has suggested that in the United States an underclass has developed, especially an African-American underclass characterized by poverty and unemployment. It has no accessible avenues to improve its condition and therefore posesses little hope. There may also be a continuing impact of slavery on black culture, because education was punished and families were constantly in danger of separation (Staub, 1995). Violence and discrimination against black people continued afterwards with little genuine attempt by society, through quality education and otherwise, to help create a culture of greater enablement.

The Evolution of Violence in U.S. Culture

A variety of forms of aggression have increased within U.S. society, these changes mutually supporting each other, creating changing norms and standards of behavior, changes in institutions, and a change in the cultural milieu.

Violence in TV programs and films has greatly increased, compared to the 1950s or 1960s. Starting in the mid-1980s, youth violence has greatly increased, including murder by young adolescents. Another societal change is the availability of guns even to adolescents (Summary Report of the APA's Commission on Violence and Youth, 1993). The greater lethal violence by youth in the United States relative to other countries is to a large extent accounted for by violence inflicted by guns (Prothrow-Stith, 1991).

There has also been a substantial increase in reported cases of maltreatment of children from 1980 to 1989 (Gelles & Conte, 1990; National Center on Child Abuse and Neglect, 1988), a 58% increase in physical abuse, and more than a tripling of sexual abuse. However, Straus and Gelles (1986) found a 47% decline in parents' self-report of very severe violence between 1975 and 1985 against children living with both parents. It is unclear what combination of increase in reporting of abuse to authorities, increase in incidence, and decrease in parents' willingness to report severe mistreatment has occurred in the past decade. To the extent that there has been a genuine increase in child maltreatment, the factors that account for it may include the changing roles of men and women in the family and difficulties negotiating them and adjusting to them, divorce and single parenting, stepfamilies and people living together without blood ties, the decrease in felt obligation toward children, and changing societal norms and the greater acceptance of aggression.

In genocidal societies mistreatment and violence against victims result in changes in the personality of individuals, in social norms, and in the behavior of bystanders. They also lead to the creation of institutions that propagate violence (Staub, 1989). We may be witnessing a similar phenomenon in the United States: different types of violence, both symbolic and real, without a particular target group, join to create progressive change in society's standards and institutions. This has contributed to the development of more violent persons and to the acceptance of violence and passivity by bystanders and by society as a whole.

Subculture of Violence

This is a concept that has been used to describe subgroups of society in which (usually due to poverty, unemployment, and discrimination) violence has become acceptable, and even valued or required. The vulnerability created by such conditions may lead to the development of cultures in which people, especially men (Sanday, 1981), need to create a feeling and image of invulnerability and strength. Recently such subcultures have expanded to include many schools. With increases in drug use and drug dealing, subcultures of drug-related violence have developed.

The lack of structure and order in their neighborhoods, the insecurity created, and the intimate closeness to violence that occurs in front of their eyes can have profound effects on youth. It can desensitize them to violence and reduce emotional responsiveness in general. This can reduce their concerns about others' lives or deaths as well as their own.

Gangs are aspects of these subcultures and contribute to youth violence. Presumably gangs fulfill important needs that are not fulfilled in the family or school, including the needs for connection and identity formation (Staub & Rosenthal, 1995). Gangs develop their own standards and values, which are often in opposition to the traditional values of society. When they become prevalent in a neighborhood, the need for security becomes another reason for joining them (Prothrow-Stith, 1991).

There can be many deeply rooted subcultural origins of violence as well. In the southern United States, especially in certain regions, violence in response to insult and as a form of protection has been much higher than in the rest of the country (Nisbett, 1993). Nisbett suggests that it is especially high in traditional herding areas of the South and proposes as its origin the vulnerability of the herd to theft and the need to protect it.

REVERSING THE TREND: LOVING CHILDREN AND HEALING THEIR TRAUMAS

What can we do to increase positive socialization of children by parents —and by schools?

Parent Training

Providing parents with knowledge about children and improved skills in rearing them can bring about a number of benefits, like changed assumptions about children, greater self-assurance about setting standards and guiding children, and the willingness and ability to use positive discipline.

Early Intervention Programs

These have been designed to prepare children from disadvantaged populations for school. However, in addition to contributing to school success they have social benefits such as reducing delinquency (Ziegler et al., 1992). This may be partly due to children's increased ability to participate in school life and greater connection to school. However, effective intervention programs also involve parents. The direct and incidental training as well as support that parents receive may increase nurturance and positive guidance by them and decrease hostility and abuse.

Caring Schools

The school environment can provide affection and nurturance and to some extent counteract neglect and hostility in the home. Early day care can to some degree balance negative relations to parents. The attachment classification of infants to parents and to caretakers in day care are independent of each other (Scarr & Eisenberg, 1993). Children with insecure attachment at home can benefit from secure attachment to caregivers. Good quality child care promotes the development of children from stressed, disadvantaged, dysfunctional homes (Scarr & Eisenberg, 1993).

Teachers can use positive socialization practices, such as affection, reasoning, guidance, and positive discipline (Staub, 1979, 1981, 1989). They can help children learn responsibility to others and a sense of their own value, for example, by involving them in creating rules for the classroom. They can create a community that includes all children, including potentially marginal ones. Shared responsibilities, from taking care of pets to collecting money for charity, can be used for community building. Teachers can involve children in activities that benefit others within the classroom or school, or guide them to engage in such activities in the community.

Cooperative learning techniques (Deutsch, 1993; Johnson, Maruyama, Johnson, Nelson, & Skon, 1981) can be introduced as one avenue for creating cross-cutting relations (Deutsch, 1973; Staub, 1988, 1989), that is, deep engagement with each other of children from different racial, ethnic, or religious groups. This diminishes the differentiation of "us" and "them," the devaluation and prejudice that can lead to violence. Schools can invite parents to join in furthering school efforts to develop caring, positive identity and reduce aggression. An alliance with the school and other parents can provide valuable support and community to many parents.

Changing Conditions in the Parents' Lives

Social programs that improve parents' lives can improve their parenting. Greater economic security can reduce violence, especially by single parents (Gelles, 1981). When the conditions of mothers' lives change, the attachment classifications of infants change, with improved conditions creating more secure attachment (Sroufe, 1979). Providing parents with social support through community building can also be expected to improve parenting.

Create Awareness of People's Role as Bystanders

In the case of group violence like genocide or mass killing, the passivity of bystanders affirms the perpetrators and contributes to the evolution of greater violence (Staub, 1989). In the case of violence against children or sexual abuse, the passivity of the other parent, relatives, teachers, and at times of strangers allows its continuation and evolution.

Mothers at least sometimes know about father-daughter incest (Scott & Flowers, 1988) and often have the opportunity to know, but their own needs lead them to close their eyes to it (Staub, 1991a), which enhances the trauma (Browne & Finkelhor 1986). Bystanders can affect the behavior of other bystanders, and even of perpetrators, by what they do (Hallie, 1979; Latane and Darley, 1970) and by what they say (Staub, 1974). Information can create awareness in people that the other parent, a family member, a stranger, or even an adolescent peer has the potential to exert influence and diminish hostile behavior against and promote respect for children and youth. Respect for the rights of parents may be one inhibitor of such intervention. Changing societal values and laws have begun to eliminate the right to harm children.

Helping Abused, Traumatized Children Heal

Since victims often become perpetrators, it is important to help abused and traumatized children and youth deal with their trauma, not only for their own sake, so that they lead better lives, but also for the sake of their children and the quality of community life. When traumatized children and adolescents are identified, therapists, teachers, and others can help them experience empathy with themselves and help them learn that children who are victimized are not bad people but innocent victims, and that not all people are victimizers.

With aggressive adolescents, caring adults need to be persistently accepting but not naíve, aware of the manipulative maneuvers many of them have acquired. They must also be able to exercise control and provide guidance (Staub, 1971).

Positive connections to other people and feeling cared about are essential to inhibit the development of aggressiveness. When affective ties to parents do not develop or are broken early in life, relationships with caring adults (Garmezy & Rutter, 1983) or connections to other children (Freud and Dann, 1951) can create human ties that are the basis for caring about others' welfare. Children or youth caring for or teaching younger kids (Staub, 1975, 1979; Whiting & Edwards, 1988) can be another means for creating human ties.

CONCLUSION

This article has focussed on familial sources of helpful versus aggressive behavior in children and youth and on social-cultural influences on parents and families that contribute to parental behavior and family functioning that lead to aggression. It has not explored in detail the origins and role of violence in neighborhoods and the peer culture. These also require attention. Learning and personal evolution are continuous. Even if the origins of caring and helping (and hostility and aggression) are rooted in the family, interactions with peers and the environment contribute to a continuing evolution that shapes the personality and behavior of children, youth, and adults.

REFERENCES

Agnew, R. (1990). The origins of delinquent events: An examination of offender accounts. *Journal of Research in Crime and Delinquency, 27,* 267–294.

Bandura, A., & Walters, R. H. (1959). *Adolescent aggression: A study of the influence of child training practices and family interrelationship.* New York: Ronald Press.

Bandura, A. (1986). *Social foundations of thought and action: A social cognitive theory.* Englewood Cliffs, NJ: Prentice-Hall.

Bandura, A., & Cervone, D. (1983). Self-evaluative and self-efficacy mechanisms governing the motivational effects of goal systems. *Journal of Personality and Social Psychology, 45,* 1017–1028.

Batson, C. D. (1990). How social an animal? The human capacity for caring. *American Psychologist, 45,* 336–347.

Baumeister, R. F. (1992). *Meanings of life.* New York: Guilford.

Baumeister, R. F., Chesner, S. P., Senders, P. S., & Tice, D. M. (1988). Who's in charge here? Group leaders do lend help in emergencies. *Personality and Social Psychology Bulletin, 14,* 17–22.

Baumrind, D. (1967). Child care practices anteceding three patterns of preschool behavior. *Genetic Psychological Monographs, 75,* 43–88.

Baumrind, D. (1971). Current patterns of parental authority. *Developmental Psychology, 4,* 1–101.

Baumrind, D. (1975). *Early socialization and the discipline controversy.* Morristown, NJ: General Learning Press.

Bellah, P. N., Madsen, R., Sullivan, W. M., Swindler, A., & Lipton, S. M. (1985). *Habits of the heart: Individualism and commitment in american life.* New York: Harper & Row.

Belsky, L., & Vondra, L. (1992). Lessons from child abuse: The determinants of parenting. In Cichetti, D. and Carlson, V. (Eds.), *Child maltreatment.* New York: Cambridge University Press.

Boone, S. L. (1991). Aggression in African-American boys: A discriminant analysis. *Genetic, Social, and General Psychology Monographs, 117*(2), 203–228.

Bowlby, J. B. (1980). *Attachment and loss: Vol. 3, Loss, sadness and depression.* New York: Basic Books.

Browne, A., & Finkelhor, D. (1986). Impact of child sexual abuse: A review of the research. *Psychological Bullentin, 99*(1), 66–77.

Buss, A. H. (1966). The effect of harm on subsequent aggression. *Journal of Experimental Research in Personality, 1,* 249–255.

Buss, A. H. (1971). Aggression pays. In J. L. Singer (Ed.), *The control of aggression and violence.* New York: Academic Press.

Coopersmith, S. (1967). *Antecedents of self-esteem.* San Francisco, CA: Fremont.

Copeland, A. (1974). Violent black gangs: Psycho-and sociodynamics. *Adolescent Psychiatry, 3,* 340–353.

Deutsch, M. (1973). *The Resolution of Conflict: Constructive and Destructive Processes.* New Haven, CT: Yale University Press.

Deutsch, M. (1993). Educating for a peaceful world. *American Psychologist, 48,* 510–517.

DiLalla, L. F., Mitchell, C. M., Arthur, M. W. & Pagliococca, P. M. (1988). Aggression and delinquency: Family and environmental factors. *Journal of Youth and Adolescence, 73,* 233–246.

Dodge, K. A. (1993). Social cognitive mechanisms in the development of conduct disorder and depression. *Annual Review of Psychology, 44,* 559–584.

Dodge, K. A., Bates, J. E., & Pettit, G. S. (1990). Mechanisms in the cycle of violence. *Science, 250,* 1678–1683.

Dodge, K. A., & Frame, C. L. (1982). Social cognitive biases and deficits in aggressive boys. *Child Development, 53,* 620–635.

Eisenberg, N. (1992). *The caring child.* Cambridge, MA: Harvard University Press.

Elder, G. H., Jr., & Caspi, A. (1985). Economic stress in lives: Developmental perspectives. *Journal of Social Issues, 44,* (4), 25–45.

Eron, L. D., Walder, L. O., & Lefkowitz, M. N. (1971). *Learning of aggression in children.* Boston: Little, Brown.

Etcheson, C. (1984). *The rise and demise of democratic Kampuchea.* Boulder, CO: Westview Press.

Feinberg, J. K. (1978). *Anatomy of a Helping Situation: Some Personality and Situational Determinants of helping in a conflict situation involving another's psychological distress.* Unpublished doctoral dissertation, University of Massachusetts, Amherst.

Finkelhor, D. (1979). *Sexually victimized children.* New York: The Free Press.

Friedrich, L. K., & Stein, A. H. (1973). Aggressive and prosocial television programs and the natural behavior of preschool children. *Monographs of the Society for Research in Child Development, 38* (4), (Serial No. 151).

Freud, A., & Dann, S. (1951). An experiment in group upbringing. In R. Eissler et al. (Eds.), *The Psychoanalytic Study of the Child,* Vol.6. New York: International University Press.

Garbarino, J., Dubrow, N., Kostelny, K., & Pardo, C. (1992). *Children in Danger.* San Francisco, CA: Jossey-Bass.

Garmezy, N., & Rutter, M. (1983). *Stress, coping, and development in children.* New York: McGraw-Hill.

Gelles, R. J. (1981). Child abuse and violence in single parent families: Parent absence and economic deprivation. *American Journal of Orthopsychiatry, 59,* 492–502.

Gelles, R. J., & Conte, J. R. (1990). Domestic violence and sexual abuse of children: A review of research in the Eighties. *Journal of Marriage and the Family, 52,* 1045–1058.

Gibbs, N. C. (1989). Wilding in the night. *Time,* May 8, pp. 20–21.

Gillooly, D., & Bond, T. (1976). Assaults with explosive devices on superiors. *Military Medicine, 141* (10), 700–702.

Goldstein, J. H., Davis, R. W., & Herman, D. (1975). Escalation of aggression: Experimental studies. *Journal of Personality and Social Psychology, 31,* 162–170.

Greven, P. (1991). *Spare the Child: The religious roots of punishment and the impact of physical abuse*. New York: Alfred A. Knopf.

Grodman, S. M. (1979). *The role of personality and situational variables in responding to and Helping an individual in psychological distress*. Unpublished doctoral dissertation, University of Massachusetts, Amherst.

Grusec, J. E. (1982). The socialization of altruism. In N. Eisenberg (Ed.), *The development of prosocial behavior* (pp. 139–166). New York: Academic Press.

Grusec, J. E., Kuczynski, L., Rushton, J. P., & Simutis, Z. M. (1978). Modeling, direct instruction, and attributions: Effects on altruism. *Developmental Psychology, 14*, 51–57.

Hallie, P. P. (1979). *Lest innocent blood be shed: The story of the village of Le Chambon, and how goodness happened there*. New York: Harper & Row.

Hammond, R., & Yung, B. (1991). Preventing violence in at risk African-American youth. *Journal of Health Care for the Poor and Undeserved, 2*, 359–373.

Harris, M. B. (1972). The effects of performing one altruistic act on the likelihood of performing another. *Journal of Social Psychology, 88*, 65–73.

Hartup, W. W. (1970). Peer interaction and social organization. In P. H. Mussen (Ed.), *Carmichael's manual of child psychology*. New York: Wiley.

Health, L., Krutt Schnitt, C., & Ward, D. (1986). Television and violent criminal behavior: Beyond the Bobo doll. *Violence & Victims, 1*, 177–190.

Herman, J. L., & Hirschman, L. (1981). *Father-daughter incest*. Cambridge, MA: Harvard University Press.

Hoffman, M. L. (1970a). Conscience, personality, and socialization technique. *Human Development, 13*, 90–126.

Hoffman, M. L. (1970b). Moral development. In P. H. Mussen (Ed.), *Carmichael's manual of child development*. New York: Wiley.

Hoffman, M. L. (1975a). Altruistic behavior and the parent-child relationship. *Journal of Personality and Social Psychology, 31*, 937–943.

Hoffman, M. L. (1975b). Developmental synthesis of affect and cognition and its implications for altruistic motivation. *Developmental Psychology, 11*, 607–622.

Huesmann, L. R., & Eron, L. D. (1984). Cognitive processes and the persistence of aggressive behavior. *Aggressive Behavior, 10*, 243–251.

Huesmann, L. R., Eron, L. D., Lefkowitz, M. M., & Walder, L. O. (1984). Stability of aggression over time and generations. *Developmental Psychology, 20*(6), 1120–1134.

Janoff-Bulman, R. (1992). *Shattered assumptions*. New York: The Free Press.

Johnson, D. W., Maruyama, G., Johnson, R., Nelson, D., & Skon, L. (1981). The effects of cooperative, competitive and individualistic goal structures on achievement: A meta analysis. *Psychological Bulletin, 89*, 47–62.

Kaufman, J., & Zigler, E. (1987). Do abused children become abusive parents? *American Journal of Orthopsychiatry, 57*, 186–192.

Keogh, T. (1993, January/February). Children without a conscience. *New York Age Journal*.

Kinard, E. M. (1979). The psychological consequences of abuse for the child. *Journal of Social Issues, 35*(2), 82–100.

Kohlberg, L., & Candee, L. (1984). The relationship of moral judgment to moral action. In W. M. Kurtines, & J. L. Gewirtz (Eds.), *Morality, moral behavior, and moral development* (pp. 52–73). New York: Wiley-Interscience.

Latane, B., & Darley, J. (1970). *The unresponsive bystander: Why doesn't he help?* New York: Appleton-Crofts.

Lefcourt, H. M. (1976). *Locus of control: Current trends in theory and research.* Hillsdale, NJ: Lawrence Erlbaum.

Lefkowitz, M. M., Eron, C. D., Walder, L. O. & Heussmann, L. R. (1977). *Growing up violent.* New York: Pergamon Press.

Lewis, D. O., Mallouh, C., & Webb, V. (1989). Child abuse, delinquency, and violent criminality. In D. Cicchetti & V. Carlson (Eds.), *Child maltreatment: Theory and research on the causes and consequences of child abuse and neglect.* New York: Cambridge University Press.

McCord, J. (1988). Parental behavior in the cycle of aggression. *Psychiatry, 51,* 14–23.

Miller, A. (1983). *For your own good: Hidden cruelty in child-rearing and the roots of violence.* New York: Farrar, Straus, and Giroux.

Milner, J. S., Robertson, K. R., & Rogers, D. L. (1990). Childhood history of abuse and adult child abuse potential. *Journal of Family Violence, 5,* 15–34.

Morgan, H. (1993). *Spouse abuse.* Unpublished doctoral dissertation, University of Massachusetts, Amherst.

National Center on Child Abuse and Neglect. (1988). *Study findings: Study of national incidence and prevalence of child abuse and neglect.* Washington, DC: U.S. Department of Health and Human Services.

National Center for Health Statistics. (1992). Unpublished data tables from the NCHS Mortality Tapes, FBI-SHR, Atlanta, GA: Centers for Disease Control.

Newman, D. E. (1974). The personality of violence: Conversations with protagonists. *Mental Health and Society, 1,*(5–6), 328–344.

Nisbett, R. E. (1993). Violence and U.S. regional culture. *American Psychologist, 48,* 441–450.

Offer, D., Marohn, R. C., & Ostrov, E. (1975). Violence among hospitalized delinquents. *Archives of General Psychiatry, 32*(9), 1180–1186.

Oliner, S. B., & Oliner, P. (1988). *The altruistic personality: Rescuers of Jews in Nazi Europe.* New York: The Free Press.

Olweus, D. (1979). Stability and aggressive reaction patterns in males: A review. *Psychological Bulletin, 86,* 852–875.

Patterson, G. R. (1982). *Coercive family processes.* Eugene, OR: Castilia Press.

Patterson, G. R. (1986). Performance models for antisocial boys. *American Psychologist, 41,* 432–444.

Patterson, G. R., Littman, R. A., & Bricker, W. (1967). Assertive behavior in children: A step toward a theory of aggression. *Monographs of the Society for Research in Child Development, 32* (Serial No. 113).

Prothrow-Stith, D. (1991). *Deadly consequences: How violence is destroying our teenage population and a plan to begin solving the problem.* New York: Harper Collins.

Radke-Yarrow, M. R., Zahn-Waxler, C., & Chapman, M. (1984). Children's prosocial dispositions and behavior. In P. H. Mussen (Ed.), *Carmichael's manual of child psychology,* 4th ed. (vol. 4, pp. 469–545). New York: Wiley.

Rausch, H. (1965). Interaction sequences. *Journal of Personality and Social Psychology, 2,* 487–499.

Rodriguez, J. (1990). Childhood injuries in the United States. *American Journal of Diseases of Childhood, 144,* 627–646.

Rosenhan, D. (1970). The natural socialization of altruistic autonomy. In J. Maesuley and L. Berkowitz (Eds.), *Altruism and Helping behavior.* New York: Academic Press.

Sanday, P. R. (1981). The socio-cultural context of rape: A cross-cultural study. *Journal of Social Issues, 37,* 5–27.

Scarr, S., & Eisenberg, M. (1993). Child care research issues, perspectives, and results. *Annual Review of Psychology, 44,* 613–644.

Scheidlinger, S. (1992). *On adolescent violence: Some preliminary group process observations.* Unpublished manuscript on file with the author, Albert Einstein College of Medicine, Bronx, NY.

Scott, R. L., & Flowers, J. V. (1988). Betrayal by the mother as a factor contributing to psychological disturbance in victims of father-daughter incest: An MMPI analysis. *Journal of Social and Clinical Psychology, 6*(1), 147–154.

Shaffer, D. R. (1988). *Social and personality development.* Monterey, CA: Brooks-Cole.

Sroufe, L. A. (1979). The coherence of individual development: Early care, attachment, and subsequent developmental issues. *American Psychologist, 34,* 834–842.

Staub, E. (1970). A child in distress: The effects of focusing responsibility on children on their attempts to help. *Developmental Psychology, 2,* 152–154.

Staub, E. (1971). The learning and unlearning of aggression: The role of anxiety, empathy, efficacy and prosocial values. In J. Singer (Ed.), *The control of aggression and violence: Cognitive and physiological factors.* New York: Academic Press.

Staub, E. (1974). Helping a distressed person: Social, personality and stimulus determinants. In L. Berkowitz (Ed.), *Advances in experimental social psychology* (Vol. 7). New York: Academic Press.

Staub, E. (1975). To rear a prosocial child: Reasoning, learning by doing, and learning by teaching others. In D. DePalma, & J. Folley (Eds.), *Moral development: Current theory and research.* Hillsdale, NJ: Erlbaum.

Staub, E. (1978). *Positive social behavior and morality: Social and personal influences,* Vol. 1. New York: Academic Press.

Staub, E. (1979). *Positive social behavior and morality: Socialization and development,* Vol. 2. New York: Academic Press.

Staub, E. (1981). Promoting positive behavior in schools, in other educational settings, and in the home. In J. P. Rushton & R. M. Sorrentino (Eds.), *Altruism and helping behavior.* Hillsdale, NJ: Erlbaum.

Staub, E. (1986). A conception of the determinants and development of altruism and aggression: Motives, the self, the environment. In C. Zahn-Waxler (Ed.), *Altruism and Aggression: Social and Biological origins.* Cambridge, MA: Cambridge University Press.

Staub, E. (1988). The evolution of caring and nonaggressive persons and societies. *Journal of Social Issues, 44*(2), 81–100.

Staub, E. (1989). *The Roots of Evil: The Origins of Genocide and Other Group Violence.* New York: Cambridge University Press.

Staub, E. (1991a). Psychological and cultural origins of extreme destructiveness and extreme altruism. In W. Kurtines & J. Gewirtz (Eds.), *The Handbook of Moral Behavior and Development.* Hillsdale, NJ: Lawrence Erlbaum Associates.

Staub, E. (1991b). Values and helping. Unpublished manuscript on file with the author, University of Massachusetts, Amherst.

Staub, E. (1992). The origins of caring, helping and nonaggression: Parental socialization, the family system, schools, and cultural influence. In S. Oliner & P. Oliner et al. (Eds.), *Embracing the other: Philosophical, Psychological and Historical Perspectives on altruism.* New York: New York University Press.

Staub, E. (1993a). Bystanders, perpetrators and heroic helpers. *International Journal of Intercultural Relations, 17,* 315–341.

Staub, E. (1993b). Individual and group selves, motivation and morality. In T. Wren & G. Noam (Eds.), *Morality and the self.* Cambridge: MIT Press.

Staub, E. (1995). The cultural-societal roots of violence: The examples of genocidal violence and of contemporary youth violence in the United States. *American Psychologist, 51,* 117–133.

Staub, E. & Feinberg, H. (1980). Regularities in peer interaction, empathy, and sensitivity to others. Presented at the symposium Development of Prosocial Behavior and Cognitions. American Psychological Association meeting, Montreal.

Staub, E., & Rosenthal, L. (1995). Mob violence: Social-cultural influences, group processes and participants. In *Summary report of the American psychological association's commission on violence and youth,* Vol. 2. Washington, DC: American Psychological Association.

Steinberg, M. D. & Dodge, K. A. (1987). Attributional bias in aggressive adolescent boys and girls. *Journal of Social Clinical Psychology, 1,* 312–321.

Stone, L. (1977). *The family, sex and marriage in England, 1500–1800.* New York: Harper & Row.

Strauss, M., & Gelles, R. F. (1986). Societal change and change in family violence from 1975 to 1985 as revealed in two national surveys. *Journal of Marriage and the Family, 48,* 465–479.

Strauss, M. A., Gelles, R. J., & Steinmetz, S. K. (1980). *Behind closed doors: Violence in the American family.* Garden City, NY: Anchor Press/Doubleday.

Stromquist, V. J., & Strauman, T. J. (1992). Children's social constructs: Nature, assessment, and association with adaptive and maladaptive behavior. *Social Cognition, 9,* 330–358.

Summary Report of the American Psychological Association's Commission on Violence and Youth. (1993). *Violence and youth: Vol. 1, Psychology's response.* Washington, DC: American Psychological Association.

Tajfel, H. (1982). Social psychology of intergroup relations. *Annual Review of Psychology, 33,* 1–39.

Tec, N. (1986). *When light pierced the darkness: Christian rescue of Jews in Nazi-occupied Poland.* New York: Oxford University Press.

Theiss, A. (1985). Self-esteem and attitudes towards violence: A theory about violent individuals. Dissertation paper presented at the University of Massachusetts, Amherst.

Thompson, W. R., & Grusec, J. (1970). Studies of early experience. In P. H. Mussen (Ed.), *Carmichael's manual of child psychology,* 3rd ed. (Vol. 2). New York: Wiley.

Toch, H. (1969). *Violent men.* Chicago, IL: Aldine.

Troy, M., & Sroufe, A. (1987). Victimization among preschoolers: Role of attachment relationships. *Child and Adolescent Psychiatry, 26,* 166–172.

Vissing, Y. M., Straus, M. A., Gelles, R. J. & Harrop, J. W. (1991). Verbal aggression by parents and psychosocial problems of children. *Child Abuse and Neglect, 15,* 223–235.

Waters, E., Wippmann, J., & Sroufe, L. A. (1979). Attachment, positive affect, and competence in the peer group: Two studies in construct validation. *Child Development, 50,* 821–829.

Weiss, B., Dodge, K. A., Bates, S. E., & Pettit, G. S. (1992). Some consequences of early harsh discipline: Child aggression and a maladaptive social information processing style. *Child Development, 63,* 1328–1333.

Werner, E. E. (1987). Vulnerability and resiliency in children at risk for delinquency: A longitudinal study from birth to young adulthood. In J. D. Burchard & S. N. Burchard (Eds.), *Primary prevention of psychopathology, 10,* Prevention of delinquent behavior (pp. 16–43). Newbury Park, CA: Sage.

Whiting, B. B., & Edwards, C. P. (1988). *Children of different worlds: The formation of Social Behavior.* Cambridge, MA: Harvard University Press.

Whiting, J. W. M., and Whiting, B. (1975). *Children of six cultures.* Cambridge, MA: Harvard University Press.

Widom, C. S. (1989a). Does violence beget violence? A critical examination of the literature. *Psychological Bulletin, 106*(1), 3–28.

Widom, C. S. (1989b). The cycle of violence. *Science, 224,* 160–166.

Wilson, J. Q., & Herrnstein, R. J. (1985). *Crime and Human Nature.* New York: Simon and Schuster.

Wilson, W. J. (1987). *The truly Disadvantaged: The inner city, the Underclass and Public policy.* Chicago: University of Chicago Press.

Yarrow, M. R. & Scott, P. M. (1972). Limitation of nurturant and non-nurturant models. *Journal of Personality and Social Psychology, 8,* 240–261.

Youngblade, L. M., & Belsky, J. (1990). Social and emotional consequences of child maltreatment. In R. T. Ammerman, & M. Hersen (Eds.), *Children at risk: An evaluation of factors contributing to child abuse and neglect.* New York: Plenum Press.

Zahn-Waxler, C., Cummings, R. & Ianoppi, P. (Ed.)(1986). *Altruism and aggression: Social and biological origins.* Cambridge, England: Cambridge University Press (in press).

Ziegler, E., Taussig, C., & Block, K. (1992). Early childhood intervention: A promising preventive for juvenile delinquency, *American Psychologist, 47* 997–1006.

3 | ADVERSITY IN ADULTHOOD

7 ADULT SURVIVORS OF CHILDHOOD SEXUAL ABUSE

Diagnostic and Treatment Challenges

Richard P. Halgin and Jeanine M. Vivona

During the past decade, we have been bombarded with accounts of the sexual abuse of children. Public awareness of the magnitude of the problem of child sexual abuse heightened during the 1980s, due in part to publicity surrounding one of the longest and most expensive criminal trials in U.S. history—the McMartin Preschool trial in California. In 1984, seven people connected with the McMartin school were indicted on charges of sexual molestation of as many as 100 children, some as young as 2 years of age, over a 10-year period. Other alarming accounts of child sexual abuse have been widely publicized as well. One startling retrospective account involved Richard Berendzen, former president of American University. Following his arrest in 1990 for making "obscene" telephone calls from his university office, Berendzen explained his shocking behavior as a result of a long history of sexual abuse perpetrated by his psychotic mother; his telephone calls to day care workers inquiring about sexual practices with children become more understandable in light of Berendzen's early experiences. In his recent book, *Come Here,* he relates, in pained autobiographical detail, his journey from the "middle bedroom" of the family home, where he was repeatedly sexually abused, to his arrest and precipitous decline, a prominent and respected professional forced to the brink of suicide.

Such personal accounts of childhood sexual abuse have become all too common; we are no longer stunned when celebrities and public figures step forward to share secrets they had hidden, sometimes from themselves as well as from others, for decades. Increasingly, survivors report memories of childhood sexual abuse that they had forgotten, or repressed, only to be recovered many years later, often during the course of therapy. Two highly publicized examples of the repression of sexual abuse memories involve Roseanne Barr and former Miss America Marilyn Van Derbur, both of whom retrieved memories of extensive childhood incest that they had repressed until adulthood. Despite a growing number of accounts of repressed and recovered childhood sexual abuse memories, however, the veracity of such memories is the subject of contentious debate among mental health and legal professionals. Recently, the controversy has been fueled by a few widely publicized court cases brought against psychotherapists by clients and, more commonly, their families; these cases allege that false sexual abuse memories are "implanted" by therapists, who then encourage clients to charge their parents or other trusted adults with sexual abuse, wreaking havoc on significant relationships and irrevocably tarnishing reputations.

As a society, we have become increasingly aware that some children are subjected to traumatic and abusive experiences that were regarded as unspeakable, if not inconceivable, only decades ago. Through the social service system and public education, we have taken steps to prevent the occurrence of such tragedies and have developed interventions with victimized children and adult survivors to ameliorate both the immediate suffering and the long-lasting effects of childhood sexual abuse. With the current controversy raging over repressed memories of childhood sexual abuse, however, well-established treatment techniques with adult survivors have come under fire. In this chapter, we discuss the prevalence of childhood sexual abuse and its common sequelae in adulthood. We outline therapeutic strategies for intervening with adults who were sexually abused as children, with particular emphasis on the treatment challenges presented by the repression of childhood sexual abuse memories.

PREVALENCE OF CHILDHOOD SEXUAL ABUSE

Methodological problems in determining the prevalence and long-term effects of childhood sexual abuse are legion. Central to these difficulties is the fact that the definition of sexual abuse varies from one study to the next. For example, some investigators consider a range of coercive sexual experiences, while others focus primarily on invasive sexual acts, particularly intercourse. Furthermore, researchers who investigate the impact of childhood abuse in adults must negotiate challenges presented by the repression of abuse memories, the vagaries of retrospection, and the difficulty of separating out the deleterious effects of the abuse itself from the impact of other family characteristics that may have left scars (Dempster & Roberts, 1991; Schetky, 1990). Nevertheless, some shocking statistics are commonly accepted by professionals in the field. Russell (1986) studied a community sample of 930 women in San Francisco and found that 16% of her sample reported having had at least one incestuous experience during childhood. Briere (1992) summarized two additional studies of childhood sexual abuse in females (Finkelhor, Hotaling, Lewis, & Smith, 1989; Wyatt, 1985) and concluded that between 20% and 30% of the women studied had experienced sexual contact, ranging from fondling to intercourse, with someone at least five years older than herself before the age of 13.

The statistics for males are lower, but still striking, with the prevalence of childhood sexual abuse experiences in men ranging from 10%–15% (Finkelhor, 1979; Finkelhor et al., 1989). This gender difference in the prevalence of childhood sexual abuse experiences may be explained in part by the fact that boys are less likely to be victims of incest than are girls (Finkelhor, 1990). However, although boys and girls are subjected to different types of sexual abuse, the long-term impact of child abuse in adulthood seems surprisingly similar for men and women (Finkelhor, 1990).

CLINICAL PRESENTATION OF ADULT SURVIVORS

The prevalence of childhood sexual abuse among adults presenting for mental health services has been estimated at between 36% and 70% (see Briere, 1992, for a review); thus psychotherapists must be familiar with the clinical presentation of sexual abuse survivors. A wide range of disturbance has been reported in adults who have experienced childhood sexual abuse, although each individual presents a unique amalgam of strengths and difficulties. The most common difficulties experienced by childhood sexual abuse survivors include symptoms of posttraumatic stress, dissociation, cognitive distortions, affective disturbances, an impaired sense of self, avoidance behaviors, and troubled interpersonal relationships.

Posttraumatic stress disorder (PTSD) has received increased attention in the years since the Vietnam war. People with posttraumatic reactions continually reexperience past traumas, despite desperate efforts to forget them. They suffer from a variety of physiological symptoms of anxiety, including trembling, sleep disturbance, and hypersensitivity. Psychological symptoms include intrusions into one's thoughts, dreams, and emotions. Daytime thoughts may be disrupted by horrifying flashbacks of the traumatic event; sleep may be contaminated by terrifying nightmares. Many adults who were sexually abused as children manifest PTSD features, particularly intrusive symptoms such as sensory flashbacks and nightmares. In fact, some experts consider PTSD to be the most appropriate diagnostic framework from which to consider the sequelae of childhood sexual trauma in adults (e.g., McCann & Pearlman, 1990; van der Kolk, 1987).

Also evident among some adult survivors of childhood sexual abuse is dissociation (Briere, 1992; Spiegel, 1990), separation of painful memories, thoughts, or feelings from the core of consciousness. Dissociative experiences range from occasional feelings of detachment from one's emotions to complete amnesia for lengthy periods of one's life. For example, a man may complain that he feels detached from others, and that it is difficult to immerse himself in intimate relationships. Or a woman may experience dramatic shifts in her cognitive and emotional state such that she feels and acts like different people at different times. Recently, this latter condition, dissociative identity disorder, has received a vast amount of public and professional attention. It is argued that the overwhelming majority of people with dissociative identity disorder have experienced severe abuse during childhood, often involving physical torture, psychological victimization, or sadistic sexual abuse (Coons et al., 1989; Ross, 1989; Terr, 1991; Wilbur & Kluft, 1989). Other selves, or "alters," develop as a defense against the horror of such trauma, allowing the child to escape into a self-hypnotic state and to create, through fantasy, a happier, safer, or stronger self. When a child uses dissociation successfully to ward off intensely painful feelings, it may become an integral component of his or her defensive structure. Thus, dissociation enables abuse survivors to escape reality, to contain traumatic memories and emotions outside conscious awareness, to detach from the abuse experiences so that they seem to have happened to someone else, and ultimately to reduce the pain (Putnam, 1989).

The thought processes of abuse survivors may be warped by cognitive distortions that impair their ability to see themselves and others accurately (Fish-Murray, Koby, & van der Kolk, 1987); survivors of sexual abuse may be perplexed about who they are. Bowlby's (1982) classic work on attachment, which highlights the centrality of secure attachment to parental figures to the development of a positive and cohesive sense of self, illuminates the mechanism by which a child abused by parents may develop a self that is fragmented, disorganized, or otherwise inadequate. Furthermore, survivors struggle to understand and incorporate the knowledge that they were sexually abused as children, desperately seeking explanations for inexplicable events. They may be afflicted by guilt, shame, self-blame, self-hatred, and low self-esteem if as children they concluded that they deserved the abuse, that they rather than their abusive parents were the "bad" ones. Self-hatred and self-blame inhibit feelings of potency and autonomy, and survivors may develop a sense of helplessness that sets the stage for subsequent revictimization. Survivors' perceptions of others, forged in the context of their early abuse experiences, may be tainted by a view of people as inevitably rejecting, abandoning, punishing, and cruel.

Depression, a common mood disturbance among survivors of childhood sexual abuse (Beitchman et al., 1992), is certainly associated with the cognitive distortions of self-blame, self-hatred, and helplessness. Exacerbating depression may be feelings of chronic anxiety, manifested by constant worry, and somatic symptoms such as unexplained headaches, stomach pain, nausea, appetite problems, and sleep disturbance.

Escape from psychic pain may become a priority for the adult suffering the effects of childhood sexual abuse; he or she may compulsively seek a soothing ointment to apply to the psychological wound. Abuse survivors attempt to distract themselves from abuse memories in order to attenuate the painful consequences of remembering, to reduce tension, and to restore a sense of control. Drugs or alcohol may provide temporary relief for some. A yearning for comfort and safety may manifest itself as an insatiable sexual appetite, or food may take on heightened significance for the survivor who struggles to satisfy unmet needs for nurturance. Some survivors engage in self-mutilation, perhaps cutting their wrists or scratching their skin, in an attempt to transform psychological into physical pain. In its most extreme form, the desire to escape pain wrought by childhood sexual abuse may lead to suicidal behavior.

Given this diversity of potential disturbances, it is not surprising to find the interpersonal relationships of some adults who have been abused as children to be colored by insecurity, apprehension, and distrust. Intimacy may be an emotionally charged endeavor that is approached with great reservation, if at all; survivors' childhood experiences have prepared them to expect exploitation, violence, or coercion from others, particularly significant others. Because they have intensely negative expectations of relationships and fear they will be exploited by others, survivors may resort to manipulative or adversarial interactions in an attempt to provoke dramatic expressions of concern and affection (Briere, 1992). In some cases, particularly with male survivors, rage may take the form of uncontrollable aggression, possibly resulting in destructive behavior toward others that perpetuates the cycle of abuse.

DIAGNOSTIC CHALLENGES

Clinicians treating survivors of childhood sexual abuse encounter several difficult challenges, the first of which is the problem of accurate diagnosis. As the list of difficulties enumerated above illustrates, the diagnostic features manifested by abuse survivors nearly encompass the spectrum of adult psychopathology; thus any of a number of diagnostic categories may apply for a given client. In fact, "victims [of sexual abuse in childhood] manifest such a large variety of symptoms that there is no single set of symptoms that can be considered characteristic" (Finkelhor, 1990, p. 329), and thus no common diagnostic label can apply uniformly. Clearly, those who present with prominent PTSD or dissociative features should receive the appropriate diagnoses. Furthermore, several possible characteristics of survivors are also associated with borderline personality disorder. In fact, one study of female inpatients found 40% of childhood sexual abuse survivors to be diagnosed with borderline personality disorder (Shearer, Peters, Quaytman, & Ogden, 1990). A clinician working with a borderline client cannot confidently conclude that symptoms are attributable to childhood sexual abuse, however; it is possible, for example, that these result from a personality disorder for which the client carries a genetic predisposition.

THE THERAPEUTIC CHALLENGE OF REPRESSED MEMORY

The prevalence of repressed memories among adult survivors of childhood sexual abuse, estimated to range from 18% to 59% (Loftus, 1993), challenges clinicians to determine the veracity of abuse memories. The traditional view, originating with Sigmund Freud, maintained that reports of childhood sexual experiences reflect fantasy. Interestingly, Freud originally took for truth the childhood sexual experiences revealed by his female analysands, then abandoned his seduction theory, or trauma theory of neurosis, relegating women's memories of childhood sexual exploitation to the realm of fantasy and wish. The surge in reports of childhood sexual abuse experiences during the 1970s and 1980s necessitated a reevaluation of this notion, however, and with feminist theorists leading the charge, clinicians have moved increasingly toward accepting as fact their clients' reports of childhood sexual trauma. Indeed, the uncovering of repressed abuse memories is the foundation of many well-established trauma-centered approaches to therapy (e.g., Briere, 1992; Chu, 1991; McCann & Pearlman, 1990; Sgroi, 1989). Much work with adult survivors involves active recovery and integration of repressed trauma memories and associated affect as a central component of the work, in which sexual abuse experiences may be viewed as the primary etiologic force behind clients' present difficulties (Haaken & Schlaps, 1991).

Some have begun to question, however, whether the pendulum has swung too far. The most strenuous opposition to the widely accepted view that memories of childhood sexual abuse are commonly repressed and recovered has come from the False Memory Syndrome Foundation, an advocacy group for individuals who have been charged with childhood sexual abuse after their alleged adult victims have uncovered repressed abuse memories in therapy. One notable foundation member is Elizabeth Loftus, an experimental psychologist and memory researcher who frequently speaks and writes against repressed memory (e.g., Loftus, 1993). Clearly, this backlash against therapists, fueled by a few highly publicized court cases charging overzealous therapists with unethical implantation of "false" sexual abuse memories (e.g., Loftus, 1993; Wakefield & Underwager, 1992), is a powerful reminder that competent psychotherapists use caution and deference when assessing clients who present for treatment with little memory of or corroborating evidence for childhood sexual abuse, however suggestive the clinical presentation may be of a sexual abuse history.

For very different reasons, some mental health professionals have begun to advocate a reevaluation of treatment approaches centered upon an unremitting search for repressed abuse memories. While many clinicians who work with survivors of sexual abuse (e.g., Briere, 1992; Chu, 1991; Herman, 1992; McCann & Pearlman, 1990) accept that memories of childhood sexual abuse may be repressed, this does not imply consensus regarding treatment strategies for use with adult survivors. For example, some clinicians advocate adoption of active measures, such as hypnosis, to uncover repressed trauma memories (Siegel & Romig, 1990); others assert that because memories surface only once clients are able to assimilate them, such active uncovering techniques are neither necessary nor particularly effective (Briere, 1992; Dinsmore, 1991; Meiselman, 1990; Sgroi, 1989). Furthermore, many clinicians who work with childhood sexual abuse survivors believe a unilateral therapeutic emphasis on recovering and integrating memories of abuse represents an unnecessarily circumscribed treatment focus. Increasingly, therapists embed trauma-specific techniques within integrationist approaches to treatment (Herman, 1992; Schwarz & Prout, 1991); some examples include the use of Ericksonian hypnosis within a systemic paradigm (Olio & Cornell, 1993), and an eclectic amalgam of cognitive-behavioral, psychodynamic, and memory recovering techniques (Briere, 1992; McCann & Pearlman, 1990). Some clinicians argue cogently for an approach that combines traditional psychodynamic techniques involving transference and countertransference interpretations and working through of painful affects with abuse-focused techniques of memory recovery and assimilation. Moreover, Haaken and Schlaps (1991) assert that the client, and not the therapist, should determine the centrality of the abuse experiences to the therapeutic endeavor; they contend that "to urge women along some predetermined path to recovery is to repeat the survivor's experience of self-negation and submission to repressive authority, however wrapped it may be in good therapeutic intentions" (p. 47).

Given these challenges from both within and without the therapeutic community, clinicians who attempt to treat adult survivors of childhood sexual abuse are confronted with a difficult treatment dilemma. The problem is exacerbated by the fact that some clients have no memory of abusive experiences in childhood, although their clinical presentation is suggestive of a trauma history. Increasingly, clients present for therapy with questions about their own repressed abuse history, influenced by the tremendous media attention paid to childhood sexual abuse in recent years, as well as by omnipresent self-help books that attest to the prevalence of both childhood sexual trauma and its repression (e.g., Bass & Davis, 1988). When clients present for therapy with few or questionable specific memories of abuse, a dogged pursuit of repressed abuse memories may not be an appropriate initial treatment strategy. For instance, the experimental research into "false memory" reveals that highly hypnotizable people are likely to report false memories in response to leading questions, whether or not they are under hypnosis (Barnier & McConkey, 1992), although when monetary rewards for accurate reporting of memories are offered, false memory reports decline (Murrey, Cross, & Whipple, 1992). Thus personality characteristics and social context influence the reporting of "memories" of events that did not occur. Memory research, then, may support the hypothesis that some clients may unwittingly elaborate vague memories in response to therapists' questions and statements about their past experiences; this may be particularly likely to occur given the power differential between therapist and client, and the relief a client may experience from obtaining a possible explanation for his or her distress. On the other hand, there is no empirical evidence that memories of traumatic experiences, such as childhood sexual abuse, have been or can be created through the course of psychotherapy (Olio, 1994). There is one point, however, upon which both skeptics of repressed memory (Loftus, 1993; Wakefield & Underwager, 1992) and believers (Briere, 1992; McCann & Pearlman, 1990) agree: allegations of childhood sexual abuse, both actual and fraudulent, are most likely to arise during psychotherapy.

THERAPY WITH SURVIVORS OF CHILDHOOD SEXUAL ABUSE

In defining a treatment approach for abuse survivors, we believe an integrative approach to be eminently sensible. Pragmatic blending (Halgin, 1989) provides a theoretical framework for incorporating divergent techniques into a treatment approach that is responsive to the unique needs of clients. A treatment strategy that incorporates varying degrees of exploratory, directive, supportive, and interpersonal techniques is of particular benefit with adult survivors of childhood sexual abuse. We agree with Briere's (1992) excellent suggestion that clinicians treating survivors adopt a treatment philosophy characterized by a sensitive respect for the inner experience of the client in which his or her current behaviors are viewed as logical, reasonable responses to childhood trauma that have become maladaptive in adulthood. Psychotherapy with abuse survivors, with all clients in fact, involves a combination of covering and uncovering techniques that takes place within a relationship built upon trust and safety. On the one hand, the client learns to contain the trauma and to reduce the disruptive power of intrusive memories. On the other, the desire for cleansing catharsis is addressed through reliving, within the safe context of the therapeutic relationship, the horror of past abusive experiences. Thus, treatment with survivors of childhood sexual abuse involves reintegration of dissociated affects, cognitions, and experiences rather than simple symptom removal.

Exploratory work focuses on helping the survivor to understand how experiences of childhood sexual abuse, as well as other life experiences, exert their influence on thoughts, emotions, behaviors, and relationships in adulthood. Implicit to exploratory and psychodynamic techniques is the utilization of the transference as a basis for elucidating and understanding relationship conflicts, especially those involving caretaking, dependency, trust, blame, guilt, power, and abandonment. Certainly in any psychotherapy, the therapeutic relationship is the principal curative factor. Of critical importance is the maintenance of appropriate boundaries in the therapeutic relationship so that the abuse survivor is assured that therapy will not result in revictimization. Abuse survivors may be especially sensitive to interactions with important persons, particularly those in positions of power. It is not surprising that a handful of disturbed psychotherapists prey sadistically on abuse victims by encouraging dependency, and in extreme cases engaging in unethical exploitation. For these reasons, therapy with abuse survivors must provide a safe place in which the content and the style of the work being conducted are routinely open to discussion. Clients must be respected as autonomous individuals and encouraged to discuss their thoughts and feelings about the therapeutic relationship in an open and uncensored manner, without fear of reprisal.

For uncovering of repressed memories, the therapist can guide the client through verbal and sensory aspects of abuse memories, perhaps using hypnotic techniques or guided imagery. Of course, a procedure that might cause the client to feel a dangerous loss of control should be approached with great caution and preceded by sensitive, detailed discussion. An alternative to techniques such as hypnosis is reliance on the traditional psycho-therapeutic dialogue; such an approach is preferable for the client who is threatened by a possible loss of control. Accompanying the exploration of abuse memories is the working through of the associated painful affects, during which the therapist works to foster healthy, nondissociated feelings through cathartic work. During this process, a supportive therapeutic stance may be particularly effective, as the therapist validates emotional expression while discouraging dissociation. For example, the client can be urged to describe his or her immediate feelings and to try to "stay with" those feelings, while the therapist normalizes the experience of strong feelings. When the goal of treatment is to reduce dissociation and to reintegrate experiences, the client is likely to undergo heightened distress as painful memories and affects are uncovered during treatment.

Clients in crisis may need more than exploration and support; they may need to learn what to do in their everyday lives in order to manage each day without feeling overwhelmed, incapacitated, or inept. In such cases, directive and cognitive behavioral techniques may be most expedient and effective. For example, through cognitive restructuring, clients learn to think and act in ways that are more healthy and fulfilling. They can revise the faulty cognitions they formed in order to adapt to an abusive environment during childhood. In this way, abuse survivors can come to view themselves differently, to realize that they were not responsible for or deserving of sexual abuse in childhood, and to acknowledge that they are not preordained to suffer unrelenting pain throughout adulthood.

Finally, with the current acknowledgment, among mental health professionals and the public alike, that memories of untoward childhood experiences may be repressed for decades, clients may present for therapy without a clear sense of having experienced childhood sexual abuse, and then raise the question of abuse during therapy as a potential explanation for their current difficulties and concerns. An important area for exploration with such a client is the meaning of the question of abuse for him or her. Certainly, many who seek psychotherapy experience significant distress in myriad areas of their lives for which they seek both relief and explanation. Clients who feel passive, helpless, and victimized may search for the basis of their problems in external forces; with the legitimate emphasis on childhood sexual abuse found in the media, it is not surprising that some clients would invite exploration of this question as a means of potentially alleviating their distress. Furthermore, as Chu's (1991) case examples clearly demonstrate, when therapy is viewed as a search for the *cause* of a client's difficulties, locating an external source of distress diverts blame that both client and therapist might otherwise impute to the client. When a client without trauma memories raises the question of a repressed abuse history, the therapist is presented with an important opportunity to explore the meaning of this rich question while taking a neutral stance toward the veracity of the abuse itself. Such exploration may reveal a client's unconscious identification with the victim as a way of coping with disavowed aggression, by the reversal of active into passive (MacGregor, 1991). The client may, consciously or unconsciously, seek revenge, rescue, or absolution for his or her difficulties through adoption of the victim role. Such a search is understandable in light of client difficulties that may be long-standing and debilitating, and must not be construed as an attempt at conscious manipulation of the therapist or the therapeutic situation.

CONCLUSION

The psychotherapist who treats adult survivors of childhood sexual abuse is faced with a number of difficult challenges. Survivors tell us that they find therapy most effective when their disclosed memories of traumatic experiences are validated by the therapist (Armsworth, 1989). Certainly, all aspects of the client's story must be treated with deference; most adult survivors of childhood sexual abuse have experienced skepticism, if not outright rejection, regarding the verity of their abuse memories, and the repetition of this dynamic is undoubtedly countertherapeutic. We certainly do not advocate a return to the victim-blaming that resulted in memories of childhood sexual abuse being habitually construed as fantasy. Nor do we condone an attitude of skepticism or dismissal toward clients' revelations in therapy. We further regard the "base rate" approach suggested by Wakefield and Underwager (1992), which attempts to assess the veracity of clinical material using probabilistic and legalistic means, as shockingly insensitive and likely harmful to clients. Nevertheless, responsible clinicians must remain cognizant of the possibility, however remote, that some clients may unknowingly create "memories" of untoward experiences in childhood, particularly clients who, in the context of the supportive yet authoritative therapeutic relationship, experience desired relief upon finding a possible explanation for their long-standing difficulties and distress.

When a client's abuse memories are vague or the clinical presentation is merely suggestive of abuse, it is the ethical responsibility of the therapist to take a neutral stance toward the veracity of the trauma. Furthermore, it may be important to acknowledge with the client that memories of the past may not be completely recovered (Olio & Cornell, 1993); inaccuracies, reconstructions, and elaborations are a normal part of memory processing (Loftus, 1993). Instead of an assiduous search for repressed memories, a thorough understanding of the meaning of a client's questions concerning abuse experiences and his or her identification with the victim role may be the most responsible approach to treatment. Trust, the foundation upon which the therapeutic relationship is founded, is engendered when the therapist remains empathically attuned to a client's unique needs and strengths; a priori acceptance or rejection of the possibility of childhood sexual abuse with any given client is clearly unacceptable. Regardless of the degree of memory for childhood trauma to which a client has access, the clinician's task remains the same: to facilitate the client's movement beyond feelings of helplessness and shame to the realization of a sense of empowerment, mastery, and control.

REFERENCES

Armsworth, M. W. (1989). Therapy of incest survivors: Abuse or support? *Child Abuse and Neglect, 13,* 549–562.

Barnier, A. J., & McConkey, K. M. (1992). Reports of real and false memories: The relevance of hypnosis, hypnotizability, and context of memory test. *Journal of Abnormal Psychology, 101,* 521–527.

Bass, E., & Davis, L. (1988). *The courage to heal.* New York: Harper & Row.

Beitchman, J. H., Zucker, K. J., Hood, J. E., DaCosta, G. A., Akman, D., & Cassavia, E. (1992). A review of the long-term effects of child sexual abuse. *Child Abuse and Neglect, 16,* 101–118.

Berendzen, Richard. (1993). *Come here.* New York: Villard Books.

Bowlby, J. (1982). *Attachment and loss: Vol. 1, Attachment* (2nd ed.). New York: Basic Books.

Briere, J. N. (1992). *Child abuse trauma.* Newbury Park, CA: Sage Publications.

Chu, J. A. (1991). The repetition compulsion revisited: Reliving dissociated trauma. *Psychotherapy, 28,* 327–332.

Coons, P. M., Bowman, E. S., Pellow, T. A., & Schneider, P. (1989). Post-traumaic aspects of the treatment of victims of sexual abuse and incest. *Psychiatric Clinics of North America, 12,* 325–335.

Dempster, H. L., & Roberts, J. (1991). Child sexual abuse research: A methodological quagmire. *Child Abuse and Neglect, 15,* 593–595.

Dinsmore, C. (1991). *From surviving to thriving: Incest, feminism, and recovery.* Albany, NY: State University of New York Press. Finkelhor, D. (1979). *Sexually victimized children.* New York: The Free Press.

Finkelhor, D. (1990). Early and long-term effects of child sexual abuse: An update. *Professional Psychology: Research and Practice, 21,* 325–330.

Finkelhor, D., Hotaling, G., Lewis, I. A., & Smith, C. (1989). Sexual abuse and its relationship to later sexual satisfaction, marital status, religion, and attitudes. *Journal of Interpersonal Violence, 4,* 379–399.

Fish-Murray, C. C., Koby, E. V., & van der Kolk, B. A. (1987). Evolving ideas: The effect of abuse on children's thought. In B. A. van der Kolk (Ed.), *Psychological trauma* (pp. 89–110). Washington, DC: American Psychiatric Press.

Haaken, J., & Schlaps, A. (1991). Incest resolution therapy and the objectification of sexual abuse. *Psychotherapy, 28,* 39–47.

Halgin, R. P. (1989). Pragmatic blending. *Journal of Integrative and Eclectic Psychotherapy, 8,* 320–328.

Herman, J. L. (1992). *Trauma and recovery.* New York: Basic Books.

Loftus, E. F. (1993). The reality of repressed memories. *American Psychologist, 48,* 518–537.

MacGregor, J. R. (1991). Identification with the victim. *Psychoanalytic Quarterly, 15,* 53–68.

McCann, I. L., & Pearlman, L. A. (1990). *Psychological trauma and the adult survivor.* New York: Brunner/Mazel.

Meiselman, K. C. (1990). *Resolving the trauma of incest: Reintegration therapy with survivors.* San Francisco: Jossey-Bass.

Murrey, G. J., Cross, H. J., & Whipple, J. (1992). Hypnotically created psuedo-memories: Further investigation into the "memory distortion or response bias" question. *Journal of Abnormal Psychology, 101,* 75–77.

Olio, K. A. (1994). Truth in memory. *American Psychologist, 49,* 442–443.

Olio, K. A., & Cornell, W. F. (1993). The therapeutic relationship as the foundation for treatment with adult survivors of sexual abuse. *Psychotherapy, 30,* 512–523.

Putnam, F. W. (1989). *Diagnosis and treatment of multiple personality disorder.* New York: Guilford Press.

Ross, C. A. (1989). *Multiple personality disorder: Diagnosis, clinical features, and treatment.* New York: John Wiley & Sons.

Russell, D. E. H. (1986). *The secret trauma: Incest in the lives of girls and women.* New York: Basic Books.

Schetky, D. H. (1990). A review of the literature on the long-term effects of childhood sexual abuse. In R. P. Kluft (Ed.), *Incest-related syndromes of adult psychopathology* (pp. 35–53). Washington, DC: American Psychiatric Press.

Schwarz, R. A., & Prout, M. F. (1991). Integrative approaches in the treatment of post-traumatic stress disorder. *Psychotherapy, 28,* 364–373.

Sgroi, S. M. (1989). Stages of recovery for adult survivors of child sex abuse. In S. M. Sgroi (Ed.), *Vulnerable populations: sexual abuse treatment for children, adult survivors, offenders and persons with mental retardation* (pp. 111–130). Lexington, MA: Lexington Books.

Shearer, S. L., Peters, C. P., Quaytman, M. S., & Ogden, R. L. (1990). Frequency and correlates of childhood sexual and physical abuse histories in adult female borderline inpatients. *American Journal of Psychiatry, 147,* 214–216.

Siegel, D. R., & Romig, C. A. (1990). Memory retrieval in treating adult survivors of sexual abuse. *American Journal of Family Therapy, 18,* 246–256.

Spiegel, D. (1990). Trauma, dissociation, and hypnosis. In R. P. Kluft (Ed.), *Incest-related syndromes of adult psychopathology* (pp. 247–261). Washington, DC: American Psychiatric Press.

Terr, L. C. (1991). Childhood traumas: An outline and overview. *American Journal of Psychiatry, 148,* 10–20.

van der Kolk, B. A. (1987). The psychological consequences of overwhelming life experiences. In B. A. van der Kolk (Ed.), *Psychological trauma* (pp. 1–30). Washington, DC: American Psychiatric Press.

Wakefield, H., & Underwager, R. (1992). Recovered memories of alleged sexual abuse: Lawsuits against parents. *Behavioral Sciences and the Law, 10,* 483–507.

Wilbur, C. B., & Klutt, R. P. (1989). Multiple personality disorder. In T. B. Karasu (Ed.), *Treatment of psychiatric disorders* (pp. 2197–2216). washington, DC: American Psychiatric Association.

Wyatt, G. E. (1985). The sexual abuse of Afro-American and white American women in childhood. *Child Abuse and Neglect, 9,* 231–240.

8 | ADVERSITY IN THE LIVES OF THE ELDERLY

Susan Krauss Whitbourne, Michelle Jacobo, and Maria-Teresa Muñoz-Ruiz

The elderly are the fastest growing segment of the American population, particularly the "old-old," who are over the age of 85 years. Although improved health and financial security have made the later years of life more comfortable and rewarding for many older Americans, there are nevertheless many elders who experience adversity in their daily lives on an ongoing basis. The experience of adversity is particularly pronounced for those over 85 years of age, who are at higher risk for severe and chronic health problems, poverty, isolation, and institutionalization.

In this chapter, we outline several important sources of adversity in the lives of elderly people, including those that affect the elderly generally and those that affect particular target populations based on age, gender, race, ethnicity, and sexual orientation. These sources of adversity range from the risk of encountering injury through falls, vulnerability to depression, the experience of caregiver burden, elder abuse, and suicide to specific concerns of minority elders and the gay and lesbian elderly community. Although each of these sources of adversity presents a particular challenge to older individuals, many elders are able to cope successfully with these challenges. Our chapter, therefore, ends with a look at some of the forms of coping with adversity used by the fortunate and resourceful individuals referred to by gerontologists as "successful agers."

At the outset of this discussion, it is important to note that gerontologists differentiate between physical and psychological changes in the individual due to what is considered "normal aging" and those changes that are due to disease (Whitbourne, 1996b). Not all sources of adversity are inherent in the aging process so that not all elders are afflicted with diseases such as arteriosclerosis, heart or respiratory disease, cancer, or Alzheimer's. It is also important to recognize that when these diseases occur, they occur against a backdrop of age-related reductions in coping resources associated with the normal aging process. By the same token, by the time they have reached the late 70s and 80s, many older adults have developed an amazing resiliency and repertoire of coping skills. A lifetime of experiences coping with changes in their personal lives, and in their families, communities, and the world at large, gives them the potential to be far more creative and resourceful in managing to overcome adversity than younger individuals whose coping skills have not yet been put to the test.

SOURCES OF ADVERSITY IN LATER LIFE

Falls

There are a number of physical changes associated both with normal aging and disease that create a heightened risk of falling among older adults. When a young person falls, the result may be minor inconvenience or perhaps even painful physical consequences such as a sprained ankle or bruised knee. When an older adult falls, the experience is much more likely to have long-term disabling consequences such as a hip fracture, leaving the individual at risk of enforced dependency, further health problems, and institutionalization.

One way to consider falls as a serious source of adversity is to examine the prevalence of falling in the over-65, community-dwelling population. These estimates range from a low of approximately one-third (Tinetti, Speechley, & Ginter, 1988) to as many as one-half of all older adults (Walker & Howland, 1991). These rates of falling translate into a figure of over 250,000 individuals who are hospitalized each year in the United State for treatment of a fractured hip (Allegrante, MacKenzie, Robbins, & Cornell, 1991). In addition to the need for hospitalization, a fall often has a permanent effect on the older individual's everyday life. If the individual survives the fall and the long-term hospitalization that may follow, physical pain and disability remain enduring problems (Wade, Lindquist, Taylor, & Treat-Jacobson, 1995). Of those who experience a fall, it is estimated that about one-quarter significantly restrict their daily activities to avoid future accidents (Tinetti, et al., 1988).

As impressive as these statistics are, it is nevertheless true that not all older adults are victims of falling. There are a number of risk factors that increase the likelihood of an older adult's suffering a disabling fall. Those elderly who are most at risk of falling include people who suffer from visual impairment, neurological deficits, gait disturbance, and loss of muscle strength and coordination (Lord, Clark, & Webster, 1991; Morse, Tylko, & Dixon, 1987). Cognitive impairments, particularly those associated with

Alzheimer's disease, contribute further to heightened risk of falling (Morris, Rubin, Morris, & Mandel, 1987). Psychological factors, such as anxiety and depression also increase the older individual's risk of falling (Tinetti, Richman, & Powell, 1990). Disability and a history of smoking are two final contributing risk factors (Vetter & Ford, 1989).

The experience of a fall can lead to a vicious cycle in which one fall leads the individual to become fearful of more falls and, as a result, to walk less securely and confidently. This loss of a sense of security can serve to increase the risk that older people will lose their balance and actually make them more likely to fall in the future. The experience of falling can also lead individuals to develop a low "self-efficacy" about themselves as being unable to avoid a fall, further impairing their balance and gait. Apart from the physical risk factors, these psychological variables related to elders' attitudes toward their abilities and sense of security can serve as important contributors to the likelihood of older individuals suffering a fall (Tinetti & Powell, 1993).

Depression

Depression is a serious form of psychological disorder that can afflict the individual at any age in adulthood. Although not necessarily more prevalent among older adults, those who suffer from the feelings of dysphoria that accompany depression experience a form of adversity that places heightened demands on their coping resources. Feelings of depression may also occur in an older individual who is reacting to life circumstances such as poverty, illness, and family difficulties that overwhelm his or her coping capacity. The existence of depression in an older individual may be seen as a reaction to adversity involving distress, a sense of personal failure, and the perception that one's resources are insufficient to meet the demands of a stressful situation. Depression, then, can be seen as a cause of adversity as well as a reaction to specific forms of adversity that may arise in later adulthood.

It is estimated that between one-tenth and one-quarter of the over-65 population report clinically significant symptoms of depression. Major risk factors for depression in old age are the experience of illness and disability (Bruce & McNamara, 1992; Goldstein & Hurwicz, 1989). Depressive feelings of pessimism and hopelessness, for example, are particularly characteristic of Parkinson's disease and arthritis, two highly disabling conditions that are more frequently suffered by the elderly (Gotham, Brown, & Marsden, 1986).

The psychological symptoms of depression are often linked to bodily complaints and other physical conditions that make it difficult to diagnose true cases of depression in the elderly. Not only can illness cause depression, but depression can cause somatic symptoms that resemble those of other illnesses such as appetite or sleep disturbances (Rozzini, Bianchetti, Carabellese, & Inzoli, & Trabucchi, 1988). The older adult suffering from symptoms of depression may find it difficult to seek treatment due to an unwillingness to admit to emotional problems. In fact, only a small minority (1%) of the elderly report having received mental health treatment from a specialist (Kennedy, Kelman, Thomas, & Wisniewski,1989). Rather than seek treatment for depression, the individual may try to find help for physical complaints considered more acceptable as a focus of treatment (Blazer et al., 1988). Further complicating the situation is the fact that symptoms of physical illness can actually mask those of depression, so that the clinician treating the older adult is unaware of underlying depressive symptomatology (Rosenberg, Wright, & Gershon, 1992). Finally, cognitive loss due to depression may appear to be very much like dementia, a condition known as pseudodementia (Teri & Reifler, 1987). The older individual may be misdiagnosed as having dementia due to Alzheimer's disease. The benefits of psychotherapy or somatic treatment are not available for such individuals, and the depression only continues to progress, perhaps leading to an exacerbation of physically based diseases.

Life experiences and adversity in the social realm heighten the risk of depressive symptoms that arise in old age. These experiences can include environmental stressors such as isolation, poverty (Dean, Kolody, Wood, & Matt, 1992; Krause, 1987a), and geographical relocation (Zamanian, Thackrey, Starrett, & Brown, 1992); multiple losses such as loss of a spouse due to marital separation, divorce, or death (Kennedy et al., 1989; Siegel & Kuykendall, 1990); as well as loss of one's greater social network. These life experiences may result in a cumulative bereavement or adaptation process placing elderly people at risk for increased emotional distress.

Caregiving Burden

The term *caregiving* is used in a variety of contexts with regard to the elderly. Caregiving burden is the subjective experience of distress faced by an individual due to the constant needs to care for an infirmed relative. Recent studies point to burden as a source of adversity in the elderly that leads to psychological symptoms such as loneliness, low life satisfaction, and depression (Lawton, Moss, Kleban, Glicksman, & Rovine, 1991). The wealth of such contemporary investigations is testimony to the importance of this source of adversity for elders; these studies have highlighted what is undoubtedly a most painful subjective experience for older caregivers themselves.

A typical response of an elderly caregivers is to describe the effects of caregiving as stressful, overwhelming, and in some cases devastating (Wilson, 1990). In fact, the existence of mental health problems has been documented in as many as 50% of a sample of caregivers in one study (Lichtenberg & Barth, 1989). The mental health problems reported by these caregivers include depression and dysthymia, disorders seen in only 1% of age-matched controls in the same time period (Dura, Stukenberg, & Kiecolt-Glaser, 1990).

The causes of distress in caregivers include negative emotional reactions such as inadequacy and guilt, feelings of responsibility for the patient, and feelings of abandonment by the rest of the family. Caregiving interferes with the individual's daily schedules and social relationships with others, and creates financial problems (Smith, Smith, & Toseland, 1991; Wilson, 1990). Apart from these effects in the emotional and pragmatic realms, caregiving puts the individual at risk for loss of a sense of self, as the individual becomes totally immersed in providing for the well-being of another. Without external sources of self-verification, the individual is left without outside sources of self-evaluation, thus intensifying the impact of experiences within the caregiver role (Skaff & Pearlin, 1992).

Some of the factors that exacerbate the experience of caregiver burden include depression or mental impairment of the elder receiving care, chronicity of illness, and physical disabilities that demand extensive time and attention (Baillie, Norbeck, & Barnes, 1988; Liptzin, Grob, & Eisen, 1988; Rosenthal, Sulman, & Marshall, 1993; Schulz, Tompkins, Wood, & Decker, 1987). Disruptive behavior such as wandering, aggression, and incontinence by the recipient of care present particular risk for emotional strain in the caregiver (Deimling & Bass, 1986; Given et al., 1990). Additionally, caregiving over a prolonged period leads to greater distress, particularly when the caregiver has little social support, is in poor health or is otherwise vulnerable, and lacks adequate resources (Given et al., 1990; Hinrichsen, 1991; Pruchno, Kleban, Michaels, & Dempsey, 1990; Vitaliano, Russo, Young, Teri, & Maiuro, 1991). Stressors not directly associated with caregiving such as work stress and stresses involving social relationships (Chiriboga, Weiler, & Nielsen, 1989; Rankin, 1990) increase the extent to which caregiving becomes a burden to the elder. Finally, family conflict is predictive of depression in the caregiver. Criticisms of the caregiver and disagreement on issues such as the amount of attention, assistance and care the patient should receive cause the caregiver to question her competence and ultimately feel like a failure. At the same time, feelings of depression caused by the experience of burden may heighten the caregiver's sensitivity to comments and reactions on the part of other family members (Semple, 1992).

The caregiving experience is recognized to be more prevalent for women (Skaff & Pearlin, 1992), who are more likely to be regarded as helpers in general (Chang & White-Means, 1991). Women outnumber men by almost a 3 to 1 ratio in frequency of performing the caregiving role (Zarit, Todd, & Zarit, 1986). Although the demands placed upon women may be perceived as more stressful, women have greater experience taking on multiple roles (Jutras & Veilleux, 1991) and may be more likely to adjust to the role of caregiver. Within female relatives, daughters usually assume the caregiving role (Hinrichsen, 1991), in part because they maintain more contact with elderly parents. Even divorced women are more likely to maintain supportive ties with former in-laws (Goetting, 1990). If the daughter is married, the burden is reduced somewhat, as she can share her burden with her spouse (Brody, Litvin, Hoffman, & Kleban, 1992). Interestingly, daughters are more likely to be regarded as sources of both positive and adverse social contacts for elders (Spaid & Barusch, 1991).

Although caregiver burden is usually interpreted to mean burden experienced *by* the caregiver, it can also apply to distress on the part of the caregiving recipient. Household caregiving arrangements can have adverse effects on the mental health of the elderly if exchange of instrumental services between caregivers and care receivers is not encouraged (Dunkle, 1985).

Families who experience caregiver burden are more likely to institutionalize the elder relative in an effort to alleviate the burden and provide better care for the infirmed relative (McFall & Miller, 1992). However, by moving the older person to an institution, the experience of stress is not necessarily removed (Deimling, Bass, Townsend, & Noelker, 1989). Although caregivers for institutionalized family members have less responsibility for and contact with their relatives, they tend to experience caregiving events as more stressful than caregivers for noninstitutionalized family members (Stephens, Kinney, & Ogrocki, 1991). This may be in part because the role of caregivers does not stop once the family member has become institutionalized, but instead it continues with a different set of responsibilities and stress (Zarit & Whitlatch, 1992). For example, competing demands on the caregivers' time and the lack of flexibility in their lives continue to cause distress. Furthermore, although caregivers no longer have to be the primary provider of assistance in activities of daily living, they still feel responsible for the well-being of their relatives and the care they are receiving (Brody, Dempsey, & Pruchno, 1990).

Elder Abuse

When caregiving burden is unrelenting, and under certain family circumstances, the caregiver may respond by abusing the elder relative. A report by the United States House of Representative Select Committee on Aging indicated that about 4% of the people over 65 years of age may be victims of abuse by caretakers through physical violence, neglect, financial exploitation, or psychological abuse. A survey of over 2,000 elderly in one urban area showed that 32 persons per 1,000 had suffered mistreatment through physical abuse, verbal aggression, or neglect (Wolf, 1988).

The perpetrator of abuse is most likely to be a spouse, and since victims are more likely to be female, the perpetrator is generally the husband (Pillemer & Finkelhor, 1989; Wolf, 1988). The female victim of abuse is more likely to be of advanced age and highly dependent on the caregiver. Elder abuse is most likely to occur when the caregiver has experienced a series of life crises, is an abuser of alcohol or drugs, is inexperienced at caregiving, has economic problems, and lacks support from other family members. Conditions such as pre-existing marital conflict and discord also increase the likelihood of elder abuse. Several components of the victim's behavior may put one at increased risk for abuse, including alcohol use as well as the victim's behavior of making multiple demands on the caregiver and being highly critical of the care that is provided (Hirst & Miller, 1986; Kosberg, 1988; Steinmetz, 1988).

Interactive factors within the family as a whole that increase risk of elder abuse include interdependence between the victim and perpetrator due to loss of or abandonment by other family members in the system. Social isolation and the financial dependency of the perpetrator on the elderly person also present further risk factors (Godkin, Wolf, & Pillemer, 1989). Finally, lack of preparation within the family for caregiving, unresolved family conflicts, and negative attitudes toward the disabled also increase the likelihood that a caregiver will resort to abuse (Steinmetz, 1988; Wolf, 1988).

Suicide

The taking of one's own life can be seen as an extreme reaction of the elder to adversity. The elderly population has a suicide rate that is 50% higher than that of the young (Osgood, 1987). Furthermore, compared to younger individuals, older persons are more likely to carry out a suicide attempt (McIntosh, 1992). The population for whom the risk of suicide is particularly pronounced is white men over the age of 85 years, for whom the rate is 66 per 100,000, the highest reported for any age or sex group within the U.S. population (USDHHS, 1991).

The fact that white males are at heightened risk of committing suicide may be due to gender differences in coping with stress and feelings of depression, or to norms of suicidal behavior (Canetto, 1992). Widowhood and divorce are additional risk factors for white men (McIntosh, 1992), either leading to or compounding difficulties due to late-onset major depression (Lyness, Conwell, & Nelson, 1992) and feelings of helplessness, and hopelessness (Osgood, 1987).

Elders who are grieving for a suicide victim might experience another form of adversity, in that there is less support available to help them through the bereavement period. They are likely to receive less emotional support for their feelings of depression and grief than natural death survivors (Farberow, Gallagher-Thompson, Gilewski, & Thompson, 1992).

TARGET POPULATIONS AT RISK FOR ADVERSITY

Minority Elders

As mentioned at the outset of this chapter, the elderly population of age 65 and older is the fastest growing segment of the American population. Among the elderly, the proportion of minority aged is growing faster than their nonminority counterparts (Wood, 1989). It is estimated that currently about 10% of the people 65 years of age and older are members of ethnic minorities. By the year 2025, 15% of the elderly population are projected to be of minority status and by 2050, this proportion will rise to 20% (U.S. Senate, 1989). Although the demographic trends show that minority groups constitute a high percentage of the elderly population, elder minorities are considered to be in a disadvantaged position among the general population because of linguistic and communication barriers. As a result, they are typically faced with economic and social discrimination. In addition, current public policies are dictated by the needs of a homogeneous population comprised mostly of white Americans failing to acknowledge the need of diverse groups (Wray, 1991). This presents obstacles for minorities that prevent them from obtaining equal access to social and economic opportunities.

The double-jeopardy hypothesis is a theoretical perspective proposed to describe the discrimination faced by those aged who are of ethnic minority status. It was first proposed by the National Urban League in 1964 to describe the effects of discrimination experienced by aged blacks. Recently, the concept of double jeopardy has become a central theme of much of the research related to minority elders and has broadened its meaning to describe the minority aged population in general. The concept of double jeopardy refers to the fact that minority elders not only have to deal with the consequences of being old, but also with the hazards resulting from discriminations against minorities in areas such as education, health services, housing, and income.

Minority elders tend to experience employment and economical disadvantages compared to nonminority groups. Aged minority remain among the most economically disadvantaged and chronically ill in society and the most in need of social support and health services (Jackson & Perry, 1989; Torres-Gil & Hyde, 1990). For example, Taylor and Chatters (1988) argue that blacks experience lower levels of economic well-being than whites at every stage of their life cycle continuing into old age, thus negatively affecting the socioeconomic conditions of aged blacks. This pattern established throughout their lives results in high rates of poverty among aged blacks and similarly among other aged minority.

Elderly minority are disproportionately represented among individuals with incomes below the federal poverty line. Despite the fact that the number of elderly considered to be living on the minimum income required to maintain an acceptable standard of living has decreased in the past years, the percentage of minority elderly living on these conditions is still substantially great compared to the majority white elderly. In their review of demographic and socioeconomic characteristics of the minority elderly, Markides and Mindel (1987) show figures representing the difference in income between minority and nonminority elderly. In 1983, 12% of white elderly were in poverty compared to 23.1% of aged Hispanics and 36.3% of aged blacks. These figures indicate that the percentage of minority elders living in poverty is almost twice and three times as much as it is for white elders living in the same conditions. In 1985 the poverty rate for aged blacks and Hispanics was about 32% and 24% respectively (Wray, 1991).

The fact that the elderly minority group is highly represented in the percentage of people below the poverty line may be correlated with their underrepresentation in institutional long-term care services and public health services. In general, minority elders are in most need of economic resources for health services because they are less likely to have health insurance and to have a routine place for health care than their nonminority counterparts (Solis, 1990; Wray, 1991). Due to less stable work histories, elderly members of minority groups are less likely to have health insurance plans. Many of them came from different countries and held jobs that were not within the Social Security Medicare-covered system. In addition, some were faced with social and job discrimination that affected their work opportunities. Even those who have medical insurance still have trouble obtaining adequate services because deductibles of publicly funded health care are too high for some minority elderly to afford within their level of income (Wray, 1991).

Another problematic aspect of aged minorities' low income is the availability of money they have upon retirement. In 1986, 93% of white elderly received Social Security upon retirement compared to 88% of aged blacks and 81% of aged Hispanics. Low income and lack of available funds after retirement result in many minority elders being cared for at home, mostly by spouses and children, causing in turn further economical burden for the families (Wray, 1991).

The fact that minority elders do not frequent health services results in higher rates of mortality at earlier ages for this group compared to nonminorities. In 1987, life expectancy at birth for all individuals was on average 75 years old, ranging from 65 years of age for black males to 79 years for white females (Wray, 1991). However, around age 75 there is a reversal of this trend known as the racial crossover effect. At this point the life expectancy of minorities increases and surpasses that of whites. Researchers hypothesized that this effect may be due to "selective survival"; that is, those minority individuals who live to be 65 are so resilient that they outlive not only their cohort group but also the white elderly. It has been suggested that this crossover effect may be related to the overall economic status of older blacks and to the disproportionately higher rates of poverty, malnutrition, and poor health (Markides & Mindel, 1987; Torres-Gil & Hyde, 1990). The crossover effect is true for blacks and whites but not for Hispanics and non-Hispanic whites.

Minorities are more likely to suffer from chronic conditions at younger ages than their nonminority counterparts (Crimmins, Saito, & Ingegneri, 1987). Prevalent chronic conditions among minorities such as blacks and Hispanics are heart disease, malignant neoplasms, diabetes, and high prevalence of infective and parasitic diseases. Compared to elderly whites, aged blacks are more likely to suffer from cognitive disability and show higher levels of severe impairment (Palmore, Nowlin, & Wang, 1985). Krause (1990) suggests that the older minority individual's higher risk of developing physical health problems may be related to higher exposure to stressful experiences as compared to members of nonminority groups. Stressful events include incidents such as poverty, malnutrition, and accidents.

Stresses associated with environmental conditions can, then, differentially affect the minority elderly's mental condition that can lower the individual's life expectancy. In addition, people from minority groups also are more likely to die at younger ages as consequences of homicides and accidents. It has been suggested that the higher mortality rates among minorities and their higher prevalence of chronic disabling disorders at an earlier age than whites may be indirectly related to their economic disadvantages (Wray, 1991). Minorities may tend to get sicker as a result of detrimental living conditions. It is also possible that because of differential opportunity costs and language barriers they tend to underutilize health services for prevention and early detection of diseases (Solis, 1990). Finally, caregiving burden might be expected to be considerably higher for minorities than for nonminorities. In current research being conducted by two of the authors, the experience of depression as related to caregiver burden is being studied in minority caregivers (Muñoz-Ruiz & Whitbourne, in progress). The findings of this study should have significance for implementing caregiver support programs targeted for this high-risk group.

The demographic and socioeconomic trends presented here have repercussions for social support services. The discussion of the areas in which minority elders are faced with adverse situations serve to support the hypothesis of the double jeopardy and to demonstrate how being a minority living in the United States may be a further source of adversity in old age.

Gay and Lesbian Experience

The elderly gay and lesbian population over 60 years of age is the last generation to have lived much of their lives prior to the social and political ramifications of Stonewall, an event which marks the beginning of the gay and lesbian liberation movement. Before this event, being gay was almost never disclosed outside of this subculture, as there was essentially no outside social support for the gay or lesbian individual (Adelman, 1990; Lee, 1989). Therefore, gay and lesbian elders may have unique stressors that cause them to experience adversity in their daily lives.

Although a majority of the gay and lesbian older population have passed through the same historical time period marked by oppression, there is no one elder gay identity. Adjustment in gay adults can be related to the individual's identification and expression of himself or herself as gay, the influence of stigma for that individual, and his or her psychosocial resources (Adelman, 1990). The majority of research focuses on elder gays and lesbians who are comfortable with identifying themselves as gay and are therefore more willing to volunteer to participate. There is an overrepresentation of white, high socioeconomic status and well-educated individuals and an underrepresentation of working class and minority gays and lesbians. Very little research on gay and lesbian elders includes people over the age of 70 years (Quam & Whitford, 1992).

Given these qualifications, a look at the available research offers some suggestions regarding risk factors for the gay and lesbian elderly. A primary risk for this group is isolation, particularly following the loss of a partner among those elders who have become estranged from their families and the larger society due to disapproval of their lifestyle (Kehoe, 1990; Lipman, 1986). Moving from private to public living situations presents another risk factor, causing the gay elder to feel unsafe and alone. For example, a gay or lesbian elder moving to an institution may feel less connected to others, after having been closeted and living all of his or her adult life in the gay community (Kimmel, 1992). Added to this sense of isolation may be the fear of homophobic responses and lack of safety if others in the institution discover his or her gayness (Adelman, 1990; Deevey, 1990).

Another source of risk in the gay and lesbian elderly are threats to one's gay identity due to a generational conflict within the gay population regarding the values associated with the gay liberation movement. Gay rights are viewed as values of the young that may contradict the values of privacy espoused by individuals in the older gay generation. For the gay or lesbian elder who is no longer connected to his or her community and has never been connected to the heterosexual community, there is the threat of complete social invisibility (Lee, 1989).

The primary concerns of the gay elderly, however, remain comparable to those of the heterosexual older adult. Although gay and lesbian elders report fears of sexual preference discrimination and rejection by adult children and grandchildren, their primary concerns are those of the heterosexual elder: avoiding loneliness, poor health, and poverty (Lee, 1987; Quam & Whitford, 1992). Some researchers have suggested that growing up gay has better prepared the gay or lesbian individual for challenges that arise in the later years due to social discrimination against the elderly (Friend, 1990). Having been victims of lifelong discrimination, the elderly gay population may be more resilient to some of the challenges involved in abandoning major social roles and dealing with ageism. Additionally, gay and lesbian elders may have an easier time adjusting to the many ways in which one has to provide self-care when alone because they have become more flexible regarding gender roles (Friend, 1990). Gay and lesbian elders may also be able to rely upon a larger network of friends than heterosexual elders, who have been more involved in their adult lives with family members (Friend, 1987; Lipman, 1986). In fact, integration into a supportive network of gay friends, political involvement, and connection with gay and lesbian community centers and organizations can help keep the gay elderly individual autonomous and able to live independently (Kimmel, 1992; Lipman, 1986; Quam & Whitford, 1992).

SUCCESSFUL AGING: COPING WITH ADVERSITY

Like other forms of stress, adversity presents a challenge to the individual's ability to cope. An overall framework for studying the reaction of older adults to adversity is provided by a cognitive model of coping, in which stress is defined in terms of the individual's perception that a situation is threatening because it overwhelms the individual's ability to meet the situation's demands (Lazarus & DeLongis, 1983). Some of the sources of adversity in later life relevant to the study of coping include bereavement, poor health, caregiving, fears of aging, risks to personal safety, threats to self-esteem, and uncertainty of life beyond death (Fry, 1990).

The importance of coping with adversity and other stressful situations can be seen from research investigating the effects of inadequate coping strategies on health status in the elderly. In one investigation, the relationship was examined between stress, social support, coping, and immune function in a sample of older adult women. The respondents were classified as either having experienced marked adversity in the past year or as being free of major stress. Those women who had been highly stressed had poorer immune functioning than women who had not experienced stresses, and a significant proportion of the variation in immune system markers was accounted for by psychosocial variables indicative of social support (McNaughton, Smith, Patterson, & Grant, 1990). Coping difficulties and lack of social support were also found to be predictive of hospital readmissions for a sample of elderly cardiac patients (Berkman, Millar, Holmes, & Bonander, 1991). The subjective experience of stress, particularly on a daily basis, was also related to prescription drug misuse among another sample of elders (Folkman, Bernstein, & Lazarus, 1987). Thus coping strategies can significantly influence the outcome of an older adult's experience with adversity.

In a cognitive model of stress and coping, Lazarus and Folkman (1984) have identified two major coping strategies: problem-focused and emotion-focused coping. In problem-focused coping, the individual attempts to reduce stress by changing a feature of the situation or the self. Problem-focused coping strategies include confrontation and planful problem-solving. Emotion-focused coping is used when individuals attempt to change the way they view a stressful situation. Some emotion-focused coping strategies include wishful thinking, distancing, and positive reappraisal. Which of these coping strategies is more adaptive varies according to the situation and there is no one generally accepted successful way to reduce stress. However, observations of the reactions of elders to stress and adversity lead to general characterizations of unsuccessful and successful coping strategies in later life.

Passive, emotion-focused coping strategies appear to characterize the reactions of elders who are less successful in managing stress. These strategies include self-blame, wishful thinking, avoidance, fantasy, and escape into drugs and alcohol (Gass, 1987; Smith, Smith, & Toseland, 1991). Unfortunately, people tend to attribute mild, short-term symptoms to aging, leading them to adopt more passive coping strategies (Leventhal & Prohaska, 1986), and it is these strategies that ultimately can reduce health status even further (Lohr, Essex, & Klein, 1988).

By contrast, successful elders use more active coping strategies, including sport and physical recreation, interacting with others for social support, and keeping busy by participating in social groups and learning new skills. Successful copers see themselves as in control of their experiences, view themselves positively, and take a confrontive, optimistic, and self-reliant approach to stressors. In cases of chronic illness, they accept restrictions, but still look for new possibilities in life. An active, problem-focused coping style seems, then, to be positively associated with handling adversity in later life (Fry, 1990; Gass, 1987; Herth, 1990; Johnson, Lund, & Dimond, 1986; Kahana, Kahana, & Young, 1987; Krause, 1987b; Kruse & Lehr, 1989; O'Brien & Conger, 1991). However, this style of coping does not necessarily involve close self-scrutiny, introspection, or an intensive process of life review. A positive orientation to one's past life based on involvement with family and a focus on past successes may help the older adult view the future more positively (Whitbourne & Powers, 1994). For some individuals, prayer may prove beneficial and for those individuals who tend to rely on external sources of control in their lives, dependency and reliance on other people may form the basis for successful coping (Reich & Zautra, 1991). Intelligence may also play a role in helping older individuals manage their everyday needs (Poon, Messner, Martin, & Noble, 1992).

There are significant ethnic and cultural variations in coping strategies which researchers have only recently begun to investigate. The black elderly are in some ways better prepared to cope with stress, having had a lifetime of rehearsal in using social support during times of stress and developing flexible ways to seek help than is true for many whites. Furthermore, a lifetime of poverty and adversity makes blacks better able to handle uncertainty (Gibson, 1986). Friends appear to provide an important source of coping for elderly blacks, more so than is the case for whites, who rely more heavily on relatives. Older, high-income whites may actually be at greatest risk for not having social support during times of stress (Ulbrich & Warheit, 1989).

The ability to cope with stress has also been investigated among rural elders, who show some distinctly adaptive strategies (Kumar-Reddy & Ramamurti, 1990). They are more likely to seek information or advice about health problems, and use problem-focused coping to deal with economic stresses. Men in particular are more likely to use cognitive strategies such as redefinition of the problem and logical analysis in dealing with stress, particularly that associated with social relationships, and a strategy of resigned acceptance in dealing with family stresses.

In conclusion, there are many reasons to regard the experiences associated with aging, particularly in target populations, as sources of adversity in the later years of the life course. However, the experience of adversity is not inevitable, nor is it irreversible. The maintenance of a sense of identity over time contributes to the older adult's ability to put the events in later life, even those involving adversity, into an adaptive framework. (Whitbourne, 1996a), They may regard as a credit to their adaptive ability that they can cope flexibly with adversity. Successful agers find ways to adapt methods of coping with stress to reduce the adversities they encounter in their daily lives. They also take advantage of the principle "use it or lose it!" in which they discover or find ways to compensate for physical and psychological changes associated with the normal aging process that can potentially interfere with the ability to perform daily activities and to cope successfully with environmental stressors. Some of these compensatory activities include regular and consistent involvement in physical exercise, the seeking of intellectual stimulation, and the willingness to take advantage of commercially available prostheses such as proper hearing aids and eyeglasses (Whitbourne, 1996b). Going beyond the concept of coping, which implies a responsiveness to externally produced events, some elders seek new levels of personal growth and development through constant searching for new opportunities to learn and stay involved in the world around them (McLeish, 1983). Awareness of these successful coping strategies can provide a source of optimism to those of younger generations who observe the aging of their elders, and methods of prevention and education for current cohorts of older adults.

REFERENCES

Adelman, M. (1990). Stigma, gay lifestyles, and adjustment to aging: A study of later-life gay men and lesbians. *Journal of Homosexuality, 13*, 7–32.

Allegrante, J. P., MacKenzie, C. R., Robbins, L., & Cornell, C. N. (1991). Hip fracture in older persons: Does self-efficacy-based intervention have a role in rehabilitation? *Arthritis Care and Research, 4*, 39–47.

Baillie, V., Norbeck, J. S., & Barnes, L. E. (1988). Stress, social support, and psychological distress of family caregivers of the elderly. *Nursing Research, 37*, 217–222.

Berkman, B., Millar, S., Holmes, W., & Bonander, E. (1991). Predicting elderly cardiac patients at risk for readmission. Special Issue: Applied social work research in health and social work. *Social Work in Health Care, 16*, 21–38.

Blazer, D., Schwartz, M., Woodbury, M., Manton, K. G., Hughes, D., & George, L. K. (1988). Depressive symptoms and depressive diagnoses in a community population. *Archives of General Psychiatry, 45*, 1078–1084.

Brody, E. M., Dempsey, N. P., & Pruchno, R. A. (1990). Mental health of sons and daughters of the institutionalized aged. *Gerontologist, 30,* 212–219.

Brody, E. M., Litvin, S. J., Hoffman, C., & Kleban, M. H. (1992). Women's sense of responsibility for the care of old people: "But who else is going to do it?" *Gerontologist, 32,* 58–67.

Bruce, M. L., & McNamara, R. (1992). Psychiatric status among the homebound elderly: An epidemiologic perspective. *Journal of the American Geriatrics Society, 40,* 561–566.

Canetto, S. S. (1992). Gender and suicide in the elderly. Special Issue: Suicide and the older adult. *Suicide and Life-Threatening Behavior, 22,* 80–97.

Chang, C. F., & White-Means, S. I. (1991). The men who care: An analysis of male primary caregivers who care for frail elderly at home. *Journal of Applied Gerontology, 10,* 343–358.

Chiriboga, D. A., Weiler, P. G., & Nielsen, K. (1989). The stress of caregivers. Special Issue: Aging and family caregivers. *Journal of Applied Social Sciences, 13,* 118–141.

Crimmins, E. M., Saito, Y., & Ingegneri, D. G. (1987). Changes in life expectancy and disability-free life expectancy in the United States. *Population and Development Review, 15,* 235–267.

Dean, A., Kolody, B., Wood, P., & Matt, G. E. (1992). The influence of living alone on depression in elderly persons. *Journal of Aging and Health, 4,* 3–18.

Deevey, S. (1990). Older lesbian women: An invisible minority. *Journal of Gerontological Nursing, 16,* 35–38.

Deimling, G. T., & Bass, D. M. (1986). Symptoms of mental impairment among elderly adults and their effects on family caregivers. *Journal of Gerontology, 41,* 778–784.

Deimling, G. T., Bass, D. M., Townsend, A. L., & Noelker, L. S. (1989). Care-related stress: A comparison of spouse and adult-child caregivers in shared and separate households. *Journal of Aging and Health, 1,* 67–82.

Dunkle, R. E. (1985). Comparing the depression of elders in two types of caregiving arrangements. *Family Relations Journal of Applied Family and Child Studies, 34,* 235–240.

Dura, J. R., Stukenberg, K. W., & Kiecolt-Glaser, J. K. (1990). Chronic stress and depressive disorders in older adults. *Journal of Abnormal Psychology, 99,* 284–290.

Farberow, N. L., Gallagher-Thompson, D., Gilewski, M., & Thompson, L. (1992). The role of social supports in the bereavement process of surviving spouses of suicide and natural deaths. Special Issue: Suicide and the older adult. *Suicide and Life Threatening Behavior, 22,* 107–124.

Folkman, S., Bernstein, L., & Lazarus, R. S. (1987). Stress processes and the misuse of drugs in older adults. *Psychology and Aging, 2,* 366–374.

Friend, R. A. (1987). The individual and social psychology of aging. *Journal of Homosexuality, 4,* 307–331.

Friend, R. A. (1990). Loneliness and the aging homosexual: Is pet therapy an answer. *Journal of Homosexuality, 13,* 43–71.

Fry, P. S. (1990). A factor analytic investigation of home-bound elderly individuals' concerns about death and dying, and their coping responses. *Journal of Clinical Psychology, 46,* 737–748.

Gass, K. A. (1987). Coping strategies of widows. *Journal of Gerontological Nursing, 13*(8), 29–33.

Gibson, R. C. (1986). Older black Americans. *Generations, 10,* 35–39.

Given, B. A., Stommel, M., Collins, C. E., & King, S. K. (1990). Responses of elderly spouse caregivers. *Research in Nursing and Health, 13,* 77–85.

Godkin, M. A., Wolf, R. S., & Pillemer, K. A. (1989). A case-comparison analysis of elder abuse and neglect. *International Journal of Aging and Human Development, 28,* 207–225.

Goetting, A. (1990). Patterns of support among in-laws in the United States: A review of research. Annual Meetings of the American Sociological Association (1989, San Francisco, California). *Journal of Family Issues, 11,* 67–90.

Goldstein, M. S., & Hurwicz, M. L. (1989). Psychosocial distress and perceived health status among elderly users of a health maintenance organization. *Journals of Gerontology, 44,* 154.

Gotham, A. M., Brown, R. G., & Marsden, C. D. (1986). Depression in Parkinson's disease: A quantitative and qualitative analysis. *Journal of Neurology, Neurosurgery and Psychiatry, 49,* 381–389.

Herth, K. (1990). Relationship of hope, coping styles, concurrent losses, and setting to grief resolution in the elderly widow(er). *Research in Nursing and Health, 13,* 109–117.

Hinrichsen, G. A. (1991). Adjustment of caregivers to depressed older adults. *Psychology and Aging, 6,* 631–639.

Hirst, S. P., & Miller, J. (1986). The abused elderly. *Journal of Psychosocial Nursing and Mental Health Services, 24*(10), 28–34.

Jackson, J. J., & Perry, C. (1989). Physical health conditions of middle-aged and aged blacks. In K. S. Markides (Eds.), *Aging and health: Perspectives on gender, race, ethnicity, and class.* Newbury Park, CA: Sage.

Johnson, R. J., Lund, D. A., & Dimond, M. F. (1986). Stress, self-esteem and coping during bereavement among the elderly. *Social Psychology Quarterly, 49,* 273–279.

Jutras, S., & Veilleux, F. (1991). Gender roles and care giving to the elderly: An empirical study. *Sex Roles, 25*(1–2), 1–18.

Kahana, E. F., Kahana, B., & Young, R. (1987). Strategies of coping and postinstitutional outcomes. *Research on Aging, 9,* 182–199.

Kehoe, M. (1990). Loneliness and the aging homosexual: Is pet therapy an answer? *Journal of Homosexuality, 20*(3–4), 137–142.

Kennedy, G. J., Kelman, H. R., Thomas, C., & Wisniewski, W. (1989). Hierarchy of characteristics associated with depressive symptoms in an urban elderly sample. *American Journal of Psychiatry, 146,* 220–225.

Kimmel, D. C. (1992). The families of older gay men and lesbians. *Generations* (Summer).

Kosberg, J. I. (1988). Preventing elder abuse: Identification of high risk factors prior to placement decisions. *Gerontologist, 28,* 43–50.

Krause, N. (1987a). Chronic financial strain, social support, and depressive symptoms among older adults. *Psychology and Aging, 2,* 185–192.

Krause, N. (1987b). Chronic strain, locus of control, and distress in older adults. *Psychology and Aging, 2,* 375–382.

Krause, N. (1990). Illness behavior in later life. In R. H. Binstock & L. K. George (Eds.), *Handbook of aging and the social sciences* (pp. 228–244). New York: Academic Press.

Kruse, A., & Lehr, U. (1989). Longitudinal analysis of the developmental process in chronically ill and healthy persons: Empirical findings from the Bonn Longitudinal Study of Aging (BOLSA). *International Psychogeriatrics, 1,* 73–85.

Kumar-Reddy, B. S., & Ramamurti, P. V. (1990). Stress and coping strategies of the rural aged. *Journal of Personality and Clinical Studies, 6,* 171–175.

Lawton, M. P., Moss, M. S., Kleban, M. H., Glicksman, A., & Rovine, M. (1991). A two-factor model of caregiving appraisal and psychological well-being. *Journal of Gerontology: Psychological Sciences, 46,* 181–189.

Lazarus, R. S., & DeLongis, A. (1983). Psychological stress and coping in aging. *American Psychologist, 38,* 245–254.

Lazarus, R. S., & Folkman, S. (1984). *Stress, appraisal, and the coping process.* New York: Springer.

Lee, J. A. (1987). What can homosexual aging studies contribute to theories of aging? *Journal of Homosexuality, 13,* 43–71.

Lee, J. A. (1989). Invisible men: Canada's aging homosexuals: Can they be assimilated into Canada's "liberated" gay communities? *Canadian Journal on Aging, 8,* 79–97.

Leventhal, E. A., & Prohaska, T. R. (1986). Age, symptom interpretation, and health behavior. *Journal of the American Geriatrics Society, 34,* 185–191.

Lichtenberg, P. A., & Barth, J. T. (1989). The dynamic process of caregiving in elderly spouses: A look at longitudinal case reports. *Clinical Gerontologist, 9,* 31–44.

Lipman, A. (1986). Homosexual relationships. *Generations, 10,* 51–54.

Liptzin, B., Grob, M. C., & Eisen, S. V. (1988). Family burden of demented and depressed elderly psychiatric inpatients. *Gerontologist, 28,* 397–401.

Lohr, M. J., Essex, M. J., & Klein, M. H. (1988). The relationships of coping responses to physical health status and life satisfaction among older women. *Journal of Gerontology; Psychological Sciences, 43,* 54–60.

Lord, S. R., Clark, R. D., & Webster, I. W. (1991). Physiological factors associated with falls in an elderly population. *Journal of the American Geriatrics Society, 39*(12), 1194–1200.

Lyness, J. M., Conwell, Y., & Nelson, J. C. (1992). Suicide attempts in elderly psychiatric inpatients. *Journal of the American Geriatrics Society, 40,* 320–324.

Markides, K. S., & Mindel, C. H. (1987). *Aging and ethnicity.* Newbury Park, CA: Sage.

McFall, S., & Miller, B. H. (1992). Caregiver burden and nursing home admission of frail elderly persons. *Journal of Gerontology: Social Sciences, 47,* S73-S79.

McIntosh, J. L. (1992). Epidemiology of suicide in the elderly. Special Issue: Suicide and the older adult. *Suicide and Life-Threatening Behavior, 22,* 15–35.

McLeish, J. B. (1983). *The challenge of aging.* Vancouver, BC: Douglas and McIntyre.

McNaughton, M. E., Smith, L. W., Patterson, T. L., & Grant, I. (1990). Stress, social support, coping resources, and immune status in elderly women. *Journal of Nervous and Mental Disease, 178,* 460–461.

Morris, J. C., Rubin, E. H., Morris, E. J., & Mandel, S. A. (1987). Senile dementia of the Alzheimer's type: An important risk factor for serious falls. *Journal of Gerontology, 42,* 412–417.

Morse, J. M., Tylko, S. J., & Dixon, H. A. (1987). Characteristics of the fall-prone patient. *Gerontologist, 27,* 516–522.

Muñoz-Ruiz, M. T., & Whitbourne, S. K. (in progress). *Depression and Caregiving Burden in elderly Hispanic Caregivers.* Unpublished manuscript on file with the authors, University of Massachusetts at Amherst.

O'Brien, S. J., & Conger, P. R. (1991). No time to look back: Approaching the finish line of life's course. *International Journal of Aging and Human Development, 33,* 75–87.

Osgood, N. J. (1987). Suicide and the elderly. Special Issue: Death and bereavement. *Generations, 11,* 47–51.

Palmore, E. B., Nowlin, J. B., & Wang, H. S. (1985). Predictors of function among the old-old: A 10-year follow-up. *Journal of Gerontology, 40,* 244–250.

Pillemer, K., & Finkelhor, D. (1989). Causes of elder abuse: Caregiver stress versus problem relatives. *American Journal of Orthopsychiatry, 59,* 179–187.

Poon, L. W., Messner, S., Martin, P., & Noble, C. A. (1992). The influences of cognitive resources on adaptation and old age. *International Journal of Aging and Human Development, 34,* 31–46.

Pruchno, R. A., Kleban, M. H., Michaels, E. J., & Dempsey, N. P. (1990). Mental and physical health of caregiving spouses: Development of a causal model. *Gerontologist, 30,* 192–199.

Quam, J. K., & Whitford, G. S. (1992). Adaptation and age-related expectations of older gay and lesbian adults. *Gerontologist, 32,* 367–374.

Rankin, E. D. (1990). Caregiver stress and the elderly: A familial perspective. *Journal of Gerontological Social Work, 15*(1–2), 57–73.

Reich, J. W., & Zautra, A. J. (1991). Experimental and measurement approaches to internal control in at-risk older adults. *Journal of Social Issues, 47,* 143–158.

Rosenberg, D. R., Wright, B., & Gershon, S. (1992). Depression in the elderly. *Dementia, 3,* 157–173.

Rosenthal, C. J., Sulman, J., & Marshall, V. W. (1993). Depressive symptoms in family caregivers of long-stay patients. *Gerontologist, 33,* 249–257.

Rozzini, R., Bianchetti, A., Carabellese, C., Inzoli, M., & Trabucchi, M. (1988). Depression, life events and somatic symptoms. *Gerontologist, 28,* 229–232.

Schulz, R., Tompkins, C. A., Wood, D., & Decker, S. (1987). The social psychology of caregiving: Physical and psychological costs of providing support to the disabled. *Journal of Applied Social Psychology, 17,* 401–428.

Semple, S. J. (1992). Conflict in Alzheimer's caregiving families: Its dimensions and consequences. *Gerontologist, 32,* 645–655.

Siegel, J. M., & Kuykendall, D. H. (1990). Loss, widowhood, and psychological distress among the elderly. *Journal of Consulting and Clinical Psychology, 58,* 519–524.

Skaff, M. M., & Pearlin, L. I. (1992). Caregiving: Role engulfment and the loss of self. *Gerontologist, 32,* 656–664.

Smith, G. C., Smith, M. F., & Toseland, R. W. (1991). Problems identified by family caregivers in counseling. *Gerontologist, 31,* 15–22.

Solis, J. M. (1990). Acculturation, access to care, and use of preventive services by Hispanics: Findings from NHANES 1982–84. *American Journal of Public Health, 80*(supplement), 11–19.

Spaid, W. M., & Barusch, A. S. (1991). Social support and caregiver strain: Types and sources of social contacts of elderly caregivers. *Journal of Gerontological Social Work, 18*(1–2), 151–161.

Steinmetz, S. K. (1988). Elder abuse by family caregivers: Processes and intervention strategies. Special Issue: Coping with victimization. *Contemporary Family Therapy, An International Journal, 10,* 256–271.

Stephens, M. P., Kinney, J. M., & Ogrocki, P. K. (1991). Stressors and well-being among caregivers to older adults with dementia: The in-home versus nursing home experience. *Gerontologist, 31,* 217–223.

Taylor, R. J., & Chatters, L. M. (1988). Correlates of education, income, and poverty among aged blacks. *Gerontologist, 28,* 435–441.

Teri, L., & Reifler, B. V. (1987). Depression and dementia. In L. L. Carstensen & B. A. Edelstein (Eds.), *Handbook of clinical gerontology* (pp. 112–122). New York: Pergamon Press.

Tinetti, M. E., & Powell, L. (1993). Fear of falling and low self-efficacy: A cause of dependence in elderly persons. *Journals of Gerontology, 48*(special issue), 35–58.

Tinetti, M. E., Richman, D., & Powell, L. (1990). Falls efficacy as a measure of fear of falling. *Journals of Gerontology, 45,* 239.

Tinetti, M. E., Speechley, M., & Ginter, S. F. (1988). Risk factors for falls among elderly persons living in the community. *New England Journal of Medicine, 319*(26), 1701–1707.

Torres-Gil, F. M., & Hyde, J. C. (1990). The impact of minorities on long-term care policy in California. In P. Liebig & W. Lammers (Eds.), *California policy choices for long-term care.* Los Angeles, CA: University of Southern California.

Ulbrich, P. M., & Warheit, G. J. (1989). Social support, stress, and psychological distress among older black and white adults. *Journal of Aging and Health, 1,* 286–305.

United States Department of Health & Human Services (1991). Births, marriages, and death for 1990. *Monthly Vital Statistics Report, 39,* (12).

U. S. Senate, (1989). *Aging America: Trends and projections. Information paper to the Special Committee on Aging*. Washington DC: Government Printing Office.

Vetter, N. J., & Ford, D. (1989). Anxiety and depression scores in elderly fallers. *International Journal of Geriatric Psychiatry, 4*, 159–163.

Vitaliano, P. P., Russo, J., Young, H. M., Teri, L., & Maiuro, R. D. (1991). Predictors of burden in spouse caregivers of individuals with Alzheimer's disease. *Psychology and Aging, 6*, 392–402.

Wade, M. G., Lingquist, R., Taylor, J. R., & Treat-Jacobson, D. (1995). Optical flow, spatial orientation, and the control of posture in the elderly. *Journal of Gerontology: Psychological Sciences, 50B*, 51–58.

Walker, J. E., & Howland, J. (1991). Falls and fear of falling among elderly persons living in the community: Occupational therapy interventions. *American Journal of Occupational Therapy, 45*, 119–122.

Whitbourne, S. K. (1996a). *The aging individual: Physical and psychological perspectives.* New York: Springer.

Whitbourne, S. K. (1996b). Psychological perspectives on the normal aging process. In L. L. Carstensen & B. A. Edelstein (Eds.), *Handbook of the practice of clinical gerontology.* Beverly Hills, CA: Sage Publications.

Whitbourne, S. K., & Powers, C. B. (1994). Older women's constructs of their lives: A quantitative and qualitative exploration. *International Journal of Aging and Human Development, 38*, 298–306.

Wilson, V. (1990). The consequences of elderly wives caring for disabled husbands: Implications for practice. *Social Work, 35*, 417–421.

Wolf, R. S. (1988). Elder abuse: Ten years later. *Journal of the American Geriatrics Society, 36*(8), 758–762.

Wood, J. B. (1989). Communicating with older adults in health care settings: Cultural and ethnic considerations. *Educational Gerontology, 15*, 351–362.

Wray, L. A. (1991). Public policy implications of an ethnically diverse elderly population. *Journal of Cross-Cultural Gerontology, 6*, 243–257.

Zamanian, K., Thackrey, M., Starrett, R. A., & Brown, L. G.(1992). Acculturation and depression in Mexican-American elderly. Special Issue: Hispanic aged mental health. *Clinical Gerontologist, 11*(3–4), 109–121.

Zarit, S. H., Todd, P. A., & Zarit, J. M. (1986). Subjective burden of husbands and wives as caregivers: A longitudinal study. *Gerontologist, 26*, 260–266.

Zarit, S. H., & Whitlatch, C. J. (1992). Institutional placement: Phases of the transition. *Gerontologist, 32*, 665–672.

9 | BIOLOGICAL FACTORS IN RELATIONSHIP AGGRESSION

Paul Gearan and Alan Rosenbaum

Marital or relationship aggression is a relatively new research area with a history dating back only 15–20 years. The initial research was aimed at identifying the parameters of marital aggression, the incidence and prevalence, as well as the inter- and intrapersonal characteristics associated with the problem. We now know that marital aggression, once thought to be a very infrequent occurrence, is in actuality one of the most serious health problems confronting society today (Browne, 1987; Stark & Filcraft, 1988). Research into the causes of relationship aggression has also proliferated over the past two decades, with the initial source of information being the female victims. Increasingly, information obtained directly from batterers has become available. More recently, increased attention has been paid to the mechanisms by which aggression evolves in relationships. The cyclic pattern of relationship aggression (Walker, 1979) and the influence of attitudes and beliefs regarding gender roles in a patriarchal society have been emphasized. Broader models conceptualizing multiple determinants for aggression are now receiving greater attention in the theoretical and research literature.

Research in the area of marital violence has been constrained by a number of factors. Marital aggression is both a behavioral phenomenon of interest to social scientists and a provocative sociopolitical issue. Research findings in this area are thus subjected to examination not only on the merits of their scientific rigor, but also on their political implications. Ethical and practical limitations inhibit potential experimental designs which could illuminate some etiological questions regarding individual or dyadic processes underlying marital violence (Rosenbaum, 1988). Limited access to collateral information sources has often forced reliance on self-report data, casting some doubt on the validity of reporting based solely on either victim or batterer reports. Longitudinal research studies, especially those concerning treatment outcome, are often beset with problems. Specifically, follow-up contact with batterers, whose life-styles are often extremely unstable, is difficult.

Despite the obstacles and limitations, the data regarding the scope of domestic violence have grown substantially over the past two decades. However, the data are often inconsistent or contradictory, and there is no consensus regarding the specific mechanisms involved in the onset and maintenance of relationship aggression. Correspondingly, there must be a willingness among researchers to challenge or expand existing paradigms to accommodate new research findings. Data from a variety of disciplines, including neuropsychology and psychophysiology, must be evaluated for their potential contributions to the understanding of this complex and dangerous problem.

EPIDEMIOLOGY AND CHARACTERISTICS OF RELATIONSHIP AGGRESSION

Regardless of the sample, the incidence and prevalence figures for domestic violence are remarkably consistent. Twelve percent of women in two nationwide surveys reported being victims of physical aggression during the previous year (Straus & Gelles, 1986; Straus, Gelles, & Steinmetz, 1980). O'Leary et al. (1989) found, in a longitudinal study with a community sample, that after 30 months of marriage, 25% of women reported being victims of aggression within the previous year. Summarily, best estimates are that approximately one-third of all married couples will experience some form of marital aggression at some point in the marital relationship (Straus, Gelles, & Steinmetz, 1980).

Violence also occurs in nonmarital relationships and, in fact, occurs at a fairly alarming rate even among casually dating couples (Sugarman & Hotaling, 1989). By "casually dating couples" we mean couples who are not in committed relationships. Currently, the Marital Treatment and Research Program at the University of Massachusetts Medical Center (UMMC) is conducting a longitudinal study at three local colleges assessing the effectiveness of a relationship aggression prevention program. During the first year of the study, 36.9% of female undergraduate students at these three institutions reported that they had been aggressed against in the previous year in their dating relationships.

It is important to keep in mind when we talk about relationship aggression that much of the popular perception of batterers is shaped by the media. The media, unfortunately, are drawn to the most sensationalized cases and so one could easily get the impression that all batterers are stalking, maiming, and eventually killing their partners. Certainly these individuals do exist, and the resulting injuries and deaths from their behaviors are tragic. However, we now know that the majority of batterers are quite different from the ones depicted in the news media, film, or television. Incidents involving pushing, grabbing, and slapping are more characteristic of the typical batterer than are repeated beatings and the use of weapons. Battering is a widespread and troubling phenomenon that includes a broad range of behaviors. Although physical aggression is what is commonly thought of when referring to either marital or relationship aggression, it is also important to keep in mind that there are other forms of aggression. These include emotional abuse, sexual abuse, and the destruction of a partner's pets and property.

For the most part, however, when researchers look at marital aggression they tend to focus primarily on physical aggression. The referents of physical aggression generally examined are those acts included in the Conflict Tactics Scale (CTS) developed by Straus (1979). CTS is widely used for quantifying aggression. It assesses the frequency of occurrences of: (1) throwing something at the partner; (2) pushing, grabbing, or shoving; (3) slapping; (4) kicking, biting, or hitting with a fist; (5) hitting or trying to hit the partner with something; (6) beating the partner up; (7) threatening the partner with a knife or gun; and (8) using a knife on the partner or firing a gun at the partner. These are the behaviors that are considered when it is stated that 30% of couples will use some form of aggression at some point in their relationship. Consequently, the occurrence of even one slap or push would cause a couple to be classified as physically aggressive.

Most of the research into the characteristics of abusive men and abusive couples has focused on the characteristics and backgrounds of the male batterer, the female victim, and on the characteristics of the dyadic relationship. Several characteristics have been found to be associated with abused women, batterers, and couples. Regrettably, early research seemed to imply that certain women were somehow responsible for the aggression perpetrated against them because of certain personality characteristics (e.g., passivity). However, in an overview of the literature, the only factor which consistently distinguished abused from nonabused women across studies was the witnessing of aggression between parents (Hotaling & Sugarman, 1986).

Witnessing violence in the family of origin either as a recipient of abuse or corporal punishment by either parent (Caesar, 1988; Hotaling & Sugarman, 1986; Rosenbaum & O'Leary, 1981) or, even more predictive, as an observer of interparental aggression (Caesar, 1988; Hotaling & Sugarman, 1986; Kalmuss, 1984) is characteristic of many batterers as well. Bandura's (1973) theoretical work regarding the development of aggression via the modeling of the actions of significant individuals lends a conceptual framework to these findings. The clinical experiences of those who have conducted sessions of the Men's Educational Workshop Program at UMMC reflect the profound effects witnessing parental violence has had on these men. Despite the fact that the majority of the men detested their own father's abuse of their mothers, many also admit that through adolescence and early adulthood they viewed this behavior as a natural component of marital conflict.

Beyond the witnessing of parental violence, several other factors have been identified as common characteristics of batterers. Rosenbaum (1988) found that abusive men tend to have undifferentiated sex-role identities (i.e., scoring low on scales for both masculinity and femininity). Further studies indicate that these men also have poor self-concepts and low self-esteem (Goldstein & Rosenbaum, 1985; Neidig, Friedman, & Collins, 1986). Batterers are often comparatively lacking in verbal skill as compared to their wives (Ganley, 1981; Rounsaville, 1978), and further reveal deficits in verbal assertiveness in their relationships (Dutton & Strachan, 1987; Maiuro, Cahn, & Vitaliano, 1986; Rosenbaum & O'Leary, 1981). Although no consistent batterers' profile has emerged, some studies have noted elevated psychopathological features in batterers such as borderline characteristics (Hamberger & Hastings, 1991).

The role of alcohol and substance use in the development of relationship aggression has been a source of some controversy. O'Leary, Arias, Rosenbaum, and Barling (1985) found that alcohol abuse was significantly related to physical aggression in both men and women. In a review of studies that examined the relationship of wife abuse and alcohol, Kantor and Straus (1986) found a wide range of incidence figures on the occurrence of alcohol-influenced aggression. In all studies that compared abusive to non-abusive males, abusive men had significantly greater alcohol use. Several other studies conducted subsequent to this review have provided supporting data for this relationship (Roberts, 1988; Tollman & Bennett, 1990; Van Hasselt, Morrison, & Bellak, 1985). However, Kantor and Straus also found that the vast majority of aggressive episodes (74%) did not involve alcohol use by either party at the time of the incident. Conner and Ackerly (1994) reiterated these contradictions in their review, but also maintained that the existing findings were compelling enough to warrant adding an alcohol component to existing batterers' treatment programs.

Summary conclusions drawn from these and other studies indicate that there is a great deal of alcohol use in violent relationships, but the majority of violent episodes cannot be explained by proximate alcohol use. Thus the role of alcohol and other substances might be explained in several ways.

First, alcohol and substance abuse might be one of several risk factors in the development of relationship aggression; the disinhibiting effects of alcohol use might increase the likelihood of aggressive behavior but not be a unitary cause. Substance abuse could clearly be seen as another symptom of a personality structure that also carries a high tendency for abusive behavior. Substantial alcohol use might provoke stress in relationships and correspondingly create financial problems for the couple. Alcohol use might also be utilized as a functional technique for the abuser to disavow responsibility for his actions. Finally, particularly for chronic alcohol or substance abusers, substance use might inflict structural damage to the brain or functional disruption to neurochemical processes that would facilitate the onset of aggressive impulses and actions.

BIOLOGICAL INFLUENCES OF RELATIONSHIP AGGRESSION

Despite the aforementioned evidence of the role of substance use and the fact that biological factors have been shown to be associated with generalized aggression in numerous studies with both animal and human subjects (Brown & Linnoila, 1990; Coccaro, Siever, & Klar, 1989), there has been relatively little emphasis on biological factors in analyzing the phenomenon of marital aggression. Most of the characteristics focused upon have been psychological and sociocultural in nature. General theories of aggression, which almost always include biological factors, have been ignored, as if to say that relationship aggression is different from other forms of aggression. One important reason why biological factors have generally been discounted is the concern that if batterers can attribute their aggression to a physical problem, it will help to absolve them of some responsibility for their behavior. For theorists who view relationship aggression purely in terms of gender power and control issues, the potentiality of factors other than these sociological and attitudinal influences can seem a threat to what they view as the correct genesis of marital violence.

A few researchers have examined the role biological factors play in the development of relationship aggression. Elliot (1977) summarized the historical research and clinical findings that linked episodes of explosive rage to a variety of physical disorders such as rabies, multiple sclerosis, Huntington's chorea, temporal lobe epilepsy, viral encephalitis, and brain tumors. Elliot observed that in several patients with an organic form of "dyscontrol syndrome"—marked by poor impulse control in a number of areas of functioning—aggressive episodes of speech and behavior can be initiated by rather minor stimuli. Other cerebral trauma, such as closed head injury, has also been linked to the onset of violence in previously normal individuals. Lewis and her colleagues (1986, 1988) in their examination of juvenile and adult death row inmates, all of whom had committed extremely violent crimes, found that neurological trauma was nearly ubiquitous in the adult sample and that the majority of adolescents had suffered some head trauma in their lives. Although Lewis et al.'s sample is not composed of individuals perpetrating crimes of domestic violence, these studies provide compelling analogues for research into relationship aggression. However, interpretation of their results must be done with caution due to several methodological limitations, including small sample size, lack of comparison groups, and the potential for experimenter bias in the assessment procedures (i.e., awareness of the aggressive history of the subjects).

Several authors have investigated the profound effects that head injury can have on psychosocial functioning and familial relationships. Fahy, Irving, and Millac (1967) gathered collateral information from family members of individuals who had suffered a head injury five to six years prior to assessment. Although these relatives reported a variety of cognitive and functional problems in the head-injured individual, the changes most troubling to relatives occurred in the area of personality and temperament changes. Most of the head-injured individuals displayed increases in irritability. Panting and Merry (1972) correspondingly found relatives were most concerned with episodic moments of rage exhibited by the head-injured individual. These behavioral changes in husbands can subsequently effect the psychological well-being of their wives. Rosenbaum and Najenson (1976) found that wives of brain-injured men when compared with wives of paraplegic men reported greater levels of depression. While wives of paraplegic men reported losses of sexual functioning in their relationship as well, wives of head-injured men attributed the decrements in sexual activity to their own diminished interest in sexual contact because of the personality changes that had occurred in their husbands. Given these data, it is reasonable to assume that the potential for verbal, and perhaps physical, conflict increases when a family member suffers a head injury.

RESEARCH CONDUCTED AT UMMC

Initial interest in examining potential biological influences on the occurrence of domestic aggression at the Marital Research and Treatment Program of UMMC began with informal clinical observation. The procedure at the Psychiatric Outpatient Department required a medical history as part of the intake evaluation. An inordinate number of batterers referred to the batterers treatment program reported some incident of head injury sometime in their lives. After observing this trend among batterers, Rosenbaum and Hoge (1989) assessed the prevalence of significant head injury among batterers in a more formal study and found that 61% of the 31 batterers evaluated reported a positive history of significant head injury. These findings were concordant with the work of Lewis, Pincus, et al. (1986, 1988), who reported a positive history of head injury in most of the violent criminals they studied. Lacking generally accepted lifetime prevalence figures for head injury, Rosenbaum and Hoge generated an estimate based on the annual incidence figures and the average age of the sample. Even allowing for the most liberal estimates of annual incidence, the 61% finding by Rosenbaum and Hoge is more than three times as high as their estimates of prevalence in the general population. Although the results of these initial studies are provocative, methodological problems including small sample size, lack of appropriate comparison groups, and a failure to control for experimenter bias in the assessment of head injury suggest a need for further investigation.

Two additional studies that corrected some of the methodological problems of this initial study have recently been completed (Rosenbaum et al., in press; Warnken, Rosenbaum, Fletcher, Hoge, & Adelman, in press). Rosenbaum and his colleagues compared 53 male batterers to groups of maritally satisfied men and maritally discordant nonviolent men. All subjects were evaluated for a past history of head injury by a physician blind to group membership and aggression history of the subject. Additionally, a psychologist blind to the medical history assessed the subject's dating and marital history, alcohol and drug use, family history, education, occupation, police record, and psychiatric history with a focus on childhood antisocial behavior.

The results indicated that 53% of the abusive males had a history of significant head injury compared to only 25% of discordant, nonviolent males and 16% of the dissatisfied nonviolent men. Further analyses confirmed that head injury was a significant predictor of being a batterer. A history of significant head injury increased the chances of marital aggression almost sixfold. Examination of the temporal order of the head injury and the aggression indicated that for 93% of the head injured batterers, the head injury preceded the first incident of marital aggression. Further, in the 13 head-injured subjects with a history of arrest for assault and battery, the head injury preceded the assault and battery in every case. The most common causes of injuries were motor vehicle accidents (34%), followed by falls (25%), sports-related injuries (17%), and fighting (13%). The results of this study support the earlier findings of Rosenbaum and Hoge (1989) and strengthen the hypothesis that head injury may play a role in the development of relationship aggression.

The strength of the association between head injury and marital aggression in a battering population suggests that we should also find an increased frequency of marital aggression among individuals who have sustained a significant head injury. Warnken et al. (in press) conducted a computer search of the medical records at the University of Massachusetts over the past six years, and screened for both head injury and orthopedic injury diagnoses. All males 18 years or older who had sustained either a significant head injury or significant orthopedic injury were contacted by mail to solicit their participation in a written survey. A substantial number of potential subjects could not be contacted because of inactive or inaccurate addresses, death, or unresponsiveness to the mailing and follow-up telephone calls. In total, 235 men were contacted; 130 (or 58%) of these subjects completed and returned the forms. In addition to being at least 18 years of age at the time of injury and having sustained either a significant head injury or orthopedic injury, subjects of both groups were required to be involved in a heterosexual relationship and to have had no history of relationship aggression prior to their accident. Many of the 130 men who completed the questionnaires were excluded on the basis of at least one of these criteria. The final sample included 33 head-injured men and 42 orthopedically injured men. Although their participation was not a prerequisite for the subject's participation, the female partners of these men were also asked to complete questionnaires similar to those of the men. Completed questionnaires were received from 65 women, 27 of whom were partners of head-injured men and 38 of whom were partners of orthopedically injured men.

Although the results of this study did not confirm the relationship between the head injury and relationship aggression, there were significant between-group differences on many variables that might be expected to either precede, or co-occur, with battering. Specifically, head-injured males and their female partners were more likely to show status incompatibility, with the female partner having the higher status job; head-injured males also reported more postinjury problems with temper, reduced self-control, more arguments with both female partner and others, and more yelling. These postinjury changes were confirmed by their female partners who, in addition, felt that the head-injured men were more likely to smash things and to get into more frequent fights. The women of head-injured subjects also reported more postinjury verbal abuse by the men. Head-injured men had lower self-esteem, more difficulty communicating, and more difficulty expressing themselves verbally.

Alcohol use, which has been implicated as a factor in relationship aggression (Kantor & Straus, 1986; Maiuro, Vitaliano, Cahn, & Hall, 1987), was also more of a problem for the head-injured males. Head-injured men reported that they were drinking more postinjury and also that they were more affected by the alcohol, (i.e., they got drunk on fewer drinks). Finally, head-injured men and their female partners reported that the men were more depressed and angry postinjury, that they had experienced more negative changes in the relationship, and that they felt less close to each other.

How do we account for the fact that despite the presence of differences between head-injured men and their orthopedically injured counterparts on a host of risk factors for aggression, we do not find between-group differences in terms of physical aggression? One possible explanation concerns the amount of time that elapsed between the injury and our assessments. The mean number of years between the injury and the assessment was 2.85 years for the head-injured men, and 5.12 years for the orthopedically injured men. Although these means are not significantly different, it is possible that given a longer time frame more aggression would have occurred among the head-injured men, especially considering the numbers of risk markers and negative relationship changes being reported.

The possibility that there may be a link between physiological factors such as head injury and battering should not be seen as a threat to models that focus on power, control and sociocultural influences. Just as all men, irrespective of their sociocultural background and upbringing, are not batterers, neither are all head-injured individuals aggressive. Head injury may be one of a number of factors, such as alcohol consumption, that reduce an individual's ability to control aggressive impulses, thus increasing the probability of an aggressive response under certain circumstances, such as when he is feeling angered or provoked. Those circumstances are still very much a product of learning and sociocultural influences.

FUTURE DIRECTIONS

The studies done to date strongly support the need for further research into the relationships between biological factors and relationship aggression. Continued research along these lines of inquiry is currently underway at the Marital Research and Treatment Program. Two studies funded by the National Institute of Mental Health are in progress which examine in greater detail the relationship between head injury and subsequent marital aggression. Rosenbaum et al.'s (in press) finding that head injury preceded the first instance of aggression in 93% of the subjects is consistent with a causal model between head injury and aggression; this also minimizes the potential that a third variable could account for these two phenomena. However, the design model of this study did not allow for causal inferences;

rather, it suggested a number of risk factors for further research. Thus, the first of the studies being conducted currently employs a prospective, longitudinal design for examining the effects of head injury on domestic violence. Utilizing the emergency rooms of the major trauma centers of Worcester-area hospitals as data sources, subjects are being recruited at the point of injury and followed with their partners for a period of two years. During this time period, the couples will be assessed for development of marital discord and aggression. Assessment consists of an interview with the couple, individual interviews with both partners to confirm the information given in the couple interview, and collection of additional individual historical information about the male, as well as a written questionnaire battery. This battery includes measures that evaluate the frequency and severity of relationship aggression, marital satisfaction, experienced hostility, and current psychiatric symptomatology. As in previous studies, a comparison group of orthopedically injured men is being employed. Those with a prior head injury or marital aggression preceding the head or orthopedic injury are excluded from the study. Any individual who was under the influence of a substance at the time of his injury is also excluded. The criteria for inclusion as head-injured subjects are a loss of consciousness and posttraumatic amnesia for at least one minute; for those individuals reporting such experiences while under the influence, these factors could also be primarily attributed to alcohol or drug intoxication rather than neurological trauma. Approximations from subject recruitment to this date indicate that 50% of individuals appearing at these emergency rooms with a head or orthopedic injury serious enough to meet criteria for inclusion are eliminated on the basis of substance use.

In addition to providing information about the role of head injury in the development of marital aggression, this study will also allow for the potential identification of the mechanisms that mediate this relationship. Several hypotheses can be offered to explain this connection. Injuries to the frontal and temporal lobes may lead to the disinhibition of aggressive impulses that previously were controlled by the individual. Under this formulation, individuals are not classified as aggressive or nonaggressive, but are seen as having aggressive impulses that under normal conditions are inhibited from behavioral enactment. However, when physiologically impaired, for example through central nervous system (CNS) trauma or alcohol and drug use, the probability for aggression increases. Elliot's (1977, 1987) theory of the "episodic dyscontrol syndrome" would be consonant with this hypothesis.

Alternatively, the head injury may stimulate personality changes that contribute to the development of marital discord, increase irritability, or produce psychosocial stressors that impact the marital relationship (Brooks,

1984; Jennett, 1972; Rosenbaum & Najenson, 1976). Many of these potential difficulties were identified by Warnken et al. (in press) as being significantly worse for head-injured men as opposed to orthopedically injured men. McKinlay et al. (1981), in their longitudinal study of head-injured patients, reported patients' families complained that these individuals became more irritable and impatient following their injuries. Since the current study will track a number of psychological symptoms (e.g., depression, somatization, anxiety) and situational changes (e.g., job status, marital discord), this will allow for the exploration of many variables that may mediate the effects head injury has on marital violence.

There has been significant evidence supporting a relationship between reduced levels of the neurotransmitter serotonin and aggression in animals and humans (Brown & Linnoila, 1990; Coccaro et al., 1989). Coccaro et al. reviewed several studies examining this relationship and found that nearly all findings suggest that reduced concentrations of the serotonin metabolite CSF 5-HIAA correlate with aggression, hostility, irritability, or criminal activity. Lidberg et al. (1985) found that men who had murdered their sexual partners, and were not alcoholics, had reduced levels of CSF 5-HIAA. In a small number of studies of animal dominance (Raleigh, McGuire, Brammer, & Yuwiler, 1984) and human aggression (Fishbein, Lozovsky, & Jaffe, 1989; Stoff et al., 1992) either a positive relationship or no relationship at all between serotonergic activity and aggressive actions has been found. However, these are uncommon exceptions; the preponderance of data supports the association of low levels of serotonin with elevated aggression. There is also one study that suggests a link between head injury and low serotonergic activity (Woerkom et al., 1977). Woerkom et al. found that individuals with frontotemporal lobe contusions had lower levels of CSF 5-HIAA than comparison subjects. This finding raises the possibility that the effects of head injury on aggression may be mediated through the serotonergic system.

In another study being conducted at UMMC, we are examining whether batterers have reduced levels of serotonergic activity, and whether this relationship is interactive with the existence of a previous head injury. Four groups of 25 men each are being recruited. These groups are: (1) maritally aggressive and head injured; (2) maritally aggressive and not head injured; (3) maritally nonaggressive and head injured; and (4) maritally nonaggressive and not head injured. Subjects in the first two groups are being drawn from referrals to the Men's Educational Workshop at UMMC, a batterers' treatment program. Subjects in the latter two groups are being recruited via newspaper advertisement (although a significant percentage of those who have entered the study by responding to the advertisement have in fact been placed in the maritally aggressive group by virtue of the score on the Conflict Tactics Scale [Straus, 1979]).

Subjects are evaluated for a history of head injury and for the presence of any exclusion criteria. Those subjects meeting requirements for one of the four groups are scheduled for two appointments at UMMC, during which blood samples will be drawn throughout the day. During one of the days, subjects are given fenfluramine following the drawing of their first blood sample. Fenfluramine releases endogenous amounts of serotonin and blocks its reuptake into the presynaptic terminal (Garattini et al., 1975), which increases serotonergic activity and eventually leads to the release of prolactin. The prolactin response serves as the index of pre- and postsynaptic serotonergic activity. On the other day of participation, the subjects are given a placebo following the first blood sample. Administration of fenfluramine and placebo is randomly counterbalanced and both subjects and personnel involved in the data collection are blind to the order of presentation.

We hope that both of these studies will increase our understanding of how CNS trauma and neuroendocrine activity affect relationship aggression. Domestic violence is certainly a complex and disturbing situation that touches all segments of society regardless of race, socioeconomic status, or education. By identifying the neurochemical and neuroanatomic influences on certain behaviors, we may discover important contributors, in at least a subset of cases, to this multidetermined phenomena.

PRACTICAL IMPLICATIONS FOR BIOLOGICAL FACTORS

The possibility that physiological factors may play a role in facilitating aggression in relationships holds out the promise that biological interventions might some day augment our current psychoeducational intervention strategies. Certain classes of medications such as the serotonin re-uptake inhibitors and beta blockers may also prove to be effective for the treatment of relationship aggression. Eames (1988) suggests that the anticonvulsant medication carbamezepine may be an effective treatment for violent episodes resulting from head injury. Lithium, believed to be a serotonin enhancing agent, has effectively reduced aggression in some cases (Morrison et al., 1973). Trazadone, which blocks the re-uptake of serotonin as well as certain serotonin receptors, has been effective in lowering aggressiveness when used in combination with the serotonin precursor tryptophan (Wilcock, Stevens, & Perkins, 1987). Other frequently used selective serotonin re-uptake inhibitors, such as Prozac, Zoloft, and Paxil, may also prove valuable in the treatment of relationship aggression. If serotonin or other neurotransmitters are found to be associated with increased levels of marital aggression, this may provide a psychopharmalogical adjunct to existing treatment modalities. Given the limited resources available and the great importance of intervention in marital violence, these pharmacological interventions may prove invaluable in facilitating the acquisition of other coping techniques in short-term treatment models.

Beyond psychopharmacological interventions, if head-injured males are indeed at risk for battering, preventive strategies may be effectively incorporated into post head-injury rehabilitation protocols, hopefully short-circuiting the development of relationship aggression. Knowledge regarding the effects of head injury on emotional expression and cognitive ability would also be helpful for clinicians treating these men in psychotherapeutic or psychoeducational contexts. The injured patients and their families may benefit from information regarding these possibilities, which would encourage them to seek earlier intervention to help them cope with these potential behavior changes.

REFERENCES

Bandura, A. (1973). *Aggression: A social learning analysis.* Englewood Cliffs, NJ: Prentice-Hall.

Brooks, N. (1984). Head injury and the family. In N. Brooks (Ed.), *Closed head injury: Psychological, social and family consequences* (pp. 123–147). New York: Oxford University Press.

Brown, G. L., & Linnoila, M. I. (1990). CSF serotonin metabolite (FOHIAA) studies in depression, impulsivity, and violence. *Journal of Clinical Psychiatry, 51,* 31–41.

Browne, A. (1987). *When battered women kill.* London: Macmillan.

Caesar, P. L. (1988). Exposure to violence in the families-of-origin among wife-abusers and maritally nonviolent men. *Violence and Victims, 3,* 49–62.

Coccaro, E. F., Siever, K. J., & Klar, H. M. (1989). Serotonergic studies in patients with affective and personality disorders: correlates with suicidal and impulsive aggressive behavior. *Archive of General Psychiatry, 46,* 587–599.

Conner, K. R., & Ackerly, G. D. (1994). Alcohol-related battering: developing treatment strategies. *Journal of Family Violence, 9,* 143–155.

Dutton, D. G., & Strachan, C. E. (1987). Motivational needs for power and spouse specific assertiveness in assaultive and nonassaultive men. *Violence and Victims, 3,* 145–156.

Eames, P. (1988). Behavior disorders after severe head injury: Their nature and causes and strategies for management. *Journal of Head Trauma Rehabilitation, 3,* 1–6.

Elliot, F. A. (1977). The neurology of explosive rage: the dyscontrol syndrome. In M. Roy (Ed.), *Battered women*, pp. 98–109. New York: Van Nostrand Reinhold.

Elliot, F. A. (1987). Neuroanatomy and neurology of aggression. *Psychiatric Annals, 17,* 385–388.

Fahy, T. J., Irving, M. H., & Millac, P. (1967). Severe head injuries: A six year follow-up. *Lancet, 2,* 475–479.

Fishbein, D. H., Lozovsky, D., & Jaffe, J. H. (1989). Impulsivity, aggression, and neuroendocrine responses to serotonergic stimulation in substance abusers. *Biological Psychiatry, 25,* 1049–1066.

Ganley, A. L. (1981). *Court-mandated counseling for men who batter: A three-day workshop for mental health professionals.* Washington, DC: Center for Women's Policy Studies.

Garattini, S., Buczko, W., Jori, A., & Samanin, R. (1975). The mechanism of action of fenfluramine. *Postgraduate Medical Journal, 51,* 27–35.

Goldstein, D., & Rosenbaum, A. (1985). An evaluation of the self-esteem of maritally violent men. *Family Relations, 34,* 425–428.

Hamberger, L. K., & Hastings, J. E. (1986). Personality correlates of men who abuse their partners: A controlled comparison. *Violence and Victims, 3,* 31–48.

Hamberger, L. K., & Hastings, J. E. (1991). Personality correlates of men who batter and nonviolent men: Some continuities and discontinuities. *Journal of Family Violence, 6,* 131–147.

Hotaling, G. T., & Sugarman, D. B. (1986). An analysis of risk markers in husband to wife violence: The current state of knowledge. *Violence and Victims, 1,* 101–124.

Jennett, B. (1972). Late effects of head injuries. In M. Critchley, B. Jennett, & J. O'Leary (Eds.), *Scientific foundations of neurology* (p. 444). London: Heinemann.

Kalmuss, D. (1984) The intergenerational transmission of marital aggression. *Journal of Marriage and the Family, 46,* 11–19.

Kantor, G. K., & Straus, M. A. (1986). *The drunken bum theory of wife beating.* Paper presented at the National Alcoholism Forum Conference on Alcohol and the family, San Francisco.

Lewis, D. O., Pincus, J. H., Bard, B., Richardson, E., Prichep, L. S., Feldman, M., & Yeager, C. (1988) Neuropsychiatric, psychoeducational, and family characteristics of 14 juveniles condemned to death in the United States. *American Journal of Psychiatry, 145,* 584–589.

Lewis, D. O., Pincus, J. H., Feldman, M., Jackson, L., & Bard, B. (1986). Psychiatric, neurological, and psychoeducational characteristics of 15 death row inmates in the United States. *American Journal of Psychiatry, 143,* 838–845.

Lidberg, L., Tjck, J., Asberg, M., Tomba, G. P., & Bertilisson, L. (1985). Homicide, suicide and CSFHIAA. *Acta Psychiatr. Scand., 71,* 230–236.

Maiuro, R. D., Cahn, T. S., & Vitaliano, P. P. (1986). Assertiveness and hostility in domestically violent men. *Violence and Victims, 1,* 279–289.

Maiuro, R. D., Vitaliano, P. P., Cahn, T. S., & Hall, G. C. (1987). *Anger, depression, and coping in alcohol abusing versus non-alcohol abusing domestically violent men.* Paper presented at the Third National Family Violence Research Conference, Durham, NH.

McKinlay, W. W., Brooks, D. N., Bond, M. R., Martinage, D., & Marshall, M. M. (1981). The short-term outcome of severe blunt head injury as reported by relatives of the injured persons. *Journal of Neurology, Neurosurgery and Psychiatry, 44,* 527–533.

Morrison, S. D., Erwin, C. W., Gianturco, D. T., & Gerber, C. J. (1973). Effect of lithium on combative behavior in humans. *Disease of the Nervous System, 34,* 186–189.

Neidig, P. H., Friedman, D. H., & Collins, B. S. (1986). Attitudinal characteristics of males who have engaged in spouse abuse. *Journal of Family Violence, 1,* 223–233.

O'Leary, K. D., Arias, I., Rosenbaum, A., & Barling, J. (1985). *Premarital physical aggression.* Unpublished manuscript on file with the authors. State University of New York, Stony Brook.

O'Leary, K. D., Barling, J., Arias, I., Rosenbaum, A., Malone, J., & Tyree, A. (1989). Prevalence and stability of physical aggression between spouses: A longitudinal analysis. *Journal of Consulting and Clinical Psychology, 57,* 263–268.

Panting, A., & Merry, P. (1972). The long-term rehabilitation of severe head injuries with particular reference to the need for social and medical support for the patient's family. *Rehabilitation, 38,* 33–37.

Raleigh, M. J., McGuire, M. T., Brammer, G. L., & Yuwiler, A. (1984). Social and environmental influences on blood serotonin concentration in monkeys. *Archive of General Psychiatry, 41,* 405–410.

Roberts, A. R. (1988). Substance abuse among men who batter their mates: The dangerous mix. *Journal of Substance Abuse Treatment, 5,* 83–87.

Rosenbaum, A. (1988). Methodological issues in marital violence research. *Journal of Family Violence, 3,* 91–104.

Rosenbaum, A. (1994) Dating aggression on college campuses. Unpublished manuscript on file with the author. University of Massachusetts Medical Center.

Rosenbaum, A., & Hoge, S. K. (1989). Head injury and marital aggression. *American Journal of Psychiatry, 146,* 1048–1051.

Rosenbaum, A., Hoge, S. K., Adelman, S. A., Warnken, W. J., Fletcher, K. E., & Kane, R. (in press). Head injury in partner-abusive men.

Rosenbaum, A., & O'Leary, K. D. (1981). Marital violence: Characteristics of abusive couples. *Journal of Consulting and Clinical Psychology, 49,* 63–71.

Rosenbaum, M., & Najenson, T. (1976). Changes in life patterns and symptoms of low mood as reported by wives of severely brain-injured soldiers. *Journal of Consulting and Clinical Psychology, 44,* 881–888.

Rounsaville, B. (1978) Theories in marital violence: Evidence from a study of battered women. *Victimology: An International Journal, 3,* 11–31.

Stoff, D. M., Pasatiempo, A. P., Yeung, J., Cooper, T. B., Bridger, W. H., & Rabinovich, H. (1992). Neuroendocrine responses to fenfluramine and aggression in disruptive behavior disorders of children and adolescents. *Psychiatry Research, 43,* 263–276.

Stark, E., & Filcraft, A. (1988). Violence among intimates: An epidemiological review. In V. B. Van Hasselt, R. L. Morrison, A. S. Bellack, & M. Hersen (Eds.), *Handbook of family violence* (pp 293–319). New York: Plenum.

Straus, M. A. (1979). Measuring intrafamily conflict and violence: The Conflict Tactics (CT) scales. *Journal of Marriage and the Family, 41,* 75–88.

Straus, M. A., & Gelles, R. J. (1986). Societal change and change in family violence from 1975 to 1985 as revealed by two national surveys. *Journal of Marriage and the Family, 48,* 465–479.

Straus, M. A., Gelles, R. J., & Steinmetz, S. K. (1980). *Behind closed doors: Violence in the american family.* New York: Anchor Books.

Sugarman, D. B., & Hotaling, G. T. (1989). Dating violence: prevalence, context, and risk markers. In M. A. Pirog-Good & J. E. Stets (Eds.), *Violence in Dating Relationships: Emerging Social Issues* (pp. 5–11). New York: Praeger.

Tollman, R. M., & Bennett, L. W. (1990). A review of quantitative research on men who batter. *Journal of Interpersonal Violence, 5,* 87–118.

Van Hasselt, V. B., Morrison, R. L., & Bellak, A. S. (1985). Alcohol use in wife abusers and their spouses. *Addictive Behaviors, 10,* 127–135.

van Woerkom, T. C. A. M., Teelken, A. W., & Minderhoud, J. M. (1977). Differences in neurotransmitter metabolism in front temporal-lobe contusion and diffuse cerebral contusion, *Lance* (April).

Walker, L. E. A. (1979). *The battered woman.* New York: Harper & Row.

Warnken, W. J., Rosenbaum, A., Fletcher, K. E., Hoge, S. K., & Adelman, S. A. (in press). Head injured males: A population at risk for relationship aggression?

Wilcock, G. K., Stevens, J., & Perkins, A. (1987). Trazadone/tryptophan for aggressive behavior. *Lancet, 1,* 929–930.

AUTHORS' NOTE

This chapter was supported in part by NIMH Grant No. MH44812 to Alan Rosenbaum, Ph.D.

10 | ADVERSE (AND BENEFICIAL) CONSEQUENCES OF IMPULSIVE BEHAVIOR

Scott J. Dickman

Impulsivity is the tendency to act with less forethought than other individuals of equal ability and knowledge. This tendency can impair the individual's ability to cope with a variety of personal and occupational demands.

Attempts to clarify the adverse effects of impulsivity on psychological functioning have been hampered by the fact that investigators have assumed that the tendency to act with relatively little forethought has a single cause and a single set of consequences. There is evidence, however, that in certain individuals the tendency to act with relatively little forethought is actually advantageous. When these individuals are distinguished from individuals for whom impulsivity is a source of psychological difficulties, the precise nature of those difficulties becomes much clearer. This chapter reviews the evidence bearing on the distinction between these two very different types of impulsivity.

Other Uses of the Term Impulsivity

The definition of impulsivity given above is the one that has typically been used in the research literature on this trait. The term *impulsivity* is sometimes used in a broader sense to refer to a cluster of personality traits that include risk-taking, a failure to plan activities in advance, and liveliness (Eysenck & Eysenck, 1977). Although these traits are frequently present in impulsive individuals, factor analyses of self-report trait measures provide evidence that they are distinct from impulsivity (e.g., Eysenck & Eysenck, 1977; Gerbing, Ahadi, & Patton, 1987).

There are two substantial bodies of literature on impulsivity that are not discussed here because the investigators appear to be using the term impulsivity in a different sense than the way it is used here. These are the work of Kagan and his colleagues on Reflection-Impulsivity (e.g., Kagan, 1966; Kagan, Rosman, Day, & Phillips, 1964) and the work of Newman and his colleagues on syndromes of disinhibition (e.g., Newman, 1987; Newman, Widom, & Nathan, 1985).

Kagan and his colleagues measure Reflection-Impulsivity by means of the Matching Familiar Figures Test (MFFT; Kagan et al., 1964). The MFFT requires subjects to determine which of a set of line drawings is identical to an exemplar. Subjects are categorized as impulsive based on fast, inaccurate performance on this test. However, performance on the MFFT is not correlated with other measures of impulsivity, either behavioral or self-report, whereas these other measures do correlate with each other (Bentler & McClain, 1976). Thus Kagan and his colleagues appear to be studying a different trait than the one discussed here.

Newman and his colleagues have studied a phenomenon that they call "syndromes of disinhibition," which they view as related to impulsivity (e.g., Newman, 1987; Newman, Widom, & Nathan, 1985). However, the main measure they use in this research is the Extraversion scale of the Eysenck Personality Questionnaire (EPQ; Eysenck & Eysenck, 1975). This scale was derived from the Extraversion scale of an earlier questionnaire, the Eysenck Personality Inventory (EPI; Eysenck & Eysenck, 1965). While the Extraversion scale of the EPI includes a substantial number of items measuring impulsivity, these items have been removed from the EPQ version of the Extraversion scale (Rocklin & Revelle, 1981). Thus, like Kagan and his colleagues, Newman seems to be studying a somewhat different phenomenon from that studied by the investigators discussed here.

The present discussion, then, focuses on impulsivity in the sense of the self-reported tendency to make decisions with relatively little forethought. This trait has been called "narrow" impulsivity (Eysenck & Eysenck, 1977).

IMPULSIVITY AND IMPAIRED PSYCHOLOGICAL FUNCTIONING

As noted earlier, most research on impulsivity has focused on its negative effects on the individual's overall psychological functioning. The data on these effects come from such sources as hospital and court records. For example, Craske (1968) found that impulsive individuals were more likely than others to get into accidents severe enough to require emergency-room treatment. Similarly, it has been found that impulsive individuals are more likely than other individuals to get into traffic accidents (Hilakivi, Veilahti, Asplund, & Sinivuo, 1989; Loo, 1979)—and less likely than others to wear seat belts (Wilson, 1990). Impulsive individuals are also more likely to drive while drunk (Moore & Rosenthal, 1993).

Impulsive individuals are more likely than others to behave violently.

Barnett and Hamberger (1992) found that impulsive men were more likely than other men to be physically abusive toward their wives. Among individuals presenting at a psychiatric emergency room, impulsive individuals are especially likely to have to be hospitalized involuntarily because they are a danger to themselves or others (Segal, Watson, Goldfinger, & Averbuck, 1988). And on an inpatient psychiatric ward, impulsive patients are especially likely to engage in violent activity toward other patients and staff (Apter, Plutchik, & van Pragg, 1993).

The violent acts of impulsive individuals are directed at themselves as well as at others. Among depressed individuals, impulsive individuals are especially likely to make suicide attempts (Apter et al., 1993; Brent et al., 1993).

Impulsive individuals are also more likely than other individuals to suffer from eating disorders (Ryden & Johnsson, 1990). And their impulsiveness presents particular problems for these individuals when they are on restricted diets. For example, Rosenbaum and Smira (1986) studied individuals who had to follow a strict dietary regimen because they were undergoing kidney dialysis. They found that impulsive individuals were more likely than others to fail to adhere to their diet, even though they knew that this behavior could endanger their lives.

Impulsive individuals appear to have similar difficulties regulating impulses within the sexual domain. For example, impulsive college students are more likely than other college students to engage in unprotected sex (Moore & Rosenthal, 1993).

Impulsive individuals are especially likely to abuse drugs (King, Jones, Scheuer, Curtis, & Zarcone, 1990). And individuals who abuse multiple drugs are more impulsive than those who abuse a single drug (McCown, 1990).

Impulsive individuals are also especially likely to make purchases that they cannot afford (Rook, 1987). And both pathological gambling and fire-setting are classified as impulsivity-related disorders in the *Diagnostic and Statistical Manual of Mental Disorders* (DSM-IV; American Psychiatric Association, 1994).

IMPULSIVITY AND SUPERIOR PSYCHOLOGICAL FUNCTIONING

This body of data suggests that impulsivity has quite adverse effects on an individual's overall psychological functioning. However, there are other data that suggest that impulsivity may sometimes enhance such functioning.

For example, Robinson and Zahn (1988) had subjects perform a simple reaction-time task that required them to lift their fingers from a key as soon as possible after the onset of a tone. Impulsive subjects were faster on this task.

Edman, Schalling, and Levander (1985) also found that impulsive subjects were faster on a reaction-time task. These investigators required subjects to press a button to indicate which of two red lights had been illuminated. In this study, impulsive subjects' greater speed was accompanied by a reduction in accuracy. However, impulsive subjects still appeared to show overall superior performance, at least by one measure. Using Edman et al.'s (1985) speed and accuracy data, one can calculate how many correct answers subjects produced per second; impulsive subjects were superior on this measure. By responding quickly, they attempted so many items that they produced more correct answers than other subjects, even though their odds of getting a given item correct were lower.

Additional evidence for the positive effects of impulsivity on psychological functioning comes from research on the personality trait of extraversion. Extraverts tend to be more impulsive than introverts, and it appears to be this characteristic of extraverts that is primarily responsible for the differences between introverts and extraverts in their performance on a variety of cognitive tasks (Anderson & Revelle, 1983; Dickman, 1985; Dickman & Meyer, 1988; Eysenck & Levey, 1972; Loo, 1979; Revelle, Humphreys, Simon, & Gilliland, 1980).

Extraverts, like impulsive individuals, have been found to perform better than other individuals on tasks in which especially rapid responding can be associated with superior performance. For example, M. W. Eysenck (1974) found that extraverts were faster at retrieving information from semantic memory; although this greater speed was accompanied by a reduction in accuracy, this reduction was small and nonsignificant. DiScipio (1971) found extraverts to be more verbally fluent than introverts. And McLaughlin and Kary (1972) found that extraverts made more correct responses than other subjects on a recognition memory test, in spite of the fact that they also made more errors; like Edman et al.'s (1983) impulsive subjects, McLaughlin and Kary's extraverts responded so quickly that their lesser accuracy on each response was outweighed by the sheer number of responses they produced.

There are at least two possible explanations for the disparate effects of impulsivity on overall psychological functioning. It could be that a tendency to act with relatively little forethought enhances the ability to cope with some situations and impairs the ability to cope with others.

Alternately, it could be that there are two different forms of impulsivity, differing both in their causes and in their consequences for the individual.

For example, some individuals might act with relatively little forethought because of an impairment in psychological functioning that does not allow them to act more deliberately; such individuals would tend to suffer from their impulsivity. Other individuals might act with relatively little fore-thought because in the context of their life situations and their other psychological characteristics such a strategy is adaptive for them; such individuals would tend to benefit from their impulsivity.

THE TWO FORMS OF IMPULSIVITY

My own work supports the view that there are two distinct forms of impulsivity, which have in common a tendency to act with relatively little forethought, but which differ in the consequences and causes of that tendency. In one study that provided evidence for this distinction, I wrote a large set of impulsivity-related questions and administered them to a sample of undergraduates. The questions concerned the frequency with which the subject acted with relatively little forethought, the types of actions he or she carried out in this fashion, the nature of the situations in which these actions typically occurred, and whether these actions tended to have positive or negative consequences for the subject (Dickman, 1990, Study 1). Measures composed of these sorts of questions have been widely used in the study of impulsivity (e.g., Barratt, 1965; Eysenck & Eysenck, 1977; Jackson, 1967). Subjects do appear to be able to report their level of impulsivity with some accuracy, as evidenced by the correlations between self-report measures and other measures of impulsivity (e.g., Bentler & McClain, 1976).

I carried out an exploratory factor analysis of subjects' responses to these questions. One possible outcome of this analysis could have been that a single broad factor emerged (i.e., subjects who reported having one of the impulsivity-related characteristics about which I inquired tended to report having all of the characteristics). Such a finding would have suggested that there is only one form of impulsivity, and that the underlying factor which is its cause produces both positive and negative characteristics. Another possible outcome could have been the emergence of two factors; subjects who reported having one of the positive characteristics would report having the other positive characteristics, but not the negative ones, while subjects who reported having one of the negative characteristics would report having the other negative characteristics, but not the positive ones. Such a finding would suggest that the positive characteristics were all caused by one underlying factor, and the negative characteristics by a different factor, and that there are, therefore, two distinct forms of impulsivity.

The actual results of the factor analysis were consistent with the second of these two possible outcomes. Two different impulsivity factors emerged.

The questions that loaded on one of these factors clearly all referred to a tendency to suffer negative consequences due to acting with relatively little forethought. I labeled this factor "dysfunctional" impulsivity. Some examples of the questions that loaded on this factor were "I frequently make appointments without thinking about whether I will be able to keep them" and "I often get into trouble because I don't think before I act."

The questions loading on the other factor clearly involved a tendency to benefit from acting with relatively little forethought. I labeled this factor "functional" impulsivity. Some examples of questions that loaded on this factor were "I am good at taking advantage of unexpected opportunities, where you have to do something immediately or lose your chance" and "I like to take part in really fast-paced conversations, where you don't have much time to think before you speak."

The factor-analytic procedure I used (principal axis with an oblique rotation) made it possible to determine whether there was any relationship between the two factors, any tendency for someone high in one type of impulsivity to be especially high (or low) on the other. The two factors were in fact quite independent. There does not appear to be any relationship between someone's level of dysfunctional impulsivity and his or her level of functional impulsivity.

In another study (Dickman, 1990, Study 3), I looked at whether subjects' self-reported levels of dysfunctional and functional impulsivity, as measured by their responses to my questions, were actually associated with differences in the way they carried out basic cognitive tasks. In this study, I measured functional and dysfunctional impulsivity using scales derived from the factor analysis just described. Subjects were classified as high or low in each of these two types of impulsivity based on median splits of the scores on the two scales.

The experimental task was a visual comparison task. Subjects were presented with pairs of complex geometric figures and were asked to indicate whether the two figures in each pair were the same or different. They had a fixed period of time to complete as many figures as they could. The instructions to the subjects emphasized both speed and accuracy.

On this task, individuals high in functional impulsivity were faster and less accurate than individuals low in functional impulsivity. And functional impulsives' rapid style of responding did actually produce benefits for them. I calculated the total number of items subjects completed correctly in the time allotted, a measure of performance used in many tasks, including classroom examinations. Functional impulsives were superior on this measure in spite of their high error rate, due to the sheer number of items they completed.

In contrast to functional impulsivity, dysfunctional impulsivity showed no relationship to the speed or accuracy of performance on this task. I do have some data from another study that supports the view that dysfunctional impulsives show performance deficits consistent with their self-reported tendency to suffer from their impulsivity.

In this study (Dickman, 1994b), subjects carried out a visual search task. This task required them to first memorize a list of target letters (e.g., V, H, C, Q). They then were presented with strings of letters (e.g., WRMACN) and were asked to indicate whether any of the target letters were present in the string. Subjects high in dysfunctional impulsivity made more errors on this task than subjects low in dysfunctional impulsivity, while high and low functional impulsives did not differ in their performance.

THE NATURE OF FUNCTIONAL IMPULSIVITY

Functional impulsives' performance on the visual comparison task is consistent with the view that these individuals act with relatively little forethought because this is beneficial for them. On the visual comparison task, the overall effect of functional impulsives' greater speed was to increase the total number of items they completed correctly, even though that increased speed was accompanied by a higher error rate.

It is not necessarily the case that this relationship between speed and accuracy will hold for all tasks; it is likely that for some tasks, the reduction in accuracy resulting from increases in speed will be great enough so that the total number of items completed correctly will decline. Therefore, if the use of fast inaccurate strategies by functional impulsives were in part voluntary, they would not be expected to use such strategies under all circumstances. This is consistent with the finding that functional impulsives were neither particularly fast nor particularly inaccurate on the visual search task (Dickman, 1994b).

Performance Under Conditions of Extremely Rapid Responding

We have some additional data on the cognitive performance of impulsive individuals that suggests that functional impulsives can show superior performance for other reasons than being more productive by increasing their speed. In this study (Dickman & Meyer, 1988), we had subjects carry out the visual comparison task just described. However, instead of allowing subjects to determine how quickly they would respond, we manipulated the pace of the task by presenting the pairs of figures in rapid succession and requiring subjects to respond in the brief interval between presentations.

We found that when the pace was relatively slow (e.g., the figures were present for four seconds) impulsive individuals tended to be less accurate than other individuals. However, when subjects were forced to respond very rapidly (the figures were only present for half a second), impulsive individuals were actually more accurate than other individuals.

Although we did not distinguish between functional and dysfunctional impulsivity in this study, the measure we used, the EPI impulsivity scale, is correlated with both our measure of dysfunctional impulsivity and our measure of functional impulsivity (although somewhat less strongly with the latter measure; Dickman, 1990). One plausible interpretation of the findings of this study is that the superior performance of impulsive subjects in the 0.5-second condition was due to the performance of functional impulsives, while the inferior performance of impulsives in the other conditions of the study was due to the performance of dysfunctional impulsives.

From this perspective, the superior performance of functional impulsives in the 0.5-second condition was a consequence of the fact that these individuals prefer to respond very quickly in general, and therefore are accustomed to using cognitive strategies that maximize performance when responding is very rapid. Other subjects, in contrast, are likely to find their usual cognitive strategies disrupted by the requirement to respond extremely rapidly and will therefore perform poorly under these conditions. If this interpretation of the data is correct, it suggests that functional impulsives are likely to be at an advantage in general in situations in which everyone must act very quickly.

Avoiding a Tradeoff in Accuracy

Although we have no data bearing directly on this yet, it seems plausible that functional impulsives' rapid responding will not always have a cost in accuracy. Outside the laboratory, functional impulsives might well choose ecological niches in which their preferred style of responding does not result in a cost in accuracy.

For example, functional impulsives might choose to work at jobs in which the accuracy of their performance was not readily apparent, so that their mistakes would often go undetected (e.g., sales jobs in which a rapidly paced sales presentation could render it difficult for customers to detect inaccuracies). Or functional impulsives could select jobs that were so undemanding, given their level of ability, that they could respond very rapidly without sacrificing accuracy; here they are essentially sacrificing complexity of output for speed. It may be that the tendency of laboratory research to focus on the negative consequences of impulsivity is due to the fact that this research has typically relied on tasks that stress accuracy, the type of situation in which functional impulsives' strategies are likely to be least effective.

The Source of Functional Impulsivity

What causes certain individuals to become functionally impulsive? There are at least two possibilities. It could be that in order to be able to successfully adopt rapid error-prone strategies, the individual must have certain psychological characteristics, and it is individuals who have these characteristics who become functionally impulsive. It could also be that some individuals are raised in environments in which the tendency to act with relatively little forethought is advantageous, and they develop this tendency because it is rewarded.

There is some evidence bearing on the sort of psychological characteristics that might render a tendency to act with relatively little forethought an effective style of responding. I have examined the relationship between measures of functional and dysfunctional impulsivity and a variety of personality measures, including self-report measures of liveliness, activity level, and risking-taking (Dickman, 1990, Study 2).

I found that functional impulsives are especially lively, active, and willing to take risks. It might well be that individuals with these characteristics are both willing to respond very rapidly and able to do so with such effectiveness that the quantity of their output can compensate for its errorproneness.

Individuals might also become functionally impulsive if they grew up in environments in which speed was rewarded and accuracy was of less concern. For example, children raised in environments where they are able to "fast-talk" their way out of difficulties might well learn to adopt a functionally impulsive style.

THE NATURE OF DYSFUNCTIONAL IMPULSIVITY

Our visual search data provided evidence consistent with dysfunctional impulsives' report that they suffer from their tendency to act with relatively little forethought. There is other evidence that this tendency has negative consequences for dysfunctional impulsives. Dysfunctional impulsivity is associated with low self-esteem (Heaven, 1994), a tendency toward procrastination (Ferrari, 1994), and disorderliness (Dickman, 1990).

What causes dysfunctional impulsives to perform the way they do on cognitive tasks? Since the main general measures of impulsivity tap primarily dysfunctional impulsivity (Dickman, 1990), theories originally proposed to explain the characteristics of individuals high in general impulsivity can be viewed as theories of dysfunctional impulsivity.

Arousal Models of Dysfunctional Impulsivity

The theory of impulsivity that has thus far generated the most research is that of H. J. Eysenck (e.g., Eysenck, 1994). Eysenck has proposed that impulsive individuals are characterized by a low level of cortical arousal. According to this theory, one function of cortical activity is to inhibit the activity of those subcortical structures that mediate impulsive responding. The low level of cortical arousal of impulsive individuals, then, results in a failure to inhibit those lower structures and therefore in impulsive behavior.

Humphreys and Revelle (1984) have proposed a variant of this theory in which high and low impulsives differ in their circadian rhythms of arousal. According to this theory, the arousal levels of low impulsives reach their peak earlier in the day than those of high impulsives. Thus high impulsives are relatively low in arousal during the day when most psychology experiments are held, and this reduced level of arousal accounts for their performance characteristics.

The data on impulsivity do not, however, lend strong support to arousal-based theories of impulsivity. For example, studies that have examined EEG measures of cortical activity in introverts (who are low in impulsivity) and extraverts (who are high in impulsivity) have not found consistent differences (Gale, 1973).

Similarly, a number of studies have examined the effects of arousal on performance, through such techniques as the administration of caffeine. These studies have typically found that the effects of arousal on performance do not parallel the differences in performance between high and low impulsives (e.g., Anderson, Revelle, & Lynch, 1989; Smith, Rusted, Savory, Eaton-Williams, & Hall, 1991).

An Attentional Model of Dysfunctional Impulsivity

I have proposed an alternative explanation for dysfunctional impulsivity that seems to be more consistent with the available data (Dickman, 1994a). According to this theory, individuals high and low in dysfunctional impulsivity differ in the nature of the cognitive mechanisms that allocate attention. Individual differences in impulsivity reflect differences in the degree to which attention tends to remain fixed once it is directed to a particular source of information. To use the "searchlight" metaphor that is often applied to attention, high and low impulsives differ in the ease with which the beam of the searchlight can be moved from its current location; in low impulsives, that beam tends to remain fixed, whereas in high impulsives it is readily shifted.

According to this theory, the reason that dysfunctional impulsives report that they act with relatively little forethought is that they devote comparatively little of the time prior to responding to considering their response. Instead, their attention is distracted by task-irrelevant stimuli, internal and external.

This theory accounts for the seemingly paradoxical finding that dysfunctional impulsives do not consistently respond more quickly than other individuals in spite of their self-reported impulsivity (e.g., Dickman & Meyer, 1988; Matthews, Jones, & Chamberlain, 1989). If they were easily distracted, dysfunctional impulsives could respond as slowly as other individuals, and yet feel that they had not adequately considered their responses.

This theory also accounts for another seemingly paradoxical finding. Ferrari (1994) found that dysfunctional impulsives were especially likely to be procrastinators. If dysfunctional impulsives found it difficult to concentrate their attention for long periods of time, they might well put off tasks that required such concentration.

Research on the way impulsive individuals carry out a variety of cognitive tasks also lends support to this theory of dysfunctional impulsivity. This theory predicts that dysfunctional impulsives will be at a disadvantage only when the task is demanding in terms of attention. Such attentional demands could be present because subjects were required to pay attention to the task over an extended period of time, or because the task required especially intense concentration over a briefer period of time.

One source of evidence that impulsive individuals are impaired when they are required to maintain attention to a task over a long period of time is work on the way high and low impulsives carry out simple perceptual processing. In this research, subjects are asked to perform such tasks as indicating as rapidly as possible which of two lights has been turned on, or indicating which of four numbers is being displayed. High impulsives are not impaired relative to low impulsives when such tasks are relatively brief in duration (e.g., Smith et al., 1991), but they are impaired when the task lasts over half an hour (e.g., Roessler, 1973; Thackray, Jones, & Touchstone, 1974).

There is also evidence that impulsive individuals are impaired when they are required to maintain especially intense concentration over a relatively brief period of time. For example, I found that impulsive subjects showed inferior performance on a simple perceptual task when the time required to complete each task condition was less than 30 seconds.

This task required subjects to process both the fine details (the "local" level) and the gross features (the "global" level) of stimuli (Dickman, 1985). The stimuli were similar to ones that Kinchla and Wolfe (1979) and others have used in the investigation of the processing of the local and global levels of stimuli. Stimuli of this sort consist of small upper-case letters arranged so that they form the shape of a large letter; thus, small Es might be arranged in a circle to represent a large O. The small letters represent the local level of each stimulus, while the large letter represents its global level.

In each condition of this study, high and low impulsive subjects were presented with 36 stimuli. They had to determine into which of two categories each stimulus fell. In one condition, this categorization was based solely on the local level of the stimuli. Thus subjects might be asked to sort stimuli composed of small Hs into one category and stimuli composed of small Ts into the other, ignoring the larger letters formed by these Hs and Ts. In another condition, the categorization was based solely on the global level of the stimuli. Subjects might be asked to sort large Hs into one category and large Ts into the other; they could ignore the nature of the small letters whose arrangement formed the shape of an H or T. In the third condition, subjects had to integrate the information provided by the local and global levels in order to classify the stimuli. For example, subjects might be asked to sort large Hs made out of little Os into one category, and both large Hs composed of little Es and large Ts composed of little Os into the other. These stimuli could not be correctly classified based on either the local or global level alone. Subjects had to identify both the small letters and the large letter they formed, and combine the information provided by these two stimulus levels.

When the task only required subjects to pay attention to one level of the stimuli, either the local or the global, there were no differences between high and low impulsives. However, when subjects were required to integrate the information provided by these two dimensions, high impulsives showed a greater decline in performance, compared to the single-level tasks, than low impulsives did. Treisman and her colleagues have found that the integration of information from different dimensions of stimuli is especially attention-demanding (Treisman & Gelade, 1980; Treisman & Schmidt, 1982).

The Cause of Dysfunctional Impulsivity

Thus the deficits that dysfunctional impulsives show on cognitive tasks can be accounted for by assuming that in these individuals the mechanisms that allocate attention allow it to be too readily shifted. There is some evidence that speaks to the ultimate source of this characteristic of dysfunctional impulsives' attentional mechanisms.

There have been several studies of the heritability of impulsivity. These studies have found that impulsivity has a substantial genetic component (e.g., Eaves, Martin, & Eysenck, 1977; Pedersen, Plomin, McClearn, & Friberg, 1988). Assuming that the general measures of impulsivity used in these studies tap primarily dysfunctional impulsivity, these data suggest that there can be an inherited predisposition toward impulsivity.

This does not necessarily mean that an individual's level of dysfunctional impulsivity cannot be altered. However, it does seem to be the case that impulsive individuals respond less well to treatment than other individuals, due to the particular nature of their problem. Successful treatment for most disorders requires that the individuals seeking treatment carefully consider their current life situations and make well-thought-out decisions about how they want to change. These are psychological processes that are undermined by dysfunctional impulsives' difficulties in giving adequate consideration to decisions before making them.

So, for example, Hjordis and Gunnar (1989) found that impulsive individuals were especially likely to drop out of a behavioral treatment program for obesity. Sohlberg and his colleagues found that impulsivity was associated with poor progress among bulimic and anorexic patients (Sohlberg, Norring, Holmgren, & Rosmark, 1989). McCown (1990) found that impulsivity was negatively correlated with abstinence from alcohol in individuals attending a self-help group for alcoholism. Although Guerra and Slaby (1990) found some short-term benefits of cognitive therapy for impulsive individuals, they also found that these gains did not persist.

This suggests that new techniques will have to be devised for successfully treating dysfunctional impulsives. These techniques will have to provide external mechanisms to help these individuals focus their attention on their problems and their goals long enough to establish a consistent direction in treatment.

THE RELATIONSHIP BETWEEN FUNCTIONAL AND DYSFUNCTIONAL IMPULSIVITY

Eysenck has suggested that the term *impulsivity* should be restricted to dysfunctional impulsivity (Eysenck, 1994). He suggests that functional impulsivity is better thought of as *spontaneity.*

One reason to consider functional impulsivity as a form of impulsivity is that in both the research literature and in common usage, the tendency to act with relatively little forethought has been seen as the central feature of impulsivity (e.g., Eysenck & Eysenck, 1977). This tendency characterizes both functional and dysfunctional impulsives, and it therefore seems appropriate to apply the term impulsivity to both groups of individuals.

Eysenck (1994) has also argued that functional impulsivity ought not to be considered impulsivity because it lacks the emotional component usually associated with impulsivity. There do exist definitions of impulsivity that emphasize its emotional aspects. For example, according to the DSM-IV, impulsive acts involve "an increasing sense of . . . arousal before committing the act, [and] . . . an experience of either pleasure, gratification, or release at the time of committing the act" (p. 321).

However, our measures of dysfunctional impulsivity do not emphasize the emotional component of impulsivity any more than our measures of functional impulsivity do; both of these measures focus on the cognitive and behavioral aspects of impulsivity rather than on the emotional arousal on which the DSM-IV focuses. And Eysenck's own impulsivity measures, which tap primarily dysfunctional impulsivity, do not emphasize the emotional aspect of impulsivity either. Thus it does not seem possible, at least at this time, to distinguish between functional and dysfunctional impulsivity in terms of the role of emotion.

CONCLUSION

The work reviewed here suggests that in order to understand the effects of impulsivity on psychological functioning, it is necessary to distinguish between two quite different sources of impulsivity. This distinction has implications for the way our society should deal with impulsive individuals.

Some impulsive individuals actually seem to benefit from their impulsivity. It may well do such individuals no service to try to train them to be less impulsive. It seems possible that mental health professionals, who typically have spent considerable time in environments in which much emphasis is placed on avoiding mistakes (e.g., graduate and medical schools), fail to recognize the benefits of the rapid error-prone style of functional impulsives, and tend to mistake functional impulsivity for pathology.

For those individuals whose ability to cope with the demands of their daily lives *is* impaired by their impulsivity, techniques to reduce that impulsivity will have to be based on an understanding of the mechanisms that produce it. If in fact a difficulty maintaining attention underlies dysfunctional impulsivity, treatments that focus on improving concentration are likely to be much more effective than those that focus on simply encouraging these impulsive individuals to respond more slowly. Given the negative consequences of dysfunctional impulsivity, both for the individual and for the society in which he or she lives, there is clearly a need to develop such treatments.

REFERENCES

American Psychiatric Association (1994). *Diagnostic and statistical manual of mental disorders,* (4th ed.). Washington, DC: American Psychiatric Association.

Anderson, K. J., & Revelle, W. (1983). The interactive effects of caffeine, impulsivity, and task demands on a visual search task. *Personality and Individual Differences, 4,* 127–134.

Anderson, K. J., Revelle, W., & Lynch, M. J. (1989). Caffeine, impulsivity, and memory scanning: A comparison of two explanations for the Yerkes-Dodson Effect. *Motivation and Emotion, 13,* 1–20.

Apter, A., Plutchik, R., & van Pragg, H. M. (1993). Anxiety, impulsivity and depressed mood in relation to suicidal and violent behavior. *Acta Psychiatrica Scandinavica, 87,* 1–5.

Barnett, O. A., & Hamberger, L. K. (1992). The assessment of maritally violent men on the California Psychological Inventory. *Violence and Victims, 7,* 15–28.

Barratt, E. S. (1965). Factor analysis of some psychometric measures of impulsiveness and anxiety. *Psychological Reports, 16,* 547–554.

Barratt, E. S., & Patton, J. H. (1983). Impulsivity: Cognitive, behavioral, and psychophysiological correlates. In M. Zuckerman (Ed.), *Biological bases of sensation seeking, impulsivity, and anxiety* (pp. 77–116). Hillsdale, NJ: Lawrence Erlbaum Associates.

Bentler, P. M., & McClain, J. (1976). A multitrait-multimethod analysis of reflection-impulsivity. *Child Development, 47,* 218–226.

Brent, D., Johnson, B., Bartle, S., Bridge, J., Rather, C., Matta, J., Connolly, J., & Constantine, D. (1993). Personality disorder, tendency to impulsive violence, and suicidal behavior in adolescents. *Journal of the American Academy of Child and Adolescent Psychiatry, 32,* 69–75.

Craske, S. (1968). A study of the relation between personality and accident history. *British Journal of Medical Psychology, 41,* 399–404.

Dickman, S. (1985). Impulsivity and perception: Individual differences in the processing of the local and global dimensions of stimuli. *Journal of Personality and Social Psychology, 48,* 133–149.

Dickman, S. (1990). Functional and dysfunctional impulsivity: Personality and cognitive correlates. *Journal of Personality and Social Psychology, 58,* 95–102.

Dickman, S. (1994a). Impulsivity and information processing. In W. McCown, M. Shure, & J. Johnson (Eds.), *The impulsive client: Theory, research, and treatment* (pp. 151–184). Washington, DC: American Psychological Association.

Dickman, S. (1994b). The performance of functional and dysfunctional impulsives on a visual search task. Unpublished raw data.

Dickman, S., & Meyer, D. E. (1988). Impulsivity and speed-accuracy tradeoffs in information processing. *Journal of Personality and Social Psychology, 54,* 274–290.

DiScipio, W. J. (1971). Divergent thinking: A complex function of interacting dimensions of introversion-extraversion and neuroticism-stability. *British Journal of Psychology, 62,* 545–550.

Eaves, L. J., Martin, N. G., & Eysenck, S. B. G. (1977). An application of the analysis of covariance structures to the psychogenetical study of impulsivity. *British Journal of Mathematical and Statistical Psychology, 38*, 185–197.

Edman, G., Schalling, D. T., & Levander, S. E. (1985). Impulsivity and speed errors in a reaction time task: A contribution to the construct validity of the concept of impulsivity. *Acta Psychologica, 53*, 1–8.

Eysenck, H. J. (1994). The nature of impulsivity. In W. McCown, M. Shure, & J. Johnson (Eds.), *The impulsive client: Theory, research, and treatment* (pp. 57–70). Washington, DC: American Psychological Association.

Eysenck, H. J., & Eysenck, S. B. G. (1965) *Manual of the Eysenck personality inventory.* London: Hodder & Stoughton.

Eysenck, H. J., & Eysenck, S. B. G. (1975). *Manual of the Eysenck personality questionnaire.* London: Hodder & Stoughton.

Eysenck, S. B. G., & Eysenck, H. J. (1977). The place of impulsiveness in a dimensional system of personality description. *British Journal of Social and Clinical Psychology, 16*, 57–68.

Eysenck, H. J., & Levey, A. (1972). Conditioning, introversion-extraversion and the strength of the nervous system. In V. D. Nebylitsyn and J. A. Gray (Eds.), *Biological bases of individual behavior* (pp. 206–220). London: Academic Press.

Eysenck, M. W. (1974). Individual differences in speed of retrieval from semantic memory. *Journal of Research in Personality, 8*, 307–323.

Ferrari, J. (1994). Procrastination and impulsiveness: Two sides of a coin? In W. McCown, M. Shure, & J. Johnson (Eds.), *The impulsive client: Theory, research, and treatment* (pp. 265–276). Washington, DC: American Psychological Association.

Gale, A. (1973). The psychophysiology of individual differences: Studies of extraversion and the EEG. In P. Kline (Ed.), *New approaches to psychological measurement* (pp. 57–74). London: Wiley.

Gerbing, D., Ahadi, S., & Patton, J. (1987). Toward a conceptualization of impulsivity: Components across the behavioral and self-report domains. *Multivariate Behavioral Research, 22*, 1–22.

Guerra, N. G., & Slaby, R. G. (1990). Cognitive mediators of aggression in adolescent offenders: 2. Intervention. *Developmental Psychology, 26*, 269–277.

Heaven, P. C. L. (1994). Personality correlates of functional and dysfunctional impulsiveness. *Personality and Individual Differences, 15*, 191–204.

Hilakivi, I., Veilahti, J., Asplund, P., and Sinivuo, J. (1989). A sixteen-factor personality test for predicting automobile driving accidents of young drivers. *Accident Analysis and Prevention, 21*, 413–418.

Hjordis, B., & Gunnar, E. (1989). Characteristics of drop-outs from a long-term behavioral treatment program for obesity. *International Journal of Eating Disorders, 8*, 363–368.

Humphreys, M. S., & Revelle, W. (1984). Personality, motivation, and performance: A theory of the relationship between individual differences and information processing. *Psychological Review, 91*, 153–184.

Jackson, D. N. (1967). *Personality research form manual*. Goshen, NY: Research Psychologists Press.

Kagan, J. (1966). Reflection-Impulsivity: The generality and dynamics of conceptual tempo. *Journal of Abnormal Psychology, 71*, 17–24.

Kagan, J., Rosman, B. L., Day, D., & Phillips, W. (1964). Information processing in the child: Significance of analytic and reflective attitudes. *Psychological Monographs, 78*, No. 1 (Whole No. 578).

Kinchla, R. A., & Wolfe, J. M. (1979). The order of visual processing: "top-down," "bottom-up," or "middle-out." *Perception and Psychophysics, 25*, 225–231.

King, R. J., Jones, J., Scheuer, J. W., Curtis, D., & Zarcone, V. P. (1990). Plasma cortisol correlates of impulsivity and substance abuse. *Personality and Individual Differences, 11*, 287–291.

Loo, R. (1979). Role of primary personality factors in the perception of traffic signs and driver violations and accidents. *Accident Analysis and Prevention, 11*, 125–127.

Matthews, G., Jones, D. M., & Chamberlain, A. G. (1989). Interactive effects of extraversion and arousal on attentional task performance: Multiple resources or encoding processes? *Journal of Personality and Social Psychology, 56*, 629–639.

McLaughlin, R. J., & Kary, S. K. (1972). Amnesic effects in free recall with introverts and extraverts. *Psychonomic Science, 29*, 250–252.

McCown, W. G. (1988). Multi-impulsive personality disorder and multiple substance abuse: Evidence from members of self-help groups. *British Journal of Addiction, 83*, 431–432.

McCown, W. G. (1990). The effect of impulsivity and empathy on abstinence of poly-substance abusers: A prospective study. *British Journal of Addiction, 85*, 635–637.

Moore, S. M., and Rosenthal, D. (1993). Venturesomeness, impulsiveness and risky behavior among older adolescents. *Perceptual and Motor Skills, 76*, 98.

Newman, J. P. (1987). Reaction to punishment in extraverts and psychopaths: Implications for the impulsive behavior of disinhibited individuals. *Journal of Research in Personality, 21*, 464–480.

Newman, J. P., Widom, C. S., and Nathan, S. (1985). Passive-avoidance in syndromes of disinhibition: Psychopathy and extraversion. *Journal of Personality and Social Psychology, 48*, 1316–1327.

Pedersen, N., Plomin, R., McClearn, G. E., & Friberg, L. (1988). Neuroticism, extraversion and related traits in adult twins reared apart and reared together. *Journal of Personality and Social Psychology, 55*, 950–957.

Revelle, W., Humphreys, M. S., Simon, L., & Gilliland, K. (1980). The interactive effect of personality, time of day, and caffeine: A test of the arousal model. *Journal of Experimental Psychology: General, 109*, 1–31.

Robinson, T. N., & Zahn, T. P. (1988). Preparatory interval efects on the reaction time performance of introverts and extraverts. *Personality and Individual Differences, 4*, 749–761.

Rocklin, T., & Revelle, W. (1981). The measurement of extraversion: A comparison of the Eysenck Personality Inventory and the Eysenck Personality Questionnaire. *British Journal of Social Psychology, 20,* 279–284.

Roessler, R. (1973). Personality, psychophysiology, and performance. *Psychophysiology, 10,* 315–327.

Rook, Dennis (1987). The buying impulse. *Journal of Consumer Research, 14,* 189–199.

Rosenbaum, M., & Smira, K. B. (1986). Cognitive and personality factors in the delay of gratification of hemodialysis patients. *Journal of Personality and Social Psychology, 51,* 357–364.

Ryden, O., & Johnsson, P. (1990). Psychological vulnerabilities and eating patterns in a group of moderately obese patients. *Journal of Obesity and Weight Regulation, 8,* 83–97.

Segal, S. P., Watson, M. A., Goldfinger, S. M., & Averbuck, D. S. (1988). Civil commitment in the psychiatric emergency room. *Archives of General Psychiatry, 45,* 759–763.

Smith, A. P., Rusted, J. M., Savory, M., Eaton-Williams, P., & Hall, S. R. (1991). The effects of caffeine, impulsivity and time of day on performance, mood and cardiovascular function. *Journal of Psychopharmacology, 5,* 120–128.

Sohlberg, S., Norring, C., Holmgren, S., & Rosmark, B. (1989). Impulsivity and long-term prognosis of psychiatric patients with Anorexia Nervosa/Bulimia Nervosa. *Journal of Nervous and Mental Disease, 177,* 249–258.

Thackray, R. I., Jones, K. N., & Touchstone, R. M. (1974). Personality and physiological correlates of performance decrement on a monotonous task requiring sustained attention. *British Journal of Psychology, 65,* 351–358.

Treisman, A. M., & Gelade, G. (1980). A feature-integration theory of attention. *Cognitive Psychology, 12,* 97–136.

Treisman, A. M., & Schmidt, H. (1982). Illusory conjunctions in the perception of objects. *Cognitive Psychology, 14,* 141–149.

Wilson, R. J. (1990). The relationship of seat belt non-use to personality, lifestyle and driving record. *Health Education Research, 5,* 175–185.

4 | ADVERSITY IN THE BROADER SOCIETY

11 TRANSFORMING THE PSYCHOLOGY OF RISK

From Social Perception to the Geography of Communities

Linda Silka

Consider an increasingly common scenario in which the cognition of laypersons plays a part. Communities find themselves struggling with the adverse effects of local environmental problems on residents (Edelstein, 1988). These communities are disproportionately likely to be poor communities and communities of color (Bullard, 1990). In their quest to have their concerns addressed, residents take steps on their own, moving (often with considerable trepidation) into a policy arena defined by language and technology foreign to most laypeople (Littrell & Hobbs, 1989). In the process, they turn to experts who often fail to provide the assistance needed and who frequently misunderstand the context from which the concerns arise (Dietz & Rycroft, 1987). The results are often unhappy collisions between "experts" and laypeople (Bullard, 1993; Cohen & O'Connor, 1990).

Seeking to understand such collisions, psychologists have advanced a psychology of risk perception that attempts to model how laypeople perceive risks. But this psychology of risk all too rarely looks at the context of risk, or the nature of the communities in which this risk arises; in short, our psychology of risk, although increasingly precise, remains surprisingly generic.

How do we return our analysis of individual cognition of risk to the community dilemmas that were a part of the initial interest in the area? How do we do so in ways that shed light on the psychology of adversity? The present analysis begins with a discussion of the limitations of past approaches to the psychology of risk for studying communities.

PSYCHOLOGY OF RISK:
PROBLEMS AND POSSIBILITIES

From the beginning, a number of common working assumptions and strategies of approach have held together the risk perception literature (Brehmer, 1987; Cvetkovich & Earle, 1992). This rich body of work has included a focus on problematic risk perception (i.e., why people perceive risk in biased ways), and an underlying action orientation (i.e., how this research can aid laypeople in making better risk assessments). Psychology's focus on the individual is also mirrored in this work, with its emphasis on individual cognition and modeling the risk perception process through the study of heuristics and the like. And a traditional laboratory approach has been followed, guided by the attendant assumptions that the individual can be studied independent of context.

In many respects, this focus on heuristics and individual cognition has been highly productive. An internally consistent program of research has resulted that maps out models of risk perception and increases our understanding of basic judgment processes. Yet as the area has reached maturity and begun to adopt a standardized methodology and focus on a delimited line of questions, the general thrust of the paradigm has increasingly been called into question.

Cogent criticisms of the psychology of risk perception have begun to emerge over the last few years (Freudenburg, 1988). These criticisms draw from diverse ecological and scholarly perspectives but all similarly question whether the risk literature moves us any closer to producing a body of basic research that speaks to the applied problems of everyday risk perceptions.

Critics have asked whether the existing paradigm is too internalist and cognitive, too "in the head" in its way of treating people as isolated individuals confronting environmental issues (Kasperson, Renn, & Slovic, 1988). Although traditional laboratory approaches are seen as advancing an understanding of cognitions, critics question whether they tap into the underlying environmental dilemmas that people often struggle with in their communities (Cohen & O'Connor, 1990). The studies have also been criticized as insufficiently connected to analyses of environmental risks (Krimsky & Plough, 1988), and as inadequately attending to cultural and ethnic differences in environmental risk experience (Cvetkovich & Earle, 1991; Vaughan, 1993). Finally, many have commented that the work on psychology of risk remains too isolated from groundbreaking analyses of environmental risk occurring in other disciplines and various interdisciplinary contexts (Johnson & Covello, 1987).

Changes in the field in response to these criticisms have been slow and fragmented. A few researchers have picked up on the cultural thread. For example, a special issue on cultural and ethnic differences in environmental views has recently been published (Cvetkovich & Earle, 1991). Others have begun to probe differences in risk cognitions that result from variations in perspectives on justice (Opotow, 1993). Yet few attempts have been made to draw out the implication of the core assumptions that underlie the various criticisms: the supposition that environmental cognition is tied to the experience of place. In this chapter I argue for the heuristic value of tying the psychology of risk to the geography of place.

THE GEOGRAPHY OF RISK

The geography of risk assumes that location is central (for broader treatments of the effects of location on various types of social functioning, see Gregory, 1994; Rose, 1993). That is, it assumes that to understand risk responses we must look closely at place and the many factors associated with geographic location (e.g., ethnic and class differences in risk experiences, geographically based encounters with combinations of risk, the fact that encounters with risks are often neighborhood-based). The incorporation of place and its associated variables into the model we use to investigate risk is likely to enhance our understanding of people's experience of risk, the environmental dilemmas they face, and the actions they take.

Treating geography as having psychological import is far from new. Investigations of the links between cognition and geography began several decades ago, when a tradition developed of examining how people cognize their environment (Evans, 1980). These perceptions were analyzed in terms of intuitive cognitive maps (Golledge, 1987; Wood, 1992). Earlier work illustrated the value of closely examining the linkages between place and cognition (Craik & Feimer, 1987); in this chapter we look at new lines of investigation that point to the gains to be had from incorporating an explicit geographical focus into the study of risk.

By looking at risk in a geographical framework we tap into several important literatures that have thus far remained largely unconnected to basic risk perception work. Three disparate lines of research have explored geographical themes and argue for the need to situate the psychology of risk within a geographic context, including recent analyses in community psychology of place and empowerment, recent investigations of environmental racism and equity, and new spatial analysis techniques emerging in the field of geographical information systems (GIS).

Although differing in many respects, the three reflect common themes of place, culture, and social action. They point to the need to situate the risk perception work within a geographic context. They provide ideas about how to operationalize geographic context, offer suggestive possibilities for framing cultural differences in risk experiences, and reflect back on varieties of ordinary risk experiences. And they illustrate different ways of framing questions of how geographically situated cognitions are linked to social action. In short, these bodies of work offer insights into everyday risk perception and reflect back on risk perception literature in novel ways. The three areas are examined below, with the aim of sketching out the problems in risk perception made salient by a focus on geography.

COMMUNITY PSYCHOLOGY:
APPROACHES TO THE ANALYSIS OF PLACE

If we wish to look closely at geographic contexts to understand people's responses to the environmental dilemmas they face, we hardly need to reinvent the wheel to find ways to analyze settings. The gains to be had by examining geographical context are reflected in work in community psychology, an area with an extensive history of situating analyses of psychological concepts within geographic contexts, yet which remains largely untapped by those who study risk perception.

Community psychologists have long regarded laboratory approaches that isolate the individual to be inadequate for predicting responses in real life settings (Heller, 1989; Sarason, 1974). These researchers have sought other ways of exploring cognition and the links between cognition and action. Over the last several decades community psychologists have developed an extensive body of research examining people in neighborhoods, communities, and other settings (cf. Altman & Wandersman, 1987). Work in this area has been directed at developing rigorous models for exploring the nature of settings and communities (Florin & Wandersman, 1984; Heller, 1990; Levine & Perkins, 1987).

Situating the analysis of psychological concepts within geographic contexts has had considerable heuristic value. Community psychologists have begun to identify the dimensions along which settings and communities vary in order to understand how settings impact behavior and functioning (Mulvey & Silka, 1987; Novaco, Stokols, & Milanesi, 1990; Perkins, Florin, Wandersman, & Chavis, 1990). People's experiences in settings and the associated psychological experience of place have come under examination (Chavis & Wandersman, 1990). Complex characterizations of settings have been the result of these investigations (Levine & Perkins, 1987). For example, the experience of adversity has been found to be linked in complex ways to settings (Holahan & Wandersman, 1987). The fact that a community is financially impoverished, for example, is insufficient to predict community responses to problems (Rappaport, 1987). Instead, researchers have shown that a variety of mediating psychological variables (e.g., setting social support, availability of mutual assistance) are needed to account for how groups respond to adversity (Davidson & Cotler, 1993; Levine, 1988; Unger & Wandersman, 1985).

Community psychologists have also illustrated how cognitions can be tied to settings through investigations of the predictive power of constructs such as the psychological sense of community (McMillan & Chavis, 1986). Once again we see attempts being made to bridge the gap between individual processing and the community level of analysis and to tie individual cognition to group experiences (Hallman & Wandersman, 1992, 1993; Zimmerman, 1990). For example, rather than seeing individuals as central, community psychologists looked to social groupings such as families as the nexus of various community experiences. Community psychologists have begun to analyze the multiple risks that families face through their linked experiences with housing, schools, jobs, the infrastructure, and toxic waste sites (Hallman & Wandersman, 1992). Past studies have shown that these family concerns can be powerful forces for community change (Unger, Wandersman, & Hallman, 1992).

Community psychologists have also shown how the analysis of settings can be extended to include an examination of the links between cognition and social action. In other words, they have sought to answer questions about when groups will take action and how an understanding of geographical settings may aid in understanding those actions. In their attempts to identify the constructs that mediate action, community psychologists have analyzed such difficult and slippery concepts as empowerment and investigated the geographic underpinnings of how empowered groups act (Wandersman & Florin, 1990). Some researchers now argue that empowerment is shaped in part by setting variables such as connectedness (Chavis & Wandersman, 1990). Those who experience a sense of connectedness are likely to act in a variety of instrumental ways (Wandersman & Florin, 1990). In examining actions in settings, community psychologists also have attempted to move away from individual levels of analysis. For example, Brody (1988) has taken the individually based concept of self-efficacy and attempted an analysis of collective efficacy in order to better predict how people will respond to risks in work settings.

Although much of the analysis in community psychology described above lends itself to risk applications, relatively few researchers in community psychology have explored possible linkages between risk and community. Key work that has explored this linkage is that of Hallman and

Wandersman (1992). They have begun to test out a community psychology analysis of risk response that grounds itself in a geographic context and draws on concepts and findings in community psychology. Their work argues that we must understand specific community dilemmas, settings, and variables if we are to understand risk perceptions, and their work brings to the foreground questions of group experiences and collective coping strategies. Wandersman and Hallman (1993) show the ways in which individual difference variables, despite having some predictive power, fail to provide sufficient practical knowledge for the development of community intervention strategies.

Community psychologists also point to the importance of attending to complexity and here too we can see a linkage to risk perception. A classic paper in community psychology discussed the importance of paradox in analyzing communities (Rappaport, 1987), with Rappaport arguing that paradoxes are often the most revealing of the operation of complex factors and interventions that have unexpected effects. Paradoxes abound in risk perception. There is the paradox that cognitive research shows unfamiliar risks to be the most feared, yet communities are increasingly mobilizing around familiar risks (Bullard, 1993). And there is the paradox of laypeople seemingly overreacting to some hazards that involve limited risk and underreacting to others that pose much greater risk (Johnson & Covello, 1987). What we have taken to be contradictions (especially when considered simply within a heuristics framework) may upon examination turn out to reflect psychological factors mediated through geographic contexts.

The kind of setting analysis that community psychologists engage in has been relatively rare in studies of the psychology of risk, although there is some emerging convergence. Recent work in the psychology of risk has expanded to incorporate a few setting variables. We see this, for example, in research on mental models of radon in the home (Bostrom, Fischhoff, & Morgan, 1992). Rather than look just at abstract beliefs about risk, researchers here catalogue the radon risks in the setting itself and then develop models of how people actually conceive of those risks. This kind of setting approach (albeit of a highly constrained setting in the case of radon) is exactly what community psychologists—our first example of researchers using a geographical analysis—have advocated in recent years. And what is particularly instructive about the approach taken by community psychologists is that their work suggests how to avoid a deterministic stance toward settings while closely examining settings and contexts in which people encounter risks, not just in the home, but throughout their neighborhoods and communities.

The intent of this first section has been to trace how the largely untapped community psychology approach sheds light on the importance of geographical settings and illustrates one way of beginning to look at psychological variables within a geographical context. Community psychology is not the only area of theoretical analysis to provide insights into ways to incorporate a geographical focus into the study of risks. In the next section we turn to the implications for risk perception of a very different line of research, that on environmental equity, whose broad ranging implications have also not been examined and remain outside standard analyses of the perception of risk. Although the environmental equity movement shares in common with community psychology an attention to geographical settings, the environmental equity work ties those concerns more explicitly to risk. In the next section we trace recent attempts to use a geographical analysis to reframe questions about differential exposure to risk. Such an approach is beginning to reveal a variety of important demographic and cultural factors that figure in community responses to environmental dilemmas.

ENVIRONMENTAL EQUITY:
LINKING COMMUNITY DEMOGRAPHICS TO RISK

Increasingly researchers of risk have become aware of the need to turn their attention to questions of culture, race, class, and gender (Cvetkovich & Earle, 1991). Various researchers have carried out cross-cultural analyses (for example, Rosa & Kleinhesselink, 1991) and analyses of ethnic differences (Vaughan & Nordenstam, 1991). Yet, despite burgeoning work in this area, it has remained unclear why cultural and ethnic differences should contribute to differences in risk perception (are they a result of differences in schemas, salience of problems, or some other cognitive factor, for example?). What has been missing is a theoretical framework for explaining differences.

Recent interdisciplinary work outside of psychology investigating questions of environmental equity has begun to provide just such a framework (Mitchell, 1993). Analysts of environmental equity have started to ask whether cultural and racial differences in perception of risks might be a consequence of differences in geographical experiences. Thus this analysis focuses not so much on the common environmental dilemmas all people share but on disproportionate risks faced by some groups. By examining geographic distributions of risk—for example, how communities vary in their exposure to risks—these analysts argue that we will uncover marked variations in exposures as a function of race, ethnicity, and class, and will likely find poor communities and communities of color at greatest environmental risk.

Although it has long been suspected that many environmental risks are associated with living in poor, minority, urban settings, these risks are only now beginning to be documented (Bryant & Mohai, 1992). Bullard and others (Bullard, 1990, 1993; Bullard & Wright, 1990), for example, have argued that poor, minority communities are often the sites of "dirty" industries that impose elevated health risks throughout the community. This view is increasingly being confirmed. Residents of poor communities are reported to suffer disproportionate exposure to a variety of toxins such as carbon monoxide, ozone, sulfur, sulfur dioxide, and lead, as well as to emissions from hazardous waste dumps (Heritage, 1992). And recognition of environmental hazards in poor communities has been no sure path to problem amelioration. In poor, minority communities it generally takes longer for authorities to respond to and redress problems than in wealthier neighboring communities (Bullard, 1990). The resulting environmental racism may have various causes: overt racism, the lack of options in poor communities for turning down dirty industries that bring in needed jobs, or the absence of a well-organized constituency to make certain that federal and state pollution laws are observed. Whatever the causes, the costs are great (Lampe, 1992).

In expanding the psychology of risk to encompass routine community issues, the environmental equity movement offers many intriguing insights. Several are illustrated here. The community level of analysis inherent in the environmental equity movement focuses attention on combinations of risk and their inequitable distribution (Silka & Levenstein, 1993). Environmental equity has served as a reminder of the often-neglected point that environmental risks are likely to be interrelated (Bullard, 1993). In the past, risks have often been thought of as separate (e.g., one person might have an unsafe job, another person might live near a hazardous waste dump). Yet a focus on environmental equity reminds us that many risks come together to impact disproportionately poor communities and communities of color. Environmental equity highlights in a very concrete way the fact that risks may be interdependent within neighborhoods and families: at work we may be employed in an unsafe industry, at home we may be living in an older apartment where our children face a heightened risk of lead paint poisoning, and in our neighborhood we may be living near hazardous waste sites or industries that are releasing toxins into the environment. The combined risks associated with living in poor, urban communities that have antiquated housing, dirty industries, inadequate infrastructures, and a lack of code enforcement may together present a very different picture of risk than is suggested by each isolated example.

The environmental equity approach is also closely linked with social action; the original impetus for much of this work was to mobilize community residents through sharpening perceptions of risk (Hamilton, 1990). Although researchers have not empirically investigated whether perceptions of risk are indeed changed by awareness of inequities, the response to their work does suggest that an emphasis on environmental inequities can be a very powerful instigator to action (Bullard, 1993; Russell, 1989). In communities where pollution problems have been low on the list of priorities to be addressed, newly found awareness of inequities have mobilized community residents to action (Gottlieb, 1993; Heritage, 1992; Taylor, 1993). What were once isolated bits of information that acted as a barrier to mobilization can lead to activism among community residents when a more comprehensive picture of environmental risks and their inequitable distribution becomes available (Bullard, 1993).

As the points in this section suggest, various possibilities for the geographical expansion of risk perception emerge from the action-research orientation of environmental equity analysis. Through the lens of the environmental equity research we obtain a greater sense of people dealing with actual community dilemmas. As a cautionary tale on the perceived irrelevance of laboratory studies on risk, the environmental racism approach speaks volumes: examination of the growing literature shows almost no reference to the risk perception literature (cf. Heritage, 1992). Yet these community dilemmas are exactly the sort that researchers of risk perception hope to explicate. Work on perception is aimed at understanding the dynamics of perceptions enough to indicate how to change them, yet environmental equity would appear to change people's views on risk just by presenting risks in new ways that tap directly into everyday concerns. Studying perception—even in its more social forms as in the study of social amplification of risk—would seem to offer incomplete tools for explicating community contexts and may even be seen as undermining the basis of social action. Yet by adding geography and its correlates new possibilities are opened up for exploring equity or other factors. Geographical analyses may uncover unexpected relationships among variables having psychological significance.

The environmental equity movement provides a rich context for examining culture and its link to risk, yet this movement lacks tools for making geographical relationships explicit. As we see in the next section, an independent line of research has been devoted to developing tools for analyzing geographic relationships. This latter work points to a variety of possibilities for exploring risks and their perception in an explicitly geographical context that can be considered in the context of community psychology and environmental equity.

GEOGRAPHIC INFORMATION SYSTEMS: MAPPING DIFFERENCES

The analytical tools available for investigating geographical relationships have been limited until recently. This has begun to change with the introduction of computer-based geographic information systems (GIS), which are now being employed in many disciplines to analyze geographical relationships (Garson & Biggs, 1992; Scholten & de Lepper, 1991). GIS moves away from static displays to dynamic maps capable of supporting nuanced, iterative analyses; in doing so, GIS calls attention to the fact that many problems can be investigated in a spatial context (Aronoff, 1989; Huxhold, 1991). An examination of recent GIS research shows how this technology is being used to shed new light on a variety of social and environmental problems in urban settings.

The conceptual underpinnings of GIS technologies continue to develop (Huxhold, 1991), but as these technologies stand they might be likened to the spatial equivalents of computer programs that allow for causal analyses and model testing using large datasets. Rather than starting with data on various causative factors, one begins with geographical locations. Data for a variety of features at those locations can then be examined. One might have census information on income, ethnicity, and education, as well as community right-to-know information on toxic releases and hazardous sites, for example. In addition, health information on incidence of lead paint poisoning and similar problems could be available by location. Based on one's theoretical model, a variety of different types of data can be collected and juxtaposed to examine and display spatial relationships.

GIS technologies allow for the manipulation and display of this geographic information through overlays over basemaps. Once a computer basemap is in place (i.e., the physical outline, street grids, and landmarks of a community), dozens of overlays can be generated, stored, and revised, with each overlay displaying separate demographic, environmental, or other spatially tagged types of data. Selection of the overlays is often theoretically driven (e.g., questions of environmental equity might lead researchers to include geographically organized ethnicity information as one of the overlays in their environmental assessments).

The manipulation of these geographical overlays provides sophisticated opportunities for assessing and screening risk, and testing theory of various sorts (Rhind, 1991). Boolean operations can be completed on selected overlays whereby areas are identified, for example, in which low incomes and high levels of toxic releases occur together. Buffering routines can be carried out, allowing one to select target points or areas (e.g., schools) and then create buffer zones of a particular size around the targets and attempt to maximize certain characteristics (e.g., reduced drug-related activities, reduced environmental risk) around those target points. The extent to which the activities actually occurring in buffer zones violate assumptions can then be assessed. And GIS can be used to test hypotheses: Are areas with high lead paint also areas with a high prevalence of families with low income?

GIS technologies have been used to explore adversity within a geographical framework and have turned out to be useful in addressing a broad range of social and environmental problems in urban settings where complex data sets have previously proved unmanageable (Huxhold, 1991; Wiken, Rump, & Rizzo, 1992). One community employed GIS to address what had previously been an intractable problem: sifting through vast amounts of geographical data to develop a viable school desegregation plan that could be reconfigured to meet changing legal and social requirements (Wood, 1992). GIS was used in another community to uncover unexpected neighborhood disparities in the allocation of local tax dollars for services (McCullough, 1991). GIS also has been used in community policing, aiding in the identification of complex geographic patterns of crime and enhancing policy decisions in allocating resources (Garson & Biggs, 1992). Most recently, GIS has been used to test hypotheses about environmental racism (Burke, 1993).

In many of the above cases, GIS mapping procedures have been used not simply to map the community but also to involve community residents in local decision making. GIS has been used to facilitate community decision making about locations for soup kitchens, bars, and other high impact community sites where a host of variables must be taken into consideration (Sawicki, 1993; Thrall, 1993). Bertin (1981) captures this involvement by calling maps "moments in the process of decision making"; he points to the iterative possibilities inherent in GIS mapping that allow for inserting and deleting information to test out different ways of viewing community problems.

Indeed, researchers from a variety of disciplines have now begun to investigate ways that these complex mapping resources can become more explicit aids to communication. Many have argued that people are more responsive to maps than other, less visual ways of presenting risk-related information (Garson & Biggs, 1992; Monmonier, 1993). Wood (1992), for example, has described how maps showing the spread of AIDS have helped to make the risks more salient and have acted as an impetus to behavior change among high school students. Others are exploring the possibilities inherent in GIS's increased capacity for personalized communication; with this technology it is easier to customize maps that center on people's own neighborhoods and schools and that juxtapose personalized information against risks of various kinds (Garson & Biggs, 1992).

Despite the great interest in GIS in many disciplines, psychologists have yet to explore what might be learned about the risk perception process through the close study of decision making, communication, and other efforts employing GIS technologies. Yet GIS work seems directly related to many issues of longstanding interest to psychologists and will open new questions. Underlying conceptions of risks as reflected in how people respond to risks framed in local geographic terms are likely to suggest new questions about the relative salience of various risks. Iterative GIS mapping provides a spatial means of investigating the complex nature of the questions people raise about community risks. Mapping also provides a way of exploring the language of risk, differences in which have remained barriers to communication between laypersons and experts. Maps are now being used with overlays, boolean searches, and buffers, providing opportunities to examine how different people combine risks and estimate their spreading impact.

Analyses of the perception of risk have been much taken up with questions of social construction and here too the GIS mapping provides instructive parallels; researchers continue to ask why experts construct risks differently than nonexperts, and whether views of risk "map" onto real risks (Johnson & Covello, 1987; Pidgeon, 1991). Students of maps have grappled with similar issues (Monmonier, 1993). As Wood (1992) has noted, "the usual perception of the nature of maps is that they are a mirror, a graphic representation, of some aspect of the real world" (p. 18), but "no sooner are maps acknowledged as social constructions then their contingent, their conditional, their arbitrary character is unveiled" (p. 19). Every map shows certain features and not others, highlights certain concerns and not others. As Monmonier (1991) has noted, the maps for the Love Canal area still fail to show any of the environmental damage. Maps work by serving particular interests. Bringing the analysis of how people respond to maps as social constructions into the discussion of the perception of risk grounds the latter in community themes and links the geographical focus in yet another important way to questions of how perceivers construe risk.

LOOKING TO THE FUTURE:
SITUATING THE PSYCHOLOGY OF RISK
WITHIN THE GEOGRAPHY OF RISK

I began this paper by noting that researchers of risk focus on a common scenario in which communities find themselves struggling with local environmental problems. The psychological analysis of layperson cognitions is intended to augment the understanding of these community dilemmas, but this analysis often occurs in the absence of an understanding of the context of risk or the nature of the communities in which the risk arises.

Instead, within the psychological study of risk perception, too little has been done that takes geography into account in investigating how laypeople think about the risks around them. Efforts that have been made to incorporate geography in risk analysis have mostly dealt with incidents rather than with the routine, with how people perceive risks in their community in the aftermath of signal events rather than how they judge risks on a daily basis (Freudenburg & Pastor, 1992). The prototypic perception to be explained has been that of punctuated, crisis communication about unusual community hazards or the visible siting of a technological hazard (Vaughan & Seifer, 1992). Yet as we have seen throughout this chapter, recasting issues in geographical terms suggests deeper and broader linkages with geography to be explored.

Fruitful lines of inquiry are opened up by situating the psychology of risk perception within a geography of risk, as we see in the three very different lines of work examined here that have yet to figure in the literature of the psychology of risk perception. In each of these very different bodies of work, attempts have been made to come to grips with the fact that geography has a more central role than might be expected in helping account for behavior and functioning. Analyses in community psychology, environmental equity, and geographic information systems provide instructive models for what a geography of risk might look like and point to some of the theoretical and conceptual tools now available for probing geographic relationships. Although differing in many respects, the three reflect common themes of place, culture, and social action. They point to the need to situate the risk perception work within a geographical context. They provide ideas about how to operationalize geographical context, offer suggestive possibilities for framing cultural differences in risk experiences, and reflect back on varieties of ordinary risk experiences. And they illustrate different ways of framing questions of how geographically situated cognitions are linked to social action. In short, these bodies of work offer insights into everyday risk perception and reflect back on risk perception literature in novel ways.

What are the points of convergence in these three bodies of work when they are considered in the context of risk perception? In very different ways, the three lines of research discussed in this paper converge on the importance of probing combinations of risks that are associated with daily experiences in geographical locations. As we have seen, tools like GIS provide flexibility for the nuanced analyses of combinations of risks, and as well as for assessments of the ways perceivers evaluate risks that co-occur in a geographical location. Community psychology, in addition, points to the importance of explicating family and other group experiences in communities; tainted soil in the playground, poor air quality, and environmentally dangerous households may influence judgments of risk, not because of their effect on the individual, but because of their effect on the family. And environmental equity approaches to the geography of risk point to the theoretical importance of uncovering and explicating discrepancies in experience; making disproportionate and inequitable geographic risks salient —as environmental racism analysis does—may help us understand variations in experience and in perception.

Moreover, geographical analysis of the sort that we see in these three lines of research recasts demographic variables. All three areas indicate that ethnicity, class, and other variables take on different forms as predictors for perception when geographical differences in exposure are recognized as possible mediators of demographic differences. The ways of working with demographic variables shift. The mixed findings of links between demographic variables and risk perception (Vaughan & Nordenstam, 1991) become less surprising if geographical experience is taken into account as a mediating factor. And the geographical focus introduces important new hypotheses to tested. Some have asked what might account for gender differences in community activism around risks (i.e., why most grass-roots activists are female)(Seager, 1993). Examining structural differences in the geographical experience of men and women—amount of time in the home, at work, caring for children—may indicate that the risks associated with neighborhoods and communities are differentially salient to women and men (Hamilton, 1993).

By focusing on geography we also see the degree to which there are unexplored geographical underpinnings to many recent efforts aims at making technical information accessible, altering perceptions and improving the quality of community decision making. This geographical focus can be seen in the community right-to-know laws (MacLean & Orum, 1992) and in various technical assistance materials aimed at community self-help (Coogan & Greene, 1991; Neighborhood Works, 1993). Much of this work assumes that people are driven by concerns with their local community and that people will be mobilized by discussions of environmental risk that tap into geographical location (Coogan & Greene, 1991). An integrated approach to conceiving of risk perception within the geography of risk—one that takes into account past research on variables such as psychological sense of community—may help us better predict when such interventions are likely to have their intended effects of altering cognition and action. Tools like GIS provide opportunities to reframe community risk information to test various hypotheses about the ways in which people conceive of community-based risks.

Improved communication has also been a common goal of much analysis of public perceptions of risk (National Research Council, 1989). It has long been implied that if intuitive perceptions were better understood then it would be possible to create more effective communications (Slovic, Fischhoff, & Lichetenstein, 1981). A geographical framework reconfigures this analysis of communication. It suggests in general terms that geographical factors be included to understand their role in perceptions and responses to risk. It also offers up specifics like the investigation of the effects on perceptions of risk of GIS mapping manipulations as a vehicle to carry out fine-grained analyses of how a complex interactive display that omits or highlights risk information of various sorts in a geographical context.

A geographical analysis also speaks to the elusive link between perception and action. A surprising amount of the risk perception work has been intended to understand when perceptions of risk lead to social action (Vaughan & Seifert, 1992). This work has had dual aims: trying to understand "hysterical" reactions in which laypersons judge risks to be much greater than judged by experts, and explaining the lack of social action on the part of laypeople to risks perceived by experts to be great. Past efforts in this area have focused on identifying abstract dimensions that predict judgments and social actions (e.g., dimensions such as unexpectedness and dread; Slovic, Fischhoff, & Lichtenstein, 1985). The geographical approach —as we have seen in community psychology and environmental racism— points to additional alternatives to explore. Reframing risk in terms of equity taps into literatures that investigate inequities as instigators to action. Borrowing from analyses of the causal significance of concepts such as empowerment, where they have been investigated as predictors of community-based social action in other areas, is likely to be useful in the analysis of when perceived risk leads to social action. A geographical analysis can be helpful in tying the analysis of cognitions to social action, both in terms of understanding social action in communities in response to risk and in predicting likely layperson responses to the future events.

The theoretical recasting offered here can be employed in a number of ways. Several explicit recommendations can be made for those who will contribute to and draw on an expanded psychology of risk that encompasses issues of geography (and thereby adversity). These recommendations grow out of the integrative analysis put forward in this chapter, and are directed partly to basic researchers, but mostly are intended for those taking on the challenging task of integrating research and activism. For basic researchers the recommendation is this: explore these literatures to test their heuristic value for advancing a theory of risks that speaks more directly to community dilemmas. The integrative analysis here punctuates the take-home message that beyond our traditional literatures lie bodies of work that can extend our theoretical reach to encompass neglected variables. What has been offered here is a theoretical roadmap of sorts that points out specific directions for finding preexisting work that is sophisticated in geography and community analysis. Essentially we should look for theories that speak directly to variables on community life. Full examination of these conceptual analyses at the very least will add depth to what we already know; more likely such an examination will result in a reframing of basic questions about how to theorize about risk in community settings.

The recommendation to activist-researchers grows out of our own application work: explore these literatures to test out their pragmatic value for advancing a more effective approach to community dilemmas. Active application across many different settings will provide the best opportunity for evaluating the significance of a geography of risk. If our own work is any guide, this expanded analysis offers rich opportunities for bringing research into a productive association with practice in communities (Silka, 1995; Silka & Levenstein, 1993; Silka & Pash, 1994). The insights from a transformed geography of risk have directed our work in various community contexts in beneficial directions that had previously eluded us. With the guidance of community groups, we have begun using GIS tools to map environmental hazards in a target city. Complex, publicly available data about hazards such as the locations of toxic waste sites are being mapped in various ways to test strategies for bringing broad segments of the population (especially traditionally neglected groups such as youth, women, and individuals from various ethnic groups) into discussions about community risks. We are working with community groups to present these interactive maps and to assess whether people from various backgrounds find this mapping approach a useful adjunct to their community decision making. Our intent is to understand whether alternative ways of geographically displaying and organizing risk information will enhance the quality of community dialogue about environmental issues in a multiethnic city. In these applications we are finding that multiple lines of work are crucial to a broadened and deepened analysis of risk and to the application tasks that urgently need to be addressed.

This chapter began with community dilemmas. As we noted, adversity in communities has often come in the form of environmental risks. Seeking to understand these risks, psychologists have advanced a psychology of risk perception based on cognitive models. Yet, as we have seen, this psychology of risk all too rarely looks at the context of risk, or the nature of the communities in which these risks arise. In this chapter we have illustrated an alternative approach in which the links between geography and risk perception can be understood when multidisciplinary frameworks are used to identify issues and concerns. By looking for commonalities across areas of work that have remained disparate, new opportunities open up for integrating psychological approaches with the concerns that are so often central to communities.

REFERENCES

Altman, I., & Wandersman, A. (Eds.). (1987). *Neighborhood and community environments.* New York: Plenum.

Aronoff, S. (1989). *Geographical information systems: A management perspective.* Ottawa, Canada: WDL Publications.

Bertin, J. (1981). *Graphics and graphic information processing.* Berlin: de Gruyter, p. 16.

Bostrom, A., Fischhoff, B., & Morgan, M. G. (1992). Characterizing mental models of hazardous processes: A methodology and an application to radon. *Journal of Social Issues, 48,* 85–100.

Brehmer, B. (1987). The psychology of risk. In W. T. Singleton & J. Hovden (Eds.), *Risk and decisions* (pp. 25–40) New York: Wiley.

Brody, J. G. (1988). Responses to collective risk: Appraisal and coping among workers exposed to occupational health hazards. *American Journal of Community Psychology, 18,* 645–664.

Bryant, B., & Mohai, P. (Eds.). (1992). *Race and the incidence of environmental hazards: A time for Discourse.* Boulder, CO: Westview Press.

Bullard, R. D. (1990). *Dumping in Dixie: Race, class, and environmental quality.* Boulder, CO: Westview Press.

Bullard, R. D. (Ed.). (1993). *Confronting environmental racism: Voices from the grassroots.* Boston: South End Press.

Bullard, R. D., & Wright, B. H. (1990). Mobilizing the black community for environmental justice. *Journal of Intergroup Relations, 17,* 33–45.

Burke, L. M. (1993). Race and environmental equity: A geographical analysis in Los Angeles. *Geographical Information Systems* (October), 44–50.

Chavis, D. M., & Wandersman, A. (1990). Sense of community in the urban environment: A catalyst for participation and community development. *American Journal of Community Psychology, 18,* 55–82.

Cohen, G., & O'Connor, J. (Eds.). (1990). *Fighting toxics: A manual for your family, community, and workplace.* Washington, DC: Island Press.

Coogan, P. F., & Greene, T. A. (1991). *Environment and health: How to investigate community environmental health problems.* Boston: Center for Environmental Health Studies.

Craik, K. H., & Feimer, N. R. (1987). Environmental assessment. In D. Stokols &

I Altman (Eds.), *Handbook of environmental psychology* (Vol. 2, pp. 891–918). New York: Wiley.

Cvetkovich, G. T., & Earle, T. C. (Eds.). (1991). Risk and culture. *Journal of Cross-Cultural Psychology, 22,* 1–149.

Cvetkovich, G. T., & Earle, T. C. (Eds.). (1992). Public responses to environmental hazards. *Journal of Social Issues, 48* (4), 1–187.

Davidson, W. B., & Cotter, P. R. (1993). Psychological sense of community and support for public school taxes. *American Journal of Community Psychology, 21,* 59–66.

Dietz, T., & Rycroft, R. W. (1987). *The risk professionals.* New York: Russell Sage Foundation.

Edelstein, M. (1988). *Contaminated communities: The social and psychological impacts of residential toxic exposure.* Boulder, CO: Westview Press.

Evans, G. (1980). Environmental cognition. *Psychological Bulletin, 88,* 259–287.

Florin, P., & Wandersman, A. (1984). Cognitive social learning and participation in community development. A comparison of standard and cognitive social learning variables. *American Journal of Community Psychology, 12,* 689–708.

Freudenburg, W. R. (1988). Perceived risk, real risk: Social science and the art of probabilistic risk assessment *Science, 242,* 44–49.

Freudenburg, W. R., & Pastor, S. K. (1992). NIMBYSs and LULUs: Stalking the syndromes. *Journal of Social Issues, 48,* 39–61.

Garson, G. D., & Biggs, R. S. (1992) *Analytic mapping and geographic databases.* Newbury Park, CA: Sage.

Golledge, R. (1987). Environmental cognition. In D. Stokols & I. Altman (Eds.), *Handbook of environmental psychology* (Vol. 1, pp. 131–174) New York: Wiley.

Gottlieb, R. (1993). *Forcing the spring: The transformation of the American environmental movement.* Covela, CA: Island Press.

Gregory, D. (1994). *Geographical imaginations.* Cambridge, MA: Blackwell.

Hallman, W. K., & Wandersman, A. (1992). Attributions of responsibility and individual and collective coping with environmental threats. *Journal of Social Issues, 48,* 101–118.

Hamilton, C., (1990). The struggle for community: Race, class, and the environment. *Social Policy, 21,* 18–25.

Hamilton, C. (1993). Coping with industrial exploitation. In R. D. Bullard (Ed.), *Confronting environmental racism* (pp. 63–76). Boston: South End Press.

Heller, K. (1989). The return to community. *American Journal of Community Psychology, 17,* 1–15.

Heller, K. (1990). Social and community intervention. *Annual Review of Psychology, 41,* 141–168.

Heritage, J. (Ed.). (1992). Environmental racism. *EPA Journal, 18,* 6–53.

Holahan, C. J., & Wandersman, A. (1987). The community psychology perspective in environmental psychology. In D. Stokols & I. Altman (Eds.), *Handbook of environmental psychology* (Vol. 1, pp. 827–861). New York: Wiley.

Huxhold, W. E. (1991). *An introduction of urban geographical systems.* New York: Oxford University Press.

Johnson, B. B., & Covello, V. T. (Eds.). (1987). *The social and cultural construction of risk: Essays in selection and perception of risk.* Dordrecht, Holland: Reidel.

Kasperson, R. E., Renn, O., & Slovic, P. (1988). The social amplification of risk: A conceptual framework. *Risk Analysis, 8,* 177–187.

Krimsky, S., & Plough, A. (1988). *Environmental hazards: Communicating risks as a social process.* New York: The Free Press.

Lampe, D. (1992). The politics of environmental equity. *National Civic Review, 81,* 27–35.

Levine, M. (1988). An analysis of mutual assistance. *American Journal of Community Psychology, 16,* 167–188.

Levine, M., & Perkins, D. V. (1987). *Principles of community psychology: Perspectives and applications.* New York: Oxford University Press.

Littrell, D. W., & Hobbs, D. (1989). The self-help approach. In J. A. Christenson & J. W. Robinson, Jr. (Eds.), *Community Development in Perspective* (pp. 48–68). Ames: Iowa State University Press.

MacLean, A., & Orum, P. (1992). *Progress report: Community right-to-know.* Washington, DC: Working Group on Community Right-to-Know.

McCullough, M. F. (1991). Democratic questions for the computer age. *Computers in Human Services, 8,* 9–18.

McMillan, D., & Chavis, D. (1986). Sense of community: A definition and theory. *Journal of Community Psychology, 14,* 6–23.

Mitchell, C. (1993). Environmental racism: Race as a primary factor in the selection of hazardous waste sites. *National Black Law Journal, 13,* 176–188.

Monmonier, M. (1991). *How to lie with maps.* Chicago: University of Chicago Press.

Monmonier, M. (1993). *Mapping it out: Expository cartography for the humanities and social sciences.* Chicago: University of Chicago Press.

Mulvey, A., & Silka, L. (1987). A community training model incorporating history, empowerment, and ecology. *Journal of Community Psychology, 15,* 257–264.

National Research Council. (1989). *Improving risk communication.* Washington, DC: National Academy Press.

Neighborhood Works. (1993). Is your local industry a good neighbor? *16,* 24–26.

Novaco, R. W., Stokols, D., & Milanesi, L. (1990). Objective and subjective dimensions of travel impedance as determinants of commuting stress. *American Journal of Community Psychology, 18,* 231–257.

Opotow, S., & Clayton, S. (Eds.). (1994). Green justice: Conceptions of fairness and the natural world. *Journal of Social Issues, 50,* 1–197.

Perkins, D. D., Florin, P., Rich, R. C., Wandersman, A., & Chavis, D. (1990). Participation and the social and physical environment: Crime and community context. *American Journal of Community Psychology, 18,* 83–116.

Pidgeon, N. F. (1991). Safety culture and risk management in organizations. *Journal of Cross-Cultural Psychology, 22,* 129–140.

Rappaport, J. (1987). Terms of empowerment/exemplars of prevention: Toward a theory for community psychology. *American Journal of Community Psychology, 15,* 121–148.

Rhind, D. (1991). Geographical information systems and environmental problems. *International Social Science Journal, 43,* 649–659.

Rosa, E. A., & Kleinhesselink, R. R. (1991). Cognitive representation of risk perception: A comparison of Japan and the United States. *Journal of Cross-Cultural Psychology,* 11–11–28.

Rose, G. (1993). *Feminism and geography: the limits of geographical knowledge.* Minneapolis: University of Minnesota Press.

Russell, D. (1989). Environmental racism. *The Amicus Journal, 11,* 22–32.

Sarason, S. B. (1974). *The psychological sense of community: Prospects for a community psychology.* San Francisco: Jossey-Bass.

Sawicki, D. S. (1993). Mapping efforts bring hope to inner-city residents. *GIS World* (June 1), 30–33.

Scholten, H. J., & de Lepper, M. J. C. (1991). The benefits of the applications of geographical information systems in public and environmental health. *World Health Statistics Quarterly, 44,* 160–170.

Seager, J. (993). *Earth Follies: Coming to feminist terms with the global environmental crisis.* New York: Routledge.

Silka, L. (1995). *Geographic information systems: Innovative tools for theory and application in community psychology.* Paper presented at the Eastern Psychological Association Convention, Boston, MA.

Silka, L., & Levenstein, C. (1993). *Environmental racism: Innovative perspectives on community environmental and occupational problems.* Paper presented at the American Psychological Association Convention, Toronto, Canada.

Silka, L., & Pash, J. (1994). *Incorporating risk perception and local context into environmental education.* Unpublished manuscript.

Slovic, P., Fischhoff, B., & Lichtenstein, S. (1981). Informing the public about the risks from ionizing radiation. *Health Physics, 41,* 589–598.

Slovic, P., Fischhoff, B., & Lichtenstein, S. (1985) Characterizing perceived risk. In R. Kates, C. Hohenemser, & R. Kasperson (Eds.), *Perilous progress: Managing the hazards of technology* (pp. 91–125). Boulder, CO: Westview Press.

Taylor, D. (1993). Environmentalism and the politics of inclusion. In R. D. Bullard (Ed.), *Confronting environmental racism* (pp. 53–62). Boston: South End Press.

Thrall, G. I. (1993). Basic GIS software can help make urban policy. *Geographical Information Systems,* (January), 58–63.

Under, D. G., & Wandersman, A. (1985). The importance of neighbors: The social, cognitive, and affective components of neighboring. *American Journal of Community Psychology, 13,* 139–169.

Unger, D. G., Wandersman, A., & Hallman, W. (1992). Living near a hazardous waste facility: Coping with individual and family distress. *American Journal of Orthopsychiatry, 62,* 55–70.

Vaughan, E. (1993). Individual and cultural differences in adaptation to environmental risks. *American Psychologist, 48,* 673–680.

Vaughan, E. A., & Nordenstam, B. (1991). The perception of environmental risks among ethnically diverse groups. *Journal of Cross-Cultural Psychology,* 29–60.

Vaughan, E., & Seifert, M. (1992). Variability in the framing of risk issues. *Journal of Social Issues, 48*, 119–135.

Wandersman, A., & Florin, P. (Eds.). (1990). Citizen participation, voluntary organizations, and community development: Insights for empowerment through research. *American Journal of Community Psychology, 18* (1)(Special Issue).

Wandersman, A., & Hallman, W. K. (1993). Are people acting irrationally? Understanding public concerns about environmental threats. *American Psychologist, 48*, 681–686.

Wiken, E. B., Rump, P. C., & Rizzo, B. (1992, Dec. 1). GIS supports sustainable development. *GIS World, 5*(10), 55–57.

Wood, D. (1992). *The power of maps.* New York: Guilford.

Zimmerman, M. A. (1990). Taking aim on empowerment research: On the distinction between individual and psychological conceptions. *American Journal of Community Psychology, 18*, 169–177.

I 2 | SOCIAL CLASS AND THE DIMENSIONS OF FAMILY SUPPORT FOR EDUCATION

Richard L. Ochberg and Lance A. Chapman

The habit of higher education appears to be inherited. Children who come from better-educated families are more likely to start college (Christensen, Melder, & Weisbrod, 1975; Wegner & Sewell, 1970; Wolfle, 1985), and more likely to graduate (Mallinckrodt, 1988). They are also likely to attend four-year rather than two-year institutions (Astin, 1972; Clark, 1960) and more selective schools (Astin, 1982; Hearn, 1984; Karabel & Astin, 1975). Why should this be?

The simplest reason, no doubt, is money. College is expensive; better-educated parents, who tend to earn more, are better able to afford tuition. In turn, higher education is a principal conduit to the more prestigious (and lucrative) occupations. In this way, advantages in education and occupation are passed from one generation to the next (Blau & Duncan, 1967).

Yet although money is surely fundamental, this explanation seems limited. A long tradition in sociology argues that social class is not simply a matter of material advantage; it is also a way of looking at the world. Among other things, families in different social strata make different judgments about how best to get ahead. This brings us to the subject of this chapter: how parents at different socioeconomic levels estimate the value of higher education.

Any number of studies have found that well-educated parents are more likely to encourage their children's engagement with school. In turn, parental encouragement influences how much education students ultimately attain (Alexander, Eckland, & Griffin, 1975; Conklin & Dailey, 1981; Duncan, Featherman, & Duncan, 1972; Farmer, 1985; Sewell & Hauser, 1975; Sewell & Shah, 1968.)

Curiously enough, there is very little research on the reasons that better-educated families value higher education. Is it because they believe that education improves one's thinking, refines one's cultural sensitivity, and humanizes one's values? (These are among the standard virtues that liberal arts colleges claim for themselves.) Or is it, more prosaically, that better-educated families are more likely to believe that academic credentials will pay off in the job market?

We know of no studies that have explored this distinction, or indeed any other set of reasons why better-educated families value higher education. By and large, previous investigators attempted to capture the intensity—but not the rationale—of parental support for education. For example, Sewell and Hauser (1975) asked respondents whether their parents had encouraged them to go to college; Alexander, Eckland, and Griffin (1975) asked, "To what extent have you discussed going to college with your parents?" Otto and Haller (1979) asked respondents how much encouragement their parents had provided for education; Conklin and Dailey (1981) asked whether "it has just about been taken for granted that you would continue your education after you get out of high school"; and Farmer (1985) asked respondents how much each parent had encouraged them to study different types of courses in high school. While all of these studies confirm that better-educated families are more enthusiastic about education, none can tell us why parents think education is a good idea.

INTRINSIC AND EXTRINSIC VALUES OF EDUCATION

In this chapter we attempt to tease apart parents' enthusiasm for the vocational utility of higher education, and its effect on cultural, moral, and intellectual refinement. We refer to these as the extrinsic and intrinsic value of education; Figure 1 indicates their hypothetical relationship to family background and students' plans for postgraduate education.

Our interest in comparing parents' perception of the extrinsic and intrinsic value of education arises from the following considerations. It appears obvious that parents (and students themselves) value education largely because they believe that a college degree will pay off occupationally. (Anyone who doubts this need only imagine what would happen to enrollment at any college that promised the best intellectual and cultural refinement money could buy—but offered no credential that could be cashed in at an employment office or an office of graduate admissions. If education improved nothing but one's mind it would be as extravagant as collecting Fabergé eggs.)

This utilitarian view of higher education is, of course, not the perspective defended by most liberal arts colleges or their graduates. Winston

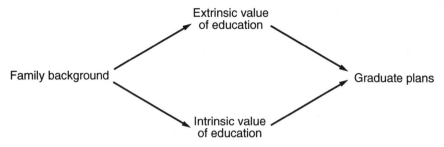

Figure 1. Hypothetical Path Model of Factors Influencing Postgraduate Plans.

Churchill, for example, declared, "The first duty of a university is to teach wisdom, not a trade." Inspiring stuff, of course, yet one wonders whether the old warhorse would have blanched at the current cost of a college education if it purchased nothing but wisdom.

We turn first, therefore, to the extrinsic value parents perceive in education. It seems likely that all parents encourage their children's academic aspirations when they believe that education leads to better jobs. In terms of our diagram, there should be a moderately strong link between the extrinsic value of education and students' postgraduate plans. Yet this in itself would not be enough to explain class differences in educational plans. In addition, we need to show that better-educated families are more likely to believe that higher education leads to occupational success. Why should this be?

One possibility is that better-educated parents are more likely to hope that their children will go into the sort of careers that require advanced education, such as the professions. Furthermore, even among parents who hold equally high occupational aspirations for their children, those with more education are likely to place more faith in the value of an academic credential. (A well-educated father who hopes that his son will thrive in business is likely to believe that an MBA will open the first door.) Therefore, we also anticipate a moderately strong link between family background and parents' belief that education is extrinsically valuable.

Is vocationally relevant training the only reason that parents encourage education? Is there no role for "wisdom" or culture in this utilitarian calculus? Perhaps there is—although perhaps for reasons no less calculating than those of the vocationally minded consumer.

A long tradition of sociological research has explored how people compare their own social class standing to that of their neighbors. These studies routinely find that income and occupation are the most important bases of comparison. Yet most people assess their class position not only in terms of the work they do or the money they earn; they also distinguish between themselves and those lower in the class hierarchy in terms of life-style. (Not surprisingly, most people think that only money—and unfounded snobbery—distinguish themselves from those higher in class position.)

Members of each class appear to claim somewhat distinct virtues for themselves. For example, working class families suggest that their superiority to the poor is based on their own greater industriousness and moral uprightness. Thus Coleman and Rainwater (1978) report, "[Working class] Americans emphasized character more than culture when judging themselves socially above others. Having 'good morals' and 'initiative' were the prime virtues they credited themselves with in contrast to those of lower standing" (p. 86; see also Kahl, 1953, pp. 189–205).

In contrast, members of the upper-middle class attach more significance to cultural sophistication. Coleman and Rainwater continue, "men and women of Upper-American standing gave most attention [to] breadth of interest and information, familiarity with the arts . . . and comfort in interaction with people like themselves" (p. 86).

In a more recent extension of these ideas, sociologists have suggested that *cultural capital*—that is, familiarity with high-brow music, art, literature, and so on—plays a decisive role in defining class membership and fostering social mobility (Bourdieu, 1977, 1984; Brubaker, 1985; DiMaggio, 1979; DiMaggio & Mohr, 1985).

Is it reasonable to imagine that a concern with cultural capital animates not only the theories of sociologists but also the practical decisions of parents? If so, we might expect upper-middle class parents—but not working class parents—to believe that higher education is important because it introduces one to a world of cultural refinement. (Let us repeat: this perspective is no less utilitarian than a concern with vocational skills—it simply takes a wider view of what class position entails.) Referring to our diagram, we might anticipate significant paths leading from family background to the intrinsic value of education, and from here to students' plans for postgraduate education.

However, a preliminary word of skepticism seems in order. Do parents at any socioeconomic level really encourage education for its cultural and intellectual value? Some families may hope that college will help their children become both better paid and more refined, but no one should harbor any illusion about what is most important. Higher education is enormously expensive and time-consuming. We suspect that by far the most important reason families consider this investment worthwhile is that it promises to pay off in the job market.

To summarize what we have said, we propose:

Hypothesis 1. Students whose parents have more education and more prestigious occupations are likely to report that their parents see more extrinsic and intrinsic value in higher education.

Hypothesis 2. Students whose parents have more education and more prestigious occupations are more likely to apply to graduate school.

Hypothesis 3. The relationship between family background and students' application to graduate school can be explained primarily by parents' perception that education is extrinsically valuable.

ELEMENTS OF THE STUDY

To test these hypotheses, we surveyed by questionnaire 162 college seniors, aged 30 or less, at the University of Massachusetts at Boston. Men and women were equally represented; about 80% identified themselves as white, with approximately equal numbers of African Americans, Hispanics, and Asians making up the balance. The following variables are of interest to us:

Family Background

Fathers' and Mothers' Education. Slightly less than half the fathers in our sample had no college education ($N = 68$); one in five had a graduate degree ($N = 32$). Mothers were somewhat less educated: 78 had no college experience; 21 had some postgraduate education.

Fathers' and Mothers' Occupation. Students reported each parent's occupation, which we coded using the most recent version of the Socioeconomic Index (Stevens and Cho, 1985). However, since many students reported no occupation for their mothers, we dropped mothers' occupation from our model.

Parents' Perceptions of the Value of Education

Students scored 17 statements regarding the value of higher education as they believed their parents would respond. They were instructed, "If you think your parents would disagree, choose the one whose opinion matters most to you." These statements were used to form two scales.

Extrinsic Value of Education (VEX) is an eight-item scale designed to measure the belief that higher education will pay off in the job market ($M = -.32$; $SD = .56$). Typical items are "People today need more education to get good careers" and "When you consider how much time and money you sacrifice, college and graduate school are not such great investments."

Intrinsic Value of Education (VEI) is a nine-item scale designed to measure the belief that higher education leads to cultural, moral, and intellectual refinement ($M = 3.63$; $SD = 1.28$). Typical items are "Well-educated people not only know more, they somehow seem more cultured" and "Education doesn't seem to help people tell right from wrong."

Students' Applications to Graduate School

Students were asked, "Which of these best describes your current plans for further education?" They were offered four choices: "I have no current plans to apply to graduate school" ($N = 18$), "I plan to work for several years and apply if and when it seems useful" ($N = 28$), "I plan to take a year off and then apply" ($N = 78$), and "I have already sent off my applications" ($N = 36$).

RESULTS OF THE STUDY

Hypothesis 1: Is There a Relationship between Family Background and Parents' Valuing of Higher Education?

Our informants suggested that their parents value education more if they are better-educated and employed at more prestigious occupations. Better-educated fathers are more likely to value education for both extrinsic reasons ($r = .224$, $p < .01$) and intrinsic reasons ($r = .345$, $p < .01$). Similarly, fathers with more prestigious occupations are likelier to believe education has extrinsic value ($r = .242$, $p < .01$) and intrinsic value ($r = .272$, $p < .01$).

Students reported similar, though slightly weaker relationships between their mothers' education and how their parents judged education's extrinsic value ($r = .167$, $p < .05$) and intrinsic value ($r = .178$, $p < .05$). This suggests that the influence of social class is primarily a matter of fathers' education and occupation. (Fathers' background was more influential than mothers' among both male and female informants.)

Hypothesis 2. Does Family Background Affect Students' Postgraduate Plans?

We expected that students would be more likely to apply to graduate school if their parents were college-educated and employed at prestigious occupations. This turned out to be true, although in a more complicated fashion than we anticipated.

Among the 50 students who aspired to more than a master's degree, those with college-educated fathers were significantly more likely to apply to graduate school ($F = 8.33$, $df = 1$, $p < .01$). (Fathers' occupation and mothers' education had no effect on students' graduate application.) However, among those students who wanted only a master's degree, those with college-educated fathers were no more ready to apply to graduate school.

Hypothesis 3. Does Parents' Perception of the Value of Education Explain the Connection between Family Background and Students' Application to Graduate School?

Our final hypothesis related to the observation that students from better-educated families are more likely to apply to graduate school. Is it because their parents think education will pay off occupationally, or because parents think education leads to intellectual and cultural refinement? To answer this question we confined our attention to the subgroup of academically ambitious students—since it is only in this group that fathers' education influences students' application to graduate school.

The relationship among fathers' education, the value parents perceive in education, and students' application to graduate school can be represented graphically by the path models shown in Figure 2. (A path model describes the influence of each variable in a sequence of events.) The three models shown suggest that parents' faith in the extrinsic value of education is a good part of the reason why young people from better-educated families are more likely to apply to graduate school. (We found that the intrinsic value of education played no significant role; therefore, we dropped it from this model.) The models also show that parents' assessment of the extrinsic value of education provides a much better explanation for young women's graduate application than for young men's.

More specifically, these models show that among young women, a rise of one standard deviation in fathers' education is associated, on average, with a rise of .66 of a standard deviation in parents' belief that education has extrinsic value. In turn, a rise of one standard deviation in extrinsic value is associated, on average, with a rise of .56 of a standard deviation in the likelihood of young women applying to graduate school. The product of these two weights—($.66 \times .56 = .38$)—describes the role played by extrinsic value as a link between fathers' education and graduate applications. Among young women, extrinsic value mediates a very large proportion of the total association between fathers' education and graduate applications (mediated covariation = .38; total covariation = .44). However, among young men, the extrinsic value of education mediates a very small proportion of this association (total covariation = .385; mediated covariation = .045).

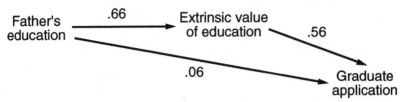

a. Academically ambitious women (n=25)

Father's education —.66→ Extrinsic value of education

.56

.06

Graduate application

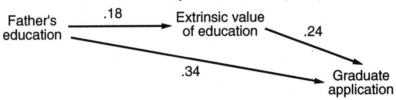

b. Academically ambitious men (n=25)

Father's education —.18→ Extrinsic value of education

.24

.34

Graduate application

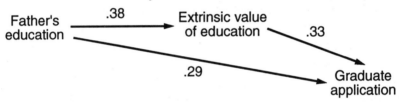

c. Academically ambitious men and women (n=50)

Father's education —.38→ Extrinsic value of education

.33

.29

Graduate application

Figure 2. Final Path Models of the Influence of Extrinsic Value of Education on Application to Graduate School.

IMPLICATIONS OF THE STUDY

Although previous research has established that better-educated families are more likely to encourage their children's educational aspirations, we know little about parents' reasons. Therefore, this study explored the distinction between believing that education will lead to a better job and believing that education makes one more intellectual, cultured, or moral. Lest our interest in refinement seem ingenuous, we note that *cultural capital* is a prominent idea in contemporary thinking about social class.

We must begin by acknowledging that there is no absolute distinction between valuing education for extrinsic and intrinsic reasons. Parents who believe education improves one's mind are also likely to believe it will pay off in the job market. However, parents' faith in the extrinsic value of education appears to carry much more weight than faith in education's intrinsic value. Students are likely to apply to graduate school when their parents believe education can land them a better job; they are not likely to apply to graduate school just because their parents think education makes one more knowledgeable or cultured.

Parents with more education and more prestigious occupations are likely to see both more extrinsic and intrinsic value in education. Interestingly enough, it seems that young men and women are more influenced by their fathers than by their mothers: as our questionnaire puts it, it is fathers' opinions "that matter most." This is as true for young women as for young men.

Family background appears to influence parental support for education more among young women than among young men. The relationship between fathers' education and the extrinsic value of education is higher among women ($r = .302$, $p < .01$) than among men ($r = .157$). It may be that parents at all socioeconomic levels believe that a college degree can help their sons' careers. Daughters, however, are a different matter. Working class families may be much less likely than upper-middle class families to picture their daughters as potential breadwinners. Therefore, working class families are considerably less likely than upper-middle class families to value education as a way of promoting their daughters' careers.

Our informants were more likely to apply to graduate school if their parents thought education would pay off financially; the intrinsic value parents saw in education had little effect. Although this result is consistent with our utilitarian prediction, it is also somewhat disappointing theoretically. As we noted, an emerging school of sociological theory holds that cultural refinement is itself a form of "capital," which may be turned to advantage in the class system. Our data suggest that a concern with cultural capital plays little role in parental support for postgraduate education. Given the prominence of Bourdieu's perspective, it is worth speculating on whether a differently designed study would have found different results.

The most obvious possibility is that a larger sample would have found a statistically significant consequence of intrinsic value. However, since results can be statistically significant (unlikely to have occurred by chance) without having substantial consequences, increasing the sample size alone would be an unimpressive strategy.

A better variation on our study might have examined the reasons and effect of parental support on students' application to college. Parents might well support undergraduate education for intellectual and cultural reasons, even if they feel that postgraduate education is worthwhile only if it can be converted into coin of the realm.

More conceptually, we wonder in retrospect whether the scales we devised really provided a fair test of the role played by cultural capital. Our extrinsic scale clearly represents the value of education as means toward some other end: a better job. In contrast, the intrinsic scale seems to represent the value of intellectual, cultural, and moral refinement as an end in itself. However, this may not represent cultural capital accurately. Bourdieu suggests that refinement is also a means to an end, no less utilitarian than pragmatic knowledge, accreditation, or indeed, money. It would have been a fairer test had our scale of intrinsic value suggested that cultural refinement via higher education would open the doors to more elegant boardrooms and bedrooms.

To put the matter this way is to underscore how insulting the proposition is likely to be. This does not make it untrue; it merely means that unusual subtlety will be required in writing questionnaire items. For example, we might have suggested: "No matter how successful you are in your career, well-educated people won't respect you unless you are educated too." A series of items in this vein might approach the idea that the invisible divisions between the classes are based partly on the appearance of cultural sophistication.

Finally, it may be worth thinking about the negative consequences of cultural sophistication. We take it for granted that all young people—and their families—find upper class membership desirable. This seems plausible, as long as class is defined in terms of material well-being. However, if class is defined in cultural terms it becomes less clear that "upward" mobility is an unalloyed virtue. A few theorists have suggested that some working class families view the upper-middle class as pretentious, and experience their children's desire for upward mobility as a form of betrayal (Hoerning, 1985; London, 1989). If this is true, a scale describing the intrinsic value of education should express, more vehemently than our's does, the negative consequences of learning to speak and act in a manner to which one was not born. Framed in these terms, the connection between schooling and "high" culture might reemerge as an explanation for class differences in parental support for higher education.

Finally we turn to the practical implications of this study. How can we go about fostering postgraduate education among working class students? Much of the research on social class and education suggests that working class families are comparatively unenthusiastic about the moral, cultural, or intellectual benefits of higher education. Were graduate applications influenced by parents' cultural, moral, or intellectual world view, then the task of promoting academic ambitiousness in working class families would be daunting indeed. However, by far the best explanation of why working class students put off applying to graduate school is that it seems a bad financial investment. If this is true, we do not need to overhaul the world view of working class parents; we simply need to make postgraduate education more affordable. Would working class students pursue advanced degrees if education were cheaper, or if low-cost loans were available? We cannot be sure, but the history of the G.I. Bill gives reason for optimism.

Is it important that this country invest in making postgraduate education affordable? Historical trends suggest that this may be the case. There was a time not that long ago when a college degree was the price of admission to most professional careers. That time is passed. Today, and no doubt increasingly in the years to come, the professions and the upper reaches of business will require postgraduate certification. If working class students continue to avoid graduate school, then education will conserve social stratification rather than serve social mobility.

REFERENCES

Alexander, K., Eckland, B., & Griffin, L. (1975). The Wisconsin model of socio-economic achievement: A replication. *American Journal of Sociology, 81,* 324–342.

Astin, A. (1972). *College dropouts: A national study.* Washington, DC: American Council on Education.

Astin, A. (1982). *Minorities in American higher education: Recent trends, current prospects, and recommendations.* San Francisco: Jossey-Bass.

Blau, P., & Duncan, O. (1967). *The American occupational structure.* New York: John Wiley.

Bourdieu, P. (1977) Cultural reproduction and social reproduction. In J. Karabel & A. Halsey, (Eds.) *Power and ideology in education.* (pp. 487–511) New York: Oxford University Press.

Bourdieu, P. (1984). *Distinction: A social critique of the judgment of taste.* Cambridge, MA: Harvard University Press.

Brubaker, R. (1985). Rethinking classical theory: The sociological vision of Pierre Bourdieu. *Theory and Society, 14,* 745–775.

Christenson, S., Melder, J., & Weisbrod, B. (1975). Factors affecting college attendance. *Journal of Human Resources, 10,* 174–188.

Clark, B. (1960). The "cooling-out" function in higher education. *American Journal of Sociology, 65,* 569–576.

Coleman, R., & Rainwater, L. (1978). *Social standing in America.* New York: Basic Books.

Conklin, M., & Dailey, A. (1981). Does consistency of parental educational encouragement matter for secondary school students? *Sociology of Education, 54,* 254–262.

DiMaggio, P. (1979). Review essay: On Pierre Bourdieu. *American Journal of Sociology, 84,* 1460–1474.

DiMaggio P., & Mohr, J. (1985). Cultural capital, educational attainment and marital selection. *American Journal of Sociology, 90*(6), 1231–1261.

Duncan, O., Featherman, D., & Duncan, B. (1972). *Socioeconomic status and achievement.* New York: Seminar.

Farmer, H. (1985). Model of career and achievement motivation for men and women. *Journal of Counseling Psychology, 32*(3), 363–390.

Hearn, J. (1984). The relative roles of academic, ascribed, and socioeconomic characteristics in college destinations. *Sociology of Education, 57,* 22–30.

Hoerning, E. (1985). Upward mobility and family estrangement among females. *International Journal of Oral History, 6*(2), 105–111.

Kahl, J. (1953). *The American class structure.* New York: Rinehart.

Karabel, J., & Astin, A. (1975). Social class, academic ability, and college quality. *Social Forces, 53,* 381–398.

London, H. (1989). Breaking away: A study of first generation college students and their families. *American Journal of Education,* 144–170.

Mallingkrodt, B. (1988). Student retention, social support, and dropout intention. *Journal of College Student Development, 29,* 60–64.

Otto, L., & Holler, A. (1979). Evidence for a social psychological view of the status attainment process: Four studies composed. *Social Forces, 57*(3), 887–915.

Sewell, W., & Hauser, R. (1975). *Education, occupation, and earnings: Achievement in the early career.* New York: Academic Press.

Sewell, W., & Shah, V. (1968). Social class, parental encouragement, and educational aspirations. *American Journal of Sociology, 73,* 559–572.

Stevens, G. & Cho, J. (1985). Socioeconomic indexes and the new 1980 occupational classification scheme. *Social Science Research, 19* 142–168.

Wegner, E., & Sewell, W. (1970). Selection and context as factors affecting the probability of graduation from college. *American Journal of Sociology, 75,* 665–679.

Wolfle, L. (1985). Postsecondary educational attainment among whites and blacks. *American Educational Research Journal, 22,* 501–525.

13 | THE ROLE OF GENDER AND ORGANIZATIONAL CONTEXT IN THE EXPERIENCE OF ADVERSITY

Sexual Harassment as a Case Example

Charlotte Mandell, Anne Mulvey, and Meg A. Bond

> *Adversity* (noun) 1: a state of hardship or affliction; 2: a calamitous event. (*The American Heritage Dictionary of the English Language* [1992])
>
> *A state of hardship:* "One of my teachers made crude sexist remarks all the time and embarrassed the women students in the class. I felt uncomfortable and tried to avoid him."
>
> *A calamitous event:* "I went to see my teacher about a problem I was having. He told me that if I came to his office my grade would improve. When I got there he put his arm on my shoulder and tried to reach into my blouse. I grabbed my books and left as quickly as I could. I dropped the class because I was afraid that I would not get a good grade." [1]

Sexual harassment is an adversity for women on college and university campuses throughout the United States (e.g., Dzeich & Weiner, 1984; Fitzgerald, Weitzman, Gold, & Ormerod, 1988; Paludi, 1991; Till, 1980). It comes in two primary forms, related yet distinct: gender or hostile environment harassment and more intrusive or coercive forms of harassment (Bond, 1988; Fitzgerald, 1991; Fitzgerald & Hesson-McInnis, 1989; MacKinnon, 1979). Gender harassment refers to generalized sexist remarks and behavior conveying degrading and sexist attitudes that are not necessarily designed to elicit sexual cooperation. This type of harassment involves behavior that creates an atmosphere of hardship and hostility for women and is an example of the first meaning of adversity. Sexualized harassment, which includes what is typically called *quid pro quo* harassment, involves either a single calamitous event or series of such events and parallels the second definition of adversity. This type of harassment refers to more coercive and imposed forms of sexual advances, ranging from unwanted flirtation to more direct pressure or force through bribes, threats, or actual physical assault. (See also the EEOC definition [Equal Employment Opportunity Commission, 1980].)

As a form of discrimination related to gender inequality, sexual harassment produces traumatic consequences for the victim in particular and creates a generalized state of adversity for women as a group. Most past research has focused on the incidence of sexual harassment, on perceptions of harassment events, or on the characteristics of victims. Such research has provided important validation of the extent of the problem and has helped to identify who might be most at risk for harassment. If we are to better understand this type of adversity and to discourage such harassment, we must also consider how group, organizational, and cultural factors influence the occurrence of and responses to harassment. On the organizational level, we need to consider how the general climate and norms of a group affect sexual harassment rates. In relation to cultural issues, we could benefit from exploring how the experience of harassment is influenced by gender. The present case study is designed to shed light on these issues.

A CASE STUDY

The analysis presented here is based on a campus-wide survey of sexual harassment of students at a large public university in the Northeast. The students attending the university come from middle-class and working-class families. Many of the students live at home with parents and are the first generation in their families to attend college. The student body is predominantly male (62%) and the majority of students are Caucasian (84%). Asians, African Americans, and Hispanics each comprise less than 5% of the student body; other ethnic minority groups (Native Americans, Cape Verdians) constitute another 5%. Most students are of traditional college age, but the university attracts a relatively large population of older returning students through a special program designed for reentry.

A questionnaire was mailed to all students at the university. It included questions concerning individual student characteristics and demographic information (e.g., age, race, major, residence), the student's experience of particular forms of sexual harassment, and the academic and social climate of the student's major department. At the end of the questionnaire, students were asked to describe any negative or unwanted experiences previously reported in the survey in their own words.

The sexual harassment items were adapted from the Sexual Experiences Questionnaire (SEQ) developed by Fitzgerald and colleagues (Fitzgerald, 1991; Fitzgerald et al., 1988). The SEQ has been demonstrated to have sufficient reliability, stability, and validity for research purposes (Fitzgerald et al., 1988). Items on this scale concerned experiences of two types of sexual harassment: gender harassment and sexualized harassment (which included seductive behavior, bribes, threats, and coercive behavior). Incidence of both types of harassment for faculty, administrators, or other staff was assessed. For sexually coercive behavior, participants were asked to include incidents perpetrated by peers as well as by faculty/staff. The items about sexual harassment events were behaviorally oriented and very specific. That is, they inquired as to whether a student had actually experienced a particular behavior. For example, one incidence item read, "Have you ever been in a situation where a faculty member directly offered you some sort of reward for being socially or sexually cooperative?" Students were asked to choose among the following response options: never, once, or more than once.

The climate scale was intended to measure the students' perceptions of the faculty in their major departments on such issues as respect for women and tolerance for diversity. The climate questions did not address the behavior of particular faculty members, but rather asked participants to generalize about the faculty of their primary department as a whole. For example, students were asked to rate their agreement with the statement, "Faculty in my major department are sensitive to the outside work obligations of students." Each item was rated on a 5-point scale, from disagree strongly to agree strongly.

Students completed 2,792 questionnaires (or 27% of the total mailed). Return rates below 50% are typical for mailed surveys concerning unpleasant or controversial topics like harassment (Rubin & Borgers, 1990). The distribution of almost all demographics within the sample were similar to the distribution within the general population of the university (i.e., age, major, race, residence, and year in school). There was, however, a relatively higher response rate among women—about half (49.5%) of the respondents were women, although women comprised only 38% of the total student population. A relatively higher response rate among women was expected given that women are far more likely than men to be victims of harassment and, thus, are more likely to have personal interest in responding to a survey on the topic.

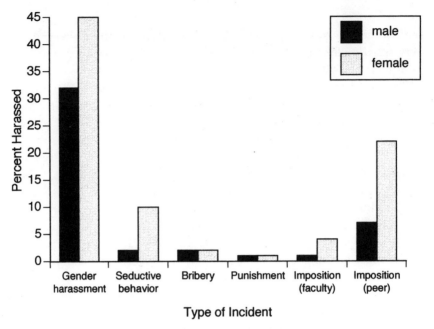

Figure 1. Incidence of Gender and Sexualized Harassment

There were some reports of every type of harassment. In general, males were the primary perpetrators. For incidents of gender harassment, threats, bribes, and seductive behaviors, male professors were reported as perpetrators more frequently than either administrators or other staff were. Incidents of coercive sexual behavior were most frequently perpetrated by male students.

Figure 1 shows incidence rates for gender harassment and four types of sexualized harassment (seductive behavior, bribes, threats, and coercion). Women reported experiencing greater rates of every type of harassment than men did. The higher numbers are consistent with the fact that women are the primary targets of sexual harassment (Paludi, 1991).

Gender differences in reports of harassment were greater for the more severe sexualized types of harassment (seductive behavior, threats, bribes, and coercion) than for gender harassment. The disparity in the more severe categories was almost 10 to 1, as opposed to 2 to 1 in the category of gender harassment (see Figure 1). One possible explanation for this phenomenon is that gender harassment often occurs in public settings, such as classrooms or meetings. Thus, although men may not be the targets of the harassment, male students are aware of its occurrence. In contrast, the more severe types of harassment often occur in more private settings, for example offices or dorm rooms. These types of harassment have particular individual targets. Thus only in those infrequent cases where the male student is the object of the harassment would more severe incidents be reported by men.

THE GENDERED CONTEXT OF HARASSMENT

At the end of the questionnaire, respondents were asked to elaborate on a negative or unwanted experience identified in the structured portion of the survey. Qualitative responses were returned by 703 survey participants; 439 (62%) were from women and 260 (38%) from men. Thus women were far more likely than men to respond to the open-ended probe, once they completed the survey.

Many respondents detailed specific incidents of gender bias, sexual harassment, or unwanted sexual incidents. Surprisingly, however, some respondents used the opportunity to describe other types of incidents negatively affecting the quality of life on campus, to indicate an absence of problems, and/or to make evaluative comments about the survey itself (see Tables 1 and 2 for prototypical female and male responses).

The predominant harassment situation described was clearly a woman being sexually harassed by a man. Women described put-downs in the classroom and violations of their space or bodies at parties and in residence halls. Many women spoke of what they should or should not have done. "I should have locked my dorm room door," or "I should not have trusted him just because I knew him from class." Women recounted varied reactions to these incidents such as pretending the event did not bother them, attempting to avoid the perpetrator, or enlisting a friend to accompany them to class or to the harasser's office. Women's stories were varied; their interpretations and concerns were, too. Nonetheless, the great majority of women saw sexual harassment and unwanted sexual attention as serious problems.

Men were much less likely to note sexual harassment as a problem. Of the men who did describe a sexual harassment incident, most reported sexual harassment that was directed at women in their presence, not at themselves or other men. Men who chose to write open-ended remarks tended to make more non-gender-related than gender-related comments about the quality of life on campus—predominantly faculty-student situations where they felt they were not treated fairly. Men's relative silence about harassment raises questions as to whether these male students were unaware of gender and sexualized harassment, or whether they observed or even participated in the harassment but did not consider it a problem.

Table 1
Women's Voices: Prototypical Comments by Female Students.

One of my teachers made crude sexist remarks and embarrassed the women students in the class. I felt uncomfortable and tried to avoid meeting him.

I almost quit school because I was completely ignored by my instructor.

One of my teachers said that the only degree I needed to worry about was the M.R.S. degree. OUTRAGEOUS!

A particular professor often plays with himself when talking to women students. He tries not to be obvious but it shows.

I was at a party and a drunken student kept trying to force himself on me. I kept pushing him away and finally I left the party with my friends.

I went to see my teacher about a problem I was having. He told me that if I came to his office my grade would improve. When I got there he put his arm on my shoulder and tried to reach into my blouse. I grabbed my books and left as quickly as I could. I dropped that class because I was afraid that I would not get a good grade.

I was working in my dorm room when a student came in. He started grabbing me and wouldn't leave me alone. I tried to fight him off but he was too strong for me. Luckily my roommate came in and he left.

Thank you for doing this survey. It is about time that someone took care of this matter.

I have not had any problems here. I hope that I never will.

I can't talk about it. It is too difficult.

A number of students (92 or 13%) took the time to write that they had never experienced a problem or that they were quite pleased with their experiences on campus—42 women and 50 men. Although the absolute numbers of women and men reporting no problems were similar, the quality of the "no problem" responses was different. Women said such things as, "I have been very lucky" or "I have not experienced any such problems *yet.*" Some women explained their lack of problems by noting, "I only spend a couple hours on campus each week in class, and I never socialize with other students." The women's comments suggested that they were aware problems existed and felt lucky or privileged to have avoided them.

Most of the men, on the other hand, confidently expressed that problems simply did not exist on campus. They used declarations like, "I have not experienced nor am I aware of such problems on campus" or "Things at this university are fine. I have no problems here."

About one-quarter of the male respondents used the space at the end of

Table 2
Men's Voices: Prototypical Comments by Male Students.

One of my professors made sexist comments in class. It was just a joke, though, and we all treated it that way.

My only problem is I could use more dates (just joking!).

Teachers at this university are not concerned with students. They treat us like we were numbers.

I am a foreign student. When I was walking on campus some rude students called out and made fun of me. There is a lot of discrimination against foreign students.

My friend was arrested for disorderly conduct for NO REASON.

I'm tired of teachers who can't teach and bore the hell out of us.

This survey is ridiculous and a big waste of my time. I have never had, nor heard of, any problems concerning sex at this university.

This survey is very biased. It only concerns women. Why was it sent to me?

One of my professors was a feminist bitch. She discriminated against the men in the class.

This survey seems to be putting down faculty and saying they are all racist and sexist. I filled it out because I was asked to, but most questions are absurd.

Things at this university are fine. I have no problems here.

the survey to voice criticisms of and/or disdain for the survey. Women's criticisms were fewer in number and qualitatively different. Some men wrote dispassionate critiques of the questionnaire (e.g., item by item analyses). Others wrote angry commentaries in which they included obscenities, personal attacks on the researchers, and sarcastic comments. The women tended to voice their concerns both less dramatically and with more qualifiers. For example, a female student wrote "Thank you for doing this survey. It shows you care." In contrast, a male student wrote, "You feminist bitches are wasting university money."

In sum, men and women wrote about different experiences of adversity on campus, in distinctively different voices. The words or "voices" of women and men students reflected gender-stratified realities as they described different types of concerns in different ways. Not only did more women describe sexual harassment, but those who described other situations also seemed to place these experiences in the context of ongoing gender biases. For example, many women stated that their unfair and abusive treatment was rooted in sex discrimination or the general devaluing of women. In contrast, the problems described by men were more often idiosyncratic to a particular class or situation. The predominant focus of men's concerns was on *personally* unfair treatment.

THE CHILLY CLIMATE AND HARASSMENT

From the responses to the open-ended question described above, we know that the gender of students influenced their experience of harassment and their reactions to it. Situational factors influenced harassment rates as well. For example, the students' residence had an important impact on their experience of harassment. Women students living in peer housing (residence halls or apartments) reported most incidents of sexual coercion, which is the most severe category of sexualized harassment. Women who lived with their parents were less likely to report this form of harassment. Finally, women who were living in their own households, with partners or children, reported less harassment of all forms. For men, it was less clear how place of residence related to incidence of harassment.

Some of the most striking findings emerged when we looked at how sexual harassment rates varied by academic departments within the university. In some of the departments the relative rates of gender harassment for women and men were comparable, whereas in other departments women reported far more gender harassment than men did. For sexualized harassment, there were differences in the overall levels of harassment reported, but women always reported far more sexualized harassment incidents than men did.

Consideration of why these differences occurred led us to explore how the culture and core values of distinct departments might be related to harassment. We suspected that gender-stratified attitudes and norms may create what has been referred to as a "chilly climate" for women and be related to incidence of sexual harassment (Hall & Sandler, 1982). Chilly climate refers to girls and women being ignored or discouraged in the classroom in a variety of ways, such as examples used to illustrate concepts, jokes initiated or condoned by an instructor, a teacher's subtle nonverbal messages to female versus male students. A recently released study, sponsored by the American Association of University Women, concluded that such informal and unspoken practices results in girls and women being "short changed" in educational settings (American Association of University Women, 1992). The study calls for dramatic changes in teaching practices and culture in educational settings.

Broadening the concept of chilly climate to include norms and experiences that occur outside the classroom is appropriate for higher education settings because many student interactions with faculty occur outside the classroom. Furthermore, while gender-stratified attitudes and norms may be related to incidence of sexual harassment, other aspects of the academic environment or climate are also likely to be important. Respect for individuals regardless of gender and support for diversity of various kinds are consistent with discouraging sexual harassment and encouraging gender and other forms of equity (Bond, in press; Fuehrer & Schilling, 1985, 1988). The presence of women, especially in positions of power, also seemed likely to be related to climate and thereby related to rates of sexual harassment (Bond, in press; Gutek, 1985). Thus we expected to find that both gender harassment and sexualized harassment would vary with aspects of departmental climate as well as with the gender composition of the department.

A preliminary analysis indicated that our climate scale measured three separate and independent clusters of items. These three clusters, referred to as climate variables, were: 1) gender stereotyping, which refers to the expression of derogatory beliefs about women in an academic context; 2) generalized student respect, which refers to tolerance for diversity; and 3) support for women's professional development.

It is important to highlight the difference between gender stereotyping (a climate variable) and gender harassment (an incidence variable). The former items were more general than the latter ones, and also differed in content. Gender stereotyping items referred to beliefs about women: for example, "Faculty expect men students to have better math skills than women students." In contrast, gender harassment items, although not obviously designed to assess solicitations of sexual cooperation, were nonetheless more sexualized in content: for example, "Have you ever been in a situation where a faculty member habitually made crude sexual remarks?"

In performing key analyses related to academic climate, we shifted the level of analysis from individual students to departments as units. We included only departments with enough respondents to provide a sense of shared perception (i.e., departments with at least 20 women respondents and more than 50 respondents in all). This limited the pool to 10 departments, with a total of 520 respondents. Using this pool, we calculated several summary scores for each department.

Scores for each of the three climate variables were computed by summing the items which comprised the cluster. For example, the gender stereotyping variable was calculated by summing 11 items. These sums were then averaged across all the respondents within a department to create a departmental mean climate score. In addition, the gender ratios of students, full-time faculty, and full professors were obtained for each department. Finally, the proportion of women who reported at least one incident of harassment by a faculty member in their major department was obtained. These summary variables are shown in Table 3.

Table 3
Incidence of Harassment among Women Undergraduate Respondents

Department	N	Gender Stereotyping	Professional Development	Respect	% Women Students	% Women Faculty	% Women Full Professors	% Women Experiencing Gender Harassment	% Women Experiencing Sexualized Harassment
1	46	19.85	10.50	14.87	29	38	0	23.9	8.7
2	129	18.74	11.17	14.78	78	53	50	18.6	5.4
3	20	20.45	9.70	13.65	13	7	0	30.0	10.0
4	28	24.64	9.89	12.25	11	0	0	39.3	3.6
5	66	16.67	10.32	13.39	24	17	33	16.7	1.5
6	68	21.69	9.52	13.34	41	42	0	30.9	4.4
7	34	18.18	10.74	14.62	56	32	22	14.7	5.9
8	59	15.53	12.27	15.24	96	100	100	6.8	0.0
9	23	22.93	8.96	12.96	35	0	0	30.1	0.0
10	47	21.00	10.15	13.26	47	33	33	14.9	2.1

Correlations of these summary variables were then performed to determine whether there was a relationship between the climate of a department, the structure of a department, and the incidence of harassment
within that department. Incidence of gender harassment was found to be
significantly correlated with all three dimensions of departmental climate.
More harassment was reported in departments where there was more gender stereotyping. Less harassment was reported in departments where there
was more support for women's professional development and more general
respect for students. There was also less harassment reported in departments
with higher proportions of women students, women faculty, and women
full professors (see Table 4). Comparable analyses revealed no significant
correlations between incidence of *sexualized* harassment and climate or
gender composition.

In essence, gender harassment was associated with departments where
faculty expressed gender-based expectations of students' styles, interests,
and academic performance. It makes sense that there would be such a
connection. This correlation is so high, however, that it raises the question
as to whether the two scales measured the same phenomenon. It is certainly
the case that if students have experienced or witnessed gender harassment,
it will effect their assessment of particular events and their assessment of the
overall climate. Less gender harassment characterized departments associated with higher levels of respectful faculty behaviors, such as giving students credit for their ideas, not making racist or demeaning comments, and
being sensitive to students' family and work obligations. The perception
that faculty and other students are supportive of women students as deve-

Table 4
Correlations between Percentage of Incidence of Gender Harassment and
Climate Variables.

| | Correlations with Gender Harassment | |
Climate Variable	Pearson r	p
Gender stereotyping	.88	< .001
Women's prof. development	−.78	< .01
Respect for students	−.71	< .02
% Women students	−.76	< .01
% Women faculty	−.73	< .01
% Women full professors	−.83	< .01

loping professionals also characterized those settings with less harassment. These findings provide additional support for the notion that incidence of gender harassment is associated with climate characteristics. The common thread here is that contexts where students are treated as people with potential for growth and development also seem to be contexts where sexist hostility toward women is not part of the accepted social fabric.

While the relationship between gender harassment and climate in this study is quite compelling, the relationship between *sexualized* harassment and climate is more difficult to assess and much less clear. Sexualized harassment is not strongly related to the climate variables. It is interesting to note, however, that sexualized harassment tends to be negatively related to the percentage of women full professors and to generalized respect for students. While these correlations are not statistically significant and are based on a small sample of academic departments, they suggest possibilities for future exploration. The relationship between sexual harrasment and climate needs to be further explored, as well as the relationship between sexual harrasment and the characteristics of individual harassers.

IMPLICATIONS

In sum, our work indicates that sexual harassment continues to be a serious adversity—in both senses of the word—for women on campus. Both gender harassment and sexualized harassment appear to result from and create *a state of hardship* for women. Our results support the need for a complex understanding of sexual harassment and the generalized adversity it represents for women.

What can be done about this? We believe the primary challenge is to faculty, administrators, and staff who occupy relatively permanent positions of status and power in the university setting. These are the people who influence the campus and classroom culture for better or worse. Faculty and staff have the power to create (or not) and enforce (or not) policies and procedures. They can and should do this in classrooms, in residence halls, and in faculty offices in order to encourage a safe and supportive campus community. Students are also encouraged to demand and support such efforts.

Our recommendations for change are directed at three different levels within higher education: the campus as a whole, classrooms, and lastly, individual students. Some ways to challenge situations that foster sexual harassment and some preventive approaches designed to discourage harassment are provided. For purposes of illustration, we have organized examples by level of intervention. It is important to note, however, that activities at these levels are not independent. They overlap and occur simultaneously, influencing each other recursively. For example, interventions that aim to change campus-wide climate will enable individuals to change. At the same time, the greater the number of enlightened individuals who are active on campus, the faster the campus climate will change to be more supportive of women.

Campus-wide Interventions

Our findings regarding the lower incidence of gender harassment in departments that are made up of large percentages of women illustrate the key role that gender balance, or proportional representation, may play in fostering a climate that encourages respect for women. It is important to work toward increasing the number of qualified women students and faculty in departments in which they are underrepresented. Perhaps even more important is ensuring that more than a few women are in positions of visible and actual power. Qualified women should be full-time faculty, should hold professor rank and should also be in high-level administrative positions across university settings. More generally, our results suggest that visibility of diverse groups of people including ethnic and racial minorities, lesbians and gay men, and people who have disabilities promotes tolerance and respect for differences, thus discouraging harassment of all forms.[2]

Another important campus-wide intervention is the creation of a diversity requirement. More and more institutions require that all students enroll in at least one course that addresses cultural diversity in some way. Exposure to such courses encourages students to learn about groups with different backgrounds and cultures. These courses also explore the destructive consequences (e.g., racism and sexism) of a single cultural standard. Such courses can be offered in many different disciplines and should, of course, be held to the same rigorous academic standards as any other courses at the university.

It is extremely important to develop campus-wide interventions that educate faculty to recognize and respond to behavior that is demeaning of women and other marginalized groups. A central goal here is to develop an expectation that faculty and staff actively promote respect and discourage intolerance and prejudice. Faculty and administrators' responses to critical incidents are important determinants of climate on campus. A few years ago, a rape was committed in a residence hall on our campus. University staff immediately called rape-crisis counselors to campus and organized a campus-wide vigil. This sort of rapid, visible response from the campus community makes a statement that such violence is unacceptable and acknowledges that it affects the entire community.

Campus-wide interventions must go beyond the academic life of the student. Our results show that living in residence halls and in off-campus apartments is associated with higher levels of harassment than is living with one's own family. We know from previous research that women students are at the highest risk of being raped during the first semester of their first year at college (Koss, 1985; Paludi, 1991). Part of this may be explained by the assumption that college is a safe community, a home away from home. It is important that orientation programs debunk this myth and directly note the frequency with which acquaintance rape and other forms of harassment occur. At the same time, information about policies and procedures regarding sexual harassment should be made accessible to all students.

We found that departments characterized by gender-stereotyped beliefs had high rates of gender harassment and that less harassment was associated with departments characterized by respect for students. Creating a campus-wide milieu of recognition of women's accomplishments is another strategy likely to discourage sexual harassment. There are numerous events that can be organized to highlight women's many accomplishments and to encourage an atmosphere of civility and respect for women including, for example, celebrating events that mark International Women's Day or Women's History Month. These events might also incorporate attention to sexual harassment through games or training sessions designed to raise awareness of the extent of sexual harassment and to equip the campus community to challenge and respond to it. Other examples worth considering are events that acknowledge women's achievements such as "Take Your Daughter to Work Day," which began in paid work settings and may easily be adapted for academic institutions.

Our results also call attention to the importance of respect for other groups (which, of course, include women), such as putting on cultural festivals and marking holidays associated with inclusion of minority groups, such as Martin Luther King Day. With events that do not specifically focus on women, it is important to acknowledge women and to make connections across different forms of oppression. One of us recently attended a conference about the full inclusion of students with learning disabilities in campus life. The opening speaker began with a famous quote about every *man* marching to the sound of *his* own drummer. While this may seem trivial, it sends a mixed message regarding inclusion, thus contradicting the theme of the conference.

In the next section, attention is focused on the classroom. A variety of examples are given to promote respect for women and to discourage sexualized and gender harassment there.

Classroom Interventions

Many studies have shown that even well-intentioned teachers who desire to create an atmosphere of equity and inclusion for women sometimes fail to do so (American Association of University Women, 1992; Hall & Sandler 1982). Our study shows that perceptions of faculty attitudes about women are closely related to rates of gender harassment. It has also been shown that faculty behavior can be modified by providing feedback using videotapes or outside observers. Faculty should be provided with opportunities and incentives for observing their own teaching styles. They should be encouraged to see who they call on, what sort of nonverbal feedback they give women and men (for example, yawns versus smiles), and ways in which their responses may be sexualized or gender-typed. Promoting respect for all students and eliminating gender-stratified ways of relating to students are both of importance in terms of inclusion.

Curricular content is also an important means of encouraging or discouraging a climate which enables sexual harassment. In *Failing at Fairness,* (Sadker & Sadker, 1994) give an example of how demeaning comments might be challenged. A teacher supervising a junior colleague heard him use the following list of oxymorons: "cold fire, hot ice, intelligent woman." The supervisor interrupted the class and pointed out to the teacher and the class the misinformation and the diminishment inherent in the last example.

Of course, teachers are usually not being observed by supervisors. Typically, students are the sole observers of their teachers. While it is hoped that teachers will be challenged by students if they provide false or demeaning information, it is the teacher's responsibility to monitor and direct the behavior of the students. Teachers should be encouraged to intervene when students engage in sexist or demeaning behavior toward each other or toward groups who may or may not be represented in the classroom (e.g., students' homophobic jokes or racial epithets). In terms of sexual harassment in particular, it is the responsibility of faculty to monitor student behavior and not to condone sexual harassment or add to it by laughing when it occurs, or dismissing it as "just a joke."

Other areas of importance in the classroom include curricular content and the use of gender-inclusive language. Are books and articles by women included throughout the syllabus? Are women guest speakers invited to class? Are issues related to women's lives being integrated throughout the curriculum? While this is easier to accomplish in liberal arts and social science courses, there are many excellent materials available for the sciences as well. When gender-fair materials are not available, the issue can be addressed directly. An example is provided by one of the authors who requires that students read B. F. Skinner's *Walden Two* (1948), for a class on learning and behavior. A classic utopian novel, *Walden Two* illustrates Skinner's behavioral principles and philosophy very effectively. Unfortunately, however, gender-stratified roles and unquestioned sexism reflect the time at which the novel was written. These aspects of the book are critiqued as part of class discussion. In terms of language itself, a number of books and manuals provide rationales for gender-fair language and also give examples of sexist language and alternatives to it (American Psychological Association, 1994; Martina, 1980; Thorne & Henley, 1975).

Individuals and Informal Interactions

The findings regarding women's and men's descriptions of negative experiences on campus point to the potential for differences and difficulties in negotiating interactions across gender. These results strongly suggest that women as a group consider sexual harassment to be a serious problem whether or not they have been victims. In contrast, many of the men who wrote of their experiences did not view sexual harassment as a problem. These gender differences argue for individual-level intervention programs that are focused on women as a group, men as a group, and on interactions between women and men. Some suggestions for each of these approaches are described briefly below.

Women should be encouraged to trust their own judgment in situations that may constitute harassment and should be provided with strategies to discourage harassment. For example, voicing objection clearly and unequivocally when an inappropriate or unwanted situation occurs can often discourage escalation. Bringing a friend to a meeting with a professor who has violated boundaries or made suggestive remarks is another way to provide personal protection and signal a potential harasser not to proceed. Documenting offensive behaviors and noting one's responses to them are good steps to take in case harassment continues and formal action becomes necessary. Information about university and criminal justice procedures should be easily accessible, and students should be encouraged to use them when necessary.

It is crucial to educate men to realize that sexual harassment is a serious problem that affects their quality of life—just as other crimes in a community do—whether or not they are the victims. Basic to this is the awareness that sexual harassment is an abuse of power that violates the target person emotionally and physically. Sexual harassment is not about sex; it is about violence that is sexualized. Helping men to put themselves in a woman's position in terms of the violation that sexual harassment represents, and in terms of safety generally, is one way to facilitate this awareness. Providing information about the law and campus rules and regulations is another. One encourages empathy and identification across differences; the other emphasizes accountability for actions via formal consequences regardless of an individual's attitude or personal intent.

Perhaps the most promising sort of intervention is one that allows women and men to explore their different views and experiences in settings that provide monitoring and "safety" for both groups, while encouraging a sense of shared commitment to address sexual harassment as a serious social and legal issue. This must involve a simultaneous concern with interpersonal communication processes and substantive information about the nature and impact of sexual harassment. Basic legal and social definitions of sexual harassment and various examples of both sexualized and gender harassment should be provided. Distinctions between legal procedures and university procedures should also be outlined, along with the advantages and disadvantages of pursuing either. Alternatives for confronting sexual harassment should be discussed. It is especially important to place the responsibility for challenging sexual harassment on the entire university community, not just on individual victims or women as a group. Our findings regarding the relationship of gender harassment and climate underscore this.

The importance of acknowledging differences between typical views of women and men regarding sexual harassment cannot be overemphasized. Situations need to be created where women and men can tell their stories and speak of their concerns, while being listened to respectfully. Using role plays or vignettes describing different types of sexual harassment can also be very illuminating. This requires skilled facilitation, however, to ensure that women's views are voiced and not dismissed by men who may see any discussion of sexual harassment as being a criticism of them, or by anyone who treats the issue as trivial. It is simultaneously important to avoid sessions dominated by criticisms of men as a group. Discouragement of blaming on both sides is necessary to allow honest dialogue toward the possibility of finding common ground.

Date Rape: Making Connections

It is not surprising that the recommendations given in the three sections above sometimes overlap with one another since individual and informal group interactions occur in the broader context of the university and of society at large. We must develop change strategies at all of these levels and work to expose the linkages among them. One theme that recurs in both our results and discussion is that women tend to see sexual harassment as a serious problem, while many men do not. Perhaps we must move to even broader levels to understand why. In order to highlight this, we use a common example of severe sexualized harassment: date rape. While date rape usually occurs in a private setting (i.e., behind closed doors) and typically involves only two people (a male perpetrator and a female victim), the larger campus culture can either condemn it or create an atmosphere conducive to it.

A culture that places women in a subordinate position often predominates on college campuses, as it does in the so-called real world. Male sports typically dominate campus-wide recreational and cultural life; they are a focus for the entire college community. Fraternities are often more visible and powerful than sororities. Male sports and fraternities are typically allocated significantly more funding than are female sports or sororities. They emphasize male prowess, bonding, and privilege (Sadker & Sadker, 1994; Sanday, 1990). When women are included, they are relegated to secondary roles. Fraternity and sports cultures have been described as particularly problematic: "after fraternities, athletic teams are most likely to be involved in gang rapes. Whether called 'brotherhood,' as in fraternity houses, or 'team work,' as in sports, the mind-set generated by male bonding can suppress independent thought and morality" (Sadker & Sadker, 1994, p. 184). Typically, such cultures define women as sexual or decorative objects, not as peers. We must examine the connections between the larger campus culture and the sexual harassment and assault of women.

CONCLUSION

Overall, our findings and recommendations illustrate the need to intervene at multiple levels if we are to prevent sexual harassment. In doing this, it is important to be aware of the recursive relationship among levels. In discussing the complexity and intransigence of racism in our culture, West

(1993) writes: "We must acknowledge that structures and behavior are inseparable, that institutions and values go hand in hand" (p. 13). This view is also useful for understanding the dynamics of sexism and its companion, sexual harassment.

It is important to understand sexual harassment not as idiosyncratic or individual events that happen to some students once in a while, but rather as a reflection of campus climate and of the devalued status of women in the larger society. Sexual harassment is related to underlying social structures and cultural values demeaning of women as a group. We must see such harassment as reflecting and adding to a dehumanized environment that ultimately affects all women and men—even those who do not consider sexual harassment to be a problem. As such, the incidence of sexual harassment constitutes a surface manifestation of a deeper reality or structure that *both* reflects and constitutes adversity for women as a group. Faculty and students alike must begin to realize this and challenge it if change is to occur. Until men as individuals and academic institutions as communities understand the reality of adversity for women not only in the letter of the law, but also in the spirit of shared community, sexual harassment will continue to be an adversity for women.

REFERENCES

American Association of University Women. (1992). *How schools shortchange girls.* Washington, DC: AAUW Educational Foundation.

American Psychological Association. (1994). *Publications Manual* (4th Ed.). Washington DC.

Bond, M. A. (1988). Division 27 sexual harassment survey: Definition, impact and environmental context. *The Community Psychologist, 21*(2), 7–10.

Bond, M. A. (1995). Prevention and the ecology of sexual harassment: Creating empowering climates. In C. Swift (Ed.), *Prevention in Human Services, 12* (2), 147–173.

Bond, M. A., Mandell, C., & Mulvey, A. (1991). *An initial report on the survey of sexual harassment of students.* Unpublished manuscript available from Chancellor, University of Massachusetts, Lowell, MA 01854.

Bond, M. A., Mandell, C., & Mulvey, A. (1991, April). *Environmental predictors of sexual harassment on campus.* Paper presented at the Eastern Psychological Association Meetings, Boston, MA.

Dzeich, B., & Weiner, L. (1984). *The lecherous professor: Sexual harassment on campus.* Boston: Beacon Press.

Equal Employment Opportunity Commission (1980). *Guidelines on discrimination because of sex.* Federal Register, 45 (219), 74676–74677.

Fitzgerald, L. F. (1991). Sexual harassment: The definition and measurement of a construct. In M. A. Paludi (Ed.), *Ivory power: Sexual and gender harassment on campus* (pp. 21–44). New York: SUNY Press.

Fitzgerald, L. F., & Hesson-McInnis, M. (1989). The dimensions of sexual harassment: A structural analysis. *Journal of Vocational Behavior, 35,* 309–326.

Fitzgerald, L. F., Shulman, S. L., Bailey, N., Richards, M., Swecker, J., Gold, A., Ormerod, A. J., & Weitzman, L. (1988). The incidence and dimensions of sexual harassment in academia and the workplace. *Journal of Vocational Behavior, 32,* 152–175.

Fitzgerald, L. F., Weitzman, L., Gold, A., & Ormerod, A. J. (1988). Academic harassment: Sex and denial in scholarly garb. *Psychology of Women Quarterly, 12,* 329–340.

Fuehrer, A., & Schilling, K. M. (1985). The values of academe: Sexism as a natural consequence. *Journal of Social Issues, 41*(4), 29–41.

Fuehrer, A., & Schilling, K. (1988). Sexual harassment of women graduate students: The impact of institutional factors. *The Community Psychologist, 21*(2), 12–13.

Gutek, B. (1985). *Sex and the workplace.* San Francisco: Jossey-Bass.

Hall, R. M., & Sandler, B. R. (1982). *The classroom climate: A chilly one for women?* Washington, DC: Project on the Status of Women, Association of American Colleges.

Koss, M. (1985). The hidden rape victim: Personality, attitudinal and situational characteristics. *Psychology of Women Quarterly, 9,* 193–212.

MacKinnon, C. A. (1979). *Sexual harassment of working women.* New Haven: Yale University Press.

Mandell, C., Mulvey, A., & Bond, M. A. (1991, June). *The determinants of quality of life on college campuses.* Poster presented at the American Association of Applied and Preventive Psychology Conference, Washington, DC.

Martina, W. (1980). Beyond the "he/man" approach: The case for nonsexist language. *Signs, 5,* 482–493.

Mulvey, A., Bond, M. A., & Mandell, C. (1992, August). Gendered voices: Student descriptions of sexual harassment and university life. Paper presented at the American Psychological Association Meetings, San Francisco, CA.

Paludi, M. A. (Ed.), (1991). *Ivory power: Sexual and gender harassment on campus.* Albany, NY: SUNY Press.

Rubin, L., & Borgers, S., (1990). Sexual harassment in universities during 1980s. *Sex Roles, 23,* 397–411.

Sadker, M., & Sadker, S. (1994). *Failing at fairness: How America's schools cheat girls.* New York: Macmillan.

Sanday, P. R. (1990). *Fraternity gang rape: Sex, brotherhood, and privilege on campus.* New York: New York University Press.

Skinner, B. F. (1948). *Walden two.* New York: Macmillan.

Thorne, B., & Henley, N. (Eds.), (1975). *Language and sex: Difference and dominance.* Rowley, MA: Newbury House.

Till, F. (1980). *Sexual harassment: A report on the sexual harassment of students.* Washington, DC: National Advisory Council on Women's Education Programs, U.S. Department of Education.

West, C. (1993). *Race matters.* Boston, MA: Beacon Press.

NOTES

[1] The vignettes above (and later student comments) are prototypical samples based on a composite of actual student remarks at the end of the survey. They are not verbatim accounts. This was done to protect confidentiality.

[2] We are not suggesting here that universities lower their standards to increase diversity. Rather, we are suggesting that universities employ proactive policies and procedures to recruit and support qualified women and members of minority groups.

AUTHORS' NOTE

Contribution of all authors was equal. Order of authors' names is random. This research was supported by a grant from the Chancellor's Office of the University of Massachusetts Lowell. We gratefully acknowledge the support of the Chancellor and the Taskforce on Sexual Harassment of the University of Massachusetts Lowell for their support of our work.

NOTES ON CONTRIBUTORS

SUSAN S. BAKER, associate professor of pediatrics at the Medical University of South Carolina, is a pediatrician who specializes in gastrointestinal and nutritional problems in infants, children, and adolescents. The author of numerous articles in peer-reviewed journals, book chapters, and three books, Baker serves on several national committees charged with making policy for children's nutrition.

ROBERT D. BAKER, associate professor of pediatrics at the Medical University of South Carolina, is presently codirector of the Division of Pediatric Gastroenterology and Nutrition and director of the Cystic Fibrosis Center. He has written many research and review papers on topics related to the gastrointestinal tract. Recently he coedited the book *Pediatric Enteral Nutrition*.

MEG A. BOND is an associate professor of psychology at the University of Massachusetts at Lowell. She is on the editorial board of the *American Journal of Community Psychology* and is a fellow of both the Society for Community Research and Action and the American Psychological Association. She has published on the topics of sexual harassment, diversity-participation paradoxes, empowerment of underrepresented groups, and feminist community psychology. Her current research focuses on the dynamics of diversity in the workplace.

LYNN COHEN BRENNAN specializes in the behavioral treatment of children with elimination disorders, sleep disorders, and autism spectrum disorders at Bedrosian Associates in Northboro and Leominster, Massachusetts.

LYNN TONDAT CARTER is professor of psychology at University of Massachusetts at Dartmouth where she has been teaching and conducting research in physiological psychology for the past twenty years. Besides authoring research articles and papers in her field, she is the first author of two editions of a workbook on cognitive skills remediation in brain-injured adults.

LANCE CHAPMAN is a resource specialist in the social work department at Beth Israel Hospital in Boston. He is an honors graduate of the University of Massachusetts at Boston. He is interested in psychobiography and life narratives. Currently he is working on a book of interviews with fathers who stay at home with their young children.

JOHN K. CONBOY is associate professor of Psychology at the University of Massachusetts at Dartmouth, where he has been teaching applied undergraduate and graduate courses in clinical psychology. His clinical and research interests are in ADHD diagnostics and treatment. He maintains a small private practice specializing in the treatment of ADHD, and consults in schools and clinics on ADHD diagnostic and treatment issues.

LAURA COSTA is a Ph.D. candidate in the Department of Psychology at the University of Rhode Island. She received her B.A. with honors in psychology from University of Massachusetts at Dartmouth.

SCOTT DICKMAN is an associate professor of psychology at the University of Massachusetts at Dartmouth. His published work is primarily on the cognitive processes underlying personality and psychopathology.

ROBERT S. FELDMAN, professor of psychology at the University of Massachusetts at Amherst, specializes in the study of nonverbal behavior and social psychological factors of education. A former Fulbright Senior Research Scholar and Lecturer, he is a fellow of the American Psychological Association and the American Psychological Society. In addition to writing numerous scientific articles and book chapters, he has edited *Fundamentals of Nonverbal Behavioral Theories and Research* and is the author of *Understanding Psychology*.

DEBORAH FRANK, associate professor of pediatrics at the Boston University School of Medicine, specializes in risk factors affecting infant development. She is founder and director of the Failure to Thrive Program at Boston City Hospital and also principal investigator of a grant from the National Institute on Drug Abuse to study cocaine-exposed children during the preschool years. She has published numerous articles and chapters and is a coauthor of *The Effects of Undernutrition on Children's Behavior* (1987).

PAUL J. GEARAN is the project director for the Marital Violence Research Program at the University of Massachusetts Medical Center. He received his masters degree in clinical psychology from the University of Connecticut, and is currently completing his doctoral studies at that institution.

SUSAN GIORDANO is an educator at the May Center for Early Intervention, providing education services to children birth to three and their families in the home and at the Center. She also provides consultation to numerous public schools regarding behavior management and curriculum development.

RICHARD P. HALGIN is a professor of psychology at the University of Massachusetts at Amherst, where he also serves as Coordinator of the Psychological Service Center. He has been awarded Diplomate status by the American Board of Professional Psychology, the highest professional distinction for clinical psychologists. He has written extensively on issues pertaining to psychotherapy, clinical supervision, and professional issues in psychology. He is also the coauthor of a textbook entitled *Abnormal Psychology: The Human Experience of Psychological Disorders* and the coeditor of a casebook entitled *Partners in Change: Growth through the Therapeutic Process.*

MICHELE JACOBO is a Ph.D. candidate in the clinical psychology program of the Department of Psychology at the University of Massachusetts at Amherst. Her current research interests are in the area of family caregiving for Alzheimer's patients, exploring the relationship between identity and attachment in caregivers and the experience of burden.

CHARLOTTE MANDELL is professor of psychology at the University of Massachusetts at Lowell, where she is currently serving as department chair. She was named Outstanding Teacher of the Year by the Massachusetts Psychological Association. She has served on the editorial board of the *Journal of the Experimental Analysis of Behavior.* She has a long-standing interest in the experimental analysis of learned behavior, and her recent work has centered on the study of the formation of stimulus equivalence relations.

JERROLD MEYER is a professor in the Department of Psychology and the Neuroscience and Behavior Program at the University of Massachusetts at Amherst. A specialist in neuropharmacology, he has published over forty articles and is a coauthor of the forthcoming second edition of *Fundamentals of Neuropsychopharmacology.* His current work on the neurobiological effects of prenatal cocaine exposure is supported by the National Institute on Drug Abuse.

MARK MIROCHNICK is an assistant professor of pediatrics at the Boston University School of Medicine and an associate neonatalogist at Boston City Hospital. A specialist in developmental pharmacology, he has published numerous articles in the leading pediatric journals. His current interests include neonatal pharmacokinetics, the biological effects of prenatal drug exposure, and the pharmacology of HIV treatment in children.

ANNE MULVEY is a professor of psychology and coordinator of women's studies at the University of Massachusetts at Lowell. She coedited a special issue of the *Journal of Community Psychology*, and has published in that journal and others, including *Women's Studies International Forum*. Dr. Mulvey is a fellow of the American Psychological Association, the Society for Community Research and Action, and the Division of the Psychology of Women. Her research interests center on sexual harassment, feminist community psychology, and neighborhood quality of life.

MARIA MUNOZ-RUIZ is a Ph.D. candidate in the clinical psychology program at the University of Massachusetts at Amherst. Her research interests are in the area of caregiving among Hispanic relatives of Alzheimer's patients; she examines the experience of caregiver distress in American and Puerto Rican families. She has presented papers at the annual meeting of the Eastern Psychological Association and at the Gerontological Society of America's annual scientific meetings.

RICHARD OCHBERG is assistant professor of psychology at the University of Massachusetts at Boston. He is interested in identity and careers. He is the author of *Middle-aged Sons and the Meaning of Work,* and the coeditor of *Storied Lives* (with George Rosenwald) and *Psychobiography and Life Narratives* (with Dan McAdams).

SUSAN RHOADS is a preschool teacher with the Granby Public School District in Granby, Massachusetts. Prior to this, she served as lead teacher/educational coordinator of the Early Childhood Learning Center, a program of the University of Massachusetts and the May Institute.

JILL RIERDAN is associate professor of psychology at the University of Massachusetts at Boston and has a private practice in psychotherapy in Cambridge, Massachusetts. Previously, she was director of a seven-year, federally funded study of adolescent girls' development at the Wellesley Center for Research on Women. She has written over fifty articles and chapters in the broad area of developmental psychopathology, and is now directing a project that applies a developmental perspective to the assessment and understanding of co-morbidities among adults being treated for a variety of psychological disorders.

FRANK R. ROBBINS is an adjunct visiting lecturer of psychology at the University of Massachusetts at Amherst and a consultant with Quabbin Valley Educational Consultants in Belchertown, Massachusetts. He has done extensive clinical work in autism and early intervention and has published book chapters and research articles in these areas. He has served as director of the Early Childhood Learning Center, a program of the University of Massachusetts and the May Institute, and is currently a member of the professional advisory board of the Autism Society of America.

ALAN ROSENBAUM is a professor of psychology at the University of Massachusetts Medical Center in Worcester, Massachusetts. He is the director of the Marital Research and Treatment Program at UMMC and has published over thirty articles on domestic violence. Rosenbaum received his doctorate in clinical psychology from the State University of New York at Stony Brook in 1979.

LINDA SILKA is a professor of psychology at University of Massachusetts at Lowell, where she also directs the Center for Family, Work, and Community. Her basic research on social cognition has been reported in numerous journal articles, as well as in her book, *Intuitive Judgments of Change* (1989). Her current work investigates the social psychology of historical inferences—how people use information about the historical past to make contemporary social judgments, including policy decisions in such areas as childrearing, alcohol and drugs, and political leadership.

ERVIN STAUB is professor of psychology at the University of Massachusetts at Amherst. His primary areas of work are the determinants and development of helping behavior and altruism, and of aggression and violence, in individuals and groups. His books on these topics are *Positive Social Behavior and Morality* (Volumes 1 and 2) and *The Roots of Evil: The Origins of Genocide and Other Group Violence*. He has also edited and coedited volumes, most recently *Patriotism in the Lives of Individuals and Groups*. He received the Otto Klineberg Intercultural and International Prize of the Society for the Psychological Study of Social Issues.

JEANINE M. VIVONA earned her Ph.D. in clinical psychology from the University of Massachusetts at Amherst and is completing a year of postdoctoral clinical training at the Institute of Pennsylvania Hospital in Philadelphia. Her research interests include exploration of the effects of childhood deprivation and trauma on the development of object relations and psychopathology. Her clinical interests include psychoanalytic psychotherapy, dissociative disorders, and personality disorders.

SUSAN KRAUSS WHITBOURNE is professor of psychology at the University of Massachusetts at Amherst. She is the author of numerous publications in the fields of gerontology and abnormal psychology, including *The Me I Know: A Study of Adult Identity, Abnormal Psychology: The Human Experience of Psychological Disorders* (with Richard Halgin), and the forthcoming *The Aging Individual: Physical and Psychological Perspectives* and *Partners in Change: Mutual Growth through the Therapeutic Process* (with Richard Halgin). She has conducted numerous research investigations and is president of Division Twenty (Adult Development and Aging) of the American Psychological Association. She has received the College of Arts and Sciences Outstanding Teaching Award.

MARTIN H. YOUNG, associate professor of pediatrics and director of the Developmental and Behavioral Consultation Program at the University of Massachusetts

Medical School, is a pediatric psychologist specializing in the psychological treatment of chronic medical conditions/diseases in children and adolescents. He and his collaborators have given presentations and published on such diverse topics as family-centered healthcare, behavioral/emotional impacts of chronic childhood illness, psychological aspects of artificial nutrition, uses of hypnosis in the treatment of chronic medical problems, enuresis, and encopresis.

BARRY ZUCKERMAN is professor and chairman of the Department of Pediatrics at Boston University School of Medicine and Boston City Hospital. He has developed and directed numerous programs for high-risk children, including the Teen and Tot Clinic, the Child Development Project, the Women and Infants Clinic, and the Family Advocacy Program. The author of over a hundred scientific articles on infant health and development, he was the 1994 recipient of the National Leadership Award from the Children's Defense Fund.

INDEX

abandonment: of caregivers for the elderly, 165; perceived, 129–130

abuse: of cocaine, 3, 17; of elderly, 161, 166–167. *See also* alcohol abuse; child abuse; sexual abuse; substance abuse

Ackerly, G. D., 186

addiction, to cocaine, 4, 6

Adelman, S. A., 190, 191, 193

adolescents: aggression in, 115–136; altruism in, 116–120; suicide among, 91–109

adrenaline, effects of cocaine on, 11

adults: childhood sexual abuse in, 147–158; impulsivity among, 199–212. *See also* elderly

affection, 117

affective disturbances, in adult survivors of childhood sexual abuse, 149

African-Americans: adolescent suicide among, 97; elderly, 168, 169–170, 174; homicide rate among, 115; violence against and among, 132

ageism. *See* discrimination, against the elderly

aggression: of children with autism, 66, 68–69, 80; effect of impulsivity on, 200–201; family impact on, 121, 123, 125–130, 185–186; motives for, 126; origins of, 120–125; role of society in, 130–134; and self-esteem, 127–128; socialization of, 128–129; and subculture of violence, 133–134; among survivors of childhood sexual abuse, 151; treatment for, 134–136; in the United States, 93, 115, 116, 132–133. *See also* relationship aggression

alcohol abuse: by adult survivors of childhood sexual abuse, 151; among the elderly, 167, 173; by head-injured males, 190–191; and impulsivity, 211; and relationship aggression, 186–187, 192; among suicidal adolescents, 95, 99, 100, 107, 109

alcoholism. *See* alcohol abuse

alcohol use. *See* alcohol abuse

Alexander, K., 242

allergies: and depression, 48; effect on children with ADHD, 46–48; incidence in children with ADHD, 45, 49–55; measuring symptoms of, 49; screening for, 55–56, 57

Allman, C., 103

altruism: family impact on, 115, 117, 118–120, 134, 135; origins of, 116–120

Alzheimer's disease, 161, 163, 164

American Association of University Women, 260

American Psychiatric Association, 45

Anderson, S. R., 70, 74

anger, 105–106, 107. *See also* aggression

animal research, on effects of cocaine on fetal development, 8–9, 12–16

antibiotics, and incidence of ADHD, 45, 51, 53, 56, 57

anxiety, 163. *See also* depression

Arias, I., 184, 186

Aro, H. M., 102

arteriosclerosis, 161

arthritis, 163

Asberg, M., 193

Asians, adolescent suicide among, 97

Asperger's Disorder, 64

attachment, 150. *See also* infant
attachment

Attention Deficit Hyperactivity Disorder
(ADHD): assessment of physical health
problems associated with, 48, 49–53;
chronic health problems associated
with, 45–58; diagnosis of, 51, 55;
effect of diet and allergies on, 46–48,
58; incidence of allergy symptoms in
children with, 45, 49–55; prevention
of physical symptoms of, 57–58;
profile of children with, 57; screening
for allergies in children with, 55–56;
treatment of, 47–48, 57; treatment of
physical symptoms of, 56, 57, 58

attention span, and impulsivity, 208–209,
210

autism: behavior management of children
with, 67, 70–71, 79–80; description
of, 64–67; diagnosis of, 63, 64, 85;
early intervention for treatment of,
67–73, 85; educational programs for
children with, 70–71, 73–84; etiology
of, 66

Avery, D., 70, 74

avoidance behaviors, of adult survivors of
childhood sexual abuse, 149

baby boomers, 92
Bailey, N., 255
Baird, M., 33
Bakow, H., 24
Balach, L., 102
Ball, L., 108
Bandstra, E. S., 11
Bandura, A., 185
Bard, B., 188, 189
Barkley, R. A., 47
Barling, J., 184, 186
Barnett, O. A., 201
Barr, Roseanne, 147
Bates, S. E., 121
Baugher, M., 102
Baumeister, R. F., 107

Bautista, D. B., 11
Bean, Z., 11
behavioral abnormalities: and ADHD,
53–54; and autism, 63–96; of children
with encopresis, 25–26, 30, 31, 33;
detection of, 6–7, 11, 28

behavior management and modification:
of children with autism, 67, 70–71,
79–80; of children with encopresis, 29

benzoylecgonine, 11
Berendzen, Richard, 147
Berman, A. L., 96, 99
Bertilisson, L., 193
Bertin, J., 229
Bettelheim, B., 66
birth defects, 9
blacks. *See* African-Americans
Bond, M. R., 193
Bonner, B. L., 29
Bonner, R. L., 106
Boston Children's Hospital, 24
Boston City Hospital, 10, 11, 12
Boston University, Human Subjects
Review Board, 28
Bourdieu, P., 249
Bowlby, J. B., 117, 150
brain tumors, and aggression, 187
Brent, D. A., 103
Briere, J. N., 149, 155
Brody, J. G., 223
Brooks, D. N., 193
Brown, L., 96
Buckley, S., 11
Bullard, R. D., 226
bystander behavior, 129–130, 135–136

Cambodians, aggression against and
among, 132
cancer, among elderly, 161
Cannon, W. B., 46
cardiovascular system, effects of cocaine
on, 4, 5
caregivers, for the elderly, 161, 164–166,
170–171

caring. *See* altruism

Carter, C. M., 47

Carter, Lynn T., 49

Carter-Conboy Auditory Vigilance Task (AVT), 51, 54

catalepsy, drug-induced, 15

catecholamines, effects of cocaine on, 10–12

Caucasians, adolescent suicide among, 97

central nervous system (CNS): effects of cocaine on, 6; trauma of, and aggression, 192, 194. *See also* nervous system

cerebral trauma, and aggression, 187–194

Chandler, M., 108

Chandra, R., 25, 32

Chaponis, D., 25

Chatters, L. M., 169

child abuse: and aggression development, 116, 121–124, 125–127, 128, 129–130, 132–133; healing of trauma from, 136; incidence of, 132–133; origins of, 130–134; of suicidal adolescents, 94, 105; therapy for, 136. *See also* sexual abuse

Child Behavior Check List (CBCL), 25, 28, 30, 31

child development: and adolescent suicide, 101–103, 109; and autism, 64–67

Childhood Disintegrative Disorder, 64

children: with ADHD, 45–58; adult survivors of sexual abuse as, 147–158; aggression in, 115–136; altruism in, 116–120; autism in, 63–86; with functional encopresis, 23–40; physical punishment of, 121, 124–125, 128, 130, 185

Children's Symptom/Health Inventory (CSHI), 45, 49, 52–55, 56, 57

Chinatown (San Francisco), social support in, 131–132

Christian, W. P., 70

Christophersen, E. R., 26, 30

chronic health problems: associated with ADHD, 45–58; of minorities, 170

Chu, J. A., 156

Churchill, Winston, 242–243

Clements, C. D., 103

Cobain, Kurt, 91

cocaine: detecting exposure to, 5, 11; pharmacology of, 3–5; prenatal effects of, 5–8, 10–17; synthetic analog of (RTI-55), 13

cocaine abuse, prevalence of, 3, 17

cocaine studies: findings from, 10–17; methodological problems in, 3, 7–8; use of animals in, 8–9, 12–16

Coccaro, E. F., 193

cognitive deficits. *See* learning ability

cognitive distortions: in adult survivors of childhood sexual abuse, 149, 150–151; among the elderly, 162–163, 170; and impulsivity, 208–210

Cole, D., 102

Coleman, R., 244

Collins, Lucille, 13

Come Here (Berendzen), 147

communication skills: and aggression, 186; of children with autism, 64–65, 66, 68, 69, 71, 74; of head-injured men, 190

communities: geography of, 219; psychology of, 221, 222–225, 231, 234–235

Conboy, John K., 49, 51

Conflict Tactics Scale (CTS), 185, 194

congenital abnormalities, due to cocaine exposure, 6, 9

Conklin, M., 242

Conner, K. R., 186

Conners, C. K., 47

Conners Parent Rating Scale (CPRS-48), 49–51

Conners Teacher Rating Scale (CTRS-28), 49–51

Conte, R. A., 47

cooperative learning techniques, 135
coping skills: among the elderly, 161,
    162, 163, 172–175; of suicidal
    adolescents, 105–106, 108, 109
cortical arousal, and impulsivity, 208,
    212
Costa, Laura, 49
crack cocaine, 4
Craske, S., 200
criminal behavior, origins of, 122
Cruikshank, B., 25, 32
cultural capital, 244, 248

Dailey, A., 242
date rape, 269
Day, D., 199, 200
delinquency, origins of, 122
dementia, 164. *See also* Alzheimer's
    disease; pseudodementia
depression: in adolescence, 109; and
    adolescent suicide, 94–95, 98, 99, 100,
    103, 105–106, 107, 108; in adult
    survivors of childhood sexual abuse,
    150–151; and allergies, 48; in
    caregivers, 165, 171, 188; in children
    with encopresis, 34; in the elderly,
    161, 163–164, 167, 168; in
    head-injured males, 191; prevalence
    of, 163; related to puberty, 94–95; and
    suicide, 167, 168
developmentally appropriate practice
    (DAP), for children, 71
Developmental Play Assessment
    Instrument, 74
deviant peer group culture, 92–93
DeWilde, E. J., 103, 108
diabetes, among the elderly, 170
Diaco, D., 102
*Diagnostic and Statistical Manual of Mental
    Disorders,* 3d ed. (DSM-III-R), 26
*Diagnostic and Statistical Manual of Mental
    Disorders,* 4th ed. (DSM-IV), 45, 64,
    201, 212
Diekstra, R. F. W., 102, 103, 108

diet, in treatment of children with
    ADHD, 47, 56, 57
DiPietro, E. K., 70
disabilities, and risk of falling, 163
DiScipio, W. J., 202
discipline of children. *See* physical
    punishment (of children)
discrimination: and aggression, 131–132;
    against the elderly, 168, 169, 172;
    against homosexuals, 172; sexual, 253–
    270
disinhibition, syndromes of, 200
disorderliness, and procrastination, 207
dissociation, in adult survivors of
    childhood sexual abuse, 149, 150,
    156
dissociative identity disorder, 150, 152
divorce: effect on adolescent suicide, 94;
    effect on aggression development, 133;
    among the elderly, 164; as risk factor
    for suicide, 94, 168; role in child
    abuse, 131
Dodge, K. A., 121
domestic violence. *See* relationship
    aggression; spouse battering
dopamine (DA), effects of cocaine on, 4,
    9, 10, 12, 13, 14–15
drug abuse. *See* alcohol abuse; cocaine
    abuse; substance abuse
drug overdoses, 96, 102
Dubrow, N., 132
Durkheim, E., 98
dyscontrol syndrome, and aggression,
    187, 192
dysphoria, 163
dysthymia, 165

Eames, P., 194
Early Childhood Learning Center
    (ECLC): behavior management at,
    79–80; curriculum at, 76–78; family
    support programs at, 80–82; fees for,
    73; institutional support for, 73;
    mainstreaming at, 78–79, 82–83;

population served, 74; program evaluation, 83–84; screening and assessment procedures at, 74; staff of, 75, 82; transition into public school from, 82–83

eating disorders, and impulsivity, 201, 211

Eckland, B., 242

Edman, G., 202

education: for children with autism, 68, 70–71, 73–84; family support for, 241–251; and positive socialization of children, 117–119, 134–135; value of, 242–245, 248–249

Edwards, G. L., 70, 74

Egger, J., 47

Eisen, L. N., 11

elderly: abuse of, 161, 166–167; caregiving for, 161, 164–166, 170–171; coping strategies for, 161, 162, 163, 172–175; depression among, 161, 163–164; description of, 161–162; fall problems of, 161, 162–163; homosexuals as, 161, 171–172; minorities as, 161, 168–171; poverty among, 163, 164, 169–170; suicide among, 161, 167–168

ELISA/ACT tests, 56, 57

Elliot, F. A., 187, 192

emotion-focused coping, 173

emotions: of the elderly, 164; of suicidal adolescents, 99, 104, 105–106

empathy, and altruism, 120

encopresis: case studies of, 34–40; definition of, 23; prevalence of, 23; studies of, 24–33; treatment of, 24, 28–30, 31–33

England, assumption about children in, 130

environmental equity, 225–227, 231

epinephrine (EPI), effects of cocaine on, 10–11

episodic dyscontrol syndrome, and aggression, 192

Ericksonian hypnosis, 153

Eron, L. D., 125

extraverts, and impulsivity, 200, 202

Eysenck, H. J., 208, 211, 212

Eysenck, M. W., 202

Eysenck Personality Inventory (EPI), 200, 206

Eysenck Personality Questionnaire (EPQ), 200

Fahy, T. J., 188

Failing at Fairness (Sadker & Sadker), 266

False Memory Syndrome Foundation, 152–153

family relationships: and aggression development, 121, 123, 125–130, 185–186; and altruism development, 115, 117, 118–120, 134, 135; and autism, 66, 69–70, 80–82; and care for the elderly, 165–166, 167; changes in, 131; of children with encopresis, 24, 32–33; effect of head injury on, 188; of suicidal adolescents, 93–94, 98, 105; and support for education, 241–251

Farmer, H., 242

fathers. See family relationships

Feingold, B. F., 46–47

Feldman, M., 188, 189

Fenton, T., 25

Ferrari, J., 209

fetus: detection of exposure to cocaine in, 5; effects of cocaine on development of, 5–7, 10–12, 17

Field, T. M., 11

"fight-or-flight" response, 11

Finland, adolescent suicides in, 102

Finney, F. W., 26

Fitzgerald, L. F., 255

Fletcher, K. E., 190, 191, 193

Folkman, S., 173

Frank, Deborah A., 10, 17

Freud, Sigmund, 152

maltreatment. *See* abuse

marginality, 92–93

Margolies, R., 29, 33

Maris, R. W., 103

marital aggression. *See* relationship aggression; spouse battering

Marital Research and Treatment Program (University of Massachusetts Medical Center), 184, 188, 191

Markides, K. S., 169

Marold, D. B., 108

Marshall, M. M., 193

Martinage, D., 193

Marttunen, M. J., 102

Matching Familiar Figures Test (MFFT), 200

Mathews, J. R., 26

May Institute, 73, 84

McCown, W. G., 211

McEachin, J. J., 67

McGee, R., 56

McKinlay, W. W., 193

McLaughlin, R. J., 202

McMartin Preschool trial, 147

McNicol, J., 47

McQuiston, S., 46

meconium, detection of cocaine metabolites in, 5, 11

Medicare, 169

memory: false, 152, 154, 157; repressed, 147–148, 152–154, 155–156, 157–158

Menninger, K., 104

Men's Educational Workshop Program (University of Massachusetts Medical Center), 186, 193

Merry, P., 188

Millac, P., 188

Milling, L. S., 29

Mindel, C. H., 169

Minderhoud, J. M., 193

minorities. *See* African-Americans; Hispanics; race

Mirochnick, Mark, 10

modeling behavior, 119, 123, 125

Moghadam, H. K., 47

Monmonier, M., 230

Moreno, A., 102

Morrow, C., 11

mothers: of children with autism, 66; and encopresis, 24; impact of drug abuse on infant development, 3, 5, 6, 7–8, 9, 11, 17

multiple sclerosis, and aggression, 187

Myers, W. C., 102

Najenson, T., 188

Nathan, S., 199–200

National Association for the Education of Young Children (NAEYC), 71

National Institute of Mental Health, 191

National Urban League, 168

native Americans, adolescent suicide among, 97

natural socialization, 118–119

neglect. *See* abuse

Neonatal Behavioral Assessment Scale (NBAS), 7, 11

neonates. *See* newborns

neoplasms, among the elderly, 170

nervous system, effects of cocaine on, 4, 5–6, 10–11

neurotransmitters: and aggression, 193–195; effects of cocaine on, 4, 6

newborns: drug addiction in, 6; effects of prenatal cocaine exposure on, 3–17; stigmatization of drug-exposed, 8, 17

Newman, J. P., 199–200

Newsweek magazine, 91

Nisbett, R. E., 134

norepinephrine (NE), effects of cocaine on, 4–5, 9, 10–12

Norring, C., 211

Offer, D., 91, 93

O'Grady, J., 102

O'Leary, K. D., 184, 186

Ormerod, A. J., 255

orthopedic injury, and relationship aggression, 190, 191, 193
Osborn, M., 102
O'Shea, J. A., 47
Otto, L., 242
Otto, T. A., 102
Overholser, J., 96
Owens-Stively, J. A., 26

packs, aggressive behavior of, 129
Panting, A., 188
parasitic diseases, among the elderly, 170
Pardo, C., 132
parenting skill: and adolescent suicide, 105; and autism, 66; and children with encopresis, 32–33; development of, 134
parents. See family relationships; mothers; parenting skill; single parents
Parkinson's disease, 163
permissive behavior, and aggression, 123
Perper, J. A., 103
personality disorder, borderline, 152, 186
Personality Inventory for Children (PIC), 49–51, 54, 55
personality traits: of altruistic people, 119–120; of suicidal adolescents, 99
pervasive developmental disorder (PDD), 64
Pervasive Developmental Disorder Not Otherwise Specified (PDDNOS), 64
Pettit, G. S., 121
Phillips, W., 199, 200
physical punishment (of children), 121, 124–125, 128, 130, 185
Piers-Harris self-esteem assessment, 26
Pincus, J. H., 188, 189
place. See geography
placental abruption, 6
political terrorism, 116
polydrug use, 8, 12, 201
Porter, S. F., 47
positive socialization, 116–120, 134–136

posttraumatic stress disorder (PTSD), 116, 149, 152
poverty: and aggression, 131–132, 135; effect on adolescent suicide, 97; among the elderly, 163, 164, 169–170
pragmatic blending (treatment approach), 154
prayer, as a coping strategy, 174
prejudice, and aggression, 131–132
Prichep, L. S., 188, 189
problem-focused coping, 173–174
procrastination, and impulsivity, 207
prosocial value orientation, 120
pseudodementia, 164
Psychiatric Outpatient Department (University of Massachusetts Medical Center), 188
psychology of risk. See risk, psychology of
psychopathology (psychological disorders): of ADHD, 45–46; of adolescent suicide, 98, 99, 100; of spouse batterers, 186
puberty, onset of, 94

rabies, and aggression, 187
race: effect on adolescent suicide, 97; and environmental equity, 225–227; and minority elders, 161, 168–171; and mortality rates, 115, 170
Rainey, S. K., 30
Rainwater, L., 244
Rapp, D. J., 47
Rappaport, J., 224
Rappaport, L., 25, 29
RAST IgE tests, 57
RAST IgG tests, 56, 57
reaction-time tasks, and impulsivity, 202
Reflection-Impulsivity, 199, 200
relationship aggression: biological influences on, 187–191; characteristics of, 184–187; effect of impulsivity on, 201; as model for children, 123–124, 185–186; pharmacological

Slaby, R. G., 211
small-for-gestational-age infants, 6
Smira, K. B., 201
Smith, T., 67
smoking, and risk of falling, 163
social class: and education, 241–251;
  effect on adolescent suicide, 97; and
  environmental equity, 225–227
social contagion effects, 93
socialization. *See* altruism; positive
  socialization; social skills
socialization void, 128–129
socializing, as a coping strategy, 174
Social Security benefits, 169–170
social skills: of aggressive children, 128–
  129; of children with autism, 64–65,
  68, 74, 76; of children with encopresis,
  25, 30–32, 33
social support: for education, 241–251;
  effect on adolescent suicide, 93–94,
  98–99; for the elderly, 171–172, 174
Sohlberg, S., 211
Soothill, J. F., 47
speech. *See* communication skills
Spirito, A., 96
spontaneity, 211
spontaneous abortions, 6
spouse battering, 123–124, 129–130,
  167, 201. *See also* relationship
  aggression
Stanton, W. R., 56
Steele, B. M., 11
Stonewall, 171
Straus, M. A., 122, 133, 185, 186
stress: and adolescent suicide, 98, 100;
  associated with homosexuality, 171; in
  caregivers for elderly, 165, 166; in
  cocaine-exposed neonates, 11; in the
  elderly, 163, 170, 172–175; and
  suicide, 167
stress mechanisms, effects of cocaine on,
  11
substance abuse: by adult survivors of
  childhood sexual abuse, 151; effect on

adolescent suicide, 95, 99, 100, 103;
  effect on aggression development, 116,
  133; among elderly, 167, 173; and
  impulsivity, 201; prevalence of, 3, 17;
  and relationship aggression, 186–187,
  192. *See also* alcohol abuse; cocaine
suicide: by adult survivors of childhood
  sexual abuse, 151; among the elderly,
  161, 167–168; and impulsivity, 201;
  motivation for, 104
Suicide: The Philosophical Issue (Clements),
  103
suicide among adolescents: continual
  vulnerability to, 101–103;
  developmental vulnerability to, 104–
  109; historical trends of, 92–95;
  intervention in, 100, 109; planning of,
  102, 104; prevention of, 97–98; rates
  of, 91–92, 108; risk factors for, 95–
  100
Sulzer-Azaroff, B., 74
Swecker, J., 255
sympathetic hyperarousal, 11, 12
sympathetic nervous system, effects of
  cocaine on, 11
synaptic transmission, effects of cocaine
  on, 4, 12
"syndromes of disinhibition," 200
Szasz, T. S., 101

Taylor, L., 169
teachers. *See* school personnel
Teelken, A. W., 193
teenagers. *See* adolescents
television, and aggression, 124, 132
temporal lobe epilepsy, and aggression, 187
therapeutic interventions: for adult
  survivors of childhood sexual abuse,
  152–157; for children with autism, 72
Tjck, J., 193
Tomba, G. P., 193
Trites, R., 47
Tryphonas, H., 47
Tyree, A., 184